Karlstadt as the Father of the Baptist Movements: The Emergence of Lay Protestantism

Professor Pater presents a revolutionary appraisal of the origins of lay Protestantism in the Radical Reformation. Karlstadt's creative contributions to the Reformation in Wittenberg are analysed, and the traditional picture of Karlstadt as an epigone of Luther, challenging his mentor purely out of spite, is discarded.

Pater shows how Karlstadt clearly influenced Ulrich Zwingli's attitudes towards celibacy and radical liturgical reform, and uncovers historical links between Karlstadt and the Swiss Baptists, including the lay theologians Felix Manz and Konrad Grebel. The author goes on to trace the influence of Karlstadt on Melchior Hoffman, who spread Baptist ideas into northern Europe. Finally Pater notes that it was via Menno Simons that Karlstadt and Hoffman had their greatest influence, for John Smyth, the founder of the Baptist movement in England, went to the Netherlands with his followers, where they applied for membership in a prominent Mennonite congregation, the Waterlander Baptist congregation in Amsterdam. Thus the impact of the Dutch Baptists (Mennonites) on the English Baptists is here established.

CALVIN AUGUSTINE PATER is Professor of Church History at Knox College, University of Toronto.

Karlstadt as rector of the University of Basel.
Copperplate engraving, 11 × 7.6 cm.
By courtesy of Universitäts-Bibliothek, Basel.
Handschriften-Abteilung

CALVIN AUGUSTINE PATER

Karlstadt as the Father of the Baptist Movements:
The Emergence of Lay Protestantism

UNIVERSITY OF TORONTO PRESS

Toronto Buffalo London

© University of Toronto Press 1984
Toronto Buffalo London
Printed in Canada
Reprinted 1986

ISBN 0-8020-555-9

Canadian Cataloguing in Publication Data

Pater, Calvin Augustine, 1939-
  Karlstadt as the father of the Baptist movements

  Bibliography: p.
  Includes index.
  ISBN 0-8020-5555-9

  1. Karlstadt, Andreas Rudolff-Bodenstein von, ca. 1480-1541.
  2. Hoffman, Melchior, d. 1543 or 4. 3. Theology,
  Protestant – History – 16th century. 4. Reformation.
  I. Title.

  BR350.K23P37   274.3'06   C83-094154-1

---

cover illustration 'Triumphus Veritatis' (1523–4). Woodcut, 17 × 42.4 cm.
By courtesy of Germanisches Nationalmuseum, Nürnberg (8° R1.1713 Postinc. und
HB 10931)

To the Buursmas:
William officially, Althea unofficially – yet both our ministers

A single photograph was all that you required to sponsor a family that others
   had passed over, because there were eight children. Those eight are
   conscious of a debt that no 'dedication' can repay.

Our deepest gratitude I express to you, also on behalf of Betty, Adrian,
   Anthony, Raymond, Claire, Casey, and Margaret.

Title-page of *Bylder* (89),
published in 1522 by Ulrich Morhart in Strassburg.
In this treatise Karlstadt divulges his reasons for opposing images,
whether they are used liturgically or as 'books for the laity.'
The horizontal pieces of the title frame depict American Indians.
By courtesy of Union Theological Seminary, New York

Contents

Preface

This study offers a radically revised appraisal of Karlstadt's theology and his impact on the origins of the Baptist movements of Reformation times.[1] On intellectual and historical grounds Karlstadt emerges as the intellectual progenitor of the Baptists. The traditional picture of Karlstadt as an epigone of Luther – and as one who challenged his more sober mentor merely out of spite – is here discarded.

In Part I Karlstadt's development towards a Baptist theology is discussed. From the beginning Karlstadt's theology differs from Luther's. Steadfastly refusing to implicate God in evil, Karlstadt all along opposes the supposition that God predestines unto heaven or hell. One's justification or condemnation before God results from human choice. In Karlstadt's view humans of themselves are unable to make a proper choice; therefore God bestows on them the light that enables them to discern good from evil and grants the power to choose. Thus divine priority and human initiative are both safeguarded.

Karlstadt's biblicism asserts itself to the detriment of tradition, and his idealization of the primitive church undercuts later historical and hierarchical accretions. Primary authority is vested in the local congregation, which elects its own shepherd after examining his doctrine and his life. This possibly subjective judgment needs objective confirmation by God, revealed to the congregation, as in Acts, through the casting of a lot. The shepherd labours 'in the sweat of his brow' on weekdays and has no special privileges apart from preaching and ordering worship. Baptism and the Lord's Supper may be administered by any member of the church. Since baptism signifies regeneration, which requires human choice and response, it should be administered to adults only.

1 The terms 'Anabaptists,' as coined by Luther, and 'Katabaptists,' as coined by Zwingli, are derogatory, and imply that the Baptists were involved in rebaptism, a charge they rightly refuted. The Baptists of continental Europe have first claim to the name 'Baptists' (Täufer, Doopsgezinden), since they used the name nearly a century before the rise of the English branch of the Baptists.

In Part II Karlstadt's impact on Switzerland is assessed. Ulrich Zwingli's attitudes towards celibacy and liturgical change were clearly influenced by Karlstadt. Like Karlstadt, the Zwinglian radicals initiated controversies on matters such as fasting and tithing. Two of the radicals, Andreas Castelberger and Konrad Grebel, exchanged letters with Karlstadt. They and their fellow radicals supported the publication of his treatises against Luther. When the printers of Basel rejected Karlstadt's dialogue on baptism as too controversial, Felix Manz took the manuscript to Zurich, incorporating most of its ideas in a manifesto to the Zurich Council. Thus Karlstadt's impact on the Reformed and Baptist movements in Switzerland is demonstrated.

In Part III Karlstadt's relationship with the northern Baptists is considered. Karlstadt exerted a tangible influence on Melchior Hoffman, though this impact was not quite as profound as in the case of the Zurich Baptists. Thus the links as well as the differences between northern and southern Baptists are illuminated. Via Menno Simons, Karlstadt and Hoffman were to have their greatest influence, however, for John Smyth and Thomas Helwys, founders of the General Baptists in England, had been deeply influenced by the Dutch Baptists (Doopsgezinden), more specifically the Waterlander Baptist Congregation in Amsterdam. Of course Smyth and Helwys came out of the English Separatist tradition, which would have predisposed them to follow the course they eventually adopted, but it was in the Netherlands that they became Baptists.

With minor exceptions, the writings of Karlstadt and Hoffman have not been reprinted since the sixteenth century; therefore it seems essential to provide separate bibliographies of their voluminous works. Thus the first and second parts of the bibliography contain the original writings of Karlstadt and Hoffman, respectively. The third part of the bibliography covers all other relevant material, including primary sources for Karlstadt's contemporaries, collections, and secondary material in books, articles, Festschriften, and so on.

Because of its controversial nature this project required full documentation, involving many materials. Consequently in the text and in the notes sources are cited in abbreviated form and the reader should turn to the bibliography for full information on any work. Works cited frequently are identified by abbreviations in small capital letters; there is a complete list of these abbreviations on pages 301–2, immediately preceding the bibliography. Works referred to only occasionally, however, are identified by author and short title. For example, full bibliographical information for 'Sider, Orlamünde Theology' is provided in the third part of the bibliography, whereas 'SIDER' is listed among the abbreviations.

Each of Karlstadt's and Hoffman's works has been given a short title, which precedes the longer title in the bibliography; in fact, in the first and second parts of the bibliography, Karlstadt's and Hoffman's works are entered alphabetically by their short titles. Where Karlstadt's writings are entered in the bibliography of

Freys and Barge (abbreviated as FB), the FB number is added in parentheses. In the text and in the notes Karlstadt's works are referred to by short title only, while Hoffman's works are referred to by author's name and short title.

For works from the sixteenth century, the letters identifying the signatures are always capitalized and the leaves within the signatures are identified by Arabic numerals, except that leaf 1 is not specified. The traditional abbreviation 'r' for recto is always omitted, but the abbreviation 'v' for verso is retained. If the reference is to several leaves in the same signature, the letter identifying the signature is not repeated. Except for title-pages (which always lack signatures), the signatures of leaves that are not identified in the original, have been supplied in brackets. Thus if a reference runs from leaf a i recto (signature not given) to leaf a iiij verso (signature not given) in Karlstadt's *Ein Sermon vom stand der Christglaubigen Seelen, von Abrahams schoss vnd Fegfeür der abgeschydnen Seelen*, listed in FB as no. 95, then the reference to it reads: *Fegfeür* (95), A–[4v].

The English translations of the quotations are my own. Wherever it has been deemed essential, the original quotations are given in the footnotes, since they are not easily accessible. Medieval Latin forms have been replaced with their classical equivalents. For modern languages, in so far as they are covered there, the practices for editing the texts follow the recommendations published in ARG 72 (1981), 299–315.

Vorred.

Ach dem yetz wie
ich bericht/neüw vnd teütſche Bib
lien/ſollen getruckt werden/vnd al
le Chriſten geiſtliche vnd leyhen/ge
lerte oder vngelerten / die heylige
ſchrifft/zůleſen oder hören leſen(vñ
in ſolchem ſtreiß)ſchuldig ſeind/ das ſy widerüb andere
Chriſten leren müge vnd wöllen/hab ich obgenanter/
viſ anregen vnd begerung etlicher gotforchtiger men⸗
ſchen/allen vnd yeglichen Chriſten/alten vnd iungen/
geweichten vnd vngeweichten/männer vñ weiber/ein
kurtze vnderricht thůn wöllen . Welche bücher/ on ye⸗
mants widerred/Götlich vnd Bibliſche ſeind/ welche
auch widerüb von etlichen mit angenomen oder züge⸗
laſſen. Damit der frum vnd getrew diener gottes/ſich
vff die allerbeſt ſchrifft legen müg/vnd der lere obligen
die inen/durch alle ketzeriſche feind tragen/vnd auß al
ler ferligkeit brenge mag. Vnd das er(wie ein klůg lein
lin)die beſt weid erſtlich ſůchē kan. Aber ich wil das al
les vffs kürtzt verſůchen. So yemāts weiter berichtůg
bedarff oder begert/der leſe mein latyniſch Büchlin de
ſcripturis Canonicis intitulirt vnd genennet/das wirt
in ferrer füren vnd verſtendigen.

Bibliſch bücher deß alten teſtamēts.

In dem alten geſatz/ſeind nachgeſchribē bücher Ca
nonici/das iſt/götlich oder bibliſche/fünff bücher Mo
y ſi/die ſelben.v.bücher ſeind zeiten von Chriſto das ge
ſätz genant. Vnd die Juden nennen auch noch heut die
ſelbe fünff bücher/das geſätz/hebraiſch thora.

A ij

Acknowledgments

It is a pleasure to express my gratitude to the following persons. Ruth Pater reproved me for my timidity, when at first I did not apply to Harvard University for graduate studies. Paul Woolley introduced me to church history, while Wilhelm Pauck's seminar on Luther stimulated me to study Karlstadt. Wilbur K. Jordan introduced me to the English Reformation, and James Samuel Preus wisely challenged me to delimit my original topic to its present dimensions. George Huntston Williams is an inspiring preceptor who, as a specialist in virtually all areas of church history, advised me when I wrote the dissertation on which this work is based, never allowing his extraordinarily heavy schedule to deter him from giving generously of his time. Later he kindly counselled me on the intricacies of having one's work published. As members of my dissertation committee Professors David Herlihy, Ian Siggins, and David Steinmetz each brought a distinctive perspective to bear on this work.

Harvard Divinity School and Harvard University provided substantial scholarships. A summer at Concordia Seminary enabled me to exploit the resources there and at the Center for Reformation Research, which granted me a fellowship. At Concordia Arthur Carl Piepkorn taught me palaeography. A year of research at the Eberhard-Karls-Universität in Tübingen depended on the encouragement given by O. Hermann Pesch and Heiko A. Oberman, as well as a generous scholarship granted by the German Academic Exchange Service (DAAD).

The librarians at Harvard were extremely helpful, as were their colleagues at the University of Tübingen, who processed nearly four hundred requests for rare works through *Fernleihe*. I received similarly efficient co-operation from librarians in Amsterdam, Augsburg, Basel, Berlin, Copenhagen, The Hague, Heidelberg, London, Munich, New Haven, New York, Prague, Providence, Sankt Gallen, Strasbourg, Toronto, Toruń, and Zurich.

During the early stage of this project Ronald James Sider generously allowed me to photocopy from his own copies of Karlstadt's writings. An intermediate draft of the present work benefited strongly from the detailed and astute criticism of Klaus Deppermann, Harry J. McSorley, and James M. Stayer.

The Presbytery of New York City permitted me to labour beyond its bounds and ordained me to minister in Westport, Massachusetts. There the members of Pacific Union Congregational Church sustained my research as well as my ministry among them.

With the encouragement of Principal J. Charles Hay and the concurrence of my colleagues and the Knox College Senate I was allowed to adjust my teaching schedule to prepare this manuscript for publication. The librarians of Knox College, Anna H. Burgess, Kathleen Waldie Gibson, and Elizabeth Kleiman, excelled with their cordial efficiency in tracking down materials or finding bibliographical references. Eileen Best, Administrator of Knox College, made all the arrangements allowing Cheryl Anne Gaver, Debra G. Hemming, and Connie Walters to work on the typescript.

Esther Jane Dille and June Isabella Rilett made a lasting contribution in proofreading and in typing. Joyce Rilett-Wood did more than anyone ought to; she combines perfectionism with a sense of humour. Jean Houston, Executive Editor of the University of Toronto Press, performs works of supererogation; she must be chided for being far too patient in answering the author's endless inquiries. Joan Bulger edited the manuscript for publication; her numerous suggestions greatly improved its style and organization. Like that of the gods, Antje Lingner's work is not always noticed; she is to be credited with carefully designing this book.

This book has been published with the help of a grant from the Canadian Federation for the Humanities, using funds provided by the Social Sciences and Humanities Research Council of Canada, and also a grant from the Andrew W. Mellon Foundation to the University of Toronto Press.

Finally I wish to thank Monica, Dorothy, and Myrna, who are more precious than books, for causing me no more trouble than I deserved. Kathryn, my wife, examined the final draft of the manuscript and shared the onerous task of reading the proofs. She realizes of course that this makes her fully responsible for any errors, like this sentence, that may have crept into the manuscript.

Knox College, University of Toronto
Summer 1982

Karlstadt as the Father of
the Baptist Movements

'Karlstadt was here, but secretly. He published six booklets, written in German, in which he teaches that there is nothing more in the eucharist than a sign of the body and blood of the Lord. The same issue caused great tumults in Bern. Here the two typesetters who printed his books have been incarcerated. This error seized the souls of all faster than a flame flies through naphtha.'   DESIDERIUS ERASMUS (Allen, Volume V, Epistle 1523:97–101; Volume VI, Epistle 1624:31–2)

'The Anabaptists are blasted windbags. They always talk about their great patience and they always shed blood. Therefore they cry that the rulers are godless and they must be extirpated. They are living devils; not human beings. Karlstadt belonged to their sect. He allowed his son to die without baptism.'   MARTIN LUTHER (TR 2, 2666a)

'And of you, servants of God, who shall stand before the treacherous judge, Dr Luther? For you have forgotten the primary articles of Dr Luther when you lived; therefore your heads ought to jump over the cold steel into the green grass. Now you are no longer martyrs but evil-doers, for Dr Luther has found the law with which he may slay the innocents.'   ANDREAS KARLSTADT (KS 2, 71:33–4, 36–40, 72:1)

Introduction

Andreas Rudolff-Bodenstein was born ca 1480 in the town of Karlstadt in Franconia.[1] In the winter term 1499–1500 he enrolled in the University of Erfurt, which was a centre of nominalism and early German humanism, completing his BA in 1502. On 17 June 1503 he enrolled as 'Andreas Karlestat' in the University of Cologne, a bulwark of Thomism, but in 1505 he transferred to the recently established University of Wittenberg.[2] Karlstadt may well have been attracted to Wittenberg by Martin Pollich von Mellrichstadt, a fellow Franconian, who with Johann von Staupitz had founded the fledgling university, which was supported, morally and financially, by Frederick, the elector of Saxony.

In August 1505 Karlstadt received from Wittenberg the degree of master of liberal arts, which qualified him to lecture on Thomistic theology and Aristotelian philosophy. Karlstadt's two treatises on Thomist logic appeared in 1507 and 1508. Although Karlstadt then revered 'the authority of Saint Thomas, which will always seem greater to me than my own mind,' he already blended Thomism with Scotism, and his *Distinctiones* contained a Greek sentence and a line in Hebrew.[3] Karlstadt would later support the Hebraist Reuchlin, who was locked in battle with the Dominicans from Karlstadt's *alma mater* in Cologne.[4]

In April 1510, Karlstadt celebrated his first mass in the town of his birth, a necessary step on the way to achieving, on 13 November, the degree of doctor of theology. He then became archdeacon of the Castle Church of All Saints in Wittenberg, and to qualify himself further he applied himself to the study of law, in addition to teaching in the university. In 1515 Karlstadt travelled to Rome, where he enrolled in the *Sapienza* (City University), receiving within a year a dual doctorate in civil and canon law (*Doctor utriusque iuris*).[5]

1 Karlstadt's hyphenated family names are explained in Bubenheimer, 'Karlstadt,' [5], [55], n3.
2 For the early history of Wittenberg University see Grossmann, *Humanism*.
3 *Distinctiones* (2), A.
4 BARGE 1, 47f; BUBENHEIMER, 38f.
5 BUBENHEIMER, 8–10, etc.

After Karlstadt returned to Wittenberg, Martin Luther prodded him to study Augustine, whose writings Karlstadt then purchased at the Leipzig book fair in January 1517. On reading Augustine, Karlstadt experienced an intellectual conversion, not without emotional overtones. He published his new insights on 26 April 1517, nailing his *151 Theses* to the door of the castle church. But, although Karlstadt gave Augustine fulsome praise, he dealt with him critically. Karlstadt's earlier veneration of Thomas Aquinas was to be transferred to Holy Scripture rather than to Augustine. Commenting on Augustine's *On the Spirit and the Letter,* Karlstadt became the first reformer to challenge the veneration of the saints.[6] In 1519 he also became the first of the Wittenberg professors to impugn the practice of mendicancy.[7] Concerned with the authority of Scripture, Karlstadt followed Jerome and Erasmus more closely than Augustine in writing his *Booklet on the Canonical Scriptures* (1520).[8]

In 1518 Karlstadt defended Luther, whose *95 Theses* were attacked by the conservative theologian Johann Eck. This literary clash led to Karlstadt's and Luther's public debate with Eck in Leipzig in 1519. Eck got full revenge, however, when he received papal permission to append Karlstadt's name to the papal edict *Exsurge Domine* (15 June 1520) that threatened Luther with excommunication. In *Of Papal Holiness* (published 17 October) Karlstadt replied, charging Pope Leo X with heresy. In April 1521 Luther appeared before the Diet at Worms and was condemned. Except for a short visit early in December, Luther was now removed from Wittenberg – for reasons of safety friends brought him to Wartburg Castle. In May and June 1521 Karlstadt was in Denmark, advising King Christian II on the reform of the Danish church. It was as a result of Karlstadt's advice that legislation was enacted exempting only *married* clergy from taxation – an irrevocable break with the past. Back in Wittenberg Karlstadt became the first reformer to repudiate monastic vows, including the vow of celibacy. In January 1522 Karlstadt married Anna von Mochau, the sixteen-year-old daughter of an impoverished noble family.

Meanwhile, on Christmas day 1521, Karlstadt had conducted the first public reformed communion service, omitting the elevation of the bread and wine, expunging the canon and all sacrificial references from the mass, and shouting in German instead of whispering in Latin the words of institution, *Hoc est corpus meum.* Before two thousand people Karlstadt, wearing lay clothing, explained the changes in the service in a sermon and, facing the congregation, distributed wine and placed the bread in the communicants' hands, giving it even to those who had not fasted. In January the reordering of the Wittenberg welfare system, advocated

6 *De Spiritu* (12), 97:4–6; Karlstadt, 'Militia Franciscana,' 72:25–75:17.
7 Ibid, 73:28–74:14.
8 *Bucher* (46), A2v.

by Karlstadt and Luther, was enacted into law by the town council. Karlstadt also published his *On the Removal of Images*, advocating their removal by legal means in order to forestall iconoclasm.[9] Nevertheless, a mob of impatient students, acting on their own, destroyed some images.

By now the Elector Frederick, under imperial pressures, had become disenchanted with the rapid pace of reform. Luther returned to Wittenberg, and suddenly sided with the conservatives, by preaching eight 'Invocavit' sermons against Karlstadt's reforms. Karlstadt's own preaching was curtailed, and a work of his was destroyed with Luther's approval by the university censors.[10] Disgraced, and with most of his reforms undone, Karlstadt continued his lectures, which were reported to be 'excellent, but infrequently given.'

Karlstadt felt betrayed by those who 'had pulled their heads out of the noose,' and he gradually withdrew to Orlamünde, becoming in effect his own vicar, for Orlamünde provided the prebend on which Karlstadt's stipend was based. Karlstadt now became disillusioned with the process of academic preparation for the ministry. Academic titles, he believed, cause distinctions among the clergy of which Christ disapproved when he said: 'Call no one master.' Known in Orlamünde as 'brother' or 'neighbour' Andreas, Karlstadt literally followed Christ's example in the synagogue of Capernaum by sitting in the midst of the congregation to explain Scripture. People were encouraged to interrupt the minister by asking for explanations or challenging the sermon and 'two or three' members of the congregation were allowed to prophesy 'as the Spirit gave them utterance.' Karlstadt translated from the Hebrew some psalms for use by the congregation of the Orlamünde brethren. Karlstadt, in collaboration with the town council of Orlamünde, removed the organ and the images from the church building. Infant baptism was abolished.

In Erfurt Karlstadt was able to publish his attack on belief in the intercession of the Virgin Mary, but other tracts were held back until December 1523, when they were published by Michel Buchfürer, a bookseller in Jena, but Luther's complaints to Frederick's chancellor Gregor Brück prevented further publications. Luther now corresponded with Brück about Karlstadt's movement, which was beginning to take on regional proportions. Luther commenced an inquisitorial tour of the region around Orlamünde, and at 7 a.m. on 22 August, to a hostile audience at the church of Jena, he preached for ninety minutes, implicating Karlstadt in the revolutionary schemes of Thomas Müntzer.[11] In the afternoon Karlstadt confronted Luther at the Inn of the Black Bear and denied his allegations. Luther tossed Karlstadt a guilder in token of a challenge, urging him to publish his

9 KT 74, 20:21–21:5.
10 BARGE 1, 452–8; 2, 526–6.
11 BARGE 2, 124–5.

views and prodding him to attack 'me as hard as you can.'[12] Luther had under-estimated Karlstadt, for although Karlstadt's polemical works, written outside of an academic context, suffered from exegetical sloppiness, they proved to be powerful enough to splinter the Reformation movement over the nature of the sacraments.

Karlstadt and his family were expelled by the regional authorities, who over-rode the town council and the congregation of Orlamünde. After vainly seeking a haven almost everywhere else, Karlstadt found a secret refuge in Rothenburg on the Tauber, but he escaped from there in 1525, when the traditionists triumphed. For the well-being of his family Karlstadt published an ambiguous recantation, and a promise to remain silent was also wrung out of him by Luther, who then gave him lodging and interceded for him with John the Elector.

Karlstadt stayed with Luther from June 1525 until he was allowed to settle in the vicinity of Wittenberg, where he eked out a living under wretched circum-stances. He was kept under surveillance, and letters of his to Kaspar von Schwenck-feld and the Nikolsburg Baptists were intercepted. Luther then demanded that Karlstadt publish an attack on Zwingli; when Karlstadt refused, he was threat-ened with life imprisonment. Karlstadt escaped in February 1529 and travelled to Holstein, finding refuge with Melchior Hoffman. Again he was expelled. He stayed in East Friesland, at the castle of Chief Ulrich von Dornum, but political pressures caused him to move again, first to Strassburg, and then to Basel, where his children went begging for food. Working out a compromise with Zwingli, Karlstadt finally found a haven in Switzerland.

In 1534 Karlstadt was called from Zurich to Basel, where he preached at the University Church of Saint Peter, occupied the Chair of Hebrew at the Univer-sity of Basel, and from time to time served as its rector. In late autumn 1541 the plague swept through Basel. Perhaps consciously affirming a tradition going back to Dionysius of Alexandria (ca 250), who reported that those who died after minis-tering to victims of the plague were regarded as martyrs (Eusebius, *Hist.eccl.* 7.22.7), Karlstadt remained in Basel. He composed a prayer, delivered in Saint Peter's Church, petitioning God to avert his rage against the city and to grant purity of will and calm to those about to die. Karlstadt died of the plague on 24 December.

The old Roman adage that one should speak nothing but good of the dead has certainly not been followed in the case of Karlstadt. Since the Wittenberg Refor-mation was the private reserve of Lutheran theologians, they reaffirmed the ver-dict rendered in Luther's *Against the Heavenly Prophets* (1524–5) and Erasmus Alber's *Against the Damned Teachings of the Karlstadtians* (1553). Karlstadt's disagreements with Luther would no longer offend most Protestants. None the less, materials in English tend to be slanted against Karlstadt because their authors

12 WA 15, 323–47.

have consulted Luther, whose writings are easily accessible in translation. However, Luther assessed Karlstadt on the basis of the following assumption: 'I no longer ask what Karlstadt says or does.'[13]

The 'Lutheran' view was the consensus until Hermann Barge published his biography of Karlstadt in 1905. Barge has tended to exaggerate Karlstadt's role in Wittenberg, arousing the ire of Lutheran theologians. Proudly asserting that 'the writer is a historian, not a theologian,' Barge has revealed the strong and weak points of such a perspective. Sharply criticized by Karl Müller, and challenged on some points by the new documentation published by Nikolaus Müller, Barge's work has nevertheless laid the foundation for modern Karlstadt research. In the period that followed, several other publications have added to our knowledge of Karlstadt.[14]

Meanwhile there was a resurgence of the view that Karlstadt was a spiritualist, a revolutionary, and an enthusiast (Schwärmer). I shall not debate Troeltsch, Holl, or Heyer, since their treatment of Karlstadt is thoroughly superficial. I note only that Troeltsch's ideal types do not necessarily correspond to historical realities, and that Holl has used the primary sources in meticulously erudite fashion when he treats Luther and Müntzer, but has dogmatized on Karlstadt. Still, Holl has recognized historical links between the so-called spiritualists and the Baptists, disregarding Troeltsch's categories.[15]

The only biography of Karlstadt in English is Gordon Rupp's treatment of him in Patterns of Reformation. Rupp dismisses Karlstadt's academic degrees, lessens his role in Wittenberg, and obscures his career in Basel. For example, after choosing an earlier date for Karlstadt's birth, Rupp notes that Karlstadt received his BA 'rather late' from Erfurt. Karlstadt's two years in Cologne are explained because of 'opportunities, and also because it was a centre of the via antiqua.'[16] However, Karlstadt did not avail himself of the opportunity to receive an MA in Cologne. He preferred to receive it in Wittenberg, soon after his arrival. Karlstadt's Wittenberg MA is also overlooked by Rupp. Karlstadt's earned doctorate in theology from Wittenberg, ignored in the main text, appears in a footnote – and as a DD, with its modern 'honorary' overtones. Karlstadt's dual doctorate in canon and civil law Rupp describes as if it were a rumour.[17] But just in case one still

---

13   WA 18, 88:8–9: 'Ich frage nu nicht mehr was D. Carlstad redt odder thut.'
14   Discussed in SIDER, 1–6.
15   Holl, 'Luther und die Schwärmer,' 424, n 1. The Schwärmer label was ultimately attached to all of Luther's opponents (WA 53, 448).
16   Rupp, Patterns of Reformation, 49.
17   Ibid, 53: 'Rumours filtered back to Wittenberg: he had left Rome after a disagreement with his supervisors, he had gone to Siena. There after a few weeks, he had obtained a doctorate in both laws from the University of Siena.' Rupp tries to be fair, but he has not overcome his earlier stigmatization of Karlstadt as 'the muddled mystic, the inveterate rebel, the Judas of the Wittenberg team.' Rupp, 'Luther and the Reformation,' 21.

wonders whether Karlstadt earned this degree, Rupp assures us that the University of Siena 'was notorious for the speed in which doctorates could be obtained.' But (and Rupp could not have known this) Karlstadt never went to Siena and he received his dual doctorate from the *Sapienza* in Rome.[18] There he debated with Italian scholars – an honour and a challenge that Erasmus had declined.

During the last decade two major studies on Karlstadt have been published, and the growing list of articles and monographs on Karlstadt reveals that he is again coming into his own as a major storm-centre of the Reformation. Ronald Sider's admirable work on Karlstadt focuses on the relationship between Karlstadt's and Luther's theology. Sider has convincingly modified or dismissed traditional allegations that Karlstadt taught 'works-righteousness' or that he was a legalist, a revolutionary, or a mystic.

Ulrich Bubenheimer, writing in the 'Oberman tradition,' has fruitfully applied the late medieval questions to Karlstadt's work, especially in the area of jurisprudence. To many of the traditional questions, as well as to the controversy provoked by Barge, Bubenheimer and Sider have given mutually confirming answers. Karlstadt, for example, contributed to the formulation of *sola scriptura*, but Luther first proposed it in a more rigorous form. The areas of consensus between Bubenheimer and Sider are even more impressive when one considers that the original research for Bubenheimer's work, published three years after Sider's, had been done concurrently.

With the work of Sider and Bubenheimer accomplished, new questions come to mind. Sider has examined Karlstadt's relationship to Luther, stressing areas of consensus: I now wish to pursue Karlstadt's peculiarities and original contributions. Bubenheimer has been very helpful in raising the issue of the context and roots of Karlstadt's outlook: I now wish to consider Karlstadt's impact on the Reformation.

My conclusions, based on an examination of Karlstadt's theology where it clashes with Luther's, establish that Karlstadt was the first proponent of a theology basic to the various Baptist movements. I have also discovered historical evidence for the links between Karlstadt and his followers. This has radical consequences for the origins of the Baptists of continental Europe.

Just as Karlstadt studies have suffered from an obsession with Luther, Baptist studies have been beclouded by confessional apologetic. Mennonite historians have provided an antidote to traditional historians in selecting for their parentage only those elements that are peaceful and compatible. This form of shunning, however, dismisses an originally wider movement to the borderline of history.[19]

---

18 BUBENHEIMER, 34f.
19 For two excellent discussions of the present status of continental Baptist research see Packull, 'Some Reflections on the State of Anabaptist History,' [313]–23; DEPPERMANN, esp 9–19.

Our understanding of the Baptist movements is now being broadened by a polygenetic approach to their origins.[20] In many respects I welcome this new consensus, for anyone who has ever been bewildered by the complexities of history knows that no movement is produced by simple causation. This caution duly applies to the Baptists, who never had as authoritative a leader or as specific a doctrine as the Lutherans or even the Calvinists. Pure monogenesis is pure nonsense.

Stayer, in examining the variety of political opinions among the Baptists, has clearly shown that modern Mennonite definitions of orthodoxy (including nonresistance, and – I would add – the modern notion of the separation of church and state) should not be projected back to the original Baptists.[21] Stayer has also shown that within a continental Baptist framework, which prefers the kingdom of heaven to the world, a variety of political responses is possible, and that the diversity of the Baptists should not be contained by arbitrary definitions. Nevertheless, definitions are useful, even necessary, as long as they are regarded as open probabilities. The only alternative is disintegration. In fact, a new synthesis, though premature at present, will probably be most satisfying for a conceptual and historical understanding of the Baptists. The edifice of Harold Bender's 'normative Anabaptism' has been crumbling, but much of it is still worth preserving.[22] Thus it seems likely that we shall move through the polygenetic phase towards re-integration. Part of the heritage of the mainline Reformers will have to be included, since the polemical sixteenth-century mind did not normally do justice, on either side, to a perspective that includes what is shared in common. When, however, we think of the *peculiarities* of the Baptist movements, Karlstadt and Thomas Müntzer stand as their two seminal genii.

Karlstadt's influence was most profound on what George Huntston Williams, in *The Radical Reformation*, defines as the 'evangelical Anabaptism' of the Swiss and Dutch variety, whereas Müntzer's legacy is most pertinent to the Baptists of central Germany. This calls for rearrangement and adjustment to historical realities and the development of a revised typology. The very imposing structure, established on a typological basis, in Williams's work will no doubt continue to inspire those who, knowing the historical complexities, aspire to order them.

The predominant tendency among Baptist scholars has been to ignore Karlstadt or to dismiss him as a revolutionary and a spiritualist. Nevertheless, there

---

20 Stayer, Packull, and Deppermann, 'From Monogenesis to Polygenesis,' 83–121.
21 Stayer, *Anabaptists and the Sword*. Stayer's new reflections on continental Baptist research have been published in the preface to the second edition and in 'Reflections and Retractions,' 196–212.
22 Bender's *Conrad Grebel* and other scholars' contributions to the influential MQR have dominated continental Baptist research for nearly three decades. *The Mennonite Encyclopedia* (1955–9) is also an impressive monument of the Bender school.

have been exceptions. In the nineteenth century Friedrich Otto zur Linden and especially Willem Izaäk Leendertz noted several instances where Karlstadt had influenced Melchior Hoffman. Karl Holl has also detected similarities between Karlstadt and the Baptists.

In 1962 two works appeared that point in a similar direction. Heinold Fast, in his work on the 'left' wing of the Reformation, classifies Karlstadt in traditional fashion, but he confesses: 'It was difficult for me to count Karlstadt among the "enthusiasts."' Next he refers to Karlstadt's 'other aspects,' his 'spiritualistic, mystical, Baptist and Reformatory traits.' Finally, Fast claims that Karlstadt's tract *Gemach* bears 'an intimate relationship to the thoughts of Konrad Grebel.'[23]

In the same year Hans Hillerbrand posed an even more trenchant challenge to the Bender school by asserting that the origin of the Baptists should not be explained simply with reference to Konrad Grebel in Zurich.[24] Besides noting the influence of Luther, Zwingli, Erasmus, and Müntzer, a large section of Hillerbrand's article deals with suggestions of Karlstadt's influence on the Baptists. Among specific instances, Hillerbrand cites the two or three letters from Karlstadt to the 'Grebel circle.'

Gordon Rupp has made the persuasive suggestion that Karlstadt influenced the baptismal theology of Hans Hut, the anti-predestinarian tracts of Hans Denck, and the *Gelassenheit* theme among some of the Baptists.[25] I agree fully with Rupp when he claims: 'So concerned have modern historians been to disentangle the first Anabaptists, the Swiss Brethren, from contamination with Thomas Müntzer, that Karlstadt's influence on them has been obscured.'[26]

Finally, H.W. Müsing has published a chapter on Karlstadt's impact on the Strassburg Baptists.[27] Müsing contends that Karlstadt's influence after his brief visit in 1524 was so strong that it was the 'first decisive break-through' for the Baptists in Strassburg, with the second break-through being the institutionalization of the Baptist community from 1526 to 1527. Thus, although my thesis that Karlstadt is the father of the Baptist movements may seem novel, it is not entirely original, and I gratefully acknowledge the debt I owe to scholars who were open to a new way of approaching Baptist origins.

I do not propose a monocausal scheme when I label Karlstadt 'the father of the Baptist movements.' As matrix one can point to the survival of mystical and ascetic forms of medieval piety, apocalypticism, and the revolutionary impulses shaped and transmitted by Müntzer. There remains the influence of Luther, especially of his translation of the Bible, and, occasionally, there was input from Erasmus.

23 Fast, *Der Linke Flügel*, 249.
24 Hillerbrand, 'The Origins of Sixteenth-Century Anabaptism,' 152–80.
25 Rupp, *Patterns of Reformation*, 81, 118, n 1.
26 Ibid, 139, n 1.
27 Müsing, 'Karlstadt und die Entstehung der Strassburger Täufergemeinde,' 168–95.

If Karlstadt's influence was greatest on the branch of the movement that Williams has defined as 'evangelical Anabaptism,' this does not imply that one must regard Karlstadt's Baptist theology as normative. The polygenists soundly regard the Baptists as a wider phenomenon, especially in the sixteenth century.[28] The followers of Hut and the other central German Baptists, as well as the revolutionary Melchiorites, are less directly connected with Karlstadt than are other Baptists. Karlstadt's influence on the Swiss and northern Baptists is not equal, for Karlstadt moulded the Grebel circle even more decisively than he influenced Melchior Hoffman.

Nevertheless, two strong points favour Karlstadt as the 'father of the Baptist movements.' The first claim rests on precedence. Before anyone else, Karlstadt developed a recognizably Baptist theology. The second point is based on the durability of Karlstadt's ideas. The dreaming apocalypticists awoke to violence and defeat, whereas the two Baptist movements most strongly identified with Karlstadt have persisted in modulated form as the Mennonites and the Baptists of the Anglo-Saxon world.

Karlstadt passes out of the history of the Baptists in 1530 when his political concern for himself and the economic well-being of his family forced him towards theological compromise. Positively, my definition of the Baptists will surface in the chapters dealing with Karlstadt's theology. There I have also resisted the intrusion of secondary material, like asceticism, which is not peculiar to the Baptists, or the sleep of the soul (pace Jean Calvin).

The arrangement of the material in the first section of this book is systematic and chronological. A purely chronological arrangement was abandoned in chapters 1 and 3, because there is enough consistency in Karlstadt's views of Scripture and his doctrine of the church that it is better to stress the continuity than to risk repetition for the sake of minor modifications. Nevertheless, within each subsection, Karlstadt's writings have been referred to chronologically whenever this was feasible. In chapters 1 and 3 the dates of Karlstadt's publications have been added in the footnotes.

The discussion of Karlstadt's influence on the Baptists in parts II and III has been limited to the Swiss Brethren and Melchior Hoffman, since they produced the two movements that proved viable.[29] Gerhard Westerburg, Karlstadt's brother-in-law, may be significant for the Baptists of the Rhineland, but he has not been considered in this study. Although Westerburg founded what briefly was, next to the Nikolsburg movement, the largest Baptist congregation (in Cologne), the Rhineland received many trends of thought, and the lines of transmission are

28 In an earlier draft of this book, which circulated on microfilm, I made several criticisms of the polygenistic position, which have now been discarded.

29 The Hutterites are related to the Swiss Baptists, but problems remain in interpreting these links. The Hutterites have survived as a minor remnant.

obscure. Moreover, except for Westerburg's publication on purgatory, the bulk of his work appeared in the 1550s, and one would expect modification by this time. Some themes Westerburg shared with others, notably Bernard Rothmann, but the problem of who influenced whom may be insoluble.

A typographical analysis of tracts not properly identified in the bibliography of Freys and Barge reveals that in the Baptist centres of Augsburg and Strassburg Karlstadt editions exceeded the output of all who can, even tangentially, be considered Baptists through 1525. The Augsburg patrician and Baptist Eitelhans Langenmantel reproduced Karlstadt's views on the Lord's Supper in his own writings. Karlstadt also influenced such diverse figures as Thomas Müntzer, Hans Hut, the Strassburg physician Otto Brunfels, and the vegetable gardener Klemenz Ziegler. Hans Denck knew of Karlstadt's rejection of predestination, though he elaborated the theme independently. In the early 1530s Melchior Hoffman made a deep impression on the Strassburg sectarians (as they did on him), and many of his and their ideas had been shaped by Karlstadt.

Much remains to be done: in view of Karlstadt's reverence for Erasmus, the latter's input is worth consideration, and Karlstadt's impact on Zwingli, Oecolampadius, Bucer, and the other Strassburg theologians is tangible enough to warrant further investigation because of its importance for the Reformed or Presbyterian tradition. Lutherans, too, would gain from a fresh appraisal of Karlstadt's gadfly role in relation to Luther, with its positive as well as its negative consequences. To accomplish this, however, Karlstadt must be made accessible. Most desirable now is a critical edition of Karlstadt's writings, which would benefit our understanding of the Reformation in all its branches.

Part One

Karlstadt's Theology

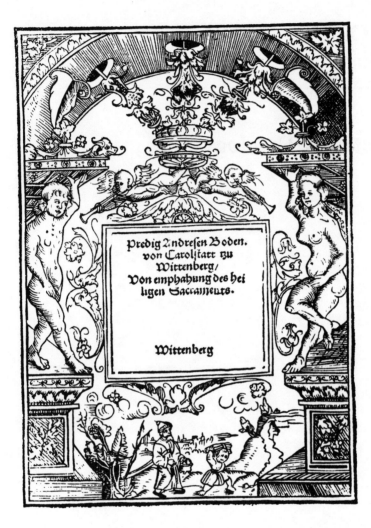

Predig Andresen Boden,
von Carolstatt zu
Wittenberg/
Von emphahung des hei
ligen Saccaments.

Wittenberg

Title-page of *Emphahung* (76),
the sermon 'on the reception of the sacrament,' which Karlstadt preached
25 December 1521 to explain the liturgical changes that he is introducing
during the first public Protestant communion service.
By courtesy of Universiteits-Bibliotheek, Amsterdam

1

Scripture and the Spirit

According to Karlstadt the original Scripture 'allows of no defect'; it is the sword that judges all things, and all are subject to it, including the political rulers.[1] Universal usage of certain Scriptures confirms, but does not establish, the canon.[2] The self-authenticating canonical Scriptures exclude the Apocrypha.[3] One may not add to or subtract from God's Word, according to Galatians 1:8: 'Even if we, or an angel from heaven, should preach to you a gospel contrary to that which we preached to you, let him be accursed.'[4] Another favourite text of Karlstadt's is Matthew 15:13: 'Every plant that my heavenly Father has not planted shall be uprooted.'[5]

Faithfulness to the Word unites the church; disobedience creates sectarianism. The sectarian factions (various monastic orders, etc) of the papal church exist because they play off one authority against another.[6] However, the true church is governed by Scripture, for

1 Credner, *Zur Geschichte des Canons*, par 3 (1518–20); *Bedingung* (36), [A4] (1520).
2 Credner, par 98: 'Postremo consuetudo ecclesiarum non videtur plus iuris illiusmodi libris contulisse, quam consensus summorum scriptorum potuit praestare, qui eos non fecerunt canonicos' (1518–20).
3 Credner, par 92: 'Ex eo consequitur, quod solus canon libros apocryphios efficit, quos excludit ... (1518–20).
4 See e.g. LÖSCHER 2, 147 (1518); *Bucher* (46), [B4v] (1520); BARGE 1, 477, th 5 (1521); *Was bann* (119), A2v (1524).
5 See e.g. *Ausslegung* (15), [D6v]–E (1519); *Leyb* (129), D2v (1524); *Messen* (131), [4v] (1524).
6 *1 Co 1* (75), A2: 'Dan wan ein versamelung gottlich wort verlosset, ists umb sie gescheen'; A3v: 'Aber wan uns das wort Gotis empffelt, und einer versucht concilien fur tzu wenden. Der ander formalitates Scoti. Der dritt das arm comment Thome. Der viert alt herkumen. Der funfft weissheit der welt und unsser vorfarn. So konden wir tzu keiner einigkeit kumen, dan das heilig evangelium ist uneinss mit allen dingen und worten' (1521).
    Karlstadt also saw schismatic tendencies in the multiplication of religious orders. See Karlstadt, 'Militia Franciscana seu militia Christi,' 75:4–7: 'Et rursus *Carolostadius*: Paulus maxime vetat schismata in ecclesia fieri [1 Cor. 1:10; 12:25]. Iam vero tot fiunt schismata, quot ordines religiosorum. Reprehendit namque quosdam, qui Petri, qui Pauli, qui Apollo dicebantur. Ait namque [1 Cor. 1:13]: "Numquid Paulus pro vobis crucifixus est?"' (1519).

it is to be noted that the biblical Scripture is worthier than the Christian church, and that the Christian church has to follow, live according to, and observe Holy Scripture; and not the contrary, that Scripture has to live according to the church and serve it.[7]

When Wittenberg was jarred by self-proclaimed prophets in 1521, Karlstadt was an ardent biblicist. He appears to censure Gabriel Zwilling when he fulminates against the dreams of false prophets who claim inspiration, preferring miracles, like the devil.[8] In January of 1522 Karlstadt alludes to Melanchthon and the Zwickau Prophets when he denounces erring prophets and their counselee:

Now God answers us through his own Word. You are not to visit prophets. But if there is someone nowadays who wants to consult doctors, masters, and bachelors in such matters, and who does not want to accept God's Word without hesitation, let him hear what follows in Ezekiel 14:9: 'I, God and Lord, have caused to err the prophet who will err, and I will eradicate him from the midst of my people.' Behold how God eradicates both the prophet who errs and causes error, as well as the counselee who takes counsels from such a prophet. Take this for an example.[9]

The Prophets' original messages, according to Karlstadt, were free of natural admixture.[10] However, this is not true of the received text of the Bible, in which Karlstadt notes contradictions and textual problems:

Neither can I ignore the fact that many an error has grown in our codices, since on the same occasion one evangelist says more, they [the copyists] have added it to the other [gospel] because they consider it important. Actually, when one [manuscript] expresses the same idea differently, he [the copyist] who had read one of the four [gospels] first, [would follow it] as an example for those he considered to have been emended. Thus it happened that all our [manuscripts] have been mixed, and in Mark many things [derive] from Luke and Matthew. Again, in Matthew much can be found that properly belongs to John and Mark.[11]

Notable is the reference to a manuscript that 'expresses *the same idea* differently.' The form of the gospels has been affected, but the ideas remain reliable.

---

7 *Bucher* (46), C3v (1520).
8 *Gelubden* (50), B2v–3 (1521).
9 *KT* 74, 15:6–13 (1522). See also SIDER, 163–5.
10 *Malachiam* (93), B2: 'Das hat got ... geleret, das menschlicher mund gotis wort redet, one alles tzutuhn und mitwircken' (1522).
11 Credner, par 142, corrected on the basis of *Scripturis* (34), L3v (1518–20).

Yet, Karlstadt does not find clarity in every verse. From obscure passages he turns to the light of Christ in the gospels.[12]

The Old Testament law does not trouble Karlstadt as it does Luther. The Ten Commandments, for example, are valid as the voice of God uttered on Mount Horeb, and proclaimed by the Prophets, Christ, and the Apostles.[13] Thus the command to make no graven images becomes basic for Karlstadt's condonation of iconoclasm, especially since Paul also opposes images (Rom. 1:20–3; 1 Cor. 5:10–11). Moreover, Karlstadt bases his social ethics on the Old Testament. He wishes to uphold a Christian interpretation of the laws of Moses.[14]

For Luther this position stamps Karlstadt as a legalist and a Judaizer. Actually Karlstadt is quite free in applying the laws of Moses, and he does so in a way that is much more progressive than the *Sachsenspiegel*, the law code of Saxony that meted out 'justice' in relation to one's standing in society. Moreover, Karlstadt pleads for a new law code, provided it reflects the principles of equity in the Mosaic code, tempered by New Testament conceptions of mercy. The Old Testament must yield to the New where the latter breaks with tradition. Unbelievers, for example, should receive more compassion:

I do *not* want [unbelievers] to be killed that way, neither do I pray in the Judaic manner: 'May sinners perish from the earth, so they will be no more' – that is, may [they] be killed. Away, away with that! Rather, let malice perish, let error be destroyed, and let the truth and knowledge of Christ replace error.[15]

Karlstadt believes that some teachings are outdated, for example, the Old Testament views of the afterlife and the concept of holy war. The proclamation of 'a sword for the Lord and Gideon' (Judg. 7:20) ceased soon afterwards.[16] Even here Karlstadt links the Old Testament with the New, for opposition to unbelievers continues, but now with the sword of Scripture. The relation between the Testaments may involve a paradox:

Christ did not subjugate anything that was pleasing to God under the old law. Christ remained within the will and the content of the old law. One who can add the following two sayings – 'by faith we overcome the law'

---

12 *Bucher* (46), [B4–v] (1520).

13 *Willen gottes* (102), [H4] (1523). Luther himself moved beyond medieval views of the Old Testament (Preus, *From Shadow to Promise*, esp 200f).

14 KS 1, 14:3–5 (1523); KS 2, 99: 24–30 (1525).

15 *Verba Dei* (26), B2: 'NON volo quod interficiantur istiusmodi, neque enim iudaice oro, pereant peccatores a terra, et non sint, hoc est, occidantur. Absit, absit, sed pereat malignitas, dispereat error, surrogetur errori, veritas et scientia Christi' (1520).

16 Credner, par 164: 'Caeterum infeliciter paulo post Gedeoni cessit, quod clamare iussit dicens: "Clamate gladius domini et Gedeonis"' (1518–20).

and 'by faith or grace we establish the law' – understands Moses, the Prophets, Christ, and Paul.[17]

Karlstadt always chooses the New Testament model for salvation, as the tracts *Priesterthum* and *Testament* establish. He also follows Augustine in distinguishing between the Testaments. The Old promises *earthly*, the New *heavenly* things. Moses proclaims Christ with figures, but in the gospels is fulfilment.[18] The New Testament radiates more clearly than the Old.[19] Basically, Karlstadt harmonizes Old and New Testament in terms of the latter.

The primacy of Scripture over human institutions is derivative. Scripture's authority comes from God who spoke through human messengers.[20] The gospel itself asserts that 'You do not speak, but the Spirit within you' (Matt. 10:20).[21] The Spirit must still speak through the Bible, for the mere letter kills, but the Spirit gives life.[22] At first Karlstadt finds the Spirit only in the Scriptures. Christ and the Spirit are included in the letter, but some never penetrate beyond the letter that they memorized.[23] Later Karlstadt scoffs at the idea of tying the Spirit to the letter as bibliolatry:

I imagined that I was a Christian when I clove profound and beautiful sayings out of Jeremiah and saved them for disputations, lectures, sermons, or other speeches and writings, and this was supposed to please God especially. But when I came to my right senses, I found that I neither knew God, nor did I love the highest Good as Goodness. I saw that I trusted, loved, and depended upon the created letter, and the same was my god,

17   KT 74, 21:27–30 (1522).
18   Credner, par 52–3 (1518–20).
19   Credner, par 156: 'Atque in primum redigendas evangelicas lampades, sive, si magis cupis, totius veritatis divinae clarissima lumina' (1518–20). Thus, despite their poor textual transmission, the gospels are the primary authority.
20   *Malachiam* (93), Bv–2v (1522).
21   Credner, par 2 (1518–20). Additional references are to Deut. 18:18; Matt. 10:20; John 14:10, 24; Rom. 1:1; Gal. 1:1. The biblical basis for Karlstadt's movement beyond Scripture should be emphasized rather than 'a Platonic devaluation of the letter' (Rupp, 'Word and Spirit,' 20). Karlstadt protests against the admixture of theology and philosophy. See e.g. KÄHLER, 34*, th 143: 'Doctrina Aristotelis in scholis theologorum facit malam mixturam' (1517). This view is expressed most crassly in 1520: 'Quid hic pontificibus, quid nonnulis doctoribus dicam, qui farinas suas sacris libris immiscuerunt, qui repurgatum triticum, qui casta et emuncta domini eloquia suis doctrinis, suis tradionibus, foedaverunt?' (Credner, introd). Col. 2:8 is also cited against the philosophers (Credner, par 3).
22   See KÄHLER, 28*, th 102–10 (1517).
23   Seitz, *Der authentische Text* 26 [Carolostadius]: 'Scire sanctam scripturam non est multas auctoritates memoriter recitare, sed spiritum introclusum in litteris et dominum nostrum Christum quaerere et gustare, insuper auctoritates ex intentione scribentium proferre' (1519).

but I did not perceive what God had spoken through Jeremiah: 'Those who keep my law do not know me,' and they have not asked for me [Jer. 2:9]. Behold, how one can enact and keep God's law and still neither know God nor acknowledge him. One knows the letter or sets one's desire upon it, but one does not know God when one's love and desire are founded upon the letter. For, those who are sons of God are driven by God; not the letter.[24]

Even so, Karlstadt follows up this passage with the rhetorical question: 'What else is such wisdom than a wisdom in human eyes, when we advance Scripture and other created things (out of which we must learn and love God) for our satisfaction?'[25] The Spirit is essential, but the letter remains the primary avenue of the Spirit, despite its defects. Some say one should chew the nut, not the shell, of the Scriptures. Karlstadt hesitates to affirm this; besides, Scripture remains clearer than 'dreams, visions, and complicated parables.'[26] The Spirit is not confined to Scripture, however, for the Bible itself points one at times directly to the Spirit.

Neither Luther nor Karlstadt could uphold the sole sufficiency of Scripture. It furnished a nice slogan against the papacy, but *sola scriptura* proved too limited a basis for a reformed church. Luther resolves the problem by augmenting Scripture with traditions that he considers compatible. Karlstadt, in contrast, does not want to add to Scripture, but he follows the example of the early church when he faces a new situation. In effect he turns to Scripture to reach beyond it:

Occasionally it does happen, however, that there are cases and matters that have not been contained in Holy Scripture; yet, no one should start or do something boldly, for we have to give an account of all of our words and works, and we have to be responsible for whether or not we sought and desired to seek God's will in such matters. Therefore I would not be displeased if Christian people would follow, and not forsake, the acts of the Apostles ... and earnestly desire to know the will of God. And when God does not want to give them enough understanding, they should cast a lot in those cases they could not understand and regulate through godly writ, following the Apostles who, by casting a lot, chose Matthias instead of Judas Iscariot (Acts 1:26).[27]

24 *Gelassen* (104), Bv (1523).
25 Ibid, Bv–2.
26 *Willen gottes* (102), D3v: 'Nu merck ich (spricht ein leeser) ... das syn gotlich gemuth in heiliger schrifft verschlossen ist wie eyn kern in einer schalenn ... Aber wie dem sey, so ist dannest gotlicher will in H. geschryfft klerlicher tzu mercken dan in dreymen, in gesichten, unde verwickelten geleychniss ... Drumb wil ich mich der lichten schrifft behelfen ...' (1523).
27 Ibid, [H4–v].

This presumes an emergency, though the casting of lots was to be part of the procedure in selecting shepherds to lead the congregation. Even here Karlstadt emulates scriptural procedure – an illustration of his primitivism, though in his writings he never appeals to a die that has been cast prayerfully.

Karlstadt's primitivism, which claims for all believers what the Apostles claimed, leads him to argue that, just as the Spirit inspired believers of old, so Christ's followers are to be inspired throughout the ages. Already in 1519 Karlstadt uses Luke 21:15 to prove Christ's continuing inspiration of believers, referring to the Holy Spirit crying in them: 'Abba, Father' (Rom. 8:15).[28] Such words confirm Scripture: 'Words of God in the Bible are words that God spoke and placed in the mouth of his servants'[29]; 'Therefore, Scripture or the Holy Spirit says ...'[30] The Spirit harmonizes with Scripture. As a believer Karlstadt is directly inspired by the Holy Spirit and, consequently, his writings are as truthful as the scriptures of the Apostles and the Prophets.[31] A shift has occurred, for Karlstadt would not have written this in 1520. Sermons, too, should be preached under direct, divine inspiration: 'Therefore all preachers should always maintain that their teaching is from God, not from themselves, and they should make such an appeal wholeheartedly, and say with profound earnestness: "thus saith the Lord."'[32]

Karlstadt's reference to 'all preachers' already (February 1522) involves more than clerics. The messenger (Malachias, German bott) was a layperson:

I think that the man whom God calls Malachi, messenger, was something of an ordinary, uncalled man like Amos, or a farmer, sheepman, or shepherd like Amos, on whom God conferred the name Malachi. Perhaps he already had another name, and God may have given him a new name. Similarly, Christ called and named simple, unlearned fishermen ... in order to confound the worldly wise, the discriminators, and men of name, to stop the mouths of all creatures, so no one would boast of himself and vaunt his own wisdom, as Paul teaches (1 Cor. 1:19f).[33]

28 *Auslegung* (15), Bv: 'Darumb sagt Christus (Luce xxi): "Ir solt nit gros furbetrachtung haben, dan weisheit wurt euch eingeben"' (1519). *Malachiam* (93), B2: 'Ir seind nit die reden, sonder der geist meines vatters, der ist welcher in euch redet. Matth. x' (1522).

29 *Malachiam* (93), B: 'Worte gotis in der biblien, seind worte, die got geret, und in den mund seiner knecht gelegt hat' (1522).

30 Ibid, B2v: 'Derhalben spricht die schrifft, aber der heylig geist.'

31 KS 2, 64:1–4 (1525).

32 *Malachiam* (93), B3v: 'Alsso solten alle predigern stetz bedingen das ire laher nicht ir selber ist, sonder gotis. Und solten disse bedinghung mit hertzen thun. Und mit grossem ernst sagen: "Das hat got geredt"' (1522).

33 Ibid, A2–v.

The layman, Peter, can solve scriptural problems with the voice of God in his heart. He does not need the 'external testimony' of a Greek grammatical argument as used by the cleric 'Gemser,' since that argument and the Spirit are in harmony. Nevertheless, those learned only in external Scripture quench the Spirit, whereas the apostolic experience of the Spirit can conquer a grammatical handicap:

> [PETER] I want to have my testimony from the Spirit, inside of myself, just as Christ promised.
> GEMSER Where?
> PETER Don't you even realize that Christ says, 'the Spirit, the Comforter, will bear witness to you' and, 'you will also be my witnesses'? Thus it went with the Apostles who were inwardly assured through the testimony of the Spirit, whereafter they preached Christ outwardly and proved through the Scriptures that Christ must suffer for us, and that the same Christ is Jesus of Nazareth who was crucified.
> GEMSER That was said about the Apostles.
> PETER Are we not to be compared with the Apostles? Why does Peter say to Cornelius that he had received the Spirit like them? Why does Paul say that we must be his imitators? Didn't Christ promise us his Spirit, as he did to the Apostles? Only the Spirit leads us to the recognition of God's words. Therefore, it follows that those who don't hear what God's Spirit says, don't understand God's words, neither are they Christians.
> As Christ says: 'Those belong to Christ, who have the Spirit of Christ.' Therefore only God's Spirit gives us the testimony and assurance (Rom 8:16).[34]

Thus the Spirit is more reliable than mere theological training that intimidates the laity. The Spirit gives theological acuity to the humble. Gemser is amazed:

> GEMSER Who taught you this?
> PETER The voice I heard and didn't see. I don't know how it came and went away.
> GEMSER Who is that?
> PETER Our Father who is in heaven!
> GEMSER Ah, if I'd only learned it from him![35]

34 KS 2, 18:30–19:8 (1524).
35 KS 2, 17:17–21 (1524).

The Spirit creates and confirms Scripture to clarify to babes what has been hidden from the wise. Because Scripture itself is derived from the Spirit, there is no contradiction.

Karlstadt's theology exhibits genuine consistency combined with a development towards radicalism. This suggests that Karlstadt was more stable than has usually been thought. His unstable situation was the result, as he saw it, of being 'a hare among the hounds,' or of having been catapulted out of Saxony 'with rifle shots.' The coherence of Karlstadt's thought derives from his biblicism; his radicalism comes from the same source, because Scripture corrodes centuries of tradition.

Karlstadt was the only reformer to publish a *Booklet on the Canon of Scripture* (1520) and his argumentation is quite sophisticated for the sixteenth century. A comparison of Karlstadt's and Luther's views on the canon is available.[36] Although Luther's Bible was crucial in shaping Protestant ideas of canonicity, Karlstadt had already faced many of the theoretical issues and Luther did not necessarily prevail over him. Perhaps it is because of Karlstadt that the book of James was kept in the Protestant canon: Luther disparaged the book, but Karlstadt staunchly defended James's canonicity,[37] and Luther's later preface to James (1546) was more moderate. Karlstadt excised the Apocrypha, including the Prayer of Manasses. Although Luther promoted the Prayer of Manasses, it did not gain currency among Protestants.[38] Striking is Karlstadt's agreement with Jerome and Erasmus that the final chapter of Mark is 'spurious' (*subditicium*).[39]

We have seen that Karlstadt favoured the New over the Old Testament. His three degrees of canonicity are also significant. Accepting the traditional Jewish tripartite division of the Old Testament, Karlstadt introduces a similar approach to the New. First are the gospels of Matthew, Mark, Luke-Acts, and John.[40] Unlike Luther, Karlstadt relegates Paul's letters to the secondary level. For Karlstadt's doctrine of the church his relative overestimation of the gospels and Acts is decisive. In practice the primary (Genesis–Deuteronomy, Matthew–Acts) and the secondary writings (Prophets, Pauline letters) are used without hesitation. This is less true of the tertiary materials (Old Testament 'Writings' and the remainder of

36 H.H. Howorth, 'The Origin.'
37 Credner, par 90–1, 147–50 (1518–20).
38 For Luther, see Howorth, 'The Origin,' 333. For Karlstadt see Credner, par 115 (1518–20). Karlstadt argues that the Prayer of Manasses is lacking in Hebrew; that it contradicts numerous biblical passages when it claims that Abraham was sinless, and that, because of its different subject matter, the Prayer was not alluded to in 2 Chron. 33:19.
39 Credner, par 131 (1518–20).
40 Credner, par 165 (1518–20). Karlstadt does not list Acts separately, for he subsumes it under Luke, citing Jerome (par 133): '[Lucas] volumen edidit quod titulo πραξεις αποστολων praenotatur' (1518–20). In *Bucher* (46), [B3], Karlstadt notes: 'Actus das seint der apostel handelung odder geschicht, hat Lucas beschrieben, derhalben seint sie evangelischmessig' (1520).

the New Testament). Karlstadt seldom cites Revelation and he well-nigh removes it from his canon.[41] He is prejudiced against apocalyptic writings and has little concern for an eschatology that goes beyond the simpler questions of personal immortality and resurrection.

From 1517 to 1519 Karlstadt teaches the supremacy of Scripture, as Bubenheimer has noted.[42] But even at this stage there are hints of a more exclusive principle. For example, Karlstadt considers limbo 'ridiculous,' not because it contradicts Scripture but because he cannot find it there.[43] Other examples could be added.[44]

However, from 1520 to 1521 the sole sufficiency of Scripture (sola scriptura) is stressed either in harmony with tradition or against tradition in general. Thus in 1520 Karlstadt rejects canon law and papal decretals because he is not supposed to add to Scripture.[45] Nevertheless, he would kiss the hands and feet of a Christian pope.[46] He also appeals to a Christian council that includes laypersons and is guided by Scripture.[47] Perhaps Karlstadt is already thinking in terms of sola scriptura, for he may have accepted a Christian papacy on the scriptural basis of the giving of the keys to Peter, and his approval of councils may have been based on Acts.

Late in 1521 the balance is clearly reversed. One's arrows should be shot from Scripture, nothing else.[48] One does not add to or subtract from Scripture.[49] A black devil with horns is not found in the Bible: therefore it is 'a lying curse.'[50] Karlstadt

---

41   Karlstadt cites negative comments from Jerome and Erasmus (Credner, par 155). He has
     already (par 69) referred to De civitate dei, 20.17, where Augustine observes that the book
     contains many obscure passages. The Apocalypse ultimately appears as the last of the tertiary
     works in the canon (par 165) (1518–20). In Bucher (46), C2–v, Karlstadt questions its canoni-
     city (1520).

42   BUBENHEIMER, 159.

43   LÖSCHER 2, 85–6, th 84–8 (1519).

44   LÖSCHER 2, 147: 'Omnem autem consuetudinem Apostolus subvertit, et abusum iudicavit,
     cum inquit: "Sed licet nos vel angelus de caelo praedicaverit vobis evangelium, praeter id quod
     praedicavimus vobis, anathema sit," et post pauca: "Nec enim ab homine accepi illud, nec
     didici, sed per revelationem Iesu Christi."' See Gal. 1:8–12.

45   Heylickeit (44), Fv (1520).

46   Ibid, [F4v]: 'Wan [der bapst] sich aber noch wolt entsinnen, und zu Christo dretten, sso wolt
     ich yhm hend und fuess kussenn.'

47   Concilio (45), [A5], rather than 'Aiij': 'Appelir ich zu dem allerheylgsten Christlichen und
     gemeynen concilio, das nicht allein bischoffen und prelaten, sunder auch weltlich hern und
     alle leyhen, so einen reynen, guten vorstand heyliger schrifft haben, begreufft' (1520); BUBEN-
     HEIMER, 298:175–7.

48   Messe (71), A3 (1521).

49   Ibid, Dv–2. Scripture may be interpreted only in its own context, or where this is not clear,
     one follows exactly (stracks) the words of Christ.

50   Ibid, [D4v]. Karlstadt also denied the existence of hobgoblins and spooks: Job VII (155), Ev (1538).

also pits Christ's words against church councils.[51] From 1521 on the principle that *human* tradition is deceitful (*humana traditio fallax*), already discernible in 1519 or 1520, is dominant.[52]

In 1521 Karlstadt calls the monastic system extrabiblical, hence antibiblical.[53] The stage is now set for conflict with Luther, who returns from the Wartburg and accepts material for a new cowl from the council of Wittenberg.[54] Luther is indifferent to extrabiblical practices, but Karlstadt condemns them. When Karlstadt applies his strict construction of *sola scriptura* to liturgy, the church, baptism, and the Lord's Supper (especially from 1522 on), he passes into his Baptist phase.

---

51   Ibid, A3v: 'Christus spricht: "Ich bin der weg, warheit, und das leben." Ehr sagt nit: "Ich bin die ubung, gebrauch, oder concilium."'
52   *Verba Dei* (26), [A4v], with reference to Col. 2:8 (1520).
53   *Coelibatu* (60), C3v (1521).
54   Luther was consistent; see his previous reaction (18 Dec 1521), BR 2, 415:25–6: 'Nam et ego in habitu et ritu isto manebo, nisi mundus alius fiat.'

2

Predestination

Traditionally Karlstadt's view of predestination has been judged on the basis of a Lutheran or Augustinian model. Jäger first interpreted Karlstadt within the framework of double predestination, although he divined a trend towards what he called a non-particularistic infralapsarianism.[1] Barge followed Jäger.[2]

Kähler is impressive in discovering Karlstadt's citations from Augustine and from pseudo-Augustinian sources, but his interpretation is flawed. He rightly assumes that Karlstadt is consistent, but Kähler serves this aim by stressing Augustine and ignoring the pseudo-Augustinian material.[3] If problems remain, Kähler checks the Augustinian context of Karlstadt's excerpts and ignores Karlstadt's selectivity.

Sider is usually solid, and therefore independent, in his interpretation of Karlstadt's theology, but on predestination he reiterates Kähler,[4] though Sider grants that some problems remain.[5] None the less, he also feels that such problems are best resolved by skipping the pseudo-Augustinian quotes.[6] But Karlstadt had used Augustine in such a way that even the genuine excerpts cited by Sider do not support unconditional double predestination.[7]

---

1 Jäger, *Andreas Bodenstein*, 348n.
2 BARGE 1, 77–9.
3 KÄHLER, 32*. An excellent summary of Augustine's views of predestination is found in McSorley, *Luther: Right or Wrong?*, ch 4.
4 SIDER, 39, n 108.
5 Ibid, 40, n 114: 'It is somewhat difficult, however, to reconcile both kinds of statements.'
6 Ibid, 39, nn 108, 112. Sometimes Karlstadt may seem more Augustinian than he really is. See e.g. KÄHLER, 21*, th 60: 'Corruit hoc, quod Augustinus contra haereticos loquitur excessive.' But note the restrictive pronoun *hoc*. Luther opposes this restriction in his *Disputatio contra scholasticam theologiam*, aiming his first thesis at a '*dictum commune*,' when he is refuting Karlstadt (WA 1, 224).
7 I would like to comment on the footnotes in SIDER, 38–40. I accept Sider's statements in nn 106, 110, 111, and 113, which establish unconditional *single* predestination for a brief phase in 1518. N 104: This indicates a final, not an unconditional, judgment. N 105: Perse-

Since Karlstadt quoted liberally from Augustine in his *151 Theses* of 26 April 1517 and published a commentary on part of Augustine's *On the Spirit and the Letter* (1517–19), Augustine's influence has been taken for granted. Kähler exag-

verance is attributed to grace alone, not to an eternal decree. N 107: God limits his grace, which is not necessarily efficacious, and which does not presuppose election or active reprobation. Karlstadt does not indicate whether the fall of the human race was predetermined. At Leipzig Karlstadt states that it was *not* predetermined. This view is implied here, for although Karlstadt appeals to God's will in th 118, which one might consider arbitrary, the use of a double negation (*non deest*) in the case of the elect is prompted by Karlstadt's refusal to imply double predestination. This is confirmed by th 111 (n 104), 'a quibusdam iuste exigit poenam.' Since God's condemnation is just, the penalty is based on the human fall. This cannot be predicated of their own fall in the case of the non-elect who were not restored to pristine grace, and by implication their exclusion must be based on the fall of the race in Adam. This establishes only conditional reprobation. N 108: Grace is resistible, and the fall of the 'sons of perdition,' who received grace for a while, is their own rather than God's work – even though God prepares for it in a passive sense. N 109: The intended stumbling of the elect does not cause their damnation. Like Kähler's (31*), Sider's translation shows that he punctuates as follows: 'Electi secundum propositum, interdum labuntur.' This reading of the text would indicate single predestination in 1517, but 'secundum propositum' modifies 'labuntur,' not 'electi.' Since Augustine does not teach effective calling in the case of the called sons of perdition, his distinction between the *vocati* and the *vocati secundum propositum* (n 110) makes sense, but not when applied to the *electi*. Thus I punctuate: 'Electi, secundum propositum interdum labuntur.' They had fallen by divine intent, based on foreknowledge that they were among the *electi*. Since the fall *secundum propositum* is restricted to the elect; this undermines unconditional reprobation. N 112: The citation unequivocally rejects double predestination. N 113: Karlstadt does not simply say that the non-elect 'were predestined with the devil into eternal fire.' His primary point is that humans cannot sift the wheat from the chaff. The phrase 'in hac vita constitui' is crucial, but ambiguous if divorced from its context. The reprobates could have been 'set up in this life' to be damned like pawns, or they could have been 'selected in this life' on the basis of their own fall (th 121, cited in n 108), or, if they have not received prevenient grace (n 107), the fall of the race would enter into God's calculations (infralapsarianism). Such a conditional form of reprobation can be called 'predestination' as Karlstadt does, but I am now refuting the view that Karlstadt taught double predestination, which presupposes unconditional election and unconditional reprobation. Karlstadt's conditional view of predestination is common in the late Middle Ages, when one could speak of predestination after foreseen merits (*post praevisa merita*). According to Biel, *Collectorium*, Prologus et I, d. 40, art. 1, not. 1: 'praedestinatio ... est praecognitio Dei de salvandis et bonis gratiae, quibus hic liberantur et in futuro coronabantur.' Later Biel introduces a restricted definition of predestination that implies single predestination. Thus Sider's problem with 'two kinds of statements' regarding predestination (n 114) parallels Oberman's discussion of whether Biel has two doctrines of predestination (*Harvest*, 187f). Since divine foreknowledge also modifies 'predestination' for Karlstadt, the parallel is instructive, as is Oberman's conclusion that Biel teaches a de facto doctrine of predestination *post praevisa merita*. Karlstadt excludes merits, but 'predestination' does follow human choice. N 114: Karlstadt rejects universalism and evades hardening. Such hardening would not *cause* damnation, for it assumes the fall. The other theses cited oppose double predestination. N 115: Karlstadt makes evil dependent on the acts of demons and one's own heart, and then there is what would have to be a conditional 'praesinitio,' and the 'cui nemo potest resistere' would allude to hardening.

gerates Augustine's impact, however, when he claims that Karlstadt ignored Johann von Staupitz's views on predestination. Staupitz (died 1524) had helped organize the University of Wittenberg as its first dean and kept up his relationship with the university. As vicar-general of the observantine Augustinians, he sent over one hundred Augustinians (including Luther) to Wittenberg. In his preface to De spiritu et littera (12) Karlstadt referred to Staupitz as his 'most meritorious preceptor and patron,' crediting Staupitz with aiding him to overcome his aversion to the idea of human inability apart from divine grace.[8] Thus Oberman rightly challenges Kähler's argument that Karlstadt held aloof from Staupitz's view of predestination.[9]

Staupitz teaches a doctrine of unconditional election and conditional reprobation (single predestination). As we shall see, Karlstadt affirms such a position in 1518, even though he would soon dilute it. Only the sole sufficiency of divine grace (sola gratia) defined the limits of his retreat.

Nevertheless, predestinarianism led to the 1518 debate with Johann Eck in Leipzig and Karlstadt's excommunication from the Roman church. Karlstadt's moderation also offended Luther. Later, Luther told some good tales about Karlstadt's arguments against unconditional reprobation, but his reminiscences are contradictory.[10] Finally, though Karlstadt did not openly relate his stance on predestination to external structures, it had sapped his confidence in the sacramental system even before his break with Rome.[11]

Towards Single Predestination, 1517 to 1519

In 1517, under the partial influence of Augustine, Karlstadt spurns several scholastic theses and affirms conditional election, sola gratia (!), and effective perseverance. God's ultimate will[12] is irresistible; showing mercy God removes the penalty of sin for some, and being just God exacts it of others. Divine foreknowledge is unchangeable. God calls many (but not all), who are illumined so that they recognize the truth and are enabled to accept or reject free will.[13]

---

8   SIDER, 18.
9   Oberman, 'Zweifrontenkrieg,' 350–1, n 64.
10   TR 4, 642:9–10 (no. 5070); TR 5, 49:5–6 (no. 5296); TR 5, 107:21–7 (no. 5375.o). An allusion to this is also found in WA 18, 207:24–6: 'Mich dunckt, D. Carlstadt [sey] eyn offentlicher feynd Gottes, und wölle ynn die helle so mehr rennen als draben.'
11   In 1518 Karlstadt does not want to discuss the relationship of (single) predestination to the power of the sacraments (KÄHLER, 95:15–17). He has something to hide. See Oberman, 'Zweifrontenkrieg,' 351, n (2).
12   'Against the Scotists,' Karlstadt argues that one should not distinguish an antecedent and consequent will in God or men; KÄHLER 31*, th 126: 'Putamus nec in deo nec in homine antecedentem voluntatem esse.' This means that God is no longer universally benevolent after Adam's fall. It also follows that God's will is based on foreknowledge.
13   KÄHLER, 29*, th 111–16.

Karlstadt distinguishes calling from election, evidently on the basis of Matthew 22:14: 'For many are called but few are chosen.' Good works, entirely derived from God, are dependent on whether one has been called. Moral behaviour is not a positive index to election, for God causes some of the elect to fall from time to time, to keep them humble, whereas even the called non-elect may persevere at length in good works before they stumble, and God does not lift them up.

The genuine criterion for election is perseverance. One cannot be sure of having this gift; therefore prayer is needed: 'Perseverance in love [dilectione] pertains to the grace of God. Therefore, Christ's prayer for Peter that he might not be lacking in faith, was not in vain.'[14] Karlstadt denounces merit on the believer's part. Even the grace of condignity, which makes one worthy before God, is effective only because God accepts his own grace. He does not owe anyone such acceptance, however.[15] Such statements seem ambiguous. Nevertheless, Kähler assumes unconditional double predestination in Karlstadt because he cites Romans 9:18: 'He has mercy upon whomever he wills, and he hardens the heart of whomever he wills.'[16] However, hardening need not imply unconditional reprobation, and later, when Karlstadt abandons single predestination, he retains a form of hardening. Therefore, Romans 9:18, cited without interpretation, is not decisive.

The image of the potter and the clay seems more persuasive.[17] Even here, however, Karlstadt's argument that 'the clay cannot resist the potter at all' must be limited to the final judgment in which the vessels are discarded, for Karlstadt never claims that the potter causes the vessels to be misshapen. In fact, the thesis of the potter illustrates a previous thesis: 'No one resists the will of God. God mercifully forgives some the penalty of sin; of others he justly exacts it.'[18] Acting in terms of sin, God's irresistible will towards the non-elect applies only to the final judgment and the intermediate hardening of existent evil.

Karlstadt asserts the immutability of divine foreknowledge, but he does not discuss eternal decrees.[19] He simply avoids active reprobation, but he accepts hardening and God's use of evil for good purpose.

14 KÄHLER, 30*, th 119: 'Perseverantia in dilectione pertinet ad gratiam dei'; th 120: 'Et ideo oratio Christi pro Petro non erat inanis, ne sua fides deficeret.' Cf th 121–3, 137.
15 KÄHLER, 32*, th 132: 'Vita aeterna non debetur iusto operanti cum gratia de condigno.'
16 KÄHLER, 32*. Regardless of the exegetical value of Kähler's view, this was not the traditional interpretation. See DENZINGER, *628.
17 KÄHLER, 29*, th 113: 'Figmentum nihil potest opponere suo figulo.'
18 KÄHLER, th 111.
19 KÄHLER, th 112. I agree with Kähler (29*) that this cannot be foreknowledge of praevisa merita, but it is not merely foreknowledge of predestination either, because Karlstadt interprets the call as enabling one to make a choice (th 115). The choice, made on the basis of prevenient grace which follows calling, would enter into God's calculations, making election conditional and necessitating foreknowledge.

Most of the apparent ambiguities can be resolved with Karlstadt's view of free will. The good we wish is entirely derived from God, but evil comes from human acts.[20] This belief precludes unconditional double predestination.

However, even election is based on foreknowledge, and this subverts unconditional single predestination. [Prevenient] grace, which enables one to see the truth, is entirely derived from God, but Karlstadt upholds one's free will to choose on the basis of this grace.[21] Although the theses on which Karlstadt rests this argument are pseudo-Augustinian, they form an integral part of the argument. Karlstadt had paved the way when he distinguished the will to do good (which comes from God) from what we will in order to do good (which also comes from God).[22] Clearly Karlstadt wants to defend salvation by grace alone, but this distinction makes sense only if one distinguishes prevenient grace (the will to do good) from human assent (what one wills in order to do good).

This is confirmed when Karlstadt opposes merits of congruity but upholds a disposition of congruity that is based on what God has already done.[23] Moreover, Karlstadt still accepts a grace of condignity, with the Augustinian modification that God does not owe salvation to those who have it.[24] This sets the stage for human choice. Since Karlstadt never interprets the choice itself as a positive good work, he can still credit God with all good works, and so we arrive at what may seem contradictory, that is, election is contingent on human choice, while God's grace is given gratuitously, though not to all.

Karlstadt has accepted many insights from Augustine, but he resists unconditional predestination. He has also broken with any doctrine of merit on the believer's part. All positive good works flow from God's grace alone.[25] Karlstadt experienced this break with scholasticism as 'vinegar to the teeth and smoke to the eyes.' He experienced this breakthrough with 'violent despair and storms of the soul concerning his eternal destiny.'[26] Barge accepts this statement, whereas

---

20 KÄHLER, 16*, th 26: 'Fecimus mala et venerunt bona.'
21 KÄHLER, 29*, th 115. This pertains only to the free will following calling, which is God's gracious gift to the called (whether elect or not). Before calling, however, God's grace batters the natural free will (KÄHLER, 17*, th 27: 'Deus est qui pulsat liberum arbitrium'), which cannot impede God (th 33), but this is the state *ante gratiam* when one does no good at all (th 34). At first sight this is confusing because Karlstadt does not develop a different nomenclature for the free will before grace, which is not genuinely free (th 33), and the truly free will after calling (KÄHLER, 29*, th 114–15).
22 KÄHLER, 16*, th 22: 'Ut bene velimus solius dei est'; th 23: 'Et quod volumus, ut faciamus bene, dei est.'
23 KÄHLER, 19*, th 46: 'Dispositiones de congruo ex parte hominis magis sunt ridende quam ponende'; th 47: 'Possunt autem ex parte dei aliquo modo poni.' Kähler does not know to what this applies (19*, n 2), but this fits the response of the elect to the call, th 115.
24 KäHLER, 19*, th 46–7.
25 KÄHLER, 32*, th 133: 'Vita aeterna est gratia data pro gratia ex misericordia et miseratione.'
26 BARGE 1, 74. See also SIDER, 17–18.

Hertzsch and Kähler trivialize this as an 'angry disappointment.'[27] Although Kähler has located a biblical precedent for Karlstadt's confession, this does not dispose of it. Proverbs and literary models have often served to universalize an experience that is nevertheless intensely personal.

If we take Karlstadt seriously, his 151 Theses of 1517 clarify why he lost certitude of salvation. Moral acts offer no index of certainty. Human choice and faith inject further insecurity, as does the hazard in divine calling. Until perseverance has been granted, one faces the threat of falling from grace. Karlstadt is recalling his views of 1517 when he notes how, at one time, his salvation seemed dependent on momentary faith.[28] Even falling resolves nothing, since God may for a while prostrate the elect to humble them.

Some late medieval schemes of election appeared to provide greater certitude, since God's antecedent will was not particularistic and his consequent will was based on merits of congruity. The pseudo-Augustinian adage that 'if you are not among the elect, make yourself elected' expresses this view.

The quest for certitude prodded Karlstadt a year later to embrace unconditional single predestination, for this position eliminated at least the human contribution to uncertainty.

The theses against Eck propounded in 1518 show a further alienation from some of the scholastics. Now Karlstadt denies that one can hold onto God's gift.[29] Congruity is Pelagian, making grace the handmaid of the human will.[30] Grace antedates human works and God's will cannot be made dependent on changeable human beings.[31]

God's calling is now efficacious. One still cannot be sure about one's election, but the old hope of doing what is within oneself (facere quod in se est) is vain, and its elimination is desirable.[32] One must suffer weakness and nothingness to join the church in praying to God alone for protection: 'Through this prayer, hope has been taken away from humanity, and this is very good, for whoever trusts humankind is accursed' [Jer. 17:5].[33]

---

27   KÄHLER, 8*, n 2.
28   Gelaub (139), A2. Referring to Christ's judgment of believers and unbelievers, Karlstadt says: 'Dise urteil hab ich vortzeiten also vernommen. Welcher an Christum glaubet, der wirt nicht gericht. Das ist war, so lang er glaubet. Widerumb, welcher nit glaubet, der ist schon gericht, das ist auch war. So lang er nicht glaubet, so lang ist er gericht.'
29   See the false thesis that the will can accept and hold on to God's gift, th 390, rejected by th 399: 'Homo non potest datam gratiam suis viribus custodire.' LÖSCHER 2, 103–4.
30   LÖSCHER 2, 91, th 250: 'Non possum a Pelagiano errore excusare eos, qui ita voluntati pedisequam faciunt gratiam, quam secundum merita de congruo dari fantur.'
31   CC 1, 55, th (153)–(4).
32   CC 1, 61, th (190): 'Qui facit quod in se est, facit quod deo displicet, mentitur, obloquitur ac sibi officit.'
33   CC 1, 60, th (176).

The adage of making yourself elect if you have not been elected could not have come from Augustine.[34] Karlstadt skips the text of the many who are called and the few who are chosen and concentrates on effective calling [Rom. 8:29, 30].[35] God confers plenary grace on one who is called (Matt. 13:12).[36] Karlstadt casts off *merits* of congruity, since calling is now efficacious, but there remains a grace of congruity before calling: 'God calls a man after he has been fitted for the call and is in harmony with it [*congruit*].'[37] Thus Karlstadt still implies a doctrine of not necessarily efficacious prevenient grace, which also affects some non-elect. God may even provide an early death for the elect so they will not fall, and God may extend the life of the non-elect so they will fall.[38] Since Karlstadt accepts original sin at this time, God must have lifted the unfallen non-elect to a state of grace for a while.[39]

The extension of life for the unelected accentuates the passive role of God in their fall. Similarly, the need to shorten the lives of some of the elect might imply that God's grace is not efficacious enough to save believers in extreme circumstances. But this would be in conflict with effective calling. Karlstadt may, however, have in mind the special circumstances of the elect in the 'days of tribulation,' or he may simply want to explain some biblical texts that would otherwise have been problematic.[40]

Karlstadt affirms a whole chain of arguments he used earlier. God does not have both an antecedent and a consequent will, but Karlstadt modifies this in terms of single predestination.[41] Election precedes our own works.[42] One cannot pray to be elected.[43] Good works are not decisive, for God's grace is poured forth despite our works.[44]

34 LÖSCHER 2, 95, th 303.
35 LÖSCHER 2, 94, th 293.
36 LÖSCHER 2, 94, th 294–5.
37 LÖSCHER 2, 103, th 385: 'Deus hominem vocat secundum quod vocationi aptus est et congruit.' In th 396f Karlstadt excludes human contributions. Thus the congruence is merely God's way of operating.
38 WA 6, 26, cited in Kähler, 'Nicht Luther,' 355, th 7: 'Iustorum alii dum iusti sunt ex huius vitae periculis, ne malitia mutet intellectum eorum auferuntur. Alii vero donec a iustitia cadunt in eisdem periculis vita productiore tenentur.'
39 LÖSCHER 2, 92, th 264.
40 E.g. Matt. 10:22, 24:22; Mark 13:20.
41 LÖSCHER 2, 95, th 308–10. Karlstadt rejects the application of 1 Tim. 2:4 on the antecedent will (th 308) as well as the consequent will (th 309). Then he casts aside the two wills of the scholastics, for 'Deus non respiciat opera futura' (th 310), and he no longer injects free choice.
42 LÖSCHER 2, 94, th 291–5. See esp th 291, where Karlstadt refers to the Book of Life and proves single predestination on the basis of Jer. 31:3: 'Perpetua charitate dilexi te, ideo miserans in misericordia attraxi te.'
43 LÖSCHER 2, 95, th 303–4. One can ask to be drawn only if one has been elected.
44 LÖSCHER 2, 94, th 289.

The moral realm is not unimportant, however, for although one's works do not cause predestination, grace produces its own works. Aristotelian ethics, based as it is on self-interest and the search for honour, must be rejected[45]; it cannot even serve theology.[46] Christian morality, expressing God's grace, differs qualitatively from the systems spun by merely human reason.

Karlstadt then discusses single predestination in terms of the will. One's 'free' will before the advent of grace leads only to sin. Since Karlstadt does not accept a vacuous concept of pure freedom, he relates it to salvation. Original human freedom is illusory, and one's own free will is evil.[47] Works are good only when God is their author.[48]

The elect still stumble seven times daily, but God upholds them in mercy.[49] Thus Karlstadt teaches election without foreseen merits. Having conceded this much, Karlstadt now tackles double predestination. Human creatures cannot cause their own election, but they do cause their own damnation: 'All that is ours, *and which God has not made* to be ours, is evil and sin' (my italics). Then Karlstadt quotes Hosea 13:9 (Vulg.): 'Israel, you cause your own misery, for your salvation alone comes from me.' For emphasis Karlstadt repeats: 'from us comes perdition: from God comes assistance, and good, and salvation.'[50]

In February of 1517 Staupitz's treatise on predestination had been printed, and there are several parallels between Karlstadt and Staupitz. Both discuss the contemplation of one's own nothingness before God.[51] Staupitz also teaches unconditional election.[52] A weak doubting of Augustine's authorship of 'If you are not predestined, make yourself predestined' leads to the dismissal of this idea.[53] Hosea 13 shows that our perdition comes from ourselves and our salvation from God alone.[54] The belief in God's infusion of love and in the consequent salvation by divine works is also found in Staupitz.[55] The morality of the natural man is contrasted with the morality of the redeemed man.[56] The theme

---

45   LÖSCHER 2, 89, th 214–19, 221–2.

46   LÖSCHER 2, 91, th 251–6.

47   CC 1, 54–5, th (149): 'Voluntas est domina et regina suorum actuum, suorum omnium scilicet malorum'; th (150): 'Quando voluntas dominatur in anima, ridet diabolus et exsultat'; th (151): 'Deus amat in nobis quod ipse fecit; at quod ipse non fecit, odit.'

48   CC 1, 53, th (142): 'Nam voluntas nostra non est regina et domina eorum operum quae deus, ut voluntatis essent, fecit.' Cf 55, th (151–2).

49   CC 1, 44–5, th (136): 'Adde, quod "septies in die iustus cadit," sed "non colliditur, quia dominus supponit manum" ...'; th (137): They are lifted from their falls by acknowledging their sins.

50   CC 1, 56, th (158)–(9).

51   Staupitz, *Fürsehung*, 139.

52   Ibid, 142.

53   Ibid, 143.

54   Ibid, 183, 185. See also Aquinas, *Summa theologiae* 1, q. 23, a. 3, ad. 2.

55   Staupitz, *Fürsehung*, 147–8.

56   Ibid, 148.

of Christ's calling many, but not all, which Karlstadt taught in 1517, is related to Staupitz's observation that the blood of Christ was poured out for many, but not for all.[57]

There are some contrasts. Staupitz is more emphatically Christocentric; his language is practical and mystical, whereas Karlstadt's arguments are made with theological precision. Staupitz is positive and irenic, but Karlstadt polemizes against the scholastics. Staupitz accepts considerable certitude that one is among the chosen. Hope means that one does not doubt one's election. Karlstadt, however, still teaches that the abandonment of such hope is essential, although Staupitz had influenced him, even if only briefly.

The first section of Karlstadt's commentary on Augustine's *De spiritu et littera* reveals Karlstadt's acceptance of single predestination. He cites a pseudo-Augustinian source to distinguish between divine foreknowledge and predestination. He accepts both for the elect, but he distinguishes them with respect to the non-elect: 'God does not predestine everything that is revealed, for evil appears but he does not predestine it, but the good he both foreknows and predestines.'[58]

Again, good works and an apparently blameless life are not an index to election, though God reveals himself through good works (Eph. 2:10), which cannot be hidden. Election becomes visible, even though not every ostensibly good work rests on election.[59] Perseverance distinguishes the elect from the outwardly good non-elect.[60] Effective calling precedes good will, and if Eck cites that 'many are called, but few are chosen,' he needs Augustine's refutation of popular misunderstanding regarding this text.[61]

Karlstadt now opposes conditional election. God does not need human assent, for the will is passive in divine election. When God converts the sinner, assent is included.[62] Karlstadt's *405 Conclusiones* (1518) and the *Defensio* (1518) teach unconditional single predestination.

Karlstadt soon abandons the doctrine of unconditional election. This reversal is understandable, for Karlstadt has three basic motivations exerting contradictory effects on his concept of single predestination. These constants are *sola gratia*, the need for certainty, and his refusal to make God the cause of evil. *Sola gratia* would drive Karlstadt towards predestination, unless he accepts a negative conditionality. The need for certainty might drive him towards unconditional predestination to eliminate the human factor, or it might drive him from it to limit divine despotism and to make man responsible for his own destiny. Although Karlstadt

57 Ibid, 155.
58 KÄHLER, 40. As Kähler notes, the citation comes from the pseudo-Augustinian *Liber hypognosticon*, PL 44, 974f.
59 LÖSCHER 2, 128.
60 LÖSCHER 2, 133: 'At ego de illis loquor fidelibus ... qui dei electi sunt, quorum nullus perit.'
61 LÖSCHER 2, 161.
62 LÖSCHER 2, 163.

has asserted that one should abandon all hope, he contains such lack of hope with a new hope that this hopelessness would become the first stage towards salvation. The need for certitude operates even in its absence! Finally, as Karlstadt admitted afterwards, the logical corollary of single predestination is double predestination. Karlstadt had written two treatises on logic, and the concept of single predestination, which is the bane of theologicians, would presently disintegrate.

Karlstadt had emphasized in mystical terms one's abandonment of hope and the negation of one's ego. This idea can be expressed on the basis of Christ's parable (Luke 15:8) as 'sweeping.' Now, Karlstadt refuses to make election dependent on a good work, 'unless it flows from the sharp, fearful, and oppressive judgment of our own sins ... When that happens, God can no longer leave the oppressed sinner at all.'

> Indeed, if someone wishes to perform a God-pleasing service, he – to sum it up – has to sweep himself with his judgment. All of God's absolutions depend and are erected on the condemnations of our own transgressions of divine commands ... As the Apostle says, 'If we condemn ourselves, God will not condemn us.'[63]

This belief rests on Augustine's *ubi non ego, ibi felicius ego* as well as on John Chrysostom's view of the sinner as *iudex sui*, who is accepted by God on the basis of his self-accusations.[64] It inaugurates the life of obedience in *gelassenheit* (self-surrender) in which one ascribes everything to God: 'Then you have surrendered and allow to take place what God does with you in accordance with his will. Thus what you claim for your ego, your self, your own, is destroyed and the blessed ego sprouts forth.'[65]

Now one's works, entirely derived from God, shine in the darkness: not in praise of self, but so that others will praise God (Matt. 5:16). The believer renounces his old self, and the Spirit of the Father works in him. This position clashes with the view of the scholastics ('the confused theologians'), 'who teach that a man produces the substance of good works.'[66] Those who have swept themselves with judgment receive a new will and good works which flow from God alone.[67]

---

63 *Ausslegung* (15), A2. Karlstadt (B–v) cites 1 Cor. 11:31 and Augustine's *De continentia* 13:29: 'Ubi enim non ego, ibi felicius ego.' *Corpus scriptorum ecclesiasticorum latinorum* 41, 179:8.
64 *Patrologia graeca*, ed J.P. Migne, 57, 450:δ'f. Karlstadt credits Chrysostom, but without specific reference to this passage in *Ausslegung* (15), [C4].
65 *Ausslegung* (15), Bv: 'so bistu gelassen, und liest geschehen, das got mit dir macht nach seinem willen. Also verdirbt dein icheit, dynheit, meinheit, und entspreust das selig mein.'
66 Ibid, Bv.
67 Ibid, E3, with reference to Ezek. 36:26.

When Karlstadt broke with scholasticism, he eliminated the antecedent will. But Karlstadt distinguishes God's alien (fremden) and proper (eigen) will: 'Alien works of God are: to suppress [human] wrath, to frighten, to create fear, to oppress, to wound, etc. Proper works of God are: to have mercy, to do good, to save, to redeem, to heal, and finally, they preserve.'[68] The distinction between God's alien and proper will is not used to rationalize double predestination. Karlstadt's choice of adjectives confirms his observation that 'all alien works serve God's proper work.'[69] Moreover, the distinction holds only for 'God's children.' Thus the hell God's alien will creates for believers serves their salvation, for in their oppression they cry out to God to rescue them.

Karlstadt uses Hosea 13:9 (Vulg.) again and adds Matthew 15:13 to prove that one's disintegration (verderben) proceeds from oneself.[70] Again, he shows how one negatively prepares for effective grace:

> As long as a man depends on and cleaves to his own power and works, he is unassisted by God. But when one ponders one's own inability or falls in one's illness, saying: 'take away my own obstruction,' then Christ speaks to him: 'my grace is sufficient for you' [2 Cor. 12:9].[71]

Karlstadt now holds to a doctrine of election, based on effective but conditional calling, and he has publicly retracted unconditional single predestination. He plans to publish a booklet on the will of God.[72] This booklet, which did not appear until 1523, contains a view so similar to what Karlstadt teaches here that he may have kept it from publication until he was free to repudiate Luther.

Karlstadt's changed views on predestination were to haunt him soon afterwards, for he became embroiled in controversy with Johann Eck, who was beginning his career of defending the old faith. To spy out the land Eck had spent some time in Wittenberg, feigning friendship with Karlstadt and Luther. But after leaving Wittenberg Eck directed his *Obelisci* against Luther. When the *Obelisci* arrived in Wittenberg, Luther had travelled to Heidelberg. Thus Karlstadt defended Luther in writing a rejoinder. The outcome was a public debate between Karlstadt and Luther on the one hand and Eck on the other. Karlstadt's position in the debate at Leipzig in 1519 was unenviable. His challenge of Eck in the *405 Conclusiones* and the *Defensio* rested on single predestination. In Auslegung he had undercut this position. If he retracted even minor points, he would appear

68 *Auslegung* (15), [B5].
69 Ibid, [B5]: 'Got macht alle fremde werck umb willen seines eygen wercks.'
70 Ibid, Ev.
71 Ibid, E2v–3.
72 Ibid, [C4v]: 'Ich wil hie von ein eygen buchlein machen von dem willen gots.' This is *Willen Gottes* (102).

to have yielded to Eck. Karlstadt did not retract. Fortunately for him Eck does not seem to have known the *Ausslegung*, and if Karlstadt narrowed the debate to the anti-scholastic element, circumventing 'sweeping,' he could uphold unconditionality and *sola gratia* without compromising himself. Should the debate spill beyond those limits, frank retraction would have been deemed capitulation. But would Eck play Karlstadt's game?

Eck played his own game as narrowly as Karlstadt did, and for his own reasons. The debate was held in the name of orthodoxy.[73] Eck, however, had been less cautious at an earlier stage when he published his *Chrysopassus*, which went so far in asserting free will that a reiteration of those arguments would have left him, not Karlstadt, besmirched with heresy.[74]

The debate was rigid and it adds little to clarify Karlstadt's views. Moreover, Karlstadt made an unfavourable impression for several reasons. For one thing, he had to be bled after a fall upon entering Leipzig, and in addition the environment was hostile. Yet, the documents relating to the debate show Karlstadt doing rather well. He manœuvred Eck into affirming that God performed the whole (*totus*) good work in the elect. And Eck's subsequent distinction between 'the whole' and 'in totality' (*totus sed non totaliter*) does not seem cogent. Despite that, Karlstadt may not have seemed convincing because he had to hide some of his own convictions.

We shall not enter into the course of the debate which has been ably treated by Sider and Moore.[75] Only a few points are new. Of interest is Karlstadt's belief that God had not predestined the original fall of humanity. Thus far this point had only been implied. If the human race had not fallen, all would still have free will, but because 'the first man' fell, the whole race fell with him.[76]

Another argument involves the image of the horse and its rider, made even more famous during Luther's battle with Erasmus. Eck cited pseudo-Augustine, saying: 'Augustine compares grace to free will as a rider to his horse.'[77] Karlstadt inverted the image: '[I reply] that the free will relates to grace as a wounded

---

73 Seitz, *Der authentische Text*, 14: [Carolostadius]: 'Primo illud testamur et ubique testatum esse volumus, nusquam ab ecclesia catholica ad latum digitum nos velle discedere.' See also Eck, ibid, 14–15, and Luther, ibid, 55–6.

74 Eck switched from his previous position that 'est enim voluntas in anima sicut regina in regno' (CC 1, 53) to saying that the free will had some activity, 'liberum arbitrium aliquid operatur.' (Seitz, 28). See also Moore, 'Between Mani and Pelagius: Predestination and Justification in the Early Writings of John Eck,' 158 and 161: '[Eck's] task was not to disprove Carlstadt, but to prevent Carlstadt from disproving him.'

75 SIDER, 70–81. See also Moore, 'Between Mani and Pelagius,' 118–58.

76 Seitz, 16, with reference to Ecclus. 15:14–15.

77 Seitz, 24: 'Et quod Augustinus ... gratiam ad liberum arbitrium velut sessorum ad equum comparat.'

invalid relates to the beast of burden on which he is borne.'[78] The latter image is genuinely Augustinian, for nature is seen as needing the support and healing of grace. None the less, the idea is foreign to Karlstadt's own development, where the authentic note is that of grace alone after self-condemnation or 'sweeping.' Karlstadt taught the *destruction* of the old self and its replacement with God's newly created ego. The *Ausslegung* rather than the debate foreshadows Karlstadt's development. Nature (flesh) is replaced by grace (Spirit).[79]

Interlude, 1520 to 1523

When Erasmus prepared to attack Luther in 1524, he reviewed the Leipzig debate, noting that he preferred Karlstadt's and Eck's 'fairly moderate debate' to the 'violent' stirrings of Luther.[80] Outsiders knew of tensions between Karlstadt and Luther. Still, the volatile external situation disallowed an open debate between the Wittenbergers. Not until 1523 does Karlstadt openly repudiate God's responsibility for evil.

Meanwhile, Karlstadt's casual comments about election are of interest. He mentions his *Anfechtungen* (inner struggles). There was a time when he had said to himself: 'Indeed, God's truths and vows are definitely just, and do not deceive anyone. But I am not among the elect,' for he suffered from *concupiscentia*. Thus he had a negative moral index to election. Good works may not indicate election, but their absence reveals that one is not elected. Nevertheless, Karlstadt overcomes such uncertainty. If he hates the many sins of his previous life (John 12:25) and prays (John 14:14), election will be granted and God will show mercy.[81] Since this merely restates the idea of 'sweeping,' coupled with his belief that God does not refuse those who repent, election is within his grasp, even if election rests on God's merciful reaction to remorseful sinners. Certainty is gained at the expense of predestination.

In election God positively draws human beings after they have become passive.[82] 'If they are driven, they suffer violence and the Spirit overpowers nature.'[83] God works first like a hammer that splinters the rock, but then through

---

78 Seitz, 27: '[Respondeo], quod liberum arbitrium habet se ad gratiam sicut infirmus vulneratus ad iumentum in quo portatur.'

79 *Ausslegung* (15), E–2.

80 Erasmus, *Opera omnia* (1706) 9, 1215: 'Nuper autem [praedestinationis controversia] renovata est per *Carolostadium* et *Eccium*, sed moderatiore conflictatione: mox autem vehementius exagitata per *Martinum Lutherum*.'

81 *Gelassenheyt* (38), [B4v].

82 *Gewaldt* (63), A3.

83 Ibid, A3v: 'Dye soen gots sein, die trybet und fhuret der geyst gotis. Werden sie getriben, so leiden sie gewald, und der geyst gewaldtiget die natur.'

faith God indwells and elects one unto daughtership or sonship, like a 'charitable father,' not a 'tyrannical king.'[84] God also uses outward means like the persecution of believers.[85]

Karlstadt harks back to John 17:9 to prove that one should not pray for the non-elect.[86] Having argued that one may pray to be elected, this is not a retraction, but he underscores that others cannot save the obstinate. The church exists to save the elect, not to pray for the damned. As it is, this view has no practical consequences, for the church does not know the elect and thus she still prays for all.

With uncertainty overridden, Karlstadt can now look back at predestination as curative for those who contemplate it.[87] It is an antidote for self-righteousness, and it leads to the birth of 'the most noble moral quality of self-denial.'[88] It has a mellowing effect, and allows one to resist usurpers, to bandage the broken, to strengthen the infirm, and to protect the strong. The 'idea of predestination' leads one to the depth of God's will where self-will is swallowed. One who has been 'formed by the knowledge of predestination' accepts what is bitter to the ego but sweet to God.[89]

Augustine argued 'strongly and impudently' when he used John 6 to prove that the elect can have certitude. Yet Karlstadt says certitude can be based on other texts, which, however, he does not cite.[90] Nevertheless, Karlstadt does not assert the power of predestination but the cure it offers to those who contemplate it. This is useful for self-denial or 'sweeping.' Karlstadt cherishes predestination for its healing influence as a model, like the classical and medieval genre of meditation on death. Thus, although predestination is not to be discounted, Karlstadt is not serious about it as such.

Next, Karlstadt holds that God does not predestine on account of future works. This, of course, is an area of common ground with Luther. Is Karlstadt being trite or is he tempted by a safe instance where he can say there is *no* predestination? The next thesis is again ambiguous. 'The prayers of the just, in so far as they have been predestined, are healthy for eternal life.'[91] As predestinarian

---

84 Ibid, A2v: 'Das wort gotis ist gleich wie eyn hammer der einen feelsch tzerknirschet ader tzemalet' (Jer. 23:29); B2v: 'Alsso geet got auch yhn die hertzen der menschen mit glauben. Und ehr wil nit ein tyrannischer konig sein, sunder eyn gutwilliger vater. Szo sollen wir dochter und soen sein.'

85 Ibid, [B4]. Karlstadt appeals to texts like John 15:20; Matt. 23:34; Heb. 11:37; Luke 11:49, etc.

86 *Gewaldt* (63), [B4], citing John 17:9.

87 Brieger, 'Thesen Karlstadt's,' 481–3.

88 Ibid, 481, th 10–11.

89 Ibid, 481–2, th 13–15.

90 Ibid, 482, th 16.

91 Ibid, 482, th 20: 'Orationes iustorum tantum praedestinatis sunt salubres ad vitam aeternam.'

as this seems, Karlstadt affirms that predestination produces visible means, and he has not touched the real question of whether predestination rests on free choice.

Finally Karlstadt says that 'the souls of the faithful who have died are in the church of the predestined.'[92] This, of course, does not clash with conditional election, but Karlstadt is reversing the doctrine of perseverance. In a truly predestinarian scheme the elect persevere because they have been predestined, but Karlstadt says that those who persevere are in retrospect seen as having been predestined. It seems that Karlstadt in 1521 covers up his rejection of unconditional predestination. The ultimate issue for Karlstadt is whether he would worship an arbitrary God who transcends human moral standards or whether his God is moral and therefore not initially partisan.

Karlstadt still clings to the position of his *Ausslegung*. In his lectures on Zechariah he discusses predestination. He emphasizes *sola gratia*, and the fact that one's conversion is dependent on God. He seems to defend unconditional single predestination until he finally comments: 'this conversion requires the mortification of the Old Man and Adam.'[93] Conditionality is here injected as 'mortification,' a synonym for sweeping.

The Final Solution, 1523 to 1525

Early in 1523 Karlstadt was meditating on freedom rather than predestination. He evaded censorship in Wittenberg by having his tract *On Purgatory* sent to Augsburg, where Philipp Ulhart printed three slightly different editions. Jörg Nadler, also of Augsburg, reprinted it; another reprint appeared in Strassburg. Gerhard Westerburg, Karlstadt's brother-in-law, had three of his own versions published. The booklet was popular, and Karlstadt no longer depended on the printing presses of Wittenberg. Michel Buchfürer would soon publish five additional works, although Luther's intervention in January 1524 prevented Karlstadt from further publication.[94] From then on, Karlstadt's tracts were primarily published in Augsburg, Strassburg, and Basel – future hearths of the Baptist movements.

The purgatory tract discloses some of Karlstadt's views on predestination. He now offers salvation beyond the grave to those who are ignorant and lacking in righteousness.[95] Karlstadt again bases salvation on God's acts and the negative

---

92 Ibid, 482, th 21: 'Anima fidelium defunctorum sunt in praedestinatorum ecclesia.'
93 BARGE 2, 568: 'Conversio illa requirit mortificationem veteris hominis et Adae.' The comment is based on Zech. 1:3.
94 See Hase, *Johann Michael*, 20–1.
95 As Williams has first noted (*Radical Reformation*, 39), and as Kleiner ('Karlstadt's Eschatology,' 1–35) has proved at length, Karlstadt had been influenced by Wessel Gansfort, whose *Farrago* was published in Wittenberg in 1522. Karlstadt accepted the argument of Wessel in this area, with an unusual lack of reservation, because Karlstadt was searching for a God who is just, even in terms of human understanding.

preparation of the sinner. One is not judged on the basis of a decree, or a forensic act, but on the basis of God's righteousness within. There are some, though they have died in Christ, who lack enough righteousness because of ignorance. They will be instructed in the city of souls, the purgatory without alchemical fire. There they are deprived of the beatific vision until they discover God in the noonday sun of clarity.[96] They may have been sincere idolators, deceived with masses and other rituals.[97] People will not be judged because of ignorance (unwissenheit) in this life, for God will deliver them from it in the grave.[98] This is not a second-chance doctrine, for Karlstadt refers only to those who never had a chance, though they sincerely wanted one: 'The experience of souls that run hither and thither is so deep that I cannot reprove nor reject them.'[99] If this argument appears subjective, it is because Karlstadt implies that his God is at least as merciful as Karlstadt himself. God has a sense of fairness: all who are sincere may choose: 'Now he who will have one will with Christ must accept God's will.'[100] God's will is no longer likened to a hammer that splinters the rock, for it is now regarded as resistible. Even so, God is not a jilted lover, ever pleading for acceptance. The encounter between God and the believer is based on mutual self-surrender. Karlstadt pleads the cause of a kindly God, but he also pleads against human self-centredness:

[God] is ready to unite himself with you today, if you are of good will and believing, and are deprived of all your powers ... He is still waiting for all who are in need to call on him with their heart, to help them, and to do all kinds of miraculous things. However, your own will has drawn you

96 Fegfeür (95), C.
97 Ibid, C3–v.
98 Ibid, C2v: 'Ich halt es dafür das sy dort studieren und leren miessen (sein sy anders versehen zur seligkait) und erkennen alle ware urtail oder sententz welche got will haben erkandt, ee er sy in hymel nymbt. Es myesten auch die todten evangeliziert werden, auf das er sy nicht urtailn [1 Pet. 4:6].' Ironically, Karlstadt had earlier rejected any notion of purgatory and of communication with the dead, th 1–22, 38–48, in BARGE 1, 495–7. Later he was to reject it again. Thus in Basel in 1539 Karlstadt harmonizes Old and New Testament teachings regarding Sheol and the intermediate state, concluding that the dead lack sensory perception and experience soul sleep (Iob VII (155), Bv–2v). Karlstadt's interest in the afterlife was confined to ideas concerning personal immortality, for he was indifferent towards apocalypticism.
99 Fegfeür (95), C3.
100 Willen gottes (102), A2v: 'Wer nu mit Christo einen willen wil haben, der muss gots willen annemenn.' Christ sets the example for this (John 5:30, 6:38). Those who follow are adopted by Christ. They are his friends and relatives. When they have been adopted, they are sinless (A2v–3): 'Welcher das thut, der ist ein freundt Christi, ja eyn angeborner freund Christi, der nit Christo auss fleischlicher geburt und sipschafft verwant, sonder auss got angeboren ist, und kan nit sundigen [1 John 3:6].'

away from his eyes, has cast you out of his divine will, and caused God not to hear you, though you cry.[101]

Although humans must respond to God, such a response already presupposes the work of the Spirit within them. Fallen human creatures cannot accomplish this by themselves:

The creatures lack enough ability to understand [2 Cor. 3:5]. Much less can they desire or long for something from God, for one's desires follow one's thoughts. And no one desires what he does not understand. Now mark that a man must desire the work, wisdom, strength, and the like that proceed from the godly Spirit. This is humanly impossible without God's merciful will. Therefore God's merciful will alone creates and works good thoughts and desires according to his Spirit. And the same fatherly will sends his Spirit to the creatures, and the Spirit is the origin of their sincere cry to God: 'Abba! Father!' [Rom. 8:15].[102]

Then when God takes the first step, potential believers must respond with self-denial. Otherwise God does not even heed their prayers. In 1521 Karlstadt urges the Wittenbergers to accept the elements of communion with their own hands. Now God enables them to accept him into their hearts, and voluntarism becomes central for Karlstadt's theology. With this scheme of salvation Karlstadt now ponders traditional problems.

Evil is man's own, not God's, problem, for God did not create sin. One chooses evil by insisting on one's own 'free' (fallen) will, or by heeding others, rather than God. The way out is through hatred of one's flesh, that is the self.[103] God allows evil, without desiring it. Only the eternal will shows God's true nature: a just and loving God. God's permissive will does not reveal God's nature, but it reveals what God does to accomplish (in subservience to the eternal will) what is necessary.[104] Humanly speaking, and in a secondary sense, God's will can be thought of as permissive, hardening, and wrathful. But then fallen human nature is abetted in its own evil schemes.[105] In fact, the permissive will seems threatening, but the persecution that it abets leads believers to contrition.

101 Ibid, [B4v].
102 *Teuffelischen falhs* (114), B2v.
103 *Willen gottes* (102), B2–v, D, Ev.
104 Ibid, Ev–3.
105 Ibid, [E4]: 'Derhalbenn spricht Paulus: "Got hat sye geben der unreynikeyt durch begirden irer hertzen" (Rom. 1:24), unnd leret also das der verhencklich will mitt den lustenn unnd begirden unsers hertzenns oder aygen wyllens uber eyn kumpt.'

Like many of the scholastics, Karlstadt again accepts a universally benevolent intent on God's part (eternal will) and he also affirms a final judgment. The temporally permissive will serves this end. One must choose, and God abets this choice, whether for good or for evil. Human inability and divine benevolence meet with human responsibility. Those who choose to be vessels of wrath, can only blame themselves, for God did not create them evil.[106]

Karlstadt overcomes righteousness based on works, however. God grants power to those who are evil, but believers are at first faced with conflict. Their wills are then annihilated in the abyss of the divine will, after a negative choice against themselves. But the positive righteousness, by which they are judged, flows from God alone. This Augustinian note preserves grace alone.

The only positive collaboration takes place between God's permissive will and unbelievers, but this causes damnation.[107] One creates, in effect, one's own hell, either in this world or the next. The reverse is also true, one's surrender to God turns even hell into heaven. Karlstadt must have thought of Psalm 139:8 when he said:

GOD'S WILL TURNS HELL TO HEAVEN. Indeed, there is no hell so awful that it cannot be turned into heaven and eternal life by God's eternal will. Should I descend into hell with full surrender of my will, and accept God's eternal will for myself, [then] hell has to become for me a kingdom of God, and death [is turned to] eternal life.[108]

Even the believer whose faith is weak can live in certainty: 'Of this I am sure and certain, that God does not allow the smallest spark of faith to perish. I see that Christ will have him unhindered, who has a small spark of the confession of Christ' (Mark 9:24).[109]

Now Karlstadt clarifies the universal intent of Christ's atonement. In sprinkling the ark with blood Moses pointed to Christ, showing that 'all men's sins would be washed in the blood of Christ.'[110] Karlstadt is not a strict universalist, however, for the atonement affects only those who *want* to be washed.

---

106 Ibid, Ev: 'Paulus hat noch nit gsagt das got in anfangk, als er alle ding in yrem schmuck und tzierung schuff, die vass des tzorns geschaffen, sonder das got sye gedult und geliden hab (Rom. 1:26, 9:22).'
107 Ibid, F2.
108 Ibid, Ev–2.
109 KS 1, 19:4–7.
110 *Priesterthum* (112), C2: 'Seintemal Moses nichts anders mit solchem blutvergissen oder besprengung gethan hat dann das er mit verdeckten geschichten antzeygett das aller menschen sunde abgewaschen wurden im blut Christi.' See also C.

Besides stressing human free choice, Karlstadt enhances Christ's work of salvation by also insisting on Christ's freedom. Though he obeyed the Father in saving the world, Christ owed no one such obedience:

The Son of God, Jesus of Nazareth, has offered himself of his own free will and out of obedience to God his Father. And he surrendered himself into the hands of Judas the traitor, and the hands of the heathens, Pilate, and the executioners. And his life and death stood mightily in his own power and will. Had he wanted to keep his soul, no one would have taken it from him [Matt. 26:53].[111]

Of his free will Christ accomplished salvation for all, and he wants to 'draw all men unto himself.' Those who accept find gradual inner justification through progressive union with the historical Christ who lived and died in Palestine. By imitating Christ's life one is united with him in his death to participate in salvation, even though, historically, justification has once and for all (uff ein mal) been accomplished on the cross.[112]

During a disputation in Wittenberg the thesis is proposed that God is the final cause of evil. Karlstadt repudiates the idea. 'The devil is a liar, and when he lies, he lies of himself' (John 8:44). Ergo, God does not cause evil. This demands further precision regarding the permissive will. When God abetted the devil in lying, did God also lie? The answer is negative, for then the devil did not lie 'of himself.' God permitted the devil to exist, but since Christ is the Truth (John 14:6), God does not cause the devil's lies, and even God's wrath does not do evil or lie.[113] In hardening a sinner God does not create evil but merely grants power or the necessary conditions, which the sinner then abuses, although God's gifts are good in themselves. Paul proves that in hardening God does not initiate evil but drives people on (Rom. 1:28).[114]

The original creation, including Satan, was good (Gen. 1). Satan's fall is like Adam's, for both were created good and they cannot blame God.[115] God endows humans with a free will, but when they trust themselves, or another, more than God, they become scholastics and believe in doing their utmost (facere quod in se est), and so they fall. They prefer natural reason to the Holy Spirit, and that is the root of their pride and lack of self-surrender (ungelassenheit).[116] Of course

111   Ibid, [B4v].
112   Ibid, F3v, C2v.
113   Teuffelischen falhs (114), A2v.
114   Ibid, B3v: 'Ists doch doben abgeredt das got umb voriger sunden willen in neue sunden treibt.'
115   Ibid, A3v–[4].
116   Ibid, [A4].

Adam and Satan are unique because their original reason was good, but it was not to be used exclusively. In addition, Satan cannot plead the otherwise legitimate excuse of ignorance. God allowed Satan and his angels to hear the proclamation of Christ, but they preferred their own creaturely powers, causing their own fall.[117]

God touches all creatures with love and compassion. God is a sweet and infinite light, in whom there is no darkness at all. The only reason for the final judgment is that, although the light shone in the darkness, the world preferred the darkness (John 3:19).[118] Judgment was not God's original intent, however, for Christ came to redeem rather than to judge the world (John 3:17, 8:15).[119]

Karlstadt again quotes Hosea 13:9 (Vulg.): 'Israel, your death comes from yourselves, but your salvation comes from me.' Evil is not a thing (therefore God did not create it), but it flows from the wrong will and attitude. To this the sophists (of Wittenberg) reply that it is logical to assume that God causes evil, because he creates those who commit evil. But if they use logic, let them pursue the argument to its bitter end to ponder what it is within God that causes evil. Then the world will know that the God of the sophists is evil.[120]

Augustine cannot always be trusted. Even Karlstadt's earlier view (1518) that God can withdraw his grace and permit the fall of others without causing it – single predestination and not fully effective prevenient grace – must be repudiated. Single predestination implies double predestination, for if God refuses to aid the needy, their falls are caused by a sin of omission.[121]

Although Karlstadt repudiates *facere quod in se est*, he appreciates the scholastics for not making God responsible for evil; besides,

Have all judgments of scholasticism been overturned? Has the article of the trinity and of the deity and incarnation of Christ, etc, also been subverted? Or might it not be that certain matters, in which the scholastics deal with God, have not been invented or imagined?[122]

As in the case of God's call, Karlstadt leaves the answer up to the individual.

117   Ibid, [A4v]: 'So gar hat got keine schuld des teuffelischen falhs.'
118   Ibid, B2: 'Das ist das Christus saget: "das lichte ist komen in die welt, und die welt hat finsternis mehr gelibt denn das lichte, drumb ist ir synn unnd will verkhert."'
119   Ibid, B.
120   Ibid, A3: 'Und must dar nach auch volgen, das got selbert nicht gut wer, die weil sich ettliche geister an seiner gotheit verseert unnd sich in ewigen falh gebracht haben.'
121   Ibid, B3: 'Nu, wenn dem also ist das unsere krefften nicht guts gedencken nach begeren vormögen, ehe sie got angreifft, und der jene fallen muss den got nit uber sich rücket, so wer je got schuldig am falh. Sih, wenn du mir nit hülffest, so ich fiel, und küntest mich retten, so werestu meines falhs schuldig.'
122   Ibid, B3v–[4].

Karlstadt often returns to these themes, but, to avoid repetition, we merely refer to the remarkable passage on how the believer prepares, on his own, to receive God, who then distributes His gifts to him according to his needs (Matt. 25:14f).[123] This gradual process of inner justification linked to God's sanctification culminates in the completion of sprinkling, through Christ's blood-baptism, on the seventh day.

Karlstadt's sermon *On Angels* contains a somatic hypothesis of the devil's fall. The devil grew jealous because Christ was to acquire a coarse, human, and mortal body, and yet he would rule over the angels at God's right hand, and he was to be called 'god.' That 'really stuck in the devil's craw,' so he revealed Christ's vulnerability by planning to slay him. Therefore, the devil is called a murderer from the beginning (John 8:44) and Christ is the Lamb slain by Satan from before the foundation of the world (Rev. 13:8, Vulg.).[124]

Believers who fall do not fall from grace. John 3:18 ('He who does not believe is condemned already') refers to deliberate, eternal unbelief. From temporal unbelief one will be delivered, provided one sins unknowingly (1 Tim. 1:13).[125] Like Eck, Karlstadt now teaches that God's prevenient grace is universally given. All people are vessels into which God pours his grace. Unbelief is like 'a broken vessel which leaks,' whereas true faith is a 'well-constructed container.'[126]

Karlstadt does not agree with Luther's purely positive definition of faith. There is true faith and false faith, for 'even the demons believe and they shudder' [James 2:19].[127] If one dies in the intermediate type of unbelief, which is caused by ignorance, one will hear the truth proclaimed in the city of souls, for 'God will judge the living *and the dead* through his word of proclamation' (John 5:25). Then comes the time of commotion when one's free choice places one among the elect or the damned.[128]

Deliberate resistance against God is a sign of damnation. Martin Luther, for example, rides his own beast, and with wilful lies about the Lord's Supper he has 'made from a drink of life, a drink of death, and from a drink of the elect, a drink of the damned.'[129] Luther, by his own previous decree, had damned Karlstadt as a Judas and a Satan.[130] Though both claimed that God should be the rider, Karlstadt

123 KS 1, 63:26–64:36.
124 *Engelen* (122), A2v–3.
125 *Gelaub* (139), A2–v.
126 Ibid, A3v: 'Der glaubig ist gegen der scharpfen gerechtigkeit gottes als ein fester stehelin berg, oder ein wol gebundten fass, da durch nichts dreiffet, das got dreyn geüsset. Gegen der lügen aber hat er einen ewigen grauen und heltet keine. Widerumb, der unglaub ist sam ein zerspalten und ungebunden fass, dadurch die warheit leüfft, so offt sie dran stosset.'
127 Ibid, Dv.
128 Ibid, B2v.
129 *Testament* (143), D–v.
130 BR 2, 448:13f.

and Luther did some riding on their own, each confirming his own thesis that this leads one in the wrong direction.

The right direction stresses the crucial importance of Karlstadt's anti-Lutheran view of predestination. Both reformers assert human inability and divine grace. Karlstadt even surpasses Luther in his pessimism about human nature, for to him nature must be destroyed and re-created by grace, not just in the realm of salvation, but in the whole of life. Yet, Karlstadt's God does not dictate one's final destiny, for God graciously enables one to choose. Good works are conferred on those who hate their old lives, whether they dwell on earth or in the city of souls. God has come down so humans might be lifted up to a relationship with God such as exists between responsible adults. One is redeemed, not as an innocent child, but as an adult, through the mercy of God.

Though this position has been recast in terms of the sole sufficiency of divine grace, much of it is found in medieval scholasticism and popular mysticism. Here Karlstadt is more conservative than Luther. Yet, there are radical elements in the Christian tradition upheld by Karlstadt. The relationship between God and humans is no longer based on the paradigm of master and slave. When Karlstadt's conception of equality among believers, and their adult relationship with God, reshapes the church and its sacramental system, the effect is more radical than Luther's programme.

3

Doctrine of the Church

Karlstadt's rupture with Rome has received thorough treatment in Ulrich Buben-heimer's *Consonantia theologiae et iurisprudentiae*. Sider has also covered Karl-stadt's doctrine of the church, moving into the Orlamünde period.[1] Sider's treatment is in general harmony with Bubenheimer's, but some depth was sacrificed to achieve the broad coverage that makes Sider's work similarly indis-pensable as an introduction to Karlstadt.

Since the doctrine of the church has quite properly been the focus of tradi-tional Baptist studies,[2] Karlstadt's development from 1519 to 1525 of a doctrine of the church that is characteristic of the Baptists is herewith presented. The reduc-tionistic phase has been so well handled by Bubenheimer that it is included in the first section as a brief summary of his main conclusions.

The Break with Rome and the Fall of the Church

On the basis of published sources Bubenheimer has explored Karlstadt's rela-tionship to the papal Curia.[3] While studying at the City University of Rome (*Sapienza*) Karlstadt obtained (in addition to his theological doctorate from Wit-tenberg) the dual doctorate in canon and civil law (*utriusque iuris*), a result also of his intensive private studies in Wittenberg. Karlstadt stood in the Italian legal tradition, favouring the secular legists over the canonists. He also served as a

---

1 SIDER, 46–59, 86–103, 135–40, 238–91.
2 Noteworthy are Heyer, *Der Kirchenbegriff der Schwärmer*; and Littell, *The Origins of Sectarian Protestantism* (1963), first published as *The Anabaptist View of the Church* (1952). Weber's and Troeltsch's distinction between 'church' and 'sect' proved helpful in these studies.
3 BUBENHEIMER, 11–66. Unfortunately I have been unable to locate new proof of Karlstadt's activities in Rome: the earliest matriculation records of the City University (*Sapienza*) appear to have been lost or destroyed, and no record of Karlstadt's appointment as viscount was located. I remain indebted to my friend Nelson Minnich who assisted me in my search.

secretary at the Curial Datary and he was rewarded with a papal benefice that entitled him to an honorary viscountcy. Thus Karlstadt can be distinguished from Luther on the basis of his papal rather than conciliar bias.

From 1518 to 1519 Bubenheimer sees Karlstadt as a scriptural theologian, loyal to the pope.[4] However, Karlstadt is ahead of Luther in his view of church councils.[5] Both Luther and Karlstadt assume Scripture's supremacy rather than its sole sufficiency from 1516 to 1519. Luther was the first publicly to challenge both popes and councils, in May of 1519, whereas Karlstadt did not do so until a year later. I would suggest that Luther's insinuation that Karlstadt was worried about his prebends is a genuine, and not necessarily dishonourable, motive.[6]

In 1516 (1518?) Karlstadt opposes the infallibility of councils, and he accepts the possibility of a heretical pope who is to be deposed if he has willingly flouted the law (ius divinum) of Scripture.[7] Against Barge, Sider and Bubenheimer rightly argue that Karlstadt was not the first in Wittenberg to defend the principle of an exclusive reliance on Scripture (sola scriptura).[8] Bubenheimer, however, credits Karlstadt with the most systematic analysis of the fundamental hermeneutical and ecclesiological issues at stake in the Wittenberg Reformation.[9]

To protect the pope Karlstadt at first reduces the scriptural basis on which a pope can be condemned. He radically restricts the literal sense of Scripture to the open and express meaning of a passage, without circumstantial aids of interpretation.[10] Contextual interpretations (sensus colligibilis), based on such factors as the historical intent of the writer, fail to offer a sound basis for declaring a pope heretical. Papal decretals do not contradict Scripture.[11]

In 1518 Karlstadt appeals to the prayers of the church, which he deems biblical.[12] A year later he ousts some prayers, but he still holds that prayers accepted by universal (not just Roman) usage are scriptural. Other prayers should be purged from the liturgy.[13] Late in 1520 all liturgical prayers recede before Scripture.[14]

---

4   BUBENHEIMER, 159.
5   BUBENHEIMER, 198: 'An einem Punkt in der Ekklesiologie, nämlich in der Entwicklung der Konzilsidee, ist Karlstadt Luther voraus, während gleichzeitig seine konservativere Haltung bezüglich der Papalidee noch bis in seine zehn Thesen vom Herbst 1520 nachwirkt.'
6   BR 1, 368:18–37.
7   LÖSCHER 2, 80, th 12–15. The theses were published in 1518, but Bubenheimer's argument (BUBENHEIMER, 67–116) that the subject matter of these theses was first debated in Rome in 1516 is convincing on historical and form-critical grounds.
8   BARGE 1, 118–21; BUBENHEIMER, 77–8, 109–16; SIDER, 46–57.
9   BUBENHEIMER, [281].
10 BUBENHEIMER, 127–37.
11 LÖSCHER 2, 100, th 358, where Karlstadt refers to 'apostolica et pontificia decreta' (1518).
12 CC 1, 38, th (102)f (1518).
13 KÄHLER, 103:32–104:26 (1518), cited in BUBENHEIMER, 144, n 286.
14 Credner, par 36. See BUBENHEIMER, 145, n 287.

Karlstadt, like Luther, jettisons the scholastic method in 1517, for theology and philosophy produce an 'evil mixture.'[15] The church Fathers retain a derivative authority, however, for where they are in harmony, they agree with Scripture.[16] In his *Defensio* against Johann Eck (1519) Karlstadt notes: 'I admit that between the sayings of the saints [i.e. church Fathers] and Scripture that is called canonical by the church Fathers, there is a profound difference, since the Fathers did not aim to reach the highest goal.'[17] In *Ablas* he notes that 'the church Fathers regret that their books are esteemed to be equal to Holy Scripture.'[18]

The application of biblical principles took time to develop. Karlstadt resigned his viscountcy and returned the title to the pope in 1520.[19] He remained locked in the prebendary system until 1524, however, because his income and appointment in Wittenberg as well as his claim to the ministry in Orlamünde depended on it. Thus Karlstadt's practice does not immediately reflect his theories.

The fundamental crisis in his relationship with the papacy occurred in 1520, when he received the censure of Luther, and when two of Karlstadt's own theses had been condemned by the University of Leuven (Louvain). Karlstadt then attacks Pope Leo X as a heretic. Moreover, Karlstadt states that the papacy has fallen and has been excommunicated since 1296 [!] during the pontificate of Alexander IV (ruled 1254 to 1261).[20] In June or July 1521 Karlstadt back-dates this to Pope Callistus II (ruled 1119 to 1124) because he decreed celibacy.[21]

In January of 1522 the fall of the church is backdated to Pope Gregory I (ruled 590 to 604) because he introduced the unbiblical notion of chanting in the services. 'The church whose head was Gregory instituted this murmuration; not the church whose head is Christ.'[22] In the autumn of 1520 Karlstadt dates the fall of the general church councils from the Council at 'Meaux' (Meaux, 845; Paris, 846), which 'erred everywhere.'[23] He now rejects canon law, but as a product of

15   KÄHLER, 34*–5*, th 143–4 (1517).

16   Ibid, 11*, th 1–6.

17   LÖSCHER 2, 117: 'Inter dicta patrum sanctorum atque scripturam (quam ecclesiastici appellitant canonicam) δίς διὰ πασῶν fateor distare, quod patres nullatenus supremam adsequi octavam instituerint' (1518).

18   *Ablas* (28), [A4]: 'Die rechten alt vetter haben ein vordriess, das yhr bücher der heyligen schrifft gleych gewirdert werden.'

19   *Heylichkeit* (44), B2: 'schick ich yhm mein vicecomitat ... widder heim.'

20   Gerdes, ed, *Scrinium* 1/1, 39, th 3: 'Alexander IV, et post eum pontifices Romani anathemate se per suas decretales percusserunt, ab anno 1296, usque ad annum 1520, nunc praesentem.' BUBENHEIMER, 290, reads: '1246.' Either way the date is wrong. Bubenheimer discusses the theses, 171–5.

21   *Coelibatu* (62), [Av] (1521). Cf DENZINGER, *711.

22   BARGE 1, 493, th 37–8: 'Ecclesia, cuius Gregorius caput fuit, haec murmura instituit. Sed non ecclesia, cuius caput est Christus' (1522).

23   Gerdes, ed, *Scrinium* 1/1, 39, th 1–2: 'Meldense concilium perperam erravit. Idem concilium excommunicationem ipso facto incurrit.' (BUBENHEIMER, 290) (1520).

his earlier training there remains his biblicism. The Scriptures are the new *ius divinum*, governing the church.

Towards a Baptist Doctrine of the Church

We have seen how a strict principle of *sola scriptura* as opposed to *all* tradition emerges in 1519. Nevertheless, Karlstadt accepts for some time many notions that a *modern* Protestant would deem unbiblical, but this may be a matter of application. Thus Karlstadt forges his new view of the church in confrontation with the pope, and it hardens during similar confrontation with Luther.[24]

Luther, too, can be cited in support of congregationalism or an *ecclesiola in ecclesia* theory, but he moves from being a challenger of the old church towards unofficial headship of the newly established church. Karlstadt's theocratic leanings indicate that at a local level he would have pursued a similar goal if he could have established the church and Christian magistracy which he had envisaged. Nevertheless, Karlstadt is first thwarted by Frederick the Elector in Wittenberg, and when his reformation, aided by the lower magistrates, takes root in the area of the Saale River, his work is again suppressed.

Karlstadt remains in opposition, and he accepts the practical consequences of his doctrine of the church when he disregards the local magistrates after his expulsion from Saxony in 1524. Thus there emerges a general pattern of opposition to clerical establishments and an advocacy of the oppressed, provided they are Christians or sympathetic inquirers.

Salvation

The process of salvation involves three states whose polar extremes are individualism and incorporation into the body of Christ. These stages can be schematized as follows: 1 / flesh (ego, old creation, Adam); 2 / spirit (annihilation, union, God); and 3 / incorporation (body, new creation, Christ).

Nature must be destroyed by grace: a new nature must be created. Through the violence that comes upon it the church is spiritually reborn. This violent scheme is a permanent feature of Christian life on earth, since stages 2 and 3 are achieved only after the death of the body.[25] Thus the believer's life is marked by persecution, sorrow, and repentance, as well as the constant violence of the pro-

---

24 Since this connection has been ignored, Preus finds 'traces of a persecution complex ... before the fact of actual persecution' (*Carlstadt's 'Ordinaciones,'* 88). Karlstadt, however, develops this view first in 1520 (see *Gelassenheyt* (38) and *Heylickeit* (44)), when he has been threatened with excommunication by Rome.

25 *Heylickeit* (44), A3 (1520).

cess of new birth. To the extent that the third step is attained the church comes into being on earth.

The new creation of the church

Preparatory to one's entrance into the church, one's old nature (Adam) must be in the process of destruction. One becomes a son of God through the violence wrought by the Holy Spirit:

> From this it follows that we do no violence to the word of God, but we are driven and suffer violence, as it is written [Rom. 8:14] 'Those who are sons of God are led and driven by the Spirit of God.' If they are driven, they suffer violence and the Spirit overpowers nature.
> The Spirit strives against flesh; and God, who creates a good will and good works in us, does violence to our nature. He softens the heart of stone and gives a new spirit.[26]

In his 'mystical' tracts Karlstadt speaks of annihilation of the ego, union with God, sonship or daughtership, etc, to describe the goal of conversion. Since this subject lies within the realm of regeneration and conversion, we refer to Sider's treatment of the topic.[27] Karlstadt's doctrine of regeneration is closely related to his view of the church, since he teaches that God's kingdom is the body of the reborn in Christ. We have seen how the Spirit annihilates nature, but since the Word is in harmony with the Spirit, both of these contribute to the creation of the church. The church is created by water (Word) and the Spirit. With this spiritualization of 'water' Karlstadt subverts the sacramental notion of baptism in 1521:

> Therefore, Christ says that no one is incorporated into the kingdom of God, unless he is reborn 'of water and the Spirit' [John 3:5]. From this it follows that God's Word is a spring from which God's Spirit flows into the believers, and renews them and fashions them into a kingdom of God or of Heaven.
> One does violence to the same when one disturbs, terrifies, and kills it. Nevertheless, it remains God's kingdom, and it rules with Christ. As Revelation says, 'those who were beheaded on account of the testimony,

26 *Gewaldt* (63), A3v: 'Daraus volget das wir gotis wort nit gewald thun, sunder betriben werden und gewald leiden, nach dem geschriben: Dye soen gots sein, die trybet und fhuret der geyst gotis. Werden sie getriben so leiden sie gewald, und der geyst gewaldtiget die natur'; [A4v]: 'Der geyst strebet wider fleisch, und got thet der natur gewalt, welcher guten willen und gutte werck yhn uns schaffet. Der das steinern hertz weich macht, und giebt uns ein nauen geyst' (1521).

27 SIDER, 212–99; see also Sider, 'A Theology of Regeneration,' 191–218, 352–76.

and for the sake of the Word of God, have lived and ruled with Christ a
thousand years' [Rev. 20:4].[28]

The Christian life is not individualistic but corporeal. Although conversion is
an intensely individual experience, it leads to one's destruction and incorporation
into the body of Christ. Karlstadt shifts in his view of what is the sign of this
incorporation: first it is the Lord's Supper, but baptism ultimately supplants the
Supper. Nevertheless, Karlstadt's concept of incorporation remains the same, and
it is already explained in his earlier writings. The bread of the Holy Supper is a
sign of *our* body of which Christ is the head.[29]

The miracle of transformation does not involve the Lord's bread but believers
who are grafted onto the body of Christ and become a community through faithful preaching:

The Apostles preached Christ and him crucified, the body that was given
and the shed blood of Christ, and many accepted such teachings and persevered. But those who persevered had a community [gemeynschafft] or
company [geselschafft] in the teaching of the Apostles, and they followed
in breaking the bread and drinking the cup. The teaching came first. From
this you must deduce the foundation of the Christian community or company, just as knowledge is the foundation for common incorporation in all
guilds [zünfften]. So the whole people of God finds, or should have, its
community in the one God whom it knows.[30]

28 *Gewaldt* (63), B3v: 'Der wegen saget Christus, das keiner gotis reich eingeleibt wirdt, ehr sei
dan wider geborn "auss dem wasser und geist." Dar auss volget, das gotis wort ein born ist, dar
aus gotlicher geist yn die glaubige fleusset, und vernauhet sie, und macht sie ein reich gotis
ader der hiemeln. Dem selben thuet man gewald, wan man ehs umbtreibet, angstiget und
ertodt. Ehs bleibet aber doch gotis reich, und regiret mit Christo, alss Apocalypsis saget: "Die
seelen, so von wegen des getzeugknis endheubt sein und von wegen des wort gottis ertodet,
haben gelebt und regirt mit Christo .M. jar"' (1521).
29 *Leyb* (129), D3v: 'Itzt kürtz halb wil ich euch einss erinnern das Paulus des hern brodt ein
zeichen oder figur unsers leibes, des Christus ein heübt ist, nennet, und spricht: "Seind wir vile
nicht ein brodt?"' (1524). Karlstadt must have in mind 1 Cor. 10:7 [Vulg.]: 'Quoniam unus
panis, unum corpus multi sumus, omnes qui de uno pane participamus.' This is crucial for Karlstadt's understanding of the signs (sacraments). It is first applied (1519) to 'the sacrament of
penance' as a sign of inner repentance which precedes (LÖSCHER 2, 112–18). Later it is applied to
baptism and, ultimately, to the Lord's Supper – the only signs Karlstadt then recognizes.
30 *Christus* (124), Cv: 'Die apostel predigten den gekreützigten Christum, den ubergeben leyb
und das vergossen blut Christi, unnd viele namen solche lere an, unnd blieben drinn. Die aber
drinn blieben, die hetten ein gemeynschafft oder geselschafft in der apostel lere, unnd folgende
im brodt brechen unnd kelch drincken. Die lere ging für. Darauss soltu den grund christlicher gemeinschafft oder geselschafft abnemen, wenn das erkentnüs in allen zünfften die
grundfeste gemeyner geselschafft ist. Als auch das gantz gross volck gottes seine geselschafft
und gemeynschafft in einem erkanten got het, oder haben solt' (1524).

The church rests on the Word, and the congregation (κοινωνία) is one in observing the same ritual as Christ intended. The church does not overlap with society. Karlstadt's secular equivalent for κοινωνία is community, company, or guild. Other favourite and biblical names are 'the Christian flock,' the 'nation of the elect,' and 'God's little congregation' (das heuflein gottes).[31] Of course, the most frequent references are to the 'body of Christ' or 'the kingdom of God.' Christ's physical body is derived from Mary, but his spiritual body encompasses all believers, on earth and in heaven. This spiritual body is revealed when believers share their goods and love with one another.[32] Believers also console one another as fellow sufferers.[33]

Because the church is made visible in its deeds, Karlstadt once makes a universal claim for the church of Wittenberg.[34] Later, he must have found such visibility elsewhere. The greatest nation in the world is the nation of the elect (Deut. 4:6–8). It consists only of those believers who, like Mary, have spiritually conceived Christ within them.[35]

The rejection of alternatives

In delineating the nature of the church, Karlstadt wards off both individualism and competing notions of corporeality. As is to be expected in the sixteenth century, Karlstadt is preoccupied with contending notions of corporeality, but his own corporeal conception counters individualism.

The elevation of Spirit and Word as sole arbiters of Christian faith and practice forestalls boundless personal creativity. Personal rights must also be subsumed to the needs of the church if they clash. One has, for example, the right of freedom, where Scripture is not explicit: 'Concerning Sunday, there is no doubt that people have instituted it; of Saturday, it is still in doubt.'[36] Karlstadt draws two inferences: first, everyone may celebrate the Sabbath any day of the week; furthermore, each day should be like a Sabbath. However, celebrating the Sabbath at will leads to chaos. Therefore, the individual right is subsumed to the needs of the community. If some use the common Sabbath for revelry, Christians should prohibit games and drunkenness.[37]

31 Verba Dei (26), [A], contains the first reference to 'gregi Christiano' (1520); Emphahung (76), [Av], first refers to the church as 'heufflyn' (1521).
32 Leyb (129), D3v (1524); KS 1, 70:6–14 (1524).
33 Fritzhans (49), [A4v]–B (1521).
34 Litera (65), Av: 'universa VVittembergensis ecclesia' (1521).
35 Verba Dei (26), Cv: 'SPIRITALITER ergo concipiunt Christum qui verbum dei auditu, diligenti reverentur, et matres Christi efficiuntur spirituales' (1520). This was a popular theme, for example, in the writings of Staupitz.
36 KS 1, 41:27–8: 'Von dem sontag ists unheimlich das ihn menschen eingesetzt haben. Von dem samstag ists noch ym tzangck' (1524).
37 KS 1, 30:35–31:2 (1524).

Karlstadt rejects several alternative notions of the church. He does not tie the church to holy places, for he polemizes against churches 'made of stone.' There are too many of them, and they symbolize false visibility.[38] Christ is more alive in Scripture than in a stone house or communion cups.[39] Living temples are better than stone churches.[40] Stone churches tie up the people's money, while living temples suffer. The income of stone churches should aid the poor.[41]

Every institutional hierarchy insulates Christ from the believer. One must turn to the Creator rather than the creation.[42] Other ties separate one from God; thus the medieval hierarchy must be bypassed, but Karlstadt also sees a threat in the new theologians. Let the laity drink from Christ's living waters instead of the theological concoctions of the scribes.[43] At times the whole multitude has gone astray.[44]

The church of equals

Karlstadt taunted Eck for preaching a more Pelagian doctrine in church than he did during the Leipzig debate. According to Karlstadt, he pressed Eck on this, and the latter retorted with a system of double truth: one doctrine for scholars, another for the multitude. Meanwhile, Karlstadt had read Erasmus's preface to the New Testament, which expresses the hope that even common people will learn to read the Scriptures.[45]

In *Verba Dei* (1519) Karlstadt affirms the need for plain people to have access to the Scriptures. Everyone should study the Word: the farmer at the plow, women, illiterates, all must come to know the truth. What is now secret must be proclaimed from the housetops (Matt. 10:27). Even in the Old Testament *all* the people were instructed in the law (Deut. 6).[46]

Thus Karlstadt accepts Luther's appeal to 'the priesthood of all believers.'[47] Karlstadt cannot carp over a biblical phrase (1 Pet. 2:9), but he, in fact, dislikes the term *priesthood*. Soon he contrasts priests and prophets, symbolized by Moses and Aaron:

38 *Gelubden* (50), D3v–[4], Fv–2 (1521).
39 *Heylickeit* (44), [E4–v] (1520).
40 *Coelibatu* (60), C3–v (1521); *Gelubden* (50), [D4] (1521).
41 KT 74, 29:14, 15: 'Auch hette ich gern gesehn, das der stenerin kirchen jerlich eynkomen tzu obvermeltem kasten und bruderlicher hilff wer gewand' (1522).
42 *Gelassen* (104), Bv: 'Gelassenhait hat alle lieb und lust on mittel, in got lautter ... Ungelassenhait hatt lust und lieb in dem, das geschaffen ist' (1523).
43 KS 2, 7 (1524).
44 *Gelubden* (50), B3v (1521).
45 See Karlstadt's summary of Erasmus in *Verba Dei* (26), D (1520).
46 Ibid, [C4v].
47 *Heylickeit* (44), D3v–[4] (1520).

Moses heard God's words directly from God, and he had to prompt his older brother, Aaron [Exod. 4:15, 16]. Thus Aaron was below and less than Moses, although Aaron was a bishop and *Pontifex Maximus* [High Priest or Pope] [Exod. 28:1].

Saint Aaron was inclined to superstition and he made a calf, while Moses waited for God's Word on the mountain. To this same calf they offered adoration and sacrifice [Exod. 32].

Afterwards, Aaron became jealous, because his brother Moses was younger and more respected, and received greater grace, and he was especially offended by the fact that he had to hear God's words first through Moses to proclaim them afterwards [Num. 12].

Thereupon Karlstadt mentions other priests like Annas and Caiaphas, 'who wish to trample and slay the Prophets and Apostles.'[48]

Though he uses it sometimes, Karlstadt is unhappy with the term *priesthood* of believers. Against the pope Karlstadt asserts 'the godhood of all believers.' The Bible does not say:

he who is a bishop or a cardinal or a wooden shoe [Franciscan] is a god. No! But it says: 'I have said to all, you are gods,' for in Christ there is neither male nor female [Gal. 3:28], neither emperor nor pope, but all are one. God shows no regard for persons; he wants all to be his sons who receive and accept Christ [John 1:12].[49]

Thus Karlstadt goes beyond the priesthood of all believers, and ultimately the phraseology does not fit his own anti-priestly view of the church.

Distinctions in rank subvert the unity of the church. For the sake of order Karlstadt accepts bishops or shepherds, but, despite their special function, their privileges are not exclusive. They are not different from others, for 'no one can be a superior or ruler of Christians, or a pope, or a bishop, unless he is weak and sick like any other poor Christian.'[50]

---

48   *Gewaldt* (63), Cv: 'Moyses horet gotis wort one mittel von got, und musset Aaron, seynen eltern bruder, gotis wort ferner eingeben, alss Exo. iiii. geschriben. Alsso was Aaron under und minder dan Moyses, wiewol Aaron ein byschoff und der oberste pontifex was. Exo. 28. Der heylige Aaron was behend tzu affterglauben, machet ein kalp weil Moyses gotis wort warttet auff dem beerg, das selbige kalp betten sie ann und opfferten yhm. Exo. 32. Darnach wurd Aaron verdriessen das sein bruder Moyses jünger und mehr angesehen, und yn grossern gnaden was, und was yhm sunderlich verdrisslich dass ehr alletzeit von Moysen, gotis wort orstlich horen, dar nach verkundigen solt.' See also C2 (1521).

49   *Heylickeit* (44), C2v–3. Karlstadt refers to the 'You are gods' passage in Ps. 82:6 (Vulg. Ps. 81:6) (1520).

50   *Heylickeit* (44), [A4v] (1520).

Ordination does not confer 'any new thing'; it merely confirms a call issued by the church.[51] All believers are 'a spiritual household, a holy priesthood, to offer a spiritual host.'[52] Karlstadt does not yet allow the laity to celebrate the Lord's Supper in church, but they can celebrate it spiritually, and that, he believes, surpasses the external observance.[53] Later, in 1521, Karlstadt affirms the right of the laity to celebrate the sacrament at home.[54]

Karlstadt clashes with Luther on the doctrine of the church, because Luther's conception of the sacrament of the altar involves the establishment of a new priesthood, with rights not accorded to the laity. Therefore Karlstadt charges the Lutherans with being 'sacramentalists' (Sacramentler).[55] The Old-Testament-style priesthood passed away when Jesus Christ became the sole priest of the Christian body. Nevertheless, with his sacrament Luther has created 'mediators of the New Testament, who want to compete with the high priest [Caiaphas] and have the same office and power to hand over the body and blood of Christ.'[56]

The Church of the Few

The medieval church asserts the operative power of the sacrament, and the church is thought to consist of the baptized. Thus when Karlstadt encounters Augustine, he reduces the scope of the church, and since Karlstadt soon moves beyond Augustine and discards the operative power of the sacrament of baptism, he further restricts his concept of the church. Before his official break with Rome Karlstadt already (1519) claims that the ties of belief cut through all earthly bonds, even those of one's own family.[57] A year later his theories are tested when his parental family begs Karlstadt to remain in the old church.[58] Karlstadt is quite pained by the clash with his family. The tract Gelassenheyt reveals his inner struggle, but he decides to surrender to God – not to his relatives:

51 Ibid, [D4].
52 Ibid, D3v. Thus Karlstadt emphasizes the spiritual level, at which he can establish complete equality.
53 Fritzhans (49), B2v: 'Got begert barmhertzickeit: nit solche fleischliche opffer und reyn-machung' (1521).
54 BARGE 1, 489, th 113, implies this, for Karlstadt says that, if there were no private masses, one would have to hold that the laity cannot celebrate by themselves, and Karlstadt still accepts private masses (th 112) (1521).
55 Testament (143), B2v (1525).
56 Ibid, C2: 'Luther und seyne nachfolger wöllen sich mitler des neuen testamentes machen, dem obersten priester gleych seyn, ain gleich ampt haben, machte haben den leyb und das blut Christi aussutaylen.'
57 Verba Dei (26), B2–v (1520).
58 Gelassenheyt (38), passim.

I know that I cannot be a disciple of Christ, unless I leave father and mother, brother and sister, and friends [Luke 14:25–7] as well as my own nature, in every respect. Whatever is in me and of me, and what separates me on earth, in soul and in body, must be surrendered [gelassen]. 'He who would imitate me [Christ] shall deny himself, carry his cross daily, and follow me' (Luke 9:23–6).[59]

At this stage (1520) Karlstadt has the academic community of Wittenberg to support him, but this is no longer true in 1522, when Luther's plan 'to tread that Satan underfoot' has succeeded.[60] Karlstadt yearns for companionship: 'I did not intend doing this on my own, but with the three councils and some of your [Luther's] companions, who made the decision. Afterwards they pulled their heads out of the noose, and they left me standing alone.'[61] Unlike Zwilling, however, Karlstadt refuses to recant. From then on, his pessimism about the number of believers deepens towards this sombre assessment of 1525: 'You are certainly not many whom I touch, and even if you were many, I do know that only a fraction will be saved.'[62]

Thus there is a conflict in the evolution of Karlstadt's idea of the church. On the one hand, there are the many biblical references to the little remnant. On the other, there is a yearning for companionship and for a church numbering more than just a few. Karlstadt's personal feelings are gradually overcome and this results in a fairly consistent development towards contraction of the true church, until it consists of 'the brethren in Orlamünde,' a few brethren in Zurich and Rothenburg, and a Swabian furrier whom Karlstadt met at the Black Cloister in Wittenberg.

Karlstadt originally hoped to see his plans for reformation established with the co-operation of the lower magistrates. In January of 1522 his and Luther's efforts bore fruit with the Wittenberg Ordinance, a draft of which was published with Karlstadt's On the Removal of Images.[63] Two years later Karlstadt received the backing of the Council of Orlamünde, which defended him even when he had been ordered to leave Saxony.[64]

59 Ibid, B3–v: 'Ich weyss das ich keyn jünger und nachfolger Christi kan geseyn, ich lasse dan vatter und mutter, brüder und schwester, und freund, und meyn aygen natur, haut und har, es muss alles seyn gelassen, das in mir und auss mir ist, alles das mich yhn hymel erdrich yn seel und leyp hyndert'; B3v: 'Welcher nach mir wil folgen, der sol sich selber vorleugnen, und trag seyn creutz teglich und folge mir. Lu. 9' (1520).
60 BR 2, 448:13f (1521).
61 WA 15, 337:16–18 (1524).
62 KS 2, 64:39–65:1: 'Ir seynd doch zwar nitt vil, die ich rür, unnd ob ir gleych vil weren, weyss ich doch wol das der wenigste teyl sälig wurd' (1525).
63 KT 74, 31–2 (1522).
64 KS 2, 56–7 (1524).

Karlstadt then tries to harmonize his exclusivistic doctrine of the church with magisterial reform, which is imposed from above. He has an egalitarian view of the church, but not of society at large. Even though Karlstadt may have thought that he was living in 'the Christian city of Wittenberg,'[65] he believes that he is living not in a city of Christians but in a city whose council imposes Christian regulations.[66]

Karlstadt's concern for social ethics also motivates him not to abandon hope for the magistracy. Even in 1524, when he travelled to Zurich, Strassburg, and Basel, and when he shunned the clergy of the established church as well as the magistrates, he may not have lost all hope in principle. At any rate, in 1525, when he went underground in the imperial city of Rothenburg on the Tauber, he appealed from the elector of Saxony to the emperor.[67] Karlstadt may not have been hopeful, but he denounced the rulers as 'princes of the world' only after they themselves had proved this point to him.

Karlstadt's appeals were thwarted, and his church was disestablished not so much in principle as by circumstances. The 'congregation of God' consists of 'all citizens of the godly city.'[68] This is not a concept of local theocracy, for even angels are included in this godly city. Thus the church as city of God has a vertical axis. If the magistrates co-operate, so much the better, but if they do not, the church asserts its independence: 'Each congregation [gemein], whether small or large, shall see for itself that it does what is right and good, and it shall wait for no one.'[69]

We have already seen that the church could, in extreme circumstances, be reduced to a household or a single individual. Not only circumstances can make such a course necessary, however. Long before Karlstadt gives up on the magistracy, he emphasizes the need for worship at home. In 1519 Karlstadt insists that the Bible be read twice daily at table. The home has a specific religious role independent of the church.[70] However, even family ties may have to be cut with Christ's sword.[71] But Karlstadt tries to harmonize religion and the family: 'For a

---

65 KT 74, [2] (1522). However, this designation also appears on tracts by Melanchthon, and the title-page on which it is used, may have been composed by the printer.

66 See the letter of Karlstadt and others to the elector, 12 Dec. 1521 (WB 84–90), where Karlstadt's view of the small persecuted remnant is again delineated.

67 *Testament* (143), A2v (1525).

68 KS 1, 25:37–26:1 (1524).

69 KS 1, 80:28–30: 'Ein jeglich gemein, sie sey klein oder gross, sol für sich sehen das sie recht und wohl thu, und auff niemants warten' (1524).

70 *Bucher* (46), [B4v]: 'wolt ich geratten haben das sie des morgens ein zeit, klein odder gross, in lesung odder anhorung heyliger evangelien, und nach mittem tag odder abent essen, ein zeit in der heyligenn schrifft altes gesetz vortryeben ja gewinnen' (1520).

71 *Gelassenheyt* (38), Bv–2 (1520).

father always has greater power to order the worship of his home, than a pope or a bishop, or even a whole community.'[72]

Even a religious act of surrendering (*gelassen*) one's family fails without love: 'But it could happen that one surrendered [*geliess*] land, meadows, elders, children, and one's wife, and one would still be unsurrendered [*ungelassen*] in one's soul, ... when one desires and loves such surrender.'[73] The remedy is to love one's family, not for its own but for God's sake. Karlstadt frowns on the easy abandonment of one's family. Consequently, one must abandon one's own abandonment (*gelassenheit in gelassenheit*) in order to love like God. Home religion is essential.

As for the established church, Karlstadt repudiates the church of Rome in 1520. To submit to a heretical pope is worse than martyrdom:

> I see two deaths before my eyes: one of these I must suffer. To the right threatens [eternal] death ... , to the left, the death of my flesh. One of these I must accept ... Is it not better, since I must die anyway and I lose no more than a brief span of life, that I accept the death of my body and flesh, and protect the [eternal] life of my spirit?[74]

Karlstadt's dismissal of Lutheranism came in 1524, two years after Luther had rejected him. The brethren in Orlamünde call Luther 'a false brother' who is not a Christian, because he is a man of abusive language and he disregards Christ's rules for church discipline.[75] Karlstadt's polemic against the 'new pope and his monkeys' is well known. Luther is outside the pale of the church; hence in 1525 Karlstadt is still praying that 'the horned ass' might see the light and repent.[76]

Karlstadt can even conceive of a lonely individual who conforms outwardly but who shuns active idolatry. Here he anticipates the *Stillen im Lande* among the Baptists. In such a situation it is helpful to have been excommunicated:

> GEMSER You haven't eaten the bread of the Lord according to the institution of the pope?

72 KS 1, 42:6–9 (1524).
73 *Gelassen* (104), [E4v]: 'Aber es möcht kumen, das ainer ecker, wysen, eltern, kinder und sein eeweyb gliess, und wer in seiner seele ungelassen ... wan er lust und lieb in sollicher ubergebung und gelasung hat' (1523).
74 *Gelassenheyt* (38), [A4]: 'Zwen tödt sehe ich vor augen: eynen muss ich leyden. Auff der rechten seyten trayhet mir der todt, meynen geyst zu todten und erwurgen, und mich ewiglich zu peynigen. Auff der lyncken stehet der todt meynes fleysch. Eynen muss ich annemen ... Ist es aber nit besser, weyl ich doch sterben muss und vorliess nicht dan ein klein und kurtze zeyt, ich fall in todt meynes leybs und fleysch, und bewar meyn leben des geystes?' (1520).
75 WA 15, 343:14f (1524).
76 KS 2, 104:1–6, 21–5 (1525).

PETER Not for twenty years.
GEMSER How come you were so lucky?
PETER I had been excommunicated by the pope for my salvation.[77]

Karlstadt practised this principle in 1525 when he returned to Saxony but eschewed the Lutheran sacrament of the altar.

Karlstadt's brethren in Orlamünde had argued that failure to excommunicate is a sign of a false church. In more moderate form this idea can be traced back to the time when Karlstadt was still in communion with Rome. Among his rights as archdeacon of the Church of All Saints was that of patronage of the church of Orlamünde. At Orlamünde Karlstadt excommunicated several persons. One case involved his vicar, Nikolaus Suppan; three other persons were excommunicated for 'worldly reasons.'[78] Bubenheimer has refuted Barge's charge that Karlstadt did not act within his rights.[79] However, we cannot determine whether Karlstadt was fair in applying those rights. Even so, Karlstadt acted with a certain amount of integrity, for he already regarded the church as too inclusivistic. His eyes had been opened to this problem by Augustine. In 1518 Karlstadt notes that there are many heretics and pretended believers in the church, when one judges according to the Bible rather than the scholastics. As Augustine observed, such heretics must be cast out of the church.[80]

These excommunications occurred before Karlstadt broke with the pope, and he alters his position on excommunication in 1520. He realizes that the pope may soon excommunicate him, and then he no longer regards excommunication as the right of a single individual. Whether the prospect of his own danger was decisive, or whether this new clarity came from what Karlstadt had previously done unto others, cannot be determined. At any rate he now elaborates a biblical procedure of excommunication.

The pope represents one extreme when he binds those who are not bound in heaven.[81] On the other hand, public punishment is essential for public sins.[82] The one who holds the keys, however, is Christ, who has delegated his authority to the whole congregation, or to an individual who truly represents the will of the congregation:

I surely know what procedure Paul observed in the expulsion and isolation of the public sinner whom he handed over to the devil, so his flesh would

77 KS 2, 22:38–23:2 (1524).
78 BARGE 1, 57–8; BARGE 2, 531–2.
79 BUBENHEIMER, 20–1.
80 LÖSCHER 2, 99, th 349–54.
81 Heylickeit (44), C3v: 'Antwort, fur das erste sag ich, der bapst yrret vielmals mit seinen panden und ketten. Ehr vorbinded, der in hymeln auff gelost is' (1520).
82 Ablas (28), B2v: 'Ich waiss das offenlich sunde, offenlich straff haben' (1520).

perish [1 Cor. 5:5]. Paul also received his procedure and word from Christ, as it is written for us in Matthew 18:15–18. From this it follows that a cleric cannot bind without a Christian congregation [hauffen], for Paul says [1 Cor. 5:4]: 'When you are assembled and my spirit is present [deliver him to Satan],' and Christ says [Matt. 18:17]: 'Tell the church. If he does not hear the church, ...' And there follows: 'All that you bind or loose on earth is bound or loosed' [Matt. 18:18]. Hence Christ conferred the key to Peter when he represented the whole congregation [hauffen], Matt. 16:19.[83]

The keys must be turned against anyone 'who leads a godless existence and life':

Christ has brought a sword [Matt. 10:34], and he especially wants to cut us off and separate us from those brethren who lead a godless existence and life. [Christ] says: 'He who does not hate father and mother and follow me cannot and may not be my servant [Luke 14:26].'
Paul has also forbidden us to have any fellowship with those who publicly live against God [1 Cor. 5:1–5; 2 Thess. 3:6, 11].[84]

83 *Emphahung* (76), [B4]: 'Ich weiss wol welch form und wort Paulus gehalten hat in auss werffung und absunderung des offenbare sonders den er dem teuffel gab zu verderbtnis seinis fleisch. 1. Co. v. Paulus hat ouch sein form und wort von Christo genumen das wir Mat. xviii. geschriben haben. Darauss volget das kein pfaff, on ein Christlichen hauffen kan binden, dan Paulus spricht: "Congregatis vobis et spiritu meo." I. Co. v., und Christus sagt: "Dic ecclesiae. Si non audierit ecclesiam etc." Volget: "Alles das ir pindet oder lossen werdet, das ist gepunden oder erlost." Matt. xviii. Sso hat Christus Petro die schlüssel geben, alss er fur den gantzen hauffen antwurt. Matt. xv"' (1521). Karlstadt first states that binding is the work of 'all Christians' in *Heylickeit* (44), C3v. He says he will elaborate this view 'if the pope presses him strongly' (1520). Karlstadt may have been influenced by Luther's reading of Matt. 16:18 in the light of Matt. 18:18 (WA 6, 411–12; WA 7, 170). However, in his references to the power of the keys Luther thinks primarily of the right to interpret Scripture. Since the keys could also be thought of as referring to excommunication, Karlstadt may have extended Luther's argument. If Luther had intended to grant the congregation the right of excommunication, as well as the free interpretation of Scripture, then he retracts in WA 10/3, 58–60, where the right of excommunication belongs to the priest. Luther notes the practice of the New Testament church, but he does not plan to reintroduce it all by himself. Besides this difference, the basic contrast between Karlstadt and Luther exists in their understanding of the function of excommunication. For Luther it is 'the motherly scourge' of the church, which is primarily remedial (WA 6, 63–75). For Karlstadt excommunication is an instrument for the reformation and purification of the church.

84 *Was bann* (119), A2v: 'Christus hat ein schwert bracht, und wil uns in sonderheit von solchen brüdern abschneiden und teylen, die ein gotloses wesen und leben füren. Und spricht: "Welcher nit vater und muter hasset und mir nachvolgt, der kan oder magk mein diener nicht sein, etc,"' with marginal references to 'Math. 10.' and 'Luce. 12. [!]'; Bv: 'Auch hat

False liturgical practices also deserve excommunication:

Paul also teaches that we have no fellowship [*gemeinschafft*] with those who honour images. 1 Cor. 5. Moreover, Paul mentions that all who use the cup or bread should flee idolatry, for it cannot be harmonized: participation in the Lord's bread and service of idols. Paul says, 'you shall have no communion with idolaters, adulterers, and the like ...'[85]

Besides moral and liturgical offences Karlstadt discusses deviations in doctrine. 'Now we are not to converse with, or greet, or invite into our homes [2 John 10] those who evade Christ's teachings. For we have been forbidden to love them as our neighbours.'[86] This injunction applies only to those who knowingly spurn Christ. A neighbour ignorant of Christ is an exception. Karlstadt will share his goods with him, 'that he may come with me into a godly community.'[87] Karlstadt also cautions against rash excommunication: 'Therefore, no banning [*bann*] or shunning [*acht*] is to be proclaimed except in affairs pertaining to God.'[88] Perhaps Karlstadt is retracting his previous excommunication of three persons for 'worldly reasons.' He also underlines the fearsome nature of shunning: 'For God's shunning [*acht*] is no small matter, as can be proved from the fact that its Hebrew equivalent is *herem*, which means: to slay, destroy, exterminate, and nullify.'[89]

Paulus uns vorbotten, das wir keine gemeinschafft mit den haben sollen, die offentlich wider got leben,' with marginal references to '1. Cor. 5' and '2. Thess. 3' (1524). See Sider's significant, if too cautious, observation (SIDER, 287): 'Perhaps these few remarks should be viewed as the initial stage of the development of congregational discipline and shunning in the left wing of the Reformation. It is interesting, however, that Karlstadt advocated exclusion from the congregation only on doctrinal grounds.' In fact, Karlstadt develops a complete procedure for excommunication, and ethical reasons predominate.

85 KT 74, 9:32–3: 'Paulus der leret auch das wir kein gemeindschafft mit den solchen haben, die bildnis eheren. 1 Cor. v' (1522). *1 Cor. 10* (142), B2: 'Ferner meldet Paulus und bittet alle die jhenen so des herren Kelch oder brott brauchen, das sy Götzen dienst flyehen sollen. Denn es steet nitt bey einander: Des herren kelch unnd brott teylhafftig seyn, unnd den götzen dienen. 1. Corinth. 6. 9 und 10. 2. Corinth. 6' (1525). KS 1, 77:27–9: 'Paulus spricht: "Ir solt kein gemeinschafft mit den götzen dienern, eebrechern, und der geleichen, haben"' (1524). The same argument occurs later in the *Brotherly Agreement* of Schleitheim.

86 KS 1, 66:22–5: 'Nun sollen wir denen nit ein freüntlich wort mitteylen, oder grüssen, noch sye zu hauss nemen, die Christi lere nit habenn. So ist unns auch verbotten solich als nechsten zu lieben' (1524).

87 KS 1, 70:6–14, 20–33 (1524). See also Sider's refutation of Holl (SIDER, 285–7).

88 *Wass bann* (119), B3: 'Drumb solt man auch keynen bann oder acht verkundigen, dann nur in göttlichen sachen' (1524).

89 Ibid, B3: 'Dann Gottis acht ist nicht ein geringe sache, das vornimb also: das hebreisch wort *herem* heisset, todt schlagen, verwüsten, vertilgen, unnd zu nicht machen.' Sometimes Karlstadt uses *acht* as equivalent to *bann*, but when he distinguishes it [B3–v], it means to be 'one achtung, also das man des menschen gar nichts mehr achten solt' The English equivalent is 'shunning' or 'avoidance.'

The practice of excommunication or shunning should be a constant warning to believers to avoid the godless:

Every believer should prefer to die rather than be among such who are godless, as one sees in the acts or sufferings of David and other servants of God.[90] One makes no covenants with the heathen.[91] Weak Christians are worse than heathen; they are twofold heathen. No compromise is possible: 'You shall not be in the communion of devils. You cannot drink both the Lord's and the devil's cup.'[92]

The devil's cup, served by Luther's clerics, must be avoided. 'We see that the devil has donned new robes, and he employs those who see but are blind.'[93] The 'old' and the 'new, twofold papists' are anti-Christians (endtchristen). Just as Karlstadt challenges his excommunication by 'the old pope,' so he scores Luther's use of the secular arm for this same purpose: 'So he comes out with rifle shots, and he shoots me out of Saxony with an edict, to harm me to no end. Therefore I am supposed to sit quietly, so he will not shoot me out of the whole world. He surely would do this if he could, and if God were dead.'[94]

Excommunication is valid only when the true church practises it according to biblical principles. Karlstadt advances many more biblical reasons for excommunication than were practised by his opponents. He wants a clearly demarcated church, and in that sense he is intolerant, although he denounces the killing of heretics.[95]

However, Karlstadt and his followers could not establish themselves, so the 'new' and the 'old papists' were more intolerant in practice. More latitudinarian in

90 Ibid, B: 'Und ein itzlicher gleubiger solt lieber sterben dann bey solchen gotlosen menschen sein, als man sihet in den geberden oder leyden Davids, unnd der andern knechten gottis.'
91 KS 1, 95:3–5: 'Disse historien zeigen klärlich an das die Juden weder verbündtnus mit den heiden machen, weder gemach thun solten altarien umb zustürtzen' (1524).
92 1 Cor. 10 (142), [C4]: 'Ir solt nichts sein in der gemeinschaft der teuffeln: ir könt nit zugleich des herren kelch trincken und des teuffels'; 'Ir künt nit zu gleich des herren tisch teylhafftig sein, und des teuffels tisch' (1525).
93 Testament (143), B3v: 'Seytemal wir sehen das der teuffel in neuen korrecken steet und understeet sich die sehenden blenden' (1525).
94 Leyb (129), [D5]: 'So platzet er mit büchsen schützen herfür, und scheüsset mich mit einem briffe, auff ein mal auss den landen zu Sachsen zu meinem unüberwintlichem schaden. Derhalben muss ich schweygen, uff das er mich nit auss der gantzen welt schiess, das er gern thet, wenn erss vermöcht, und gott gestorben wer' (1524).
95 Verba Dei (26), B2 (1520). Karlstadt is more severe towards those who pretend to be Christians than towards outright unbelievers. In view of this, and Karlstadt's preoccupation with 1 Cor. 5 on the subject of excommunication, it seems that verse 12 was influential. Thus 'false brethren' are worse than unbelievers. Already in 1522 Karlstadt says of 'the pope, cardinals, bishops, priests (Pfaffen), and monks': 'Sie seind erger dan heyden, und fechten offenlich wider gotis wort' (Malachiam (93), A3v).

some respects, they nevertheless were willing to wield the sword. This confirmed Karlstadt in his view that the church suffers violence from pretended believers.

The Life of the Church

From a certain puristic standpoint the doctrine of the church should be separated from the practical life of the church, but we ignore an artificial system of compartmentalization. In Karlstadt there is little distinction between his theories and their ultimate application in practice, and I shall consider only the essentials. The role of the sacraments, which devolved into signs, is not being treated here. Karlstadt's conception of the Holy Supper is not an essential mark of his Baptist views. Later, when his views on the Supper appear in other Baptist writers, I shall discuss such dependence there. Karlstadt's view of baptism has never been analysed, but there is such a wealth of material that a discussion of it has been relegated to the next chapter.

Anticlericalism

Besides lifting the lowly, egalitarianism implies casting down the mighty, and from the traditional standpoint Karlstadt is anticlerical. Divesting the clergy of pretence is a positive factor, however, not only for the laity, since clerical abuses hurt everyone. The priests are their own enemies, when, after a night of carousing, they lie in church and are heard to mutter: 'fill'er up,' 'I'll have another one,' or 'shuffle the deck.'[96] Worthy clerics do not fear the loss of hoary privileges, for 'a God-fearing man will love the [Minister] for the sake of truth.'[97]

Karlstadt's polemic takes three distinct forms. He may analyse the defects of clericalism (e.g. clerics tend to cow the people). Often he resorts to counter-intimidation. Ultimately, however, he strives to heal and unite the ministers and the people. This pattern may deliberately reflect the three steps of Karlstadt's scheme for conversion, where especially the second step is most violent.

Karlstadt wants to overcome the plight of the church with radical measures. Clericalism debased the church in the past. When Christ appeared before Pilate, the laity (Pilate and the crowd) wanted to free Christ, but the clerics wanted to slay him, just as they still try to slay him in their masses. The programme of the priests prevails, however, for they browbeat the people and Pilate. This is Karlstadt's summary of Mark 15:1–15. The pharisaic Roman scribes have 'lifted up' the Saviour. In farmer's language Karlstadt counters with the 'lifting up' of the

96 KS 2, 46:4–11 (1524).
97 KS 2, 14:37–8: 'Ich wil dir bürg seyn, das dich der gotfürchtig man von wegen der warheyt lieben würd' (1524).

clergy: 'Woe to you, for you shall be lifted up, like a tail above an arsehole (you who have been placed above all the nations of the earth), because you smear and desert the Saviour.'[98] Ultimately, this position leads to a Lord's Supper that affirms the once and for all sacrifice at Calvary. The elements of the Lord's Supper are no longer uplifted, and any layperson may break the bread and pour the wine just as well as the official shepherd of the congregation.[99]

The clergy should communicate with the people. Thus they should hold their services in German, but Karlstadt implicitly criticizes Luther by refusing to use chancellery-style German. Sermons should not be adorned with 'courtly, cosmetic, painted, and worldly-wise words.'[100] The origins of a word like *gelassenheit* should be sought among the common people. The chancellery style is mocked for its artificiality: 'Among our German Franconians, the word *vhelig* [rather than *sicher*, safe] is rare and strange. That's why the scribes of the chancellery use it.'[101]

The clergy also flaunt their academic and clerical titles. Karlstadt's countergambit is the rejection of all titles. Unbiblical clerical titles should be discarded. 'From this, everyone should understand the made-up lie of the word "vicar."'[102] Thus Karlstadt challenges common parlance when this reflects a theological position that he opposes. Counter-intimidation is the aim when Karlstadt asserts the godhood of all believers against the pope. Such polemic is not an end in itself, however, for it is overcome in the unity of the body of Christ. The laity have received one biblical title, which they share with the cleric who has been divested of pretence. It is 'brother Andreas' who writes to the 'brethren' in Orlamünde.[103] After Luther's *Appeal to the Christian Nobility* Karlstadt makes a similar appeal, but he implicitly emends Luther when he notes that, in the church, Christ is the corner-stone, and 'the same stone is the foundation and nobility of all who believe in him.'[104] This clarifies Karlstadt's position *vis-à-vis* Luther and Thomas

98 *Priesterthum* (112), F: 'We aber euch, denn ir musset als ein schwantz fürs trekloch gehefft werden, die weil ir unser haupt und unsern heyland also vorsprecht, und den vorlasset, der euch uber alle völker dieser erden gesetzt' (1523).
99 Referring to the one who proclaims Christ's death to the congregation (1 Cor. 11:26), Gemser asks: 'Von wem?' and Peter replies: 'Von einem derss brodt brechen wil, oder von einem andern' (KS 2, 28:30–1) (1524).
100 *Fegfeür* (95), Av (1523).
101 *Gelassen* (104), A2 (1523).
102 *Malachiam* (93), A3v: 'Darab soll yder man betrachten das edicht und erlogen worthlin vicarius, welches bepst erdicht haben, und konden nymer mher in gotlichem bevel antzeigen, das sie stathalter oder vicarien gottes seind.' Against such titles Karlstadt upholds the biblical title *Malachias*, which he translates as apostle or messenger (*bott*) (1522) Cf. *Messen* (131), [1v]–2.
103 KS 1, 3:4–6 (1523).
104 *Heylickeit* (44), D[not C]3v: 'der selb stein ist ein grund und adelkeit aller deren sso in yhn glauben' (1520).

Müntzer. Unlike Müntzer, Karlstadt is not an egalitarian in his view of society, and he accepts a special role for rulers and nobility. In the church, however, Karlstadt fosters outright egalitarian practice. Luther demands egalitarianism in the church in principle, but he negates it in practice, for he ties salvation to the sacraments as well as the Word. Thus the Lutheran priest becomes an essential link between God and the congregation. Karlstadt avoids this laity-clergy distinction at first, when he still has a high view of the sacrament, by conferring on the laity the right to celebrate the Lord's Supper at home. When Karlstadt no longer regards the Supper as a sacrament, Christ emerges as the *only* priest and there is no sacerdotal function separating believers from their shepherds.

When laypersons fear the erudition of the clergy, they should know that they themselves are often more intelligent.[105] To rouse the laity from its lethargy Karlstadt may use shock treatment. In 1521 he goes from door to door in Wittenberg to ask the people the meaning of a scriptural passage.

The role of the laity

Laypersons may arbitrate theological disputes.[106] When Karlstadt still accepts confession, he grants the right of absolution to the laity.[107] Late in 1519 Karlstadt exhorts the people to boycott false preachers, who must be wounded with God's curses.[108] The laity should instruct one another in the meaning of Scripture.[109] They must proclaim the gospel like Malachi: 'The Hebrew *Malachi* means "My messenger," "My subordinate," "My herald," "My recruiter" and "proclaimer." To sum it up: everyone who proclaims God's Word and is driven to proclaim by the Spirit of God, can be called Malach.'[110] Such messengers are apostles to their own households also: 'All householders should earnestly be zealous to teach the Word of God, so their children might learn in return.'[111] All believers are mes-

---

105 Ibid, (G5): 'Leyhen seint disse zeit verstendiger, geschickter, und gelarter in der heyligenn schrifft dan etzliche unnd viel geistliche prelaten.'
106 *Bucher* (46), C3 (1520).
107 Clemen, *Beiträge* 1, 36, th 29: 'Extra casum necessitatis (permittente evangelio) possumus laicis confiteri et ab eis iuro divino absolvi' (1521).
108 *Verba Dei* (26), Av: 'Non modo non audiendos esse concionatores, sed etiam plagis conficiendos, qui dei populum non sola divina verba docent' (1520).
109 *Bucher* (46), A2 (1520).
110 *Malachiam* (93), A2v: 'Malachi hebraisch heyset auff teutsch: "Meyn bott; Mein geschickter; Mein beveltrager; Meyn werber und verkundiger." In der summ: Ein jeder dero gots wort verkundiget, und von dem geist gotis getriben wirt tzu verkundigung gotliche wort, der mocht Malach genent werden.' Karlstadt equates *botten* and apostles, for he refers to Christ's 'zwolf boten' and he concludes (A3): 'Nuhn habt yhr gehort das alle aposteln und junger Christi (sso das wort gotis leren) gotliche boten seind' (1522).
111 Ibid, A3: 'Und solten sich alle hauss veter ernstlich befleissen das wort gotis alsso zu lernen, das sie widerumb ire kinder leren mochten.'

sengers (botten), who can speak under inspiration of the Holy Spirit.[112] They are the brethren who called Karlstadt in 1523.[113] Lay people should preach during the regular service: not in a corner, but in the centre of the congregation:

Indeed, we must all conform to Christ and follow Christ, and we must be zealous to proclaim the honour and holiness of our Father as Christ did, each according to his talent.

Therefore, one will reveal unto others the name of God, and proclaim the name of God to our brethren, – not in a corner, but in the midst of the congregation – that they may be brought to accept and praise God's Word ... One also needs the other, for God's gifts are diverse, and no one has them all.

For no one has been excluded, since God's command embraces all, and concerns itself with God's Word and love of the neighbour.[114]

Each member of Karlstadt's church has a constant mission to instruct and preach. This is not an explicit doctrine of special missions, but its effect is similar because persecution soon scatters Karlstadt's followers, who continue to instruct others wherever they go, causing a rapid dissemination of their ideas.

When laypersons correct the erring clergy, the latter should humbly receive such admonition. Karlstadt accepts such correction for himself: 'I do not want to be taught and directed only by the "big shots" [grossen hanssen] ... but even by a little child, through Holy Scriptures.'[115] The people have the right also to interrupt the sermon in church by asking questions or challenging ideas. Karlstadt justifies this with 1 Corinthians 14:26–31 ('Two or three may prophesy'). Such prophecies are explications of Scripture. Moses wants prophets to be unhindered (Num. 11:29). Amos and other prophets were shepherds (hyrten) who proclaimed the truth to priests (pfaffen). A layperson should cast the first stone at a false preacher (Deut. 13:5).[116]

112 Ibid, B2: 'Das hat got nit allein mit seiner laher geleret, das menschlicher mund gotis wort redet one alles tzutuhn und mitwircken. Sonder hat es auch mit der taht angetzeigt.' The references are to Exod. 4; Jer. 1; Mal. 1; Lev. 8, 26, 27.

113 KS 1, 3:4: 'Euch brüdern, die yr mich berufft.' See also 6:2–7:22 where Karlstadt discusses the need for a spiritual call and the use of a lot (1523).

114 KS 1, 17:18–25, 31–2, 18:18–20 (1523).

115 Concilio (45), A3: 'Ich wold mich nit allein grossen hanssen ... sunder auch ein klein kind lassen lernen und weyssen durch heylige schrifft' (BUBENHEIMER, 294:65–295:67) (1520).

116 Fürbit Marie (108), B3: 'Das aber die layen den predigern dürffen einreden und iren verstand auch offenbaren, disen gewalt gibt Paulus sagend: "Zwen oder drey mögen prophetiziern," das ist, schriften ausslegen, "die andern söllen schweygen. So aber ain sitzender oder zuhörer ain eröffnung hatt, soll der oberst," das ist der redner und prediger, "still schweygen" und hören was got dem layen offenbar gemacht hat' (1523).

The original idea of interruption is probably not Karlstadt's own. What seems to be the first recorded incident occurred on 16 February 1522 when a Discalced Franciscan twice demanded preaching from Scripture.[117] In August of the same year Nikolaus Kattelsburger, a weaver in Augsburg, interrupted the Franciscan Johann Winzler's sermon.[118] Karlstadt himself refers to the action of a 'pious man' who interrupted Georg Kirchner.[119] But Karlstadt is the first preacher to encourage such interruptions and to use Scripture to justify this new right of the laity.

Finally, any layperson who has received the gifts of the Spirit can become the shepherd of the congregation. A candidate may be 'anyone, learned or unlearned, high or low, young or old,' though the process of careful selection will take time.[120] Of course, Karlstadt does not defend theological illiteracy. Therefore, all the basic questions of theology should be discussed in the language of the people, so they can judge for themselves. This includes even such complex matters as separating the canonical Scriptures from the Apocrypha.[121]

The role of women

Protestantism proved to be mostly a setback for women in the church. By abandoning the veneration of the saints (many of whom were women) and opposing the monastic system (including convents for nuns), as well as reducing traditional Mariology and demoting mysticism (a Christian version of which especially appealed to women), Protestantism exhibited the regressive aspect of the Renaissance cry: *Ad fontes!* (To the fountainhead!). For the fountainhead of the reformers was Hebraic and the Reformation was modelled on religious ideas that assumed male domination. This change did not derive from explicit anti-feminism. Male as well as female saints were dethroned. Theological reasons determined the rejection of mysticism. Both monks and nuns became unemployed. Even so Roland Bainton's three volumes, *Women of the Reformation*, discuss a transitional phenomenon. Women theologians had been trained as nuns, or their courtly education had been inspired by the Renaissance. Their role was tertiary unless they wielded secular power. Queens, however, held a medieval office.

The situation was improved at intermediate levels. Protestantism required literacy for an understanding of the Bible. In spite of Karlstadt's lumping together

---

117 WB, 211.
118 Schottenloher, *Philipp Ulhart*, 22.
119 *Fürbit Marie* (108), A2 (1523).
120 KS 1, 11:1f (1523). Karlstadt based his argument for slow and careful selection on 1 Tim. 5:22. Persecution forced the Swiss Baptists to abandon this practice later. Cf the *Brotherly Agreement* of Schleitheim, art. 5.
121 *Bucher* (46), A2 (1520).

of old and new pope, the gap between the clergy and the laity had been reduced, in Lutheranism as well. Moreover, the wives and children of the clergy fared much better under Protestantism, when it broke with the common medieval clerical practice of loyal or serial concubinage.

Karlstadt envisions a greater role for women than other reformers. As he had said, anyone could prophesy in his gatherings. In addition, more than most reformers, Karlstadt held on to traditional mystical concepts. When Karlstadt refers to God as *Goodness, Oneness,* etc, he does not try to revive philosophical speculation, but he does retain a way of speaking about God which is not specifically male. Of course, Karlstadt continues to accept the biblical imagery of God as the heavenly Father. He is also traditional in emphasizing the church's role as Christ's bride.

Karlstadt is the first reformer to reject the intercession of the saints, but this does not derive from a hatred of female saints. Even angels are excluded from veneration and intercession.[122] A new sainthood replaces the dead saints of wood and stone – the people in church are saints, and they are addressed as such.[123] A traditional Catholic more than a modern Protestant would understand the full meaning of this for the women and men in Karlstadt's congregation.

No special day is to be reserved for angels, since they did not create time. The Creator-creature distinction is to be maintained. However, if the old angels have to step down, the people in the pews are elevated. On the basis of the Greek meaning of angel Karlstadt concludes that the people are angels or *botten* (messengers) themselves.[124] In mystical terms the people are 'sons' and 'daughters' of God.

Using traditional terms, Karlstadt emphasizes the female nature of the church. The reason why his church is unadorned is simple. The church is the bride of Christ who comes naked unto her husband. Luther scoffed at the 'naked bride of Orlamünde,'[125] but Karlstadt may well have been influenced by the bridal mysticism of Luther's own father-confessor, Johann von Staupitz, who used the not uncommon imagery of believers as the naked virgins who copulate with Christ.[126] That Karlstadt clung to such views is understandable, for his whole anti-hierarchical conception of the church rejects any form of intervention between God and the believer.

122 *Engelen* (122), [C4v]: 'sonderlich ist es ein sträffliche torheit, das man die engeln anbetten und inen opffer geben und sye feyren wil, oder soliche stuck beweysen, die doch Gott allein zustehn' (1524). *Fürbit Marie* (108), A2v, already gives the cardinal proof text, 1 Tim. 2:[5] (1523).
123 *Priesterthum* (112), A2 (1523).
124 *Engelen* (122), A2. Karlstadt uses *malach*, angel, messenger (*bott*), and apostle or disciple interchangeably (1524).
125 WA 18, 84:14f.
126 Staupitz, *Fürsehung,* 161.

Karlstadt even uses the female nature of the church to circumvent male domination in the Old Testament. On the basis of Num. 30:6–8 Karlstadt shows that husbands may annul the vows of their wives. Women are not accorded the same right in Numbers, but Karlstadt claims that the vows of men may also be annulled, for men are part of the church, and Christ has the power to annul the vows of his bride. The word 'wives,' understood spiritually, involves husbands, and since Moses depends on Christ, Christ's role of husband turns all earthly husbands into 'wives.'[127] Similarly, when the Old Testament allows fathers to annul the vows of their daughters, Karlstadt adds that sons should also be included.[128]

The case for annulling the vows of husbands also proceeds from the need to protect dependent women and children. Karlstadt fumes at men who vow to go on a pilgrimage and piously abandon their wives and children without providing for their needs. Such men have denied the faith, and they are worse than unbelievers (1 Tim. 5:8).[129]

The command to read the Bible at table is, as we have seen, addressed to husbands, but Karlstadt goes beyond the Old Testament role of the father in applying this command to 'each and every Christian, young and old, ordained and unordained, husbands and wives.'[130] Women should also be instructed in the Bible.[131]

---

127 *Gelubden* (50), G2f. This statement is also applied to men, G3v: 'Wir seind auch alle, disses valss weiber, eynem gemahell vertrauhet, der Christus ist. Ephe. v. Derhalben sollen wir, es sey mann, frau, gesell, oder mayd, bapst, bischoff, pfaffe, monich oder nonne vor allen, ehr wir geloben oder unsser gelubd erfullen, die stüm Christi ersuchen'; G3v–[4]: 'Nu saget Christus offt, das gott barmhertzigkeit fodert, nit gelubd' (1521).

128 Ibid, Gv: 'Was der text von meydlinge sagt, das soll auch meynes bedunckes von allen kindern, sso noch in obirkeit und gebieth yhrer eltern steend, verstanden werden.' Karlstadt cites Num. 30:5 without giving a reference. If a father approves of a vow which the child later regrets, the father may not insist on his own authority, for then he is a Nabal (fool), and he should be disregarded (G2), but this is also reciprocally true of wives. A father (*auss mennlicher oberkeit*) may annul his wife's vow *against her will*. Karlstadt clearly maintains the Pauline hierarchy: Christ, husband, wife, children. The father is the head of the family and his authority can be disregarded only in the name of the higher authority of Christ. In return, the husband owes support to his wife and children.
   Modern ideas of pure equality within the family would have been repugnant to Karlstadt, who would probably have interpreted them as a sign that family life had disintegrated. See Karlstadt's traditional interpretation of Adam and Eve (H3v). Thus the wife is *gleich und ungleich* in relation to her husband. Egalitarianism is possible, however, outside the relationship of the family, specifically in the life of the church. Thus, no one may interfere with the vows of widows (H).

129 Ibid, A3v: '[Das ist leychtfertig und schedlich ding, das einer gelubd brenget], sonderlich sso eyner weyb, kindern und hauss diener hatt. Dan die selbe soll man nit vorlassen von gelubd wegen. Wilcher aber sso nerrisch ist ... der soll wissen das er erger ist dan ein unglaubiger, und hatt den glauben vorlaugnet, als Paulus leret. 1. Timot. v.'

130 *Bucher* (46), A2 (1520).

131 *Verba Dei* (26), [D4] (1520).

When Karlstadt rejects the intercession of Mary, he shows no hostility towards her. In fact, to deny Mary's traditional role means to take her seriously and to follow her example: 'I like to honour Mary, but I will not cut off the honour from her Creator and Lord, and ascribe to Mary what she would repel.'[132]

Karlstadt *is* prejudiced against single adults of either sex. Believers do not wish to be barren: 'Aaron, the Levites, the Prophets, and the Apostles of Christ were married. Only the regiment of the Antichrist is in the unmarried and demonic estate.'[133] One should remember that when Karlstadt penned these words he was still single himself. Celibacy leads to such sins as onanism, sodomy, and fornication.[134] Nuns and monks must be married. Their celibate estate derives from pagan antiquity; nuns are vestal virgins.[135] Throughout Genesis one finds indications that God favours the estate of multiplication.

However, Karlstadt understands the needs of the elderly. He wants to resurrect the Pauline idea of an estate of celibate widows, sixty years and older. Karlstadt improves on Paul, however. He also includes *widowers*. The Pauline dictum 'In Christ there is neither male nor female' does not judge only Moses but even Paul himself.[136] Such a correction is made silently, however, for Karlstadt knows he is out of step with his times, and he conceals some of his shocking insights. Besides, why should Karlstadt spell out a specific role for women when his egalitarian church casts aside the traditional roles?

It is anachronistic, of course, to see Karlstadt pondering twentieth-century problems. Even so, he is unusually sensitive in according to all the equal rights on which his church is based. Nowhere in his writings does Karlstadt thoroughly examine the needs of women. His writings contain only scattered comments, but they must be taken seriously, for they are rigorously consistent.

Women's rights are asserted even though to do so causes controversy. Karlstadt commends the example of Jesus, who did not worry about causing a scandal

---

132 *Fürbit Marie* (108), [A4]: 'Ich eere Mariam gern. Ich will aber irem schöpffer und herren sein eer nit abschneyden, und Marie das zumessen, das sy von sich scheuet' (1523).

133 *Gelubden* (50), [H4v]: 'Aaron, Leviten, Propheten und Aposteln Christi sein eelich gewest; allein des Endchrist regiment is in unelichem und teuffelischem stand' (1521).

134 *Coelibatu* (62), A2v (1521).

135 *Gelubden* (50), Dv: 'Ich geschweig das unsere nonnen und monichen sso keuscheit geloben, den heyden mehr volgen dan gottlicher schrifft. Ich wolt auch gern einen sehen, der durch grundveste schrifften künd unterscheit geben tzwischen gelobdter keuscheit, sso die junckfrauen der abtgotterin Veste gethan, und itzt unsere nonnen sanct. Clara aber Benedictus thuen' (1521).

136 Ibid, Ef. On E2 Karlstadt observes: 'Solche. lx. jar (1. Timo v) gepüren auch den mennern, weil Moises das alter manss und weybs stetz gleich macht.' Karlstadt gives a clearer explanation in *Heylickeit* (44), C2v–3, where, referring to Gal. 3:28, he notes: 'dan in Christo ist weder man nach weyb, weder keysser nach bapst, ssonder allis ein ding' (1520).

to the weak when he conversed with the Samaritan woman.[137] The prominence of women in Karlstadt's movement, as well as his other radical ideas, appalled a humanist like Bonifacius Amerbach. Most northern humanists rocked the bark of Saint Peter ever so gently. They feared the radical onslaught of Karlstadt's biblicism. Amerbach wrote:

> Why is it not sufficient that we have been contaminated with Lutheran opinions, in view of the fact that there has newly arisen a sect of spirituals that absolutely proclaims the destruction of our way of life? Its founder is Andreas Karlstadt, once intimate with Luther, but now diametrically opposed to him in his opinions. The matter is discussed in many books, in which they grievously slander one another. Luther teaches that the true body of the Lord is present in the eucharistic sacrament; Karlstadt strongly denies this, holding there is nothing more than blessed bread. One teaches that idols are to be cast out of the hearts, but not out of the church; the other says, 'also out of the church.' This one says that education should be favoured; the other appears to agree with his followers that learning should be put aside and language study is to be abolished, claiming that Christian people need to know nothing except Hebrew. One teaches that there should be baptistries in the churches; the other removes them ...
>
> Why is it that this insanity does not disturb only men but even women? For there are, for instance, Cleobulines among us.[138]

In the fragments of the pre-Socratics Cleobuline appears as an oracle and composer of wise sayings, who followed the profession of her father. Thus, both laywomen and laymen prophesied in Karlstadt's services, although Karlstadt had not spelled this out in his writings. Here was another act of repression.

The defence of the oppressed

Karlstadt's attitude towards women reflects his general feelings towards the oppressed. He can cite with approval an anecdote that circulates among the Jews.[139] He feels that God often visits the community's sins with a murrain

137   KS 1, 79:30–3: 'Darauff sag ich: "Christus redet mit einer Samaritterin, und die Juden pflegten doch nicht zu reden mit den Samarittern, des auch verwunderten sich seine jünger. Aber Christus achtet ir ergernüs nicht, sonder thet frey das sein vatter wolt haben"' (1524). NB: This passage discusses the need for offence in general terms, and it is not specifically concerned with women. Precisely because Karlstadt underlines the scandalous nature of the gospel, however, he overcomes traditional stereotypes, also with respect to women.

138 Hartmann, ed, Die Amerbachkorrespondenz 3, 18:21–37.

139 Messe (71), D2 (1521). Karlstadt also considers the good kings of Judah to have been better than the kings of Christendom (KT 74, 20:33–5). The Jews are also on God's side in respect of images (KT 74, 5:28–31) (1522).

among the cattle, but the people then compound their guilt by making scapegoats of warlocks and witches.[140]

In 1516 Karlstadt encounters slavery in Italy, but, unlike Luther, he opposes slavery and serfdom:

> Now hear how this kind of sale occurs. It used to be that people could sell one another, and allow their body to be owned by the buyer. And the buyer could again sell his bought servant to another, just like somebody who sells an ox and allows the buyer to possess the body. Even nowadays this is not uncommon or strange in Naples and Rome. Such sold people together with their children are called servants. Of such servants our text speaks.

After discussing *only* Deuteronomy 15:11–12, and ignoring verses 16–17, which allow voluntary servitude, Karlstadt exclaims:

> That is what the sellers of humans are to do in Rome and in all Christian lands. They are to leave them untrammelled and free, and they are not to free them to reclaim them later for servitude. For then they anger God and besmirch the covenant and the name of God – those who so deceptively and cleverly keep Hebrew slaves, or call them back after they have been freed, or allow them to leave without support. For God considers this just as if one condemns and soils his name, glory, and command, when one treats them deceitfully.[141]

Karlstadt is a legalist in the sense that he demands compliance with the most compassionate rules, wherever he finds them: often in the New, but sometimes in the Old Testament. For the peasants he had genuine sympathy, despite his aversion to physical violence.

Karlstadt resisted Müntzer's plans for insurrection and Müntzer's strong psychological pressures, but in the end Karlstadt dislikes having to disavow Müntzer, preferring 'to praise Müntzer too much than scold him slightly with the truth.'[142] Even Karlstadt's attitude towards Luther can be viewed in this light. Karlstadt shows rancour towards the successful Luther, but in 1520 he steadfastly defended the Luther whose life was at stake.

---

140 KS 1, 30:25–9: 'Welchs laster got offt mals an dem viehe straffet, mit welchem wir sundigen, und lessets uns sterben oder verderben, und wir wollen dennest wider schult noch sund erkennen, und beschuldigen die zeuberer und zeuberynne' (1524).

141 KT 74, 27:9–15, 26–33 (1522). Luther countered the demands of the peasants for freedom by endorsing Urbanus Rhegius's *Von leibaygenschaft oder knechthait* (1525), see WA 18, 326: 13–327:10. Striking is Luther's appeal to the example of the patriarchs. In Münster the Melchiorites would use the same argument in defence of polygamy.

142 See below, Appendix I, 298.

The new clergy

The various offices of the clergy Karlstadt derives from Titus 1. The church has bishops, priests, and preachers.[143] Whether they are bishops or deacons, they must be married in view of 1 Timothy 3:2f.[144] Soon Karlstadt reformulates this view by harmonizing 1 Timothy 3 and 6 and Titus 1. He concludes: 'All elders [presbyters] are bishops [episkopoi]; some are also deacons. Thus the parish priests [parochi] are bishops, and if there are other elders [presbyters] they [also] are truly bishops.'[145] The hierarchy has been discarded. All priests are bishops or elders, although some elders perform the additional role of deacon. One is not a bishop simply by virtue of one's office: 'Personally, I say that I do not regard [the pope] as priest [pfarher] and shepherd [pastor], unless he shepherds me in the pasture of Christ ...'[146] Unbelievers should be barred from holding office in the church. Christ's disciples could not act in virtue of their office, when they lacked the faith to exorcise a demon (Mark 9), and works are the true test of faith:

It is impossible that [unbelieving clergy] personify or act in place of the church – just as the devil could not do it either. As Paul says: 'What communion do the children of Belial have with Christ?' [2 Cor. 6:15].

How can the darkness personify or represent the light? But if they stand in pretence, this has no foundation. Just as there is no basis for pretence, it also follows that there is no work produced by the pretended power.[147]

Thus Karlstadt exhorts others not to depend on him or anyone else.[148] He warns against personality cults:

143 Ochssenfart (90), A2 (1522).
144 Coelibatu (62), D4: 'Ne quis diaconus aut minister clericus ordinetur, nisi primum uxorem honeste tractarit, alueritque liberos, et domui bene praefuerit.' See also D3v: 'Caelebs indignus est episcopatu' (marginal comment) (1521).
145 Ibid, D: 'Consequitur quod omnes presbyteri sunt episcopi, caeteri autem diaconi. Sic parochi sunt episcopi, et si qui alii sunt presbyteri, illi veri sint episcopi. Reliqui vero ministri sunt diaconi.' Karlstadt is probably influenced by a similar argument in Jerome's letter to 'Evangelus' (Corpus scriptorum ecclesiasticorum latinorum 56, 308–12:5).
146 Heylickeit (44), F–v (1520).
147 Christus (124), B2v–3: 'Denn es ist unmüglich das eyn unglaubiger in der ki[r]chen person oder stedt stehe, gleich so wenig als der teufel. Als Paulus spricht: "Was gemeinschafft haben die Belials kinder mit Christo?" Wie künden die finsternus, die person und stedt des liechtes verwesen? Stehn sie aber, so stehen sie im schein, unther welchem kein grund ist. Wie aber kein grundt unther dem scheyn ist, so folget auch kein werck auss der erdichten macht' (1524).
148 See e.g. Christus (124), F4: 'drumb soll keiner uff mich füssen' (1524).

GEM[SER] But Martin Luther gave this advice himself.
PET[ER] That is really too bad, that simple folk sell themselves, because they respect a certain person. For they don't get the naked truth, but the person.[149]

Faith, rather than personality or office, is the first requirement for being a shepherd. The only other requirement is the call from God:

But what would you say to this, that nobody can write or preach or out-wardly perform any public function of God, unless God has called him to it? For Paul speaks plainly: 'I have not been called by men or a single per-son, but I have been appointed by Jesus Christ and God the Father.'[150]

But what of the cleric who performs all outward duties and who preaches sound doctrine? Even faithful preaching is false if God has not commanded it (Rom. 10:15).[151] The human call may well be deceptive, like the call of the Pharisees.[152] Therefore only God can call, and he reveals his call through the casting of a lot: 'The Apostles have not been so bold, that they elected another instead of Judas Iscariot, to witness for and proclaim Christ, before they recognized God's will by means of a lot [Acts 1:15].'[153]

The congregation does not technically call a prospective shepherd. It merely recognizes that God has called someone for it. Since those who think they recog-nize God's call in someone may be led astray by subjective factors, objective confirmation from God is required by the casting of a lot. Even the direct call from God is not limited to the clergy. All believers are called to witness for Christ. Karlstadt appeals to Acts 1:8: 'Ye shall receive the power of the Holy Spirit, and ye shall be my witnesses.' The difference between the call of a shepherd and the general call of all believers lies purely in the specific role of the shepherd, not in the quality of the call. Since the shepherd's function is nevertheless important, care should be exercised in calling: 'Therefore, this is the understanding of Paul, that the Christian congregation [gemeyn], or individual persons, whether high or low, shall be circumspect in the laying on of hands.'[154]

149 KS 2, 30:13–18 (1524).
150 KS 1, 5:39–6:1, 6:16–18 (1523).
151 KS 1, 7:7–17 (1523).
152 KS 1, 6:2–12 (1523).
153 KS 1, 7:18–21: 'Die Aposteln seind nit so vormessen gewest, das sie an Judas Iscarioths stadt, einen andern erwelten, der Christum zeuget und vorkündiget, eh sie durch ein loss gotis willen erkanten' (1523). See also Willen gottes (102), [H4–v] (1523).
154 KS 1, 11:33–6. The texts cited are 1 Tim. 5:22 (command), Acts 1:15–26 and 1 Sam. 16:1–13 (examples). The congregation must first pray to God 'with groans from the heart' (Rom. 8:26) (1523).

Only God's children have the right to call, for they can discern the spirits of others.[155] Those driven by the Spirit recognize God's Spirit:

It follows clearly that those who ordain or appoint shepherds and want to call someone to proclaim God's Word, should understand God's pleasure before they choose, so they will not choose against God's will someone whom God has rejected.

The fleshly ones cannot understand God's will and grace, as do those who are spiritual. Therefore only those are to choose, call, and appoint, whom the Spirit of God drives to do this; those who also have the Spirit of Christ, the supreme shepherd.[156]

No one is barred *a priori* from consideration for this office.[157] The shepherd must be morally perfect. This perfection is not absolute, for sins committed unintentionally are not really sins in God's sight.[158] The shepherd must have received the sevenfold spiritual sprinkling. 'In addition, I do not find that God ever pointed or led a sheep that thirsted for God's righteousness to such a devouring ecclesiastic or a stingy bishop, as those who lead an anti-Christian life.'[159] Following careful examination (1 Tim. 5:22), the shepherd is ordained with the laying on of hands. Even such ordination is no guarantee against hypocrites: '"Beware of false prophets. Beware of the leaven of hypocrites." "My sheep do not hearken to the voice of a stranger. Therefore, be wise as serpents," says Christ [Matt. 7:15, 10:16; John 10:5].'[160]

One sign that a shepherd proclaims God's Word occurs when the world opposes and mocks him: 'They will certainly be called Beelzebub, because they also called the Lord that [name].'[161] However, once such a genuine reaper (*schnitter*) has been called and is known to be faithful, God endows him with great spiritual authority:

155 KS 1, 12:1–7 (1523).
156 KS 1, 13:3–11 (1523).
157 KS 1, 18:18–20: 'Dann niemants ist auss geschlossen, die weyl gotis gebot alle menschenn und gottis unnd des nehsten lieb und ehre belangt' (1523).
158 KS 1, 14:29–31: 'Gottis wort ist rein und lauther, und die lauthere und reine soltens allein handeln, unnd kein unsaubere.' One is perfect and pure after sevenfold purification (Ps. 12:6 (Vulg 11:7); Jer. 6:27–30; Zech. 13:8–9; Luke 8:2); see KS 1, 15:28–37. This does not refer to absolute sinlessness, for 'Gutter will zu gott thut nit ubel, ab er gleich ubel thut' (KS 1, 19:15–16) (1523).
159 KS 1, 14:9–12: 'Datzu find ich nit das Got irgent ein schefflein (das nach gottis gerechtickeyt dürstig was) tzu eynem solchen fressigen ecclesiasten oder geyrischen bischoff geweyst oder geleydt, als die seind die ein wider christlich leben füren' (1523).
160 KS 1, 14:20–3 (1523).
161 KS 1, 17:5–7: 'Es ist jhe kein wunder, das sie den knecht Beeltzepub heissen, wenn sie den gerechten hern also gescholten haben' (1523).

for the true shepherds and reapers of the harvests and people, have an authority [oberkeit] above those to whom God sends them. Not that they must rule the people for evil gain, but they are above the people in the sense that they are to advance God's Word with power and with freedom, and [they must] tear out and smash and scatter and maul every heart (as it is appropriate and applicable) with God's Word, as if it were a sharp sword and a heavy hammer. Then again, the true shepherds are to gather what has been scattered, mend what has been broken, bring back what has escaped and gone astray, heal what is ill, and perform through God's Word whatever its nature commands.[162]

Thus the preacher is both prophet (reaper) and healer or 'servant of the sheep.'[163] Karlstadt has nothing else to say about the function of the clergy. Positive liturgical advice is also missing, although a few scattered facts are known. There must be preaching during the service by the minister and several laypersons. The service may take place in a home or a church building, preferably one made of wood. There does not seem to be a prescribed order. Psalm singing is permitted, provided it is done in unison, without musical accompaniment.[164] Otherwise, only brief and silent prayer is permitted.[165]

Finally, the preacher does not insist on receiving a salary. He follows the prophets, Christ, and Paul, and works in 'the sweat of his brow.'[166]

Paul says to the elders in Ephesus, 'I have desired neither silver, gold, nor garment. For you know yourself that my hands served me for sustenance.'

162 KS 1, 9:9–21: 'denn die rechten hyrtten und schnitter der ernden unnd volcks habenn ein oberkeyt uber die, tzu denen sie got schickt. Nicht das sie böses gewinss halben den leuten sollen herschen, sondern sie seind uber das volck in der weyse das sie gottis wort mechtigklich und mit freydigkeit füren, und rauffen auss unnd tzerbrechen und tzerstreyhen unnd tzerknirschen mit gotis wort (als mit eynem scharffen schwerdt und wichtigen hamer) ein igliches hertz darnoch es geschickt ist, und darnoch es trifft. Widerumb sollen die rechten hirten das tzerstraut sameln, das zerbrochen gantz machen, das flüchtig und irrige widerbringen, das krancke gesundt machen, unnd durch gottis wort alles aussrichten das sein eygenschafft foddert' (1523).
163 KS 1, 9:36–8 (1523).
164 BARGE 1, 492, th 18: 'Sic cum [canto mensurativo] et organa, tubas et tibias in theatra chorearum et ad principum aulas relegamus.' On singing in unison see 493, th 53. Karlstadt objected to such music, because of its secular connotations and his theological objections, not from a lack of aesthetic sensitivity. Earlier he had praised music; see KÄHLER, 114: 19–21: 'ipsi sunt firmamentum virtutis post resurrectionem, in quo laudamus dominum, ipsi sunt psalterium et cythara, tympanum et chorus, chorda et organum, in quibus deum laudamus, honoramus.'
165 Gelubden (50), F, on the basis of Matt. 6:7 (1521).
166 KS 2, 95:19–97:2. Men must work in the sweat of their brow (Gen. 3:19): Christ was a carpenter (Mark 6:3); prophets were farmers (Zech. 13:5); and Paul was a tentmaker (Acts 20:33–5. 2 Thess. 3:6–11).

But Doctor Luther makes out of this that the bastards [kegell] of his nest not only desire gold and silver, etc, but they violently desire the sweat and suck the blood of the poor man.[167]

Even Christ supported himself as a carpenter. To keep out the bloodsuckers the church should rely on voluntary giving. Compulsory tithes and taxes for the church should be abolished.[168] However, a shepherd or any church member should not suffer destitution. Since Karlstadt does not even countenance such injustice in society at large, he applies this also to the church. Believers should share their goods with the poor, though private property is not abolished. Some are wealthy, so they can aid the poor.[169]

This was not mere theory, and Karlstadt apparently went through the whole biblical procedure outlined for calling a shepherd. Thus the brethren of Orla-münde admonished Luther: 'If Karlstadt is not our shepherd, Paul has taught falsely, and your books are also false, for we have elected him.'[170]

The Church and the World

The church and academia

Karlstadt's hostility towards academia involves the condemnation of his old life when he collected degrees and swaggered back to Wittenberg in his Italian doctoral gown.[171] His polemic against the scholastics signals the beginning of his

---

167 KS 2, 96:36–97:1 (1525). At an earlier stage (1519) Karlstadt had used similar arguments against the mendicant orders. When in need one may accept support, but one does not demand it. See 'Militia Franciscana seu militia Christi,' ed G. Hammer, 73:28–37, 74:5–9: 'Carolostadius: Mendicitas talis etiam iure divino prohibita est. Nam in veteri testamento erat omnino prohibita, ut Deut. 15:4: "Omnino indigens et mendicus non erit inter vos, ut benedicat tibi dominus deus tuus in terra, quam traditurus est tibi in possessionem." Paulus etiam laborabat suis manibus, quo victus necessitudinem levaret, ne gravaret quemquam [1 Thess. 2:9; 2 Thess. 3:8]; insuper docuit hoc ipsum, ut manibus laboraremus; nam "qui non laborat, non manducet" [2 Thess. 3:10]. Igitur nulla in mendicitate perfectio, sed fragilitas et infirmitas, immo peccatum, quia prohibita iure divino. Ait Respondens Christum quoque mendicasse. Subridens Carolostadius dixit: Cuius ergo ostium pulsavit, ut eleemosynam acciperet, aut a quo petiit panem? Carolostadius: Quod et iure divino prohibita sit talis mendicitas (praeter superius adducta), patet per Psalmum [127:2]: "Quia labores manuum tuarum manducabis, et sic bene tibi erit." [Ps. 89:17b]: "Et opus manuum nostrarum, domine, dirige super nos" etc. Igitur labore a nobis victus quaerendus esset, et non otio. Aut quae causa vobis est in otio vitam expendere?' (1519).

168 BARGE 1, 494, 15 Theses De decimis pronunciata (1521).

169 Willen gottes (102), C2–v (1523). Cf KT 74, 23–30 (1522).

170 WA 15, 344:5–7 (1524).

171 See Luther's version, TR 6 (no. 6874), which proves that Karlstadt had been arrogant and that Luther was jealous.

disenchantment. Karlstadt had to cast aside a considerable part of his own education, and when he turned against canon law, he abandoned years of arduous compilation. Already in 1519 he curtly suggests that doctrine is more significant than academic titles.[172] Intellectual pride thwarts the destruction of one's ego advocated in the 'mystical' tracts.[173] Then there is Karlstadt's emphasis on egalitarianism.

A sharp altercation occurs when Karlstadt promotes Gottschalck Crop and Johannes Westermann to masterdom on 3 February 1523. According to Luther, Karlstadt appealed to Matthew 23:8 to oppose the use of titles in the church.[174] Luther promptly charged Karlstadt with 'blasphemy,' and this provoked further 'blasphemy.'

Karlstadt strongly defends basic education and literacy, so that even children can read Scripture. If Scripture is to be studied at home, the level of popular education must be raised.[175] A further element in Karlstadt's attacks on promotions would have been the customary oaths to which he already objected. The universities also stimulate pride: 'In the universities what else do you seek than honour from others? Therefore one becomes a Master, and the other a Doctor, and on top of that a Doctor of Holy Scriptures.'[176] The academics are so pompous and silly:

> GEMSER Who are the scarecrows?
> PETER They are called *doctores*. They wear fancy mortar boards, and they go forth in long gowns. They stand there like scarecrows of straw and wood, which have been covered with the rags of beggars.
> GEMSER Ah, cut it out.[177]

But, worst of all, academics have a purely historic faith. They know but fail to embrace the truth:

172 *Verba Dei* (26), B3v: 'Nempe, pudendus est error et exitialis dissimulatio, citra delectum, sequi titulos magis quam doctrinas' (1520).

173 *Gelassenheyt* (38), A2, B (1520); KS 1, 51:17–25 (1523); *Gelassen* (104), Bv–2v, E3v–F2v (1523).

174 *Liber decanorum*, ed Förstemann, 28, n 1. Cf TR 5 (no. 6207). Even in later life Karlstadt remained reluctant to use his titles. No doctor's title appears on *Axiomata* (153), *Themata* (154), and *Iob VII* (155). Karlstadt's title occurs in the third person in *Dialogus* (1529), no doubt an addition by Hoffman. The 'D.' before Karlstadt's name in the *Loci* (156) may have been added by the printer. Karlstadt's offer of doctorates to all of the clergy of Basel is an adaptation of continuing egalitarianism, rather than a volte-face, as supposed by Rupp, *Patterns*, 150–1.

175 *Verba Dei* (26), D2, in the margin (1520). For a useful summary see Fuchs, 'Karlstadts Wirken,' 534–6.

176 *Gelassen* (104) [E3v]: 'In den hohen schulen, was süchet man anders dann eere von den andern? Derhalben wirt ainer Magister, der ander Doctor und dartzu Doctor der hayligen geschrifft' (1523).

177 KS 2, 39:17–21 (1524).

Their understanding was somewhat like the understanding of the professors in the universities, who are masters at shoving God's Word from one end to the other. They act boldly and do not know the God who spoke it. They have their confession in their mouths, but not in their hearts.[178]

As we have seen, Karlstadt's church demands no special academic requirements from its officers beyond literacy. A prospective shepherd may or may not be educated in the traditional sense, but such a person must be a fellow believer whose gifts of the Spirit are recognized by others. Thus Karlstadt separates church and academia, and he hurls at 'the learned' and 'worldly wise' the biblical text with which he in 1520 had taunted the Aristotelians: 'For what has Christ in common with Belial? And what friendship is there between darkness and light?'[179]

The church against the world

Two positions must be distinguished for the sake of clarity, even though Karlstadt holds them concurrently, without contradiction. The grace-versus-nature scheme determines his basically theocratic position. God and his laws must rule the world. Christian rulers impose God's laws on society. Whenever Karlstadt is optimistic, his response towards the rulers is positive. He is then a hopeful, or temporarily successful, theocrat. This positive attitude towards government was never fully repressed among the Baptists of Melchiorite origin.

Such a doctrine is inherently unstable, however, for when the rulers are unchristian, they conspire with the princes of darkness. Then government is demonic, but even this conclusion is reached by imposing Christian categories on the world. Despite the potential for diametrically opposed responses towards the rulers, Karlstadt is thoroughly consistent. He does not separate church and state in the modern sense, for such a conception stabs at the basic premise of Baptist theology, with its grace *versus* nature scheme, whereas modern ideas of the separation of church and state imply a model based on either grace *and* nature or nature *without* grace. Nevertheless, Karlstadt does not unite the institutions of church and state, for they are seen as parallel entities with separate functions.

The thwarted theocratic stage is later reflected by Michael Sattler's faction among the Swiss Brethren wing of the Baptist movement. It is stated most force-

---

178 *Gelaub* (139), [A4v] (1524).
179 *Verba Dei* (26), Fv: 'Nempe quae conventio Christi ad Belial? Quae tenebrarum amicitia cum luce?' (1520).

fully in the *Brotherly Agreement* of Schleitheim. Since the treatment of Baptists varied locally, their political responses were similarly varied.[180] Unless a certain type of response coagulated into dogma, progress was possible.

The Christian city

Scripture is to rule *all* earthly authority, whether worldly or churchly.[181] Therefore, governments (*reipublicae*) should instruct men, women, and the youth of the realm in Holy Scripture.[182] Christian government rules the people in the place of God, who leads us to his laws, not human laws.[183] All rights of the rulers come from God, who appoints them.[184]

Rulers must advance the cause of Christ, and if the church forsakes Holy Writ, Christian rulers ought to trample upon the pope. Parodying the papal bull *Exsurge Domine*, Karlstadt exclaims: 'Arise, O lords, and rid us of the awful beast, and defend the faith to which you and all of us have been entrusted by sacraments and oaths.'[185] Nevertheless, the church's programme differs from the state's, and Karlstadt criticizes the pope for claiming jurisdiction over kings.[186] Moreover, the programme of the state differs also from that of the church, and only when the church forsakes its duties should the state intervene.

The church has the same right to demand that government follow its duty. In a treatise laced with anti-papal venom Karlstadt grants a Christian and biblical pope the right to harangue rulers on their duties.[187] Even then, this does not undermine the function of government. Those who disrespect government as such are worse than the devil.[188]

There are examples of how Karlstadt thought that government could regulate the church when the latter defaults. In 1521 Karlstadt went to Denmark, initiating reforms that were enacted into law. Indicative of legislation putting pressure on the church is the law forbidding celibate priests to hold property – a right

---

180 Cf Stayer, *Anabaptists and the Sword*.
181 Credner, par 3 (1520).
182 *Verba Dei* (26), D2v (margin): 'Reipublicae proderit iuventutem sanctis litteris erudire, sive vir, sive mulier, sive iuvenis' (1520).
183 *Ablas* (28), B3 (1520).
184 *Heylickeit* (44), D2v–3 [not Ciij]: 'Ihr sollet allen creaturen untertenig sein umb gottis willen, dem konig als einem ubertreffenlichen, und dem Landgraffen odder Fursten als den geschickten von got, dan alsso ist der gotlich wille' (1520).
185 Ibid, E2.
186 Ibid, D2v.
187 Ibid, F–v: 'Ich ... wil [den bapst] auch nit fur einen pfarhern und pastor halden, er ... sage das keysser, konig, unnd alle christliche fursten, got fur yhre nachlassickeit in seinem gestrengen gericht antwortten mussen.'
188 Ibid, D2v, with reference to 1 Pet. 2:13–17.

conferred on priests who are married.[189] Where the church fails, rulers should follow King Josiah, who imposed reform.[190]

Ideally, reform is the work of the whole community. Even when Melanchthon argues that the Wittenberg Augustinians can reform themselves,[191] Karlstadt prefers to act in concert with the magistrates.[192] The reform plans that Karlstadt helped to have passed by the Council of Wittenberg in January 1522 covered social as well as religious reform. Included was a new system of social insurance, with such provisions as equalization of pension payments, welfare measures for the poor, reschooling of the jobless, dowries for poor girls, the abolition of prostitution and mendicancy, and the removal of images from the churches.[193] Moreover, 'Christian government, because of its own Christian duty and action, shall seriously and zealously superintend [the needs] of widows, orphans, and the dispossessed.'[194]

For the magistrates' role in reforming the liturgy Karlstadt cites the example of King Hezekiah who (because it was being venerated) smashed Nehushtan – the only image ever made at the express command of God.[195] Similarly, Karlstadt worked with the council of Orlamünde (1523–4) to cleanse the temple through the removal of altars, organs, and images.

The Sabbath is made for men, so Karlstadt permits unbelievers to till their fields on the Sabbath. If they use the Sabbath for debauchery, however, they should be enticed to do something better. If this fails, they must be dealt with as disturbers of the peace: 'Such rabble should be hindered from its devilish way of resting.'[196]

In the Old Testament image worship is called 'spiritual adultery.' Some magistrates punish fleshly rather than spiritual adultery, and this makes Karlstadt wonder.[197] Where Christians govern, they impose reform. Gideon, Asa,

---

189 BARGE 1, 258, n 49. Priests may not possess land, 'uden de ville efterfølge St. Pauli laerdom, som han skriver udi sin første epistel, kap. 3 ad Timotheum, at de tage sig hustru og leve udi den hellige aegtestand, som deres gamle forfaedre have gjort.'

190 KT 74, 20:33–21:5 (1522).

191 WB, 47 (no. 18) (1521).

192 WB, 34 (no. 15) (1521).

193 KT 74, 31–2 (1522).

194 KT 74, [3]:25–7: 'hoch von noten ist das christliche obirkeit auss eygner christlicher pflicht und bewegnis, ernstlich und emsig auffsehen sollen haben uff witwen, wessen, und andere uberdrenckte personen.' (1522).

195 KT 74, 11:28–34.

196 KS 1, 31:1–5: 'Ein solchs gesind solt man in seiner teuffellischen ruhe hindern, und zu etwas besser reitzen, oder auch dringen. Und es were vil besser sie baueten den acker, dann das sie toppeln, fluchen, got lestern, sich vol sauffen, unkeuschen, verreden, verspotten, schlahen, stelen, und morden' (1524).

197 KS 1, 82:15–29 (1524).

Jehoshaphat, Jehu, Hezekiah, Shadrach, Meshach, and Abednego had the same attitude as Jesus Christ, who drove the money changers from the temple. They challenged merely human laws that are 'dung.'[198] Karlstadt supports magistrates who are inspired by such examples, for such magistrates join God's children in subduing nature by grace.

Anti-Christian government

Since princes rule by the grace of God, they must be opposed if they substitute their own rules for God's laws. At the same time that Karlstadt exhorts Christian rulers to follow their duty 'zealously [to] superintend the needs of widows, orphans, and other oppressed persons,' he claims that rulers who default should not count on a believer's allegiance, for the state may not be deified:

> [Hope in God] is one reason why the prophets often make the claim: 'I shall not place my hope on my bow. My sword will not make me blessed' [Ps. 44:6]. 'You shall not put your confidence in princes' [Ps. 118:9]. They do this because they do not wish to make a false god. They do not want to have an image in their hearts. They only want to confess him who cannot be depicted. For God does not permit it.[199]

Karlstadt fears that the rulers *have* defaulted, but he does not advocate violence. He waits for God to punish the rulers.[200] Should the rulers change and depose false priests, they would have to be praised.[201] The laws of Moses, rather than human laws, are the standard: 'Surely, [Luther] wants to esteem the laws of Moses like the *Sachsenspiegel*, and he wants to place human laws above God's laws. I fear, he will deny the laws of Moses, just as he has already denied the covenant of Moses.'[202] The letter of the Mosaic law may have been surpassed, but

198 KS 1, 96:37–8: 'Menschen gesatz seind der myst, den die Jüden ausserhalb iren gezelten tragen und mit erden begraben musten' (1524).
199 KT 74, 7:11–16: '[Hoffenung in got] ist eyn ursach das sich Propheten offtmalss bedingen, sagende: "Ich werde kein hoffenung uff meinen bogen setzen. Mein schwert wirt mich nit selig machen" [Ps. 44:6]. "Ir solt nit in die fursten vertrauhen" [Ps. 118:9]. Das thun sie derhalben das sie keinen frombden got wellen machen; das sie keyn bild yn yrem hertz wollen haben. Sie wollen den allein bekennen, der unverbildlich ist. Dan gott kanss nit leyden' (1522).
200 KT 74, 20:27–8 (1522).
201 KT 74, 20:29–31: 'Hetten aber unssere oberste yren gotlichem rath und beschluss volendet, und die pubische und verfurische klotzer auss den kirchen, tzugeburlicher straffe gejaget, musten wir sie loben, wie der .h. geist Etzechiam lobet' (1522).
202 KS 2, 99:27–30: 'Ja, [Luther] wolt das gesetz Mosi als den Sachssen Spyegel achten, und der menschen rechte über gottes rechte und gerichte setzen. Fürcht auch, er werd die rechte Mosi verleucken, als er den bund Mosi nu schon verleucket hat' (1525).

the spirit may not be violated. 'One of [God's] judgments deals with government, what government is, how it is to live and act.'[203] According to the fruit, the tree is known:

> But when we do not see such fruit in the rulers, or we see the opposite, for example when the ruler takes bribes and favours one person over others, snarls at and terrifies the poor, etc – then we know that he is a false judge, imprisoned by the devil, and he has a perverse inclination.[204]

Evil laws should be avoided: 'I call worldly law [*weltlich gesetz*] all teaching that is not based on the Bible, yet wishes to serve God's honour, praise, or will. Isaiah and Christ shun it like the devil.'[205]

Rulers who promote idolatry oppose the church: they are the 'violent' who persecute it, even if they are in collusion with the mob of churchmen.[206] They are like Jezebel, the pharaoh, Jeroboam, and Manasseh.[207] The church avoids them:

> The kingdom of God wants to exalt and hold above all to God's laud, honour, praise, will, justice, sufficiency, goodness, law, and rule. The kingdom of the world, the company of Satan, does not wish to hear or see this, but it rears itself up with rebellion and attempts to silence, quench, or badly belittle the kingdom of God ... Therefore the kingdom of God suffers violence.[208]

In this conflict one chooses the Lord over the lords, and, despite persecution, one continues to testify against evil rulers. In 1521 Karlstadt prays in public:

> You, [O Lord], are not like humans who promise like kings, rulers, lords, etc. [Yet], they cannot bear to be reminded of their promise, or to be

203 KS 2, 101:32–6 (1525).
204 KS 2, 102:10–12: 'Wenn wir aber solliche früchten inn den regenten nicht spüren, oder sehen das gegenspyl, als das der regent geschenck nymbt; ein person für die annderen fürderet; die armen anschnauet und erschreckt, unnd der gleychen thut. So wissen wir das er ein falscher richter des teuffels gefangen, unnd ein verkert gemüt hatt' (1525).
205 *Messe* (71), A3: 'Weltlich gesetz heyss ich alle leer die nit yn der biblien steht, und wil doch tzu gotts eere, lob, oder willen dienen, die Esaias und Christus alss eynen teuffel meidenn' (1521).
206 *Gewaldt* (63), [B4]–Cv (1521).
207 Ibid, C2v.
208 Ibid, Cv: 'Das reich gotis wil gotis lob, eher, preiss, willen, gerechtikeit, gnugheit, gutheit, gesetz, und regiment, fur alle ding stellen und halten ... Das kan das reich der weld, des teuffelss geselschafft, nit horen aber sehen, sunder ehs erhebet sich mit bitterlicher emboerung, und versucht wie ehs gotis reich stillen, dempffen, und auff das mindest schmelern kan.' 'Das ist die ursach, das gotis reich gewald leidet.'

admonished on account of the promises they have made. No, you are a different Lord.[209]

When Karlstadt aimed this prayer at the elector of Saxony, the latter was limiting liturgical reform. But Karlstadt does not always support the lower magistrates versus the higher rulers. In the already mentioned appeal to the emperor in 1525 Karlstadt petitioned the highest ruler against the lower magistrates at Rothenburg. Karlstadt consistently defends Christian rulers as opposed to anti-Christian rulers. The latter will face God's judgment:

> Christ has ordered the rulers to search out in mercy those who have strayed, and bring them back, meanwhile forsaking the ninety-nine to return the one who strayed. How that is kept in Christendom is sad to hear, and not very honourable. But this will be rewarded when the righteous Judge will sit in judgment, and will punish without mercy those who had no mercy.[210]

Conflicts with the established powers must be avoided if possible. In May 1524 Karlstadt faces the elector's demand to return to Wittenberg and to resign his post in Orlamünde. Karlstadt replies as follows:

Borna, 8 June 1524

To Frederick, Duke of Saxony, Elector, etc
From your electoral Grace's answer I understand that you do not wish to keep me in the parish of Orlamünde. Thus I do not know a more submissive way to serve you than that I humbly defer to you and resign.

According to the regulations, you may demand my return to the archdeaconate. However, here I cannot submit to your Grace, nor can I obey anyone else. In this matter my conscience burdens me especially, since I would display a new offence against the faith of those who do not know the damage and corruption that is caused by the mass and the liturgy.

Moreover, to those who do understand how God is snubbed and defamed by those abominations, I would give cause to slander the Name of God. Recently, I have clearly seen how God opposes pensions. Thus I do not want to enjoy a pension in absentia. I fear to do this because of the teaching of Christ who says: 'For one who gives offence to most believers, it

209   *Empfahern* (54), [C4]: 'Du bist nit wie die menschlichen vorheyscher als konig, fursten, unnd hern, und andere seynt, die vil verheyschen, und mugen nit leyden das man yhnen yhre zusag fur rueck, aber sie in krafft gethaner vorheyschung mane ... Neyn, du bist ein anderer herre' (1521).
210   WA 18, 464:15–21 (1525).

would be better to be drowned in the deep sea.' [Cf Matt. 18:6, Vulg.] Therefore I surrender to you and resign my archdeaconate and the rights I originally received with it, and I desire to have it surrendered and resigned on the authority of this my written letter.

Your Grace's humble servant,

Anndres Carolstatt.[211]

Karlstadt has now cut all ties with Lutheranism and the prebendary system of the medieval church. This decision would cost him dearly and he realizes this. He has respected the authorities and their traditional rights, but his view of the church permits him to challenge Frederick in practice. He plans to hold out as Orlamünde's own congregationally called shepherd. Thus the elector does not regain control until after Karlstadt's exile.

Once Karlstadt has been driven out of Saxony, he challenges the appointment of Kaspar Glatz, since he himself has been congregationally called to Orlamünde on the basis of biblical principles. Glatz is 'the wolf in Orlamünde, who has forced his way in.'[212] So Karlstadt tries to avoid conflict with the rulers, but he also follows the principle that in 'matters that pertain to God' one follows God's Word.[213] Karlstadt's position is consistent with what he had already envisaged in 1519. Government is to be obeyed even when it persecutes, but not when it requires a positive act against God's law.[214]

In the contest between the church and evil rulers Karlstadt is on the winning side. Even 'the gates of hell will not prevail' against the church, but victory is reserved for the end. Meanwhile, evil rulers may still attack him, but he is willing to suffer martyrdom, even for the differences between him and Luther.[215] Karlstadt already in 1520 was willing to follow the saint after whom he was named, in being tied to the grid for his convictions. Still, he prefers exile:

I grant that – on account of my Old Adam – I am not planning to run to the cross and I am not particularly enamoured of fire. Therefore, just as

211 Friedensburg, 'Verzicht,' 70–1 (excerpts). Karlstadt had announced his desire to resign his prebends in Dec. 1523 (Priesterthum (112), Fv: 'Ich will nit lang zyns haben, nach pfarren besitzen') (1523).

212 KS 2, 83:6–8: 'Das sey dir eingedrungnem wolff zu Orlamünde ... gesagt' (1525). However, Karlstadt may merely be countering Luther (WA 18, 94:14–15: 'Denn [Karlstadt] hat sich zu Orlamünde alls eyn wolff eyngedrungen').

213 KS 1, 74:20–5: 'Dannest muss ich euch sagen, das ir weder in disem fal, nach in andren sachen got belangend, soltet ansehen wie die grosse mennung redet oder richtet, sondern gerichts auff gottes wort sehen, den es ist je am tag, das die fürsten der schrifftgelerten, und der gantz hauff vor zeyten geirret haben und irren kunden' (1524).

214 Ausslegung (15), B3v–[4] (1519).

215 Missbrauch (135), Av. Karlstadt is willing to defend his view of the signs of bread and cup, 'es köst leben oder tode' (1524).

David fled before Absalom, I shall flee before the Lion [Leo x] of Florence, from one city to another. If I find grace in the eyes of the Lord, he will return and protect me. But if he says: 'I take no delight in you,' then I am ready, and let what is good in his will be done.[216]

Violence

Luther claimed in Jena that Karlstadt was involved with Thomas Müntzer. Karlstadt contested this point at the Inn of the Black Bear, but Luther denied having implicated Karlstadt.[217] Luther then repeated the charges in *Heavenly Prophets*.[218] Karlstadt's letters to Müntzer prove Luther wrong.[219] Still, Luther had reason to suspect Karlstadt. Karlstadt is non-violent by definition: a definition that differs from Luther's. Luther defines violence as any infraction of the public order. By that standard Karlstadt tolerates violence in one respect, for he condones iconoclasm. Moreover, Karlstadt understands the violence of legal repression. He writes to Frederick, the elector:

Dr Luther has appeared in many areas and places where my Christian, divine, demonstrable, and well-based teachings have been planted. He claims that you ordered him to refute in public and warn the people that these my teachings are void, erroneous, and seditious, as if they had sprung from an enthusiastic spirit. He also falsely embroiled me with [Müntzer's] rebellion in Allstedt, and he did his utmost to inculpate me before the people, and perhaps also before you.[220]

Here Karlstadt interprets Luther's desire to implicate him with Müntzer as an attempt to oust him with a false charge of treason. Karlstadt, however, rejects such violence, for sticks and whips do not convert. Even God's blows do not

216 *Gelassenheyt* (38), B3: 'Wie wol ich nach dem creutz, meynes alden Adams halben, nit gedenck zu lauffen; ich seen mich auch nit sonderlich nach dem feur. Derwegen wil ich [wie David vor Absolon geflogen] vor dem florentinischen lawen von eyner stat in die andern fliehen. Werde ich gnad in den augen des herren finden, sso wirt er mich wol wider brengen und behüten. Würt er aber sagen, "du gefellest mir nicht," sso byn ich gegenwertig, das soll geschehen das gut ist yn seynem willen' (1520).
217 WA 15, 335:35–7, 336:14–16 (1524).
218 WA 18, 92–3 (1524).
219 See below, Appendix I, 279–86.
220 KS 2, 53:25–34: 'Denn D. L. ist in vil enden und orten auffgetretten, da meine christliche götliche, erweyssliche, und gegründte leere eingeplantzt mit E. F. G. befell (als er sagt) abgefertiget, solliche mein leere vernichtig, irrig, auffrürisch ausszuschreien und also solt sie aus eynem schwermenden geyst entsprossen sein, offenlich zu widerlegen, unnd das volck darfür zu warnen. Mich auch mit dem auffrur zu Alstadt lügenhafftiglich eingemengt, und für allem volck so vil er vermocht, auch villeicht bey E. F. G. verdächtig gemacht.'

convert without the Spirit.[221] Karlstadt boasts of hating rebellion, and he forbids it.[222] However, the Christian community may perform acts of compassion that challenge rulers who default on their Christian obligations.[223] To Karlstadt this is not violence, that is an infraction of the law of God. Only unbelievers do violence to the Word, not those who hear and accept it.[224] God allows such violence only as a means to correct and discipline those whom he loves.

The persecuted church may not persecute in return; she must sacrifice her body and blood 'like a patient lamb.'[225] In 1520 Karlstadt still believes that Christian rulers should exile heretics and confiscate their goods.[226] Nevertheless, Christians should never kill their opponents. Karlstadt's *Gemach* is saturated with verbal violence, but God alone may act: 'That has been said about the vengeance of God, though, when it is written: "Cursed is he who keeps back his sword from blood"' (Jer. 48:10).[227]

Karlstadt lauds Epiphanius of Salamis (died 403) for having removed a cloth that people worshipped.[228] 'Where Christians rule, they will not heed any government (*oberkeit*), but they will freely swing the axe, and smash what is against God.'[229] This passage does not favour untrammelled violence. The axe smashes wood, not human beings, and in that crucial respect Karlstadt is much more peaceful than most magisterial reformers. Moreover, the axe is wielded '*where Christians rule*.' Karlstadt encourages Christian magistrates to alter the old forms of worship even when other authorities do not condone this. He intends to accomplish this in Wittenberg through the town council, when the elector opposes further reforms. Of course, from Luther's socially conservative standpoint what Karlstadt proposes is violent.

In fact Karlstadt's language can be violent. Christians fight with the sword of God's Word.[230] At times Karlstadt seems to issue a call for physical violence, but

221 KS 2, 75:40–76:10; the references are to Lev. 26:18; Isa. 1:5, 9:13; Jer. 2:30, 6:29 (1525).
222 WB, 181: 'Dass wil ich mich auch berumen, dass ich auffrur hass und flih'; WB, 200: 'habe auffrur vorkomen, sovill moglich' (1522).
223 WB, 186: '[Karlstadt und Gabriel] sagenn, das dye gemein woll macht habe, in nachlessigkeyt der oberkeyt auss einem mitleiden unnd liebe ichtes furzunemen' (1522).
224 *Gewaldt* (63), A3: 'Die unglobige und der Teuffel thuen dem wort gotis gewalt; nicht die ehs begeren tzu wissen' (1521).
225 *Ausslegung* (15), [E4] (1519).
226 *Heylickeit* (44), Ev. The rulers should reform the papacy, 'bey vorlust des bapstumbs und aller ehren und gutter' (1520).
227 KS 1, 84:8–10 (1524).
228 KT 74, 11:3–15 (1522).
229 KS 1, 96:12–15. The preceding passage (lines 6–12) refers to the Jews who were not bidden to remove images 'in der gantzen welt ... sonder in den orten ... in welchen sie herschen würden.' Similarly, iconoclastic activity is to be confined to localities 'where Christians rule.' See also KS 1, 85:22–5 (1524).
230 KS 1, 90:40–91:4 (1524). This theme is prominent.

in the end his language appears figurative.[231] Sometimes Karlstadt will vent his wrath in words so concrete that one feels he is only barely restrained from physical violence: 'The Word of God is the sword that the persecuted grab. It is the hammer with which they crush their opponents. It is the fire with which they burn their enemies.'[232]

Nevertheless, Karlstadt recoils from physical violence. Once, when he refers to weapons, he makes the gratuitous observation that the saints were martyred *with arms*.[233] Since Karlstadt restricts vows or oaths to those made directly to God (not men), one can vow to God in times of defensive war, but otherwise one remains passive:

> They should learn through the example of Jehoshaphat, King of Judah and reasonable fighter, to call from now only to God for assistance and allow Saints George and Sebastian to be kept in peace in the bosom of Abraham ... I do not say this, meaning to praise war and battles, but in the sense that when a war breaks out upon us without [our] evil intent, we shall cry to God ... and thus we shall vow to God and not to the saints.[234]

Once Karlstadt does affirm the right of magistrates to wield the law of the sword (*ius gladii*).[235] Of course, we have seen that the sword has been taken out of the hands of the magistrates in religious matters. Even prayers in support of a purely defensive war do not settle the ultimate questions. Christ has already thwarted the power of Satan's minions, for 'He threw the rulers of the world out of the world when, in deepest obedience, he took our place.'[236] Karlstadt believes Jesus spoke figuratively when he told his disciples to purchase a sword (Luke 22:35–8). Parrying papal claims that this text confers civil as well as religious power, Karlstadt comments: 'What kind of a sword is this? Listen to what Christ says: "This is the sword, that the Scripture should be fulfilled." Thus I hear that the Scripture is the sword to be chosen.'[237]

---

231 See e.g. KS 1, 85:36f (1524).

232 *Gewaldt* (63), C3v: 'Das wort gotis ist das schwert, das die vervolgte ergreuffen. Ist der hamer, damit sie yre anfechter tzerknirschen. Ist das feuer, damit sie yre fiend vorprennen' (1521).

233 *Gelubden* (50), A3v: 'Und etzliche rudische peurische menschen, rueffen zu den waffen (damit die heyligen gemartert sein)' (1521).

234 Ibid, [B4].

235 See Bubenheimer, 'Scandalum,' 333–4.

236 *Leyb* (129), [B4v]: 'In dem selben tempel und in der selben zeit, zerstöret Christus dem teüffel sein reich, und stiess den fursten der welt, auss der welt' (1524).

237 *Gelassenheyt* (38), B2: 'Was ist das fur eyn schwert? Hör wie Christus sagt, "Das ist das schwert, die schrifft muss erfuldt werden." Alsso hör ich das die schrifft das schwert ist, das wir erkeussen sollen' (1520). Although Karlstadt does not refer to this, he is making a counter-

Believers trust God who can protect a 'very small congregation' (*bloss klein heufflyn*), and who can smite an army with the rustling of leaves (1 Chron. 14:15). Trusting in arms reveals a divided faith:

They trust in their armed men together with God. That is a great sin, and all armed men shall fall because of this, just as Peter sank into the lake when he believed too little [Matt. 14:28–33]. Your hope shall stand only and entirely in God [2 Chron. 14:9–12, 16:7–9; Judg. 7].[238]

Karlstadt publicly disavows his friend Müntzer a year before the debacle at Mühlhausen. In his private letter to Müntzer he again contrasts reliance on political compacts with faith in God.[239] Karlstadt had written, but not published, a booklet on the topic: 'Whether they are all Christians, who defend God's Word with Fire-arms.' This booklet had been written 'to distinguish those who are true Christians.'[240] Karlstadt did not observe the hoary right to bear arms, and he even wore a farmer's knife with a deliberately broken scabbard.[241] When he was attacked on leaving the gates of Rothenburg, he did not defend himself, but a friend intervened.[242]

claim to the medieval church. He would have known that Boniface VIII, in his bull *Unam sanctam*, claimed that the two swords of the disciples conferred both civil and religious juris-diction on the papacy. See DENZINGER, *870, intro.

238 *Willen gottes* (102), H3v: 'Oder verlassen sich auff ir gewapendt volck, unnd uff got sampt-lich, das ist eyn grosse sunde, und solten alle krygher derhalben fallen, wye Petrus ym mehre eynsanck, alss er tzeweynigh glaubt. Matth. xiiii. Ir hoffnung solt alleyn unnd gantz yn got steen. ii. Paralip. xiiii et .xvi. Iudicum. vii.' (1523).

239 See below, Appendix I, 283–6.

240 KS 2, 58:1–6 (1524).

241 According to Erasmus Alber, Karlstadt 'trug auch ein Bauernmesser mit einer zerbrochnen Scheide' (BARGE 2, 379). From this garbled statement I deduce that Karlstadt wore a farmer's knife with which he had tampered, but he could not have removed the scabbard, for that would have been dangerous. He must have broken off the hilt to proclaim his peaceful inten-tions, while he wore the blade in the scabbard, to be used for chores on his farm. Support for this interpretation may be provided by an altar painted by Lukas Cranach the Younger in commemoration of the Lutheran Reformation in 1565. In the altar, now in Mildensee, near Dessau, Christ is pictured celebrating the Passover with eleven Lutherans. Judas (with the money-bag) is dressed simply as a peasant with prominent nose and black beard. Judas (i.e. Karlstadt) wears a farmer's knife from which the hilt has been removed.

242 Georg Spelt intervened when Schäferhans threatened to kill Karlstadt (BARGE 2, 352). Karl-stadt reports on this experience and his passive posture in Rothenburg in WA 18, 441:6–442:28 (1525). He reaffirms this in WA 18, 463:8–10: 'Was gott pflantzt, das bleybt fur wind und gewesser; was gott nicht pflantzt, das wird ausgerodt und vergeen. Da hilfft keyn wehr; dord tut keyn gewalt' (1525).

To sum up, Karlstadt is non-resistant at the personal, but not at the national level. A purely defensive war may be justifiable, but even so Christians do not trust in arms, and Christ alone settles the outcome of history. The magistracy may wield the sword in civil, but not religious, matters. Christian magistrates establish true religion, and smash images, even if others disapprove.

The church herself must endure violence as the rod of God's wrath or discipline, but she is not purely passive. She combats the world with the sword of God's Word. Karlstadt often treats this 'sword' as if it were a word of plain verbal abuse, spat at those who wronged him. Though purified with sevenfold fire, he still sins, but one hopes, from his perspective, that such sins were unintentional. If not, he sinned against the Holy Spirit, as did nearly everyone else who stabbed his pen in the acidic ink of that era.

4
Baptism

Karlstadt began his career in Wittenberg as a Thomist who was open to humanistic and Scotistic influences. In 1517 he purchased Augustine of Hippo's works, which changed his outlook considerably. This switch would not have had powerful consequences for Karlstadt's baptismal theology, however. Thomas's viewpoint on baptism was hardly different from Augustine's. A few minor developments will be pointed out.

The Council of Florence had declared baptism to be 'first among all the sacraments, ... the entrance to the spiritual life.'[1] Thomas taught that baptismal grace confers a plenary remission of all previously imputed or committed sin, and its indelible character enables the baptized to lead a Christian life in the future.[2] Nevertheless, Thomas also recognizes the spirit-baptism of repentance and the blood-baptism of martyrdom, which, in case of necessity, are sufficient for salvation. In a certain sense spirit- and blood-baptism surpass water-baptism. Whereas water-baptism is a figurative representation, deriving from latent power, spirit-baptism proceeds from a disposition (affectio) of the heart, and blood-baptism is of even greater value, being experienced in imitation of the work of Christ, and proceeding from the strongest love and affection.[3]

Two minor differences between Thomas and Augustine should be noted. Thomas stressed the indelible *character* of baptism. Augustine did refer to a 'dominical character,' but he hardly emphasized it. Karlstadt was to reject entirely the idea of character. Thomas's alternatives to water-baptism continue to play a role in Karlstadt's baptismal theology. Here Thomas reflected the ideas of Augustine as well, except for his addition of the alternative (in case of necessity) of spirit-baptism. As we shall see, Karlstadt follows Thomas, rather than Augustine,

1 DENZINGER, *1314.
2 *Summa theologiae* 3, q. 62–3.
3 *Summa theologiae* 3, q. 66, a 11–12.

on this point. When Karlstadt (unlike Augustine and Thomas) radicalizes this to the point that spirit-baptism of itself is the sacrament, he makes the first major break with tradition.

The basic problem affecting one's understanding of Karlstadt's early baptismal theology is his chameleon-like prudence. Karlstadt does not hesitate to quote Augustine in a selective way that undercuts him. He frequently quotes out of context, or he fuses quotations into a new hybrid that expresses his own thoughts rather than those of his sources. Moreover, the strictly Augustinian legacy had not been clearly defined, and Karlstadt may have received some inspiration from his friend Sebastiano de Federicis, who sponsored Karlstadt's studies in civil and canon law at the Sapienza in Rome. Sebastiano was an eminent jurist, and no mean forger of papal supplications and bulls, who atoned for his transgressions by being burned at the stake.[4] Thus Karlstadt seems torn between a desire to reveal his new insights, and the tactical need to conceal them.[5] Despite lacunae, a consistent viewpoint emerges when the baptismal references are pieced together.

Karlstadt's attitude towards baptism is illuminated by the fact that Luther (and later Melanchthon) at first approaches the subject with a rather open mind. In his *Romans Lectures* Luther is still conservative. He claims that penitence, baptism, prayer, and the fear of God cover sin. Baptism forgives all sin, and one receives faith through baptism.[6] But in his *Hebrews Commentary* (1517 to 1518) Luther stresses that the grace in baptism requires faith as a special disposition.[7] There is here at least the potential for a radical development. Melanchthon first publicly attacked the notion that baptism confers a character in 1519.[8] Karlstadt had not published his view on this issue, but by implication he must have balked sooner than Melanchthon, although he did not do so openly.

The Weakening of Sacramental Baptism, 1517 to 1519

Karlstadt's first theses on baptism (27 April 1517) show an Augustinian bias. The 'sacrament of regeneration' effectively absolves all guilt (*reatus*), but the sins remain, and, though dead, they can be resurrected to resume their characteristic

---

4   BUBENHEIMER, 51–3, 209. KS 2, 38:1–3.
5   Karlstadt refused to debate Eck on the issue of papal supremacy (BR 1, 368:19f). In his *405 Concl.*, which includes statements on baptism, he attacks Eck in the name of orthodoxy. Luther clarifies his views on papal supremacy in the Leipzig Debate, but Karlstadt bides his time for almost a year. Of course, in 1522 it is Luther who worries about tactics. Sider also sees tactical motivations in Karlstadt during the early period. See SIDER 58, n 52.
6   WA 56, 284, 298.
7   WA 57, 170; WA 2, 410.
8   *Supplementa Melanchthoniana* 6-1, 78, th 18: 'Ergo citra haeresis crimen, non credere characterem.' Note the careful wording. Melanchthon does not attack the grace of baptism.

sovereignty and domination.[9] Concupiscence, the result of hereditary sin, never becomes dormant in the baptized. Karlstadt owes to Augustine and Luther the view of post-baptismal concupiscence as sin.[10] He goes farther when he emphasizes that venial sins are properly called sins, to be taken seriously. Here Karlstadt blurs the traditional distinction between venial and mortal sins, and, a year later, Luther may have adopted this view.[11]

Unlike Augustine, Karlstadt does not refer to a 'dominical character' or special grace conferred through baptism. With his emphasis on concupiscence as sin, Karlstadt, like Luther, insists on what is seldom underlined by Augustine. To this he adds his own fear of what to others were venial sins. Such pessimism, after baptism, points to a weakening of the sacramental rite.

In *405 Conclusions* Karlstadt derives from Augustine the principle of Scripture as its own interpreter. Obscure passages need the light of clearer passages, rather than philosophy or dialectics. The acid test of one's loyalty occurs when one faces scriptural deductions that appear repugnant.[12] When such 'harsh letters' are applied to infants who die in their sins, for example, one must draw harsh conclusions. There is no 'third place' besides heaven and hell (limbo), for the Scriptures do not refer to it.[13] Since infants who die receive the penalty for original sin – even if they have not yet sinned of their own volition – children who have not been forgiven enter a fiery hell, where they burn eternally, suffering real pain.[14]

Scripture does not separate children from adults, and at the last judgment Christ does not issue separate verdicts for adults and children. They equally go to

9   KÄHLER, 14*, th 13a, 15a: 'Per sacramentum regenerationis solvitur reatus ... [et] fit plena remissio peccatorum'; th 16: '[Post sacramentum] manet tamen peccatum in membris tamquam superatum et peremptum'; th 19 '[Peccatum] reviviscit per illicitas consensiones et in regnum proprium dominationemque revocatur.'

10 Luther speaks of post-baptismal concupiscence (WA 56, 351:4f) and sin (WA 56, 271:15f), as Augustine did (*Contra Iulianum* 2.9.32). Later Luther still appeals to Augustine to prove that post-baptismal concupiscence is a sin (WA 7, 344). For a different view see SIDER, 59–61. See also Pesch, *Die Theologie der Rechtfertigung*, 93–7.

11 SIDER, 61, reverses the dependence with reference to Luther in 1518 and Karlstadt in 1519. However, Karlstadt has defended this deviation from Augustine already in 1517. See KÄHLER, 35*, th 149–50: 'Peccatum veniale proprie est peccatum. Non contemnendum sed timendum.' Perhaps Staupitz had mediated Gerson's influence, for as early as 1497–8 Staupitz, though upholding the traditional distinction, taught that *de possibili* even venial sins were mortal. So Steinmetz, *Misericordia Dei*, 54.

12 LÖSCHER 2, 93, th 275: 'Nec contra literas, tametsi graves videantur, temere latrabimus.'

13 Ibid, 93, th 274: 'Proinde sanctam honorantes scripturam, medium inter eos quos ignis cruciabit aeternus et eos in quibus erit deus omnia in omnibus, cum Augustino ignoramus (*Hyp[ognosticon] lib. v*). Melius tamen ex causa dicenda, tertium locum nescimus.' This could also be a veiled critique of purgatory.

14 Ibid, th 276: 'Etsi infantes huiusmodi proprium actionis peccatum nullum habuerunt, originalis tamen peccati damnationem carnali nativitate traxerunt.' On their sufferings see ibid, 92, th 264–7.

hell if they are found on the left hand of the judge.[15] Karlstadt has rejected the scholastic speculations concerning unbaptized children, who experience a painless alchemical fire and are deprived of the beatific vision.

Next, Karlstadt discusses those who are named in the Book of Life. Their salvation does not rest on their own works, but on God's love that has predestined them to eternal life.[16] Although children are not mentioned, single predestination would apply to them as well, since they are treated like adults.

A new development occurs in *13 Conclusions*, published three months later against Johann Eck.[17] Claiming support from Augustine (although the text cited is now attributed to Fulgentius of Ruspe),[18] Karlstadt combines two quotations, entirely out of context. Fulgentius holds that adults are saved through the sacrament of faith and penance, which he identifies with baptism, whereas children are saved through the sacrament of baptism, which rests on Christ's blood-baptism, since children are not capable of reasoning.[19] Children who die without baptism suffer eternal torment.[20]

Karlstadt now deftly twists two excerpts from Fulgentius to defend his own position: 'Children who pass through this world without the sacrament of Holy Baptism, suffer the everlasting punishment of eternal fire, *unless* they were baptized in the name of Christ by means of his blood.'[21] Here Karlstadt separates baptism in the blood of Christ from water-baptism, blood-baptism being sufficient. This quotation occurs within the context of a discussion of predestination, and it appears that some children are chosen, while others are not. The former are saved by Christ's blood-baptism, that is the forgiveness Christ bestows on them through his atoning death.[22] Water-baptism is not essential, even though it may remove sin.

But even if baptism is not essential, does it at least reassure the believer? Karlstadt replies that baptism and the good life do not guarantee that one is among

15 Ibid, 85, th 85; 92, th 272: 'Nec demonstrare eos posse scripturam credo, qua legitur iudicem sinistris aliquibus dicturum: "Ite vos adulti in poenam sensus, at vos parvuli in damni poenam."'

16 Ibid, 94, th 289–94.

17 WA 6, 26–7. For Karlstadt's authorship see Kähler, 'Nicht Luther,' 351–60. Jäger, *Andreas Bodenstein*, 55–6, has already attributed these theses to Karlstadt and excerpted several of them. His partial quotation of th 8 has led him to distort Karlstadt's position.

18 Karlstadt misquotes from *De fide ad Petrum* (PL 40, 751–80). In PL Fulgentius of Ruspe is assigned the authorship of this work. Kähler ('Nicht Luther,' 356) shows that th 8 contains two excerpts from *De fide*.

19 *De fide* 30, 73 (PL 40, 775).

20 *De fide* 27, 70 (PL 40, 774).

21 WA 6, 26, th 8: 'Parvuli sine sacramento sancti baptismatis de hoc saeculo transeuntes, *nisi* pro Christi nomine suo sanguine baptizentur, aeterni ignis sempiterno supplicio aeternaliter cruciantur.' The *nisi* is added by Karlstadt.

22 Karlstadt regards blood-baptism as a sign of divine election in *Defensio* (11), LÖSCHER 2, 133: 'Loquor [de] fidelibus, qui re et nomine fideles sunt, qui sanguine Christi dealbati sunt, qui dei electi sunt.' This statement follows a discussion on baptism.

the elect. Many respectable and baptized people are 'like the foolish maidens, without burning lamps. They are evil. They are weeds.'[23]

Despite this, Karlstadt holds that baptism suppresses sin and removes the guilt of the elect, for he still refers to 'baptized infants' whose guilt has died although it has not been buried.[24] Now Karlstadt values repentance (Thomas's spirit-baptism) more than penance. Karlstadt agrees with Eck that there is a sacrament of penance, but he ignores Eck's view of penance as the 'second plank after shipwreck.'[25] Regular repentance is as effective as the sacrament.[26] Moreover, for Karlstadt penitence itself is less effective than in scholastic doctrine, since it fails to restore to pristine grace, and sins remain.[27] Finally, Karlstadt no longer equates sacramental penance with repentance, for the penitence God works in human hearts must precede sacramental penance, or else the latter is void (inanis). Karlstadt adds a warning: 'I fear that some want to lift the sensually perceived sign to the level of Christ, even of God.' He doubts the value of the sacrament, but not the reality it signifies. 'Confession is the work of his, that is of God's, splendour, and not of men.' The absolution of the priest following penance is a transient verbal sign, whereas inner repentance wrought by God is everlasting.[28] Soon penitence loses its independence as a sacrament when Karlstadt subsumes it under baptism. Notable is the severance of res and signum in the sacrament (!) of penance. We also encounter this separation later in Karlstadt's baptismal views.

Partial Reconstruction, 1519

Having rejected the scholastics, Karlstadt begins the work of positive reconstruction, circumventing sacramental baptism and concentrating on the baptism of

---

23   LÖSCHER 2, 133: 'Non nego fideles et electos dici quos baptizatos et recte vivere novimus, multi tamen illorum in parte fatuarum sunt virginum, nec lampades ardentes habent, sed mali sunt, sed zizania sunt.'

24   LÖSCHER 2, 141.

25   Sider takes Eck's second thesis (LÖSCHER 2, 111) for a statement by Karlstadt, without noting Karlstadt's efforts to undercut the sacrament of penance, leaving the impression that Karlstadt was conservative on this point (SIDER, 70). Eck's reference to penance as 'the second plank after shipwreck' can be traced back as far as Tertullian. The Council of Trent commended the expression 'for its aptness' (DENZINGER, *1542; see also n 1).

26   LÖSCHER 2, 112: 'Adsero et confiteor ipse, sacramentalem paenitentiam cum ecclesia, sed eam non tantum, immo et alias cum eadem sanctisque patribus adstruo'; 115: 'Si adseris paenitentiam per S[anctum] S[piritum] diffundi in cordibus, tuncque ea fideles emundari et purificari. Existimo autem hoc non solum procedere de sacramentali paenitentia, sed de omni paenitentia, quam ex scripturis conligimus.'

27   This seems to be aimed at Thomas Aquinas, Summa theologiae 3, q. 89, a. 2 ad 2: 'paenitentia, quantum est de se, habet virtutem reparandi omnes defectus ad perfectum.'

28   LÖSCHER 2, 120: 'Timeo quosdam tanti sensibilia illa signa, quanti Christum, sed et quanti deum facere'; 119: 'Igitur confessio verax dei opus est. Certe nisi intranea illa cordis confessio inspirata, externam praecedat, vacua et inanis exterior erit.'

dying and rising with Christ. Following Luther, Karlstadt accepts the primacy of faith in baptism, for 'by faith Christ dwells in the interior man,' faith itself being the gracious gift of God, through which righteousness (*iusticiam*) is imputed.[29] Karlstadt at times uses Luther's *simul iustus et peccator* image, but his own view of justification is dynamic as well as static. In April 1517 Karlstadt marks off his point of departure by observing that 'the just man is both good and evil.'[30]

Here justification is linked to a concern that the just are both good and evil in the sight of the world. This position leads Karlstadt to link forensic justification with an intrinsic form of justification in which God progressively circumcises the heart or negates the ego of the believer, followed by the divine indwelling, which causes moral transformation. Karlstadt uses mystical language to express this. He links the positive aspect of law with gospel, harmonizes Paul and James, and insists that faith and love exist in a reciprocal relationship. Christ both declares and makes one just; he is both saviour and example. The just man imitates Christ:

We claim we must ascribe to justification: mortification, perdition, destruction, descent to hell, and, in contrast, vivification, salvation, renewal, [and] the return from hell ... for the Christian life is fashioned according to the acts of Christ, and whatever Christ did on the cross, [and his] death, burial, resurrection, and ascension towards heaven ought to correspond to the life of one who has been justified.[31]

This idea is derived from the baptismal passage of Romans 6:3f. Baptism represents the experience of the believer being buried and rising with Christ. In this

---

29 *Iustificatione* (13), [A4–v]: 'Fide enim corda purificantur ... Fide enim peccatores salvos Christum fecisse ... Fides non ex nobis, sed dei donum est. Fide Christus inhabitat in corde hominis interioris. Iustificamur igitur fide, vivimus fide.'

30 KÄHLER, 32*, th 138: 'Iustus ergo simul est bonus et malus.' CC 1, 44, th (134]: '[Hoc vitium] boni et mali, filii dei, habent; semper enim, dum bene facit iustus, peccat, et bonus et malus est.' See also KÄHLER, 33*. Sider sees a development from *partim iustus, partim peccator* to Luther's *simul iustus et peccator* (SIDER, 33–6; 67–8]. However, th 138 (in 1517) speaks of one who is already *iustus*, and in the later examples cited by Sider (p 63) Karlstadt not only considers the *iustus*, but also speaks of *facere iusticiam*. Karlstadt's reply to Eck (SIDER, 67, n 91] affirms that we are not judged by God (*Non iudicamur a Deo*]; in other words he upholds the forensic aspect of justification in a negative form here. Nevertheless, Karlstadt adds a quantitative and dynamic form of justification: 'Ergo quando homo iudicat peccata sua, tunc iuste iustificans deus et misericors relinquit delictum.' Of course, against Eck one would expect Karlstadt to emphasize the forensic aspect of justification; nevertheless, intrinsic justification is mentioned.

31 *Iustificatione* (13], A3: 'Iustificationi, mortificationem, perditionem, destructionem, deductum ad inferos et, ediverso, vivificationem, salvationem, instaurationem, ab inferis reductum, adscribi contendimus'; A3v: 'Nempe, vita Christiana gestis Christi configuratur, et quisquid Christus in cruce, morte, sepultura, resurrectione, ascensione ad caelum egit, iustificati vita referre debent.'

life, however, the burial needs more stress than the rising, which is its natural consequence. Mortification is justification, because it frees from sin (Rom. 6:7) and automatically leads to resurrection (Rom. 6:5).[32] *On Justification* does not end with the joy of resurrection but with a devotional litany.

Besides the Pauline theme of dying and rising with Christ, Karlstadt illustrates the 'sacrament of baptism' with the Red Sea experience of the Israelites. He cites Augustine to prove that 'the sins in one's members are drowned in baptism and they become immovable like a stone.'[33] Karlstadt's qualms about a rite not supported by repentance must be read in light of his affirmation of the rite for believers.

Meanwhile, Karlstadt revises his view on the salvation of infants. In a letter written in 1519 he argues that only the imputation of Christ's blood-baptism can save a child, and he no longer limits blood-baptism to children who lack water-baptism. In consequence, the baptismal rite does not confer its already limited benefits *ex opere operato*. Karlstadt writes to Spalatin:

> Whereas children pay for the sins of their parents, they are punished even to the third generation, unless they have been washed in the blood of Christ through faith. It is Christ's doing when children are not condemned on account of the original penalty, or when original [sin] is not imputed to them. Nevertheless, alien sins [i.e. original sin and the sins imputed to the third and fourth generation (Exod. 20:5)] and their own sins are imputed to those who do not wash their robes in the blood of Christ.[34]

Late in 1519 Karlstadt enters on a new theme in connection with the vow made by the godparents. Such vows should be made sincerely (*ex animo*), and parents should bring up their children with affection. They should caress their

32 Ibid, A3v–[4].
33 *Ausslegung* (15), C2. In 1522 Karlstadt reconsiders this Red Sea theme, but then he goes further, for he applies it to spiritual rather than sacramental baptism (*Ochssenfart* (90), A3v).
34 Gerdes, *Scrinium* 7/2, 327, ep 35: 'Quandoquidem filii parentum delicta luunt, et in tertiam generationem puniuntur, nisi Christi sanguinem per fidem lambant. Christus est qui facit, ne parvuli originalia poena damnentur, ne originale imputetur. Eis autem, qui stolas in sanguine Christi non lavant, et aliena et propria imputantur.'
    Jäger, *Andreas Bodenstein*, 14–15: 'Sehr rigoristisch besteht Carlstadt auf der Verdammnis von Kindern, die ohne Taufe sterben, th 88–92, 86, 265 ff.' See also BARGE 1, 247: 'Damals behauptete er schroff die Prädestination zum Bösen, ja die Verdammnis der ungetauften Kinder.' On the contrary, Karlstadt only speaks of infants who die in original sin (*in originali*), th 84, 264, 276. He also speaks of unbelieving children (*infideles infantes*), th 270–1. Karlstadt does not refer to children who die without (outward) baptism, but he mentions only those who die without Christ's blood-baptism. Naturally, Jäger and Barge could have shown that traditionally only unbaptized infants were thought to have died in original sin. However, Karlstadt now rejects such a viewpoint.

infants so that the love of Christ may be engraved on their hearts. Even if the children confess their faith haltingly, as it were, the young stutterers will soon grow up to become 'robust men in Christ.'[35] Their training is to be specifically Christian. Children ought to preoccupy themselves with the reading of Holy Scripture.[36]

Karlstadt's baptismal views from 1517 to 1518 may be considered a radical and selective appropriation of Augustinianism, but this is no longer true in 1519. He has denied the existence of limbo. Water-baptism is no longer necessary, nor is it particularly effective, because all believers are saved through Christ's blood-baptism, which is based on faith.

Karlstadt did not know that some of the writings he cited should not be attributed to Augustine. When he partially accepted Fulgentius in claiming that infants can go to hell, Karlstadt thought himself true to Augustine. Even then he realized that he was being selective, for he knew and cited writings in which Augustine distinguishes between the damnation of adults and of infants, with the latter enduring only the mildest punishment, or perhaps no real pain.[37] Karlstadt's manipulation of the Fulgentius text shows his willingness to deviate from 'Augustine.'

Karlstadt has not yet attacked baptismal practices and he states his views with circumspection. The frightful vista of infants burning in hell is somewhat offset by believing infants who go to heaven, rather than limbo, even without external baptism. Karlstadt has left one point obscure. Since he links Christ's blood-baptism with faith, unbaptized infants must be saved by faith, but how can they have faith? Unlike Luther, he does not accept a special 'infant faith' (fides infantium).[38] Not until 1521 does Karlstadt explicitly accept the traditional 'parental faith' (fides aliena) doctrine. Perhaps infant faith was a problem he had not yet resolved.

The Period of Crisis, 1520 to 1522

Of Holy Water and Salt (1520) contains more than its pretended subject matter, for – as Jäger has already observed – Karlstadt obliquely criticizes baptism.[39]

---

35 Verba Dei (26), D.
36 Ibid, D: 'Pueri praecipue divines litteris occupari debent.'
37 Augustine, De peccatorum meritis, 1.16. See also Contra Iulianum, 5.11.44.
38 Luther first develops this doctrine in his Hebrews Lectures (1517–18). See Brinkel, Die Lehre Luthers, 20. It is remarkable, however, that in 1522, when he is writing to Melanchthon on the problem of infant faith, Luther uses only the fides aliena argument (BR 2, 425:41f). Perhaps this is so because fides aliena and fides infantium can be mutually exclusive. Nevertheless, I prefer Brinkel to Althaus, The Theology of Martin Luther, 364f, who separates these doctrines too rigidly.
39 Jäger, Andreas Bodenstein, 80.

Water and salt are signs that may even be harmful. Similarly, smoke is a sign of fire, but as sign it merely makes one filthy. Nevertheless, Karlstadt is not motivated by a spiritualistic dualism of matter and spirit:

> I do not say that holy water and salt hurt a man, or that one should chatter lightly about things which God created. I only ridicule the foolish and blind usage to which people exalt water and salt – and place their hope in words and promises of men – so that their hope will remain only in God's Word.[40]

The Word triumphs over spirit and ritual. A text dealing with baptism is discussed in the confidential tone characteristic of Karlstadt's writings for the laity:

> Yes, dear comrade, if you knew what daily sins are, and how they are forgiven, you'd have to laugh at your claims. If you'd pour the whole Tiber, the Elbe, the Rhine, and the Danube over a sinner, you wouldn't wash away any of his daily sins. Because all things have been blessed by God, what would you lack if you'd give two pennies to the attendant at the bath-house, and so would wash body and soul really nice and clean? But if you don't believe what water means and shows, you don't obtain salvation: Mark 16:16. And such water is nothing else or more than bath water, for water without faith cannot affect the soul.[41]

Ostensibly directed at holy water and the removal of daily sins, Karlstadt's scriptural reference shows that he includes the water of baptism. Only faith determines whether the water signifies more than a bird's bath.[42] With one's sins one goes to Christ and water needs no blessing anyway. According to John 3:5 (which also refers to baptism!), one must be rejuvenated and born again in the water. Is that not enough of a blessing?[43] Although these statements reflect the tradition that the sacraments are 'sacraments of faith' that function *ex opere operantis*, nevertheless Karlstadt discusses *only* such strictures rather than positive assertions made about baptism.

40 *Wasser* (30), A3v. For the 'filthy sign' see A3.
41 Ibid, A3–v: 'Ja, lieber gesel, wan du wissest was tegliche sund seynd und wie sie vorgeben werden, du must deiner reed lachen. Schuttest due die gantz Tyber und Elb, Reyn unnd Thonau uber einen sunder, du wurdest ym kein teglich sund abwaschen. Seynt doch alle ding durch gott gebenedeyet, was solt dir gebrechen das du dem bader ii pfenning in das bade göbest, und wüschest leyb und seel gar wol und reyn. Dan so du nit glaubst was durch wasser bedeut und angetzeyget ist, so wurstu nit selig. Marci ultimo. Und ist wasser nit anders oder meher dan wasser, und ist gar nicht besser dan des baders wasser, dan wasser sonder glauben magk die seel nit anruren.'
42 Ibid, [A4]v–B.
43 Ibid, A2v.

Karlstadt returns to the oath of his godparents. He accepts it and calls it 'my oath,'[44] for such oaths are eternally valid ('remember the daughter of Jephthah'), including the oath made on behalf of the infant who is baptized.[45] This emphasis on oaths anticipates covenantal theology, and in 1520 Karlstadt was not far removed from a baptismal position that became typical of the Reformed tradition. One proof-text was John 3:5 'Unless a man is born of water and the spirit, he cannot enter the kingdom of God.' Such water need not be holy water, and since 'water without faith cannot affect the soul,' Karlstadt implies that the water of baptism as such has no value. Six months later he is explicit:

Those who have been baptized by the Spirit and the water of tribulation are truly baptized. The saying of Christ, 'Unless one is born of water and the Holy Spirit,' should be understood quite plainly. You should receive not only the element, water, but what it allegorizes, namely tribulation, which many scriptural passages call water. Spiritual tribulation is the sacrament.[46]

One's inner repentance is the sacrament, the real thing (ding or res) of which the external water is only the sign (zeychen or signum).[47] Karlstadt erases the traditional res and signum relationship. Res and signum have been severed. They may go together, but the res (spiritual tribulation) is of itself the sacrament. This is a radical change in viewpoint.

Luther attacks vows in general to enhance the vow made in baptism.[48] Karlstadt's more thorough repudiation of oaths comes somewhat later as a by-product

---

44 *Gelassenheyt* (38), [A4v]: 'Ich hab durch meyn paden oder doden (sso mich auss der tauff gehoben, als und er ich getaufft wart) got und Christlicher kirchen vorheyschen bey dem glauben zu bleyben und zu sterben. Nun ist der glaube in der heyligen geschrifft als in eynen beschlossen garten behalten. Wie kann ich dan an zerrüthtung meynes aydes und glaubens die schrifft widerruffen?'

45 Ibid, B2v: 'Gedencket das die dochter Jepte yhres vatters gelubt mit yhrem todt erfullet. Warumb solt ich nit meyner paden gelubt auch erfullen, die mich vor der tauff got vorpflicht haben?'

46 Brieger, 'Thesen Karlstadt's,' 481, th 4–6: 'Baptizati spiritu et aqua tribulationis vere sunt baptizati. Verbum Christi "Nisi quis renatus fuerit ex aqua et spiritu sancto" ubertim et plene debet intelligi, ut non solum elementarem aquam, sed etiam allegoricam, hoc est tribulationem, quam multae scripturae aquam vocant, accipias. Tribulatio spiritualis sacramentum est.'

47 In *Wasser* (30), A3, Karlstadt defines sign as follows: 'Art und eygenschafft der zeychen ist das sie den anseher oder zuhörer von sich zu andern dingen füren. Haben aber nit macht und natur der bedeutten dingen.' Jäger (*Andreas Bodenstein*, 80) rightly saw in this the germ of Karlstadt's later sacramental teachings. The distinction between sign and thing was well known through the *Sentences* of Peter Lombard. But Karlstadt's severance of the two is radical. We have already seen this severance in the case of penance (LÖSCHER 2, 120).

48 WA 6, 538:26f.

of his fight against celibacy. He had spent late May to early June 1521 in Denmark, aiding King Christian II in revising the laws governing the Danish clergy, including laws which specified a modified rejection of clerical celibacy.[49] Karlstadt soon argues that Holy Writ does not know the institution of a celibate priesthood, and even that it forbids clerical celibacy.[50] However, even if Scripture demands a married clergy, does it sanction breaking a vow, like the vow of celibacy? Karlstadt then urges that such vows be forsaken. He also realizes that his strictures on vows apply to oaths in general.[51] The traditional university oaths should be abolished in Wittenberg.[52]

A year earlier Karlstadt had clung to infant baptism by claiming that the godparents took their vow on behalf of the infant. He illustrated the seriousness of the baptismal vow with the vow of Jephthah, which was valid though it victimized his daughter (Judg. 11:29–40). Now Jephthah is thought to have made 'an evil vow,' which should have been abandoned. Jephthah set up his own word against God's Word, which says: 'thou shalt not kill.'[53] Thus Karlstadt could have discarded the baptismal vow, but since he also encourages parents to train their children in the faith, he cannot simply abandon it. Perhaps as a substitute for vows, Karlstadt now accepts the traditional fides aliena doctrine. The faith of the godparents is a proper substitute for the faith of the infant who is to be baptized.[54] Yet, since Karlstadt accepts the need for parents to rear their children as believers, he must go farther. He salvages one type of oath or vow, one made directly to God.[55] At a crucial juncture Karlstadt heroically clings to infant baptism, but

49 BARGE 1, 240f.
50 Coelibatu (62), D3: 'Non sunt ad sacros ut aiunt ordines vocandi, qui coniugia non cognoverunt.'
51 Gelubden (50), C2, where he equates 'ayden' and 'gelubden.' See also D3.
52 Friedensburg, ed, Urkundenbuch 1, 110: 'Placeret iuramenta esse sublata, quia iuramentis nemo melior, plures fiunt deteriores. Qui deum non reveretur, is nequaquam iusiurandum reverebitur; ergo facessat.' Friedensburg's own superscription implies that oaths had been abolished. Jäger, Andreas Bodenstein, 221, claims that the reference to oaths is an annotation in Karlstadt's own handwriting. Jäger must be right, for Karlstadt's use of the subjunctive reveals wishful thinking. Karlstadt's feelings were probably unique, and Melanchthon would have been opposed to this view. Hartfelder, Philipp Melanchthon, 455.
53 Gelubden (50), E3v.
54 BARGE 1, 474, th 7: 'Nihil valet uspiam sacramentum praeter fidem, proinde fides ut potissima sacramentorum vis, pro aliis credit, ita pro aliis baptizatur.' Luther had defended this viewpoint earlier (WA 6, 538:5f), but the idea can be found in Augustine (PL 44, 570), and it had been adopted by Thomas (Summa theologiae 3, q. 68, a. 9 ad 2). It became official church doctrine in 1312 (DENZINGER, *903).
55 Vota legitima are based on God's command to vow only to him (Gelubden (50), A2v–3). The 'command' is found in Ps. 76:11. See also Gelubden (50), [F4v], where Karlstadt restricts such vows. See also Coelibatu (62), [A4v].

without meaningful reference to the rite itself, and he centralizes an alien element.

The breakdown of Karlstadt's sacramental views culminates in an affirmation that must have seemed inevitable. Biblicism, rather than a form of spiritualism, leads to Karlstadt's rejection of the sacramental system:

Similarly baptism is to give precedence to preaching as Paul appears to confirm when he says, 'Christ did not send me to baptize, but to preach the gospel' [1 Cor. 1:17]. Paul was a chosen vessel, who brought the name of Christ before kings and the people. Nothing else can better explain the glory of Christ than the Word. With it [Paul] fished for men. With it he begat saints in Christ. With it he performed the inner and invisible baptism of the Spirit. With it he inflamed the hearts of his hearers. And he placed his words of proclamation above these outward baptisms to such an extent that he did not in the least hesitate to testify that he had been sent to preach, not to baptize. Thus the preaching of the Word is more excellent than baptism, and it most definitely surpasses many regulations. That can be proven with a reason derived from the Word of Christ. For Christ says: 'he who does not believe is judged already' [John 3:18]. Likewise, 'he who will have believed and will have been baptized, will be saved.' In fact, 'he who will not have believed, will be condemned' [Mark 16:16]. The gist is that the faith of believers is emphasized and it is better than baptism. Afterwards the Lord says: 'he who will not have believed will be condemned.' This final statement shows plainly how much faith surpasses baptism, and to such a degree that baptism is nothing without faith. Neither does the baptism of hypocrisy confer something more to unbelievers who have been dipped with water than a bath would to a dipper bird.[56]

---

56 *Coelibatu* (62), C: 'Baptizationem similiter cedere praedicationi, videtur Paulus adstruere, dicens, "Non misit me Christus ut baptizarem sed ut evangelizarem." Paulus erat vas electionis, quod nomen Christi coram regibus et vulgo portabat. Neque alia re poterat gloriam Christi plus illustrare quam verbo. Eo piscabatur homines. Eo genuit sanctos in Christo. Eo baptizavit intrinsecum et invisibilem spiritum. Eo corda auditorum inflammavit. Eiusque verbi publicationem externe illi baptizationi adeo proposuit, ut nihil cunctaretur testari, se missum ut praedicet, non ut baptizet. Praestat itaque verbi praedicatio baptismo, atque insigniter praestat et modis certe multis antecellit. Id quod ratione ducta e Christi dicto, probari potest. Nam Christus ait, "Qui non credit iam iudicatus est." Item. "Qui crediderit et baptizatus fuerit, salvus erit. Qui vero non crediderit condemnabitur." Summa credentium fides exsistit, et melior est fides baptismo. Propterea dominus ait, "Qui non credit condemnabitur." Haec cauda satis ostendit quam sit baptismo praecellentior fides, intantum quod baptismus sine fide nullus est, nec plusculum sanctimoniae baptizatio incredulis demersis aqua confert, quam potest immersio mergulorum eis conferre.'

Faith and the Scriptures eclipse the sacrament. On believers the baptismal rite does not confer anything of value, but an extraneous element, the oath of the godparents, becomes central.

Karlstadt now disposes of a problematic text (John 3:5) which refers to baptism by water and the Spirit. The water may not even be a simile of baptism. Physical water is unnecessary, for it may obscure the fact that the water of John 3 must be understood spiritually as God's Word, which is the well from which the Spirit flows into the believer. It also stands for persecution. 'Yea many become members of the kingdom of God in the water of persecution.'[57] Karlstadt has now (July 1521) repudiated the text that embraces sign and thing, according to the Council of Florence and Luther.[58] This is not a new position for Karlstadt, but now he is explicit: 'I am a Christian, not out of custom, but having been baptized in the divine Word.'[59]

Christian nurture is a burden, not only for parents, but also for the church. Churches have been endowed with foundational masses, and instead of providing for chanting for the souls of the dead, they should use the endowments to instruct youths in Holy Scripture. This custom from the time of Augustine and even of Bernard of Clairvaux ought to be reinstated.[60]

Karlstadt realizes that his baptismal stance is problematic. Vows to rear one's children in the faith can be made without water-baptism. Not only has the sign been divorced from the thing signified; it can even stand in the way of proper understanding. Why then continue to baptize? Baptism must be continued, because it has been based on a *command* from Christ. Karlstadt is inconsistent, for, if he had pursued his interpretation of John 3, he would have disposed of the references to baptism, even in the ending of Mark's gospel. This illustrates the desperate nature of Karlstadt's affirmation of infant baptism. In his textual criticism of Mark Karlstadt had argued that the last chapter is spurious (subditicium) and apocryphal. Thus, he realizes that he is grasping at a problematic passage.[61]

57 *Gewaldt* (63), B3v: 'Der wegen saget Christus, das keiner gotis reich eingeleibt wirdt, ehr sei dan wider geborn auss dem wasser und geist. Dar auss volget das gotis wort ein born ist, dar aus gotlicher geist yn die glaubige fleusset ... Ja vil werden yhm wasser der vervolgung, glidmas gotlichen reichs.' Note the pun on *geborn*.

58 DENZINGER, *1314; WA 2, 728.

59 *Messe* (71), A3: 'Ich bin ein Christ, nit durch gewonheit sunder in gottlichem wort getaufft.'

60 WB, 86–7: '(Fundationes) seind aber dozu vorordent und gestifft worden, das darinne die jungen leuthe in der heiligen schrifft und christlichem glauben solten ertzogen und unterweist werden.'

61 *Malachiam* (93), A3: 'Marcus ultimi saget (ists anders sein capitell) das die junger disses evangelium musten verkundigen. Welcher getaufft ist und gleubet, der wirt selig.' In *Scripturis* (34), L (Credner, par 131) Karlstadt refers to the 'spurious chapter.' In *Bucher* (46) he calls it 'unbiblical' (B2v).

Karlstadt's baptismal theology remains in suspense until 1523. Other statements add little or nothing to his view of baptism. He reasserts the baptism of conversion and persecution as a dying and rising with Christ. He also uses Paul's image of the seed that must die before it becomes fruitful (1 Cor. 15:35f). The immediate efficacy and the joyous nature of rising with Christ are now emphasized:

> This is what it means to be a baptized Christian. He has come to the life of Christ, and has died in Christ's death. His sins are dead; he has been redeemed, and he enters into a new life in faith, righteousness, and truth. He says, 'I do not live, but Christ, he lives in me.' Rom. 6.[62]

Water-baptism is no better or worse than Old Testament circumcision. Signs do not unite with God; only faith or the circumcision of the heart is effective.[63] Still, the signs are not to be discarded, 'for the faithful must accept such external signs in their own way, and use them as signs of inner righteousness and union [with God].'

> Take baptism for example, and note what one is to be told first, when one is to be baptized. Christ says, 'ye shall baptize them in the name of the Father and the Son and the Holy Ghost,' Matt. 28:19. He who allows himself to be baptized in the name takes the external baptism, because he wants to show before everyone that he confesses the triune God and accepts him as creator of heaven and earth, who can and will give him all things needful and good. Where this righteousness is not present in the Spirit, the sign is false and God does not heed it. Hence adults (die alten) cannot find consolation in their baptism if they do not feel the descent (niderganck) of their life. Thus the Spirit is not bound to an external thing, nor does inner harmony have to be attested or authenticated by the external sign. Nor [should one assume] that the Spirit cannot perform his life and work without externals, John 4:13f, but [it should be done] simply without comfort and trust in externals.
>
> Where, however, one knows some who think that eternal bliss [selickeyt] and true union depend on the external sign, to them he shall denounce and condemn the external signs, though fittingly and properly, as Paul did with circumcision.[64]

---

62 *Willen gottes* (102), F. For the similes of dying and rising and the grain to be buried see C3v–[4]. In *Gelassen* (104) Karlstadt again describes baptism as renunciation of the world, the slaying of the Old Adam, followed by discipleship and resurrection (Bv, Ev).
63 *Willen gottes* (102), G2.
64 Ibid, G2v.

Karlstadt proposes a baptismal rite for adults, who confess their faith, allow themselves to be baptized, lead a righteous life, and experience the inner harmony which derives from the will to serve God alone, eschewing the manifold allegiances of the world. The external rite (infant baptism) is valid only for believers, to whom it can be meaningful if they feel in retrospect what the sign was supposed to represent. No wonder Karlstadt's baptismal theology would collapse.

Towards Adult Baptism, 1523

From the Scriptures Karlstadt derives several spiritualizations of baptism.[65] These bypass the medieval sacramental system, but Karlstadt also accepts baptism as an external rite. This position leads to a revised form of infant baptism, dependent on the vow of the godparents or the parents' substitute faith. Such rationalizations, which did not rest on scriptural evidence, thus clashed with Karlstadt's biblicism.[66]

In the case of believers *res* and *signum* are related out of respect for 'the creatures of God.' This integration is accidental, because sacramental baptism has lost all objective power. In addition, the *res* or spiritualized conception of baptism (baptism in the Word, blood, or Spirit) is related to an adult experience, whereas the *signum* is infant baptism.

Karlstadt reacts against popular and official superstition, for to the many hypocrites baptism is only a pretended sign. Even in the case of believers, baptism refers to continual repentance, which, by itself, can be the sacrament. In spite of a certain surface consistency Karlstadt's present baptismal stance rests on at least three inner contradictions. Still, Karlstadt hesitates to resolve the tensions, and he can afford to evade the issue as long as the baptismal rite is considered trivial. Infant baptism might even be convenient, and I regard the ulterior motive of assuaging friction as decisive in Karlstadt's choice of Luther as the godfather at the baptism of his first son, Andreas Jr, late in 1522 or early in 1523.[67] In *Geschwigen* Karlstadt destroys the rationale for infant baptism when he observes that inarticulate children are sinless in the sight of God. This tract was published at the first opportunity in December of 1523. Some time in 1523 Karlstadt had become a Baptist.

---

65 For an example of the progressive spiritualization of a biblical motif (manna) see von Rad, *Genesis*, 18n. Karlstadt's spiritualizations of baptism are derived from biblical, rather than his own, models. Thus the external Word delimits the amount of spiritualization Karlstadt accepts.

66 KS 2, 29:20–1, 37:6–8.

67 See below, Appendix I, 283, n 25. Of course they would have held differing views about the significance of this occasion. Whether the rite was performed as Karlstadt wanted (without unbiblical additions), or as it was practised in Wittenberg, is a moot question

Soon after 6 January 1522 Mark Thomä, about whom little is known, entered Wittenberg proclaiming that 'children who are now baptized before they have understanding have not been baptized.'[68] Melanchthon wrote Luther for advice, but his letter has been lost, probably destroyed. Luther's reply shows that Thomä harped on one basic text, Mark 16:16: 'He who believes and is baptized shall be saved.' Since Thomä found no faith in infants, they should not be baptized.[69] It is not certain whether this led him to a doctrine of adult baptism. If Thomä advocated adult baptism, he probably exerted a delayed influence on Karlstadt. If Thomä spiritualized baptism, his definite rejection of infant baptism would have made a minor impression. Thomas Müntzer, who stood closer to the 'Zwickau Prophets,' attacked infant baptism without replacing it or discontinuing its practice.[70] Karlstadt showed no enthusiasm for the Prophets; in fact, he was censorious of them.[71]

However, Thomä may have exerted a delayed influence, for Gerhard Westerburg, who had left Cologne under the influence of Thomä, remained in Wittenberg. Westerburg spent some time in Karlstadt's home, and ultimately he married Karlstadt's sister-in-law. With such close ties to Karlstadt, he may have exerted his own influence. Yet caution seems indicated, for example, although Karlstadt (like Thomä) argued that God directly inspires believers, he already believed this before Thomä briefly sojourned in Wittenberg.[72]

Although Bender has argued that only those who were baptized as adults were true Baptists, his argument is designed simply to ward off all historical interaction.[73] Clearly the opposition to infant baptism is an essential step towards a Baptist viewpoint. Without calling the Zwickau Prophets Baptists one may be able to draw a historical line of influence from the Prophets to Müntzer, Karlstadt, and the Zurich Baptists. Karlstadt must then be credited with first opposing the sacramental nature of infant baptism, the Zwickau Prophets with first openly

---

68 WB, 161: 'die kynder, dy man ytz tauff, ee sy vernunfft haben, sey kein Tauff.'
69 BR 2, 425:41f.
70 Bender, 'Die Zwickauer Propheten,' 265.
71 Bylder (88), Jan. 1522, KT 74, 12:6–8: 'Ich beger nit das jemand auff mich bauhe, oder mir gleube. Ja der teuffel danck dirs wan du mir gleubest, oder auff mich fussest. Kere dein oren und augen auff die schrifft.' Karlstadt also speaks of God's direct inspiration, but the mouth is a 'mere instrument,' and humans may not add anything; Malachiam (93), B3: 'Ir solt nit ein wortlin tzu gotlichen worten setzen, ader von jenen nemen. Deu. iiii. Ir solt weder tzu der rechten nach zu der lincken hand wanckeln. Deu. v. Derhalben spricht Salomon. Du solt gar nicht tzu den worten gottis setzen, auff dastu nit gestrafft werdest und ein lügner erfunden. Prover. xxx. Sie seind alle puben und lügner, die ein klein punctlin tzu gotlichen ssermon setzen.'
72 BARGE 1, 404, n 197.
73 Bender, 'Die Zwickauer Propheten,' 265f.

agitating against it; Karlstadt with first refusing to baptize infants and developing a positive position on adult baptism and Grebel's or Castelberger's Karlstadt circle with initiating the first adult baptisms.

This is not to argue that the Zwickau Prophets, Müntzer, Karlstadt, and the Swiss Brethren are all part of the same movement. There were profound differences regarding Scripture, liturgy, eschatology, and violence which separated the Prophets and Müntzer from Karlstadt and the evangelical wing of the Baptists. The tension between Karlstadt and Müntzer is apparent in their correspondence, and when Müntzer recommends Nikolaus Storch in 1523, he repeatedly asks Karlstadt to cross-examine Storch.[74]

Of outside influences, that of Jakob Strauss seems most pertinent. In the late spring of 1523 Strauss published two sermons attacking practices related to infant baptism. In several respects Strauss is more conservative than Karlstadt.[75] Strauss's repeated denunciations of chrism and oil would not have amazed Karlstadt. Like Karlstadt, Strauss has difficulty in relating res and signum. Strauss also refers to several spiritualizations of baptism, while maintaining infant baptism. He bases infant baptism on the faith of parents but not on the implicit faith of children. Strauss seems to have been dependent on Karlstadt.[76]

Some of Strauss's arguments seem new, however, and they reappear in Karlstadt's later writings. Baptism is the 'highest sacrament.'[77] In The Babylonian Captivity Luther also stresses baptism, but to him the two sacraments of baptism and the Lord's Supper are essentially equal, even though Luther's references to the sacrament are always reserved for the sacrament of the altar. Neither does Strauss reiterate a medieval opinion: thus the view that baptism is the highest sacrament is a new note, not found until later in Karlstadt's publications.

Strauss claims that Christ's mercy, as well as original sin, is imputed to children without their knowledge, and he uses Romans 5[:6, 13, 18?] for support. To

---

74 See below, Appendix I, 281.

75 Strauss tolerates additions to the baptismal water, provided people do not put their trust in them, and no fee is charged. He also implies that marriage is a sacrament (Wider den tauff, B2v).

76 In Von dem Tauff faith rather than the external rite is seen as efficacious. Strauss also refers to such spiritualizations as the baptism of rebirth, of purification, and of the Spirit. Strauss considers the use of Latin 'a great danger.' Karlstadt used the same argument, but Luther rejected it. In Wider den Tauff Strauss attacks Holy Water. He notes that he is considered a schwermer. Baptism is based on a command and the Lord's Supper is not. Strauss's insistence that the baptizer should be a believer (Von dem Tauff, B) reminds one of Karlstadt's 'believing bishops.' For Strauss's possible influence on the Baptists see Oyer, 'The Influence of Jakob Strauss on the Anabaptists,' 62–82. Every possible point of influence stressed by Oyer was probably derived from Karlstadt. This confirms Luther's judgment that Strauss was a Karlstadtian; see esp pp 66–70, 74–6.

77 Von dem Tauff, A3v.

prove that the kingdom of God belongs to *baptized* children Strauss appeals to Matthew 19[:14] and Mark 10[:14]. He illustrates the incompleteness of sacramental baptism by showing that Christ continues to glean the vines grafted on him.[78]

Since Karlstadt would soon re-examine the relationship between original sin and baptism, and since he would use identical proof-texts to establish that *unbaptized* infants belong to the kingdom of heaven, Strauss's views may have been a stimulant, although Karlstadt takes the argument further.

An alternative explanation may be more plausible. Strauss had been expelled from Hall in Tirol because of 'very heated' sermons against 'the clerics, whether bishops, priests, monks, [or] nuns.' He opposed 'part of the ceremonies and customs of the church,' and he spurned the summonses of his bishop.[79] Strauss played the laity off against the clerics, and at a later stage there is considerable Baptist activity in the area where he had preached. There is no hard evidence linking the young Strauss with the Baptists, but he had sown where others reaped.

Strauss enrolled at the University of Wittenberg in the summer of 1522. In view of his disposition he probably heard Karlstadt's lectures on Jeremiah.[80] Karlstadt would have used such texts as Jeremiah 4:4 and 9:25–6 to delineate his baptismal views, and since circumcision was the traditional Old Testament parallel for infant baptism, Jeremiah's spiritualization of the rite would have been useful. Karlstadt had already used Jeremiah to illustrate his views on baptism.

Unfortunately, the Jeremiah lectures are not known to have survived, and thus the evidence is inconclusive. Even so, Strauss's comments presume infant baptism. He may have accepted Karlstadt's views of 1522, and this would explain why Karlstadt uses some of the same arguments. Nevertheless Karlstadt may have known Strauss's tracts and have appropriated some of his arguments. At any rate, although Strauss was doubtless influenced by Karlstadt, some mutual dependence cannot be ruled out.

Karlstadt may also have been stimulated by the Zwickau Prophets, but the major breakthrough in his baptismal views came independently. The inner tensions in Karlstadt's views and his new freedom in Orlamünde, coupled with a fresh exposure to popular superstition, would seem decisive. A contributory factor may have been his own fatherhood. At least we may presume that his fatherhood interfered with the facile speculations regarding original sin and infant damnation which he had embraced as a celibate.

78 Ibid, A3–v.
79 Rogge, *Der Beitrag*, 16–20.
80 Rogge, *Der Beitrag*, 27–8.

Adult Baptism, 1523 to 1525

Karlstadt's views during this period are rather consistent, and although his reconstruction may not have been achieved at once, this period is best treated as a unit.
Karlstadt no longer practised infant baptism in Orlamünde, and in August 1524
Anna Bodenstein resisted the pressure to have her second son (Andreas III) baptized, during her husband's absence.[81] Since the dialogue on baptism did not survive
in its original form, Felix Manz's *Protestation* to the Zurich Council will not be
used, even though it was based on Karlstadt's dialogue. On only one point (original
sin) I shall make explicit what is already implicit in Karlstadt by using the dialogue of the grammarian Valentin Ickelsamer, one of Karlstadt's Rothenburg converts, later influential in the circle of Pilgram Marbeck, the South-German
Baptist.[82]

In *Geschwigen*, Karlstadt proposes that 'Good will towards God does no evil,
even if it does evil. Just as a small inarticulate child does not sin, even if it sins.
Matt. 18[:12f].'[83] Though Karlstadt maintains the sinlessness of newborn infants,
he soon reverses himself on the question of unintentional sin, which can no longer
be excused. Some of the Jews, for example, crucified Jesus Christ with good
intentions, believing that they had done God a service. Nevertheless, Peter barred
them from the church, until they repented of a sin committed in ignorance (Acts
3:17f].[84] Good or indifferent acts, accompanied by evil intent, are also evil. The
godless priests, though they accomplish nothing, are guilty of slaying Christ in
their masses, because they *intend* to slay him.[85]

In spite of his reversal on unintentional sin, Karlstadt does not gloss over
Christ's words to children in Matthew 18, so he must reject the imputation of
Adam's sin. In *Sabbat* the human penance for Adam's sin is mentioned in the
form of labouring in the sweat of one's brow.[86] The result of Adam's sin remains,
but the sin itself is not imputed.

Although infants are born sinless, their condition is precarious. One sin of
ignorance or one good deed with evil intent breaks the law, that is, the whole of
the law.[87] Ickelsamer's dialogue illustrates how older boys should convert younger
boys with scare tactics:

81 See BARGE 2, 219, n 177, and below, Appendix I, 284, n 25.
82 Ickelsamer defends Karlstadt's ideas and personality against Luther in *Clag etlicher brüder*
    (1525). Ickelsamer's tract of 1529, *Vom wandel und leben der Christen*, still shows him to be
    a Karlstadtian. The preface of the *Dialogue* which we cite is dated Ascension Day (25 May)
    1525. Karlstadt was in Rothenburg at that time.
83 KS 1, 19:15–17.
84 *Priesterthum* (112), E2. Peter's view would have been based on Lev. 4.
85 *Priesterthum* (112), Ev.
86 KS 1, 46:7f.
87 *Willen gottes* (102), C2V. See James 2:10.

JOHAN. You child, give an accounting of your life to God.

JACOB. I'm too young anyways, and God still don't punish my sins.

JOHAN. God's wrath rests on all who are disobedient, including small and young children, for David asks God not to remember the sins of his youth [Ps. 25:7].

JAC. O boy, you're saying something scary and awful.

JOHAN. It's better that you know and get scared than that you don't know and go to the devil because of it.

JAC. Tell me, how often has God punished a child so awful?[88]

Johannes then relates the stories of Elisha and the bears (2 Kings 2:23f), the wicked sons of Eli (1 Sam. 2:12f, 4:11), and the command to stone disobedient children (Deut. 21:18f). Parents who fail to teach this to their offspring are 'Christians, just as Judas was an apostle.' Thus Karlstadt remains concerned about the instruction of young children, even after he revises the doctrine of original sin.[89] Using Deuteronomy 6:7, Karlstadt exhorts parents to instruct their children and other members of their household in the meaning of the Scriptures.[90]

As a consequence of the sinlessness of infants Karlstadt repudiates infant baptism. He does not become a strict Baptist, for he does not advocate believers' baptism for those baptized as infants. Exactly when Karlstadt refused to administer infant baptism in Orlamünde is not known. As late as 1527 there were still several unbaptized children in Orlamünde, which suggests that Karlstadt suspended baptism for more than just a few months.[91] Karlstadt's first open attacks on infant baptism were printed in December of 1523, but since several pamphlets were issued at the time, Karlstadt had had to wait until Michel Buchfürer's press in Jena became available. Thus Karlstadt's pamphlets were probably written somewhat earlier. It is likely that Karlstadt ceased baptizing infants in the autumn of 1523.

Although the baptism of adults who had been baptized in infancy began in Zurich within two months of Karlstadt's visit, this was a new development. Karlstadt's brother-in-law, Gerhard Westerburg, did not receive adult baptism from Henrik Rol in Münster until 1533 or 1534.[92]

---

88 *Die Evangelischen Katechismusversuche*, ed Cohrs, 1, 133–4.

89 Karlstadt may have become somewhat more pessimistic about Adam's fall in 1525. Ickelsamer's dialogue between Margreth and Anna rejects the imputation of 'alien sin,' but Adam's defective nature is passed on to his descendants. See *Die Evangelischen Katechismusversuche* 1, 139, and Ickelsamer, *Die rechte weis*, B3–v. In 1539 Karlstadt still avoids speculations concerning the imputation of Adam's sin, but he does affirm that Adam's fall brought darkness and death to the entire human race (*Iob VII* (155), Bv, 4v).

90 KS 1, 18:7–20.

91 BARGE 2, 101, n 14.

92 Cornelius, *Berichte*, 405. 'Hinricus Rollius hait doctor Westerbergh binnen Munster gedoipt in Knipperdollinghs huise, und ist umbtrent ii jar.'

Even after Karlstadt rejects infant baptism, he retains the oath of the [god-]parents. Their solemn pledge made to God is the only type of oath upheld since 1521, and Karlstadt never abandons it.[93] There is no specific evidence for this, but since Karlstadt regards the vow as desirable, even apart from infant baptism, he may have replaced infant baptism with a ceremony in which parents covenanted with God to rear their children in the faith. Although the vow remains valid, Karlstadt now openly repudiates parental faith as a substitute for the faith of their children.[94]

Karlstadt does not specify a mode of baptism. The laity as well as the clergy have the right to administer baptism.[95] This idea, though now openly affirmed for the first time, may not be new, for in 1521 – when he still accepted the real presence! – Karlstadt allowed the laity the right to celebrate their own masses. He was convinced that the benefits of the Lord's Supper, which he then valued above baptism, were communicated through both species, and their separate promises. To receive the full benefits of the Supper a person may celebrate it individually.[96] If there is a parallel here, Karlstadt may have defended the layperson's right to perform baptism several years earlier. Nevertheless, this is not certain, for the development of Karlstadt's view of the two 'sacraments' is not entirely even.

Karlstadt's defence of the layperson's right to baptize expresses a radical break with existing practice. The medieval church allowed lay baptism only in an emergency, and then because baptism was thought essential for heavenly bliss. Karlstadt is the first reformer to implement the full equality of all believers.

Baptism, unlike the mass, is based on an explicit command.[97] Since children are not possessed by demons, the baptismal rite is not to be accompanied by extraneous acts like exorcism.[98] Baptism and the Lord's Supper are to be observed exactly as prescribed in Scripture.[99]

Karlstadt keeps insisting that the mere outward rite – even for adults – lacks value. One who has experienced baptism only outwardly is at a stage between

---

93 KS 1, 31:18–21; KS 2, 8:36–40.

94 WA 18, 461:5–7: 'Darumb ist der rum und trost falsch ... von dem glauben der eltern.'

95 On the basis of Luke 9:1f; Matt. 10:1f, 28:18f; Mark 16:15f, and the practice of Peter and John (Acts 4) Karlstadt argues that all believers are sent to proclaim the gospel, to baptize, and to perform miracles; Christus (124), B2: 'Sölche unnd der geleichen werck hat Christus den seynen gebenn, wie wol sich die pfaffenn ir sonderlich anmassen.'

96 BARGE 1, 489, th. 112f. See also Barge, Orlamünde, 45. For Karlstadt's later period see KS 2, 28:30–1.

97 KS 2, 41:26–37.

98 Christus (124), B3v: 'Also auch folgen sie Christo nach, und lesen Christus wort uber die kleine kindlin, und wollen mit solichen worten teüflen auss denen verjagen, die nit besessen, und die verstockte oren unn augen auffthun, die nit verstockt noch blind sein.'

99 Leyb (129), D2: 'Vil mehr solt ir auss der leere Pauli lernen, das wir, wider mit der tauff, noch mit dem brodt, anderss handeln sollen, denn es gott verordnet hat.'

faith and unbelief. Such a person must still come to a recognition of the truth, and choose to fall or be baptized in the Spirit.[100]

Like Luther, Karlstadt removes the distinction between Old and New Testament signs and sacraments, but, unlike Luther, Karlstadt confers no objective power whatsoever on the outward rites. Baptism is a true or false sign. The Israelites crossed the Red Sea, and for some this outward baptism was a true sign of repentance, but for most it was a false sign because they continued to murmur against Moses and God.[101] External rites that obstruct God's Word should be omitted:

> This is not only to be said concerning the Lord's Table, but of baptism and all external things. He who wants to hear the external Word rightly and participate in its meaning, should divest himself of all things that hinder or darken the Word, or obstruct the ears. He who wants to take baptism in the right way, and wants to be baptized in the name of Christ, must repent, leave the old life, and put on the new (Acts 2[:38f], Rom. 6[:3]). And it is impossible to participate both in baptism and the devil at the same time, though the water bath is an external thing, and is no more than water.[102]

In spite of that the water bath may be useful: 'For all the external exercises have been instituted for the good of man, and the believer is Lord over them, and he has power to do or not to do them, as his needs dictate and his spirit understands.'[103] Elsewhere, Karlstadt discusses the Sabbath as a sign, but the believer remains Lord of the Sabbath. Similarly, signs like baptism and the Supper must be observed as God prescribed, but the potential benefits are so marginal, and the right observance may be made so difficult, that one can suspend their observance. Karlstadt does not wish to risk his life, or that of his followers, to practise water-baptism in the proper form. He also allows the usage of the word *sign* for baptism – even though the water-bath is a false sign. The word *sacrament* is frowned on as unbiblical. With its undesirable connotations it also intimidates the weak.[104] Thus the meaning of baptism (the spiritualizations based on adult experience) is carried over from the days when Karlstadt defended infant baptism. Apparently, internal baptism sums up the whole of the Christian life.

100 *Gelaub* (139), [B4]. 'Aber in mitler zeit, ehe der glantz des schwerts, und die scherpff göt-licher gerechtickeit würt erkant, steht der mensch in bewegnüssen, und schlechtem tauff des wasserss, biss er entwders im geist getaufft wirt, oder von erkanter warheit abfellet.'
101 *1 Cor. 10* (142), A3.
102 Ibid, [C4v].
103 KS 1, 35:4–7.
104 KS 2, 11:10–25.

Coming from the medieval tradition, Karlstadt not only explains the two signs of baptism and the Lord's Supper, but he also has to dispose of the other five 'sacraments.' He subsumes them under baptism, with the possible exception of matrimony and extreme unction.

Penance has become repentance and conversion, or the spirit-baptism of tribulation, the prerequisite for outward baptism. This leads to union with Christ, the spouse; at least a matrimonial image lingers here.[105] By insisting on adult baptism Karlstadt also subsumes confirmation under it. Baptism also includes ordination, for through it one is incorporated in the church, which not only teaches the priesthood of all believers in principle, like Luther, but practises it. Karlstadt speaks of Christ's ordination in the order of Melchizedek by means of his (baptismal?) oath. With all believers Christ shares this priesthood of Melchizedek, the prince of *Salem*, a priesthood founded on righteousness and peace.[106]

This still leaves the sacrament of extreme unction. Karlstadt may have discarded it, or he may have considered it to be absorbed by blood-baptism or the death of the old ego during spiritual tribulation.

The eminent role of baptism allows it to usurp characteristics that Luther attributes to the sacrament of the altar. True baptism is incorporation into the body of Christ. Karlstadt prefers the emphasis of the old pope, who proclaims baptism as 'the first among the sacraments.' The new pope (Luther) overemphasizes the Holy Supper. We must be incorporated into Christ *before* partaking of the Supper. This fellowship and incorporation are signified by baptism.[107] Baptism is an initiation into the whole of Christian life. 'Thus begins the community: One God, one faith, one baptism, one Lord, one Christ.'[108]

Outward baptism can be a meaningful sign. Ideally Karlstadt desires to integrate sign and meaning, but this is impossible because true baptism hinges on faith. Karlstadt emphasizes, however, the positive reason: 'Thus it is with the rite of baptism. Whoever refuses [to administer] baptism until the time when people believe, and keeps it from those who do not believe, exalts the primary doctrine of faith and does not quench it.'[109] From the time when he had defended infant baptism as a trivial sacrament until his final conception of adult baptism as a mere sign, which, when properly understood and experienced, encompasses the whole of Christian life Karlstadt had radically altered his doctrine of baptism.

---

105 *Gelassen* (104), A3v.
106 *Priesterthum* (112), B2v.
107 *1 Cor. 10* (142), C2v: 'Da kan ich nitt helen, das wir nicht durch das brot unnd weyn des herrn in gemeinschafft des leybes und blutes Christi kommen, sondern in der tauff, wenn wir in Christo getaufft werden, als Paulus an vil enden schreybt, Roma. 6, Ephe. 2, Gala. 3, Collo 1.'
108 *1 Cor. 10* (142), C3v.
109 KS 2, 70:13–17: 'So ist es mit den handlung des tauffs; wölcher die tauff biss auff die zeytt wegert, und denen wegert so nit glauben, biss sy glaubige seynd worden, der treybt das hauptstuck des glaubens auf, und dempffet es nit.'

Part Two

The Zurich Reformation

Zwingli at age 48.
He wears the plain academic cloak (*Schaube*) that became typical of
ministerial attire in the Reformed tradition.
By courtesy of Zentral-Bibliothek, Zurich

5

The Swiss Appropriation of Competing Reformations

The Reformation in Zurich is hardly normative for the Swiss movement at large, especially during the early years. For example, the incipient Baptist movement took on massive proportions in the countryside, and Thomas Müntzer's influence may explain its revolutionary features.[1]

This study is confined to Zurich, however, except for the issue of tithing. The first problem in studying the movements beyond Zurich is the lack of materials suitable for a genetic study of their origins. Certain basic issues are known, but there are few documents that permit a more than superficial examination. Second, this study is involved with so many areas that only careful delimitation will keep it under control. Third, there is also the decisive principle of examining movements that endured. The Baptists of the countryside are worth investigation, but their violent features did not survive, nor did they persist as popular movements. The centres of political power tended to be dominant – and this was also true of Zurich – because in sixteenth-century society popular movements succeeded only when they persuaded the governing powers. Where they failed to persuade the magistracy, they were ultimately suppressed and dispersed.

The Zurich Reformation in its Zwinglian and Baptist forms owes a debt to Karlstadt that has been ignored, even though the Baptists of Zurich immersed themselves in Karlstadt's writings and supported the printing of Karlstadt's most radical works in the fall of 1524. Moreover, in 1530, when Karlstadt made a compromise for the sake of his family, Zwingli welcomed him to Zurich. The compromise was not profound, and Zwingli considered Karlstadt an ally. Was their agreement purely coincidental, or were there firm connections?

Since the Baptists of Zurich arose in the context of the Zwinglian Reformation, Baptist origins are intertwined with Reformed origins, even though Zwingli

1 For this phase of the movement see especially Goeters, 'Die Vorgeschichte,' 239–81; Haas, 'Der Weg der Täufer,' 50–78; and Stayer, 'Reublin and Brötli,' [83]–102.

also differed from the radicals. It is the radical movement which is most relevant here, rather than the broader question of Reformed origins. Nevertheless, the issue of Reformed origins is pertinent.

Then the vital issue is whether Karlstadt influenced the Zurich Reformation from the beginning or just at a later stage. In view of genuine similarities between Karlstadt and Zwingli, the first point to be determined is whether Karlstadt's writings circulated in Switzerland during the formative years of the Reformation.[2]

Karlstadt's Books in Zwingli's Circle

Erasmus Schmid

In an article describing a single bound volume from the library of Erasmus Schmid (Fabricius), Oskar Vasella notes the presence of six booklets of Karlstadt's, covering the years 1520 to 1523.[3] These treatises are *Ablas* (29), *Wasser* (32), *Coelibatu* (60), *Gelübden* (52), *Messe* (73), and *Fegfeur* (97).[4] Only the last work is an original edition published in Augsburg; the other booklets are editions reprinted in Basel (60; 52) or Strassburg.

Schmid's annotations to *Ablas* and *Wasser* express an almost fanatical admiration for Karlstadt's arguments. Schmid concurs with Karlstadt that the pope and his followers have been excommunicated. When Karlstadt divorces the *signum* from the *res* of the sacrament in *Wasser*, Schmid exclaims:

2 The older approach is to explain the Zurich Baptists almost solely with reference to the Zwinglian context (Bender, *Conrad Grebel*; Yoder, *Täufertum*). Walton in *Zwingli's Theocracy* treats the radicals as quite distinct. So does Davis, who emphasizes in *Anabaptism and Asceticism* the medieval ascetic heritage, as well as the influence of the *Theologia Deutsch* and of Erasmus. None of these authors has considered the influence of Karlstadt. Since certain ideas of Karlstadt reappear in Zwingli, and since there appears to be an almost total dependence of the Zurich Baptists on Karlstadt, I take a mediating position between those who emphasize Zwingli's influence and those who emphasize the differences. To Walton and Davis I concede that there are few specifically Zwinglian arguments which appear in the Zurich Baptist writings of the latter half of 1524. However, there is an area of common ground that Zwingli and the Zurich Baptists shared with Karlstadt.

3 Vasella, 'Zur Biographie des Prädikanten Erasmus Schmid,' 353–66. Vasella also notes Schmid's mention of another treatise by Karlstadt which was being printed in Basel, but Schmid was mistaken in assuming that Karlstadt wrote a third attack on Franziskus Seiler. On the basis of content Vasella's suggestion that this 'third attack' refers to *Fritzhans* (49) is plausible; besides, Seiler is mentioned there, perhaps because Karlstadt still wanted to make good his earlier threat to write a real *narrenfresser* against Seiler. However, there does not seem to be an edition of *Fritzhans* published in Basel.

4 Ibid, 353–5. To these six should be added no. 10, which is a revised German version of Karlstadt's *Apologia* for Feldkirch.

Evil Christians consider the signs and not the thing, whereas we ought to go to the things themselves which are represented by the signs. Watch yourself, you cheese farmer [Franziskus Seiler]! There are many things done in church, which of themselves are neither good nor evil. One should pay attention only to their significance. Just as the shadow of a man is nothing, but it gives a picture and indication of what a man is.[5]

And in conclusion: 'Holy water and holy salt have no more power than ordinary water and salt. He who teaches differently, does not teach like a pious Christian man.'[6] In view of many such comments Vasella claims that Karlstadt exerted a 'very strong influence' on Schmid. Schmid was a friend of Zwingli: Vasella notes Bullinger's statement that Schmid, who was then a non-resident canon of the Grossmünster Church in Zurich, had pressed for Zwingli's appointment late in 1518. In 1521 Schmid returned to Zurich from Stein am Rhein, which became a radical centre (as many as two hundred persons in Stein am Rhein received communion in both species in August 1524). Vasella concludes:

Karlstadt's influence as an author in the [Swiss] Confederacy, especially with respect to the early development of the Swiss Reformation, needs to be more deeply understood. Karlstadt's influence, next to that of Luther, would have carried the strongest weight – at any rate some time before Zwingli became effective in wider circles as an author.[7]

The evidence, even for Schmid, is far from complete. The original book collections of most of the Swiss reformers were dispersed, but in parentheses we list the number of Karlstadt's works that found their way into the libraries of Basel (52), Bern (13), Zurich (43), Schaffhausen (2), and St Gallen (17).[8]

---

5 Ibid, 358 (re A III[r]): 'Signa et non res considerant mali christiani, cum tantum ex signis deberemus venire in res ipsas, quae per signa denotantur. Hüt dich kess meyer. Vil ding geschehend in der kirchen, die fur sich selbs weder gut noch böss send; alleyn das sy anzeygen, sol man betrachten; wie eyn schatt des menschen nichtsz ist, gibt aber eyn bildnuss und anzeigung des menschen wie er ist.'

6 Ibid, 360 (re D[r]): 'Weichwasser und geweicht saltz hant nitt mer krafft dann ander wasser und saltz. Welcher anderst leertt, der lert nitt wie eyn frumer kristen man.'

7 Ibid, 360.

8 In the Universitätsbibliothek of Basel the following works are found, numbered according to FB: 5, 6, 23, 26, 29 (2 copies), 32, 37, 40, 42, 43, 44, 45, 46, 47, 48 (2 copies), 49, 52 (3 copies), 65, 67, 69, 70, 73 (2 copies), 76, 78, 86, 89, 90 or 91 (since leaf 3 is missing), 93, 96, 98, 102, 108, 113, 114, 115, 118, 121, 122, 124 (2 copies), 126, 127 (2 copies), 129, 131 (3 copies), an edition similar to 134, 135 (2 copies), 136, 137, 138 (2 copies), 139, 144, 150, 151.

   The Staats- & Universitätsbibliothek of Bern holds 4, 43, 48, 52, 60, 73, 94, 112, 115, 124, 129, 135, 143.

The significance of these figures is debatable, for we cannot establish that all of these publications were originally distributed in Switzerland. Yet this seems likely for several reasons. Duplications and triplications point to a haphazard form of collecting. Since none of the booklets bear ownership stamps, they were probably not recent purchases from other libraries. Most suggestive is the circumstance that virtually all of these publications are reprints published in three centres with ready access to the Swiss market, that is, Basel, Augsburg, and Strassburg. Thus it seems clear that Karlstadt's writings were avidly collected in the Swiss Confederacy.

Ulrich Zwingli's library

Walter Köhler has made a tentative list of Zwingli's publications, although it remains incomplete.[9] His articles dealing with Zwingli's glosses are similarly unfinished.[10] Nevertheless, Köhler's references to Karlstadt's writings remain useful. Zwingli owned a copy of the Leipzig Disputation, which included Karlstadt's moderate defence of predestination.[11] Zwingli also consulted three of Karlstadt's works related to the controversy over the Lord's Supper.[12] These must be augmented by the booklets that Felix Manz distributed in Zurich.[13] The Zurich provost Jakob Frei owned a copy of the *Apologia* written for Feldkirch, and I have already noted that Erasmus Schmid owned a German version of it. As we shall see, these tracts influenced Zwingli's rejection of celibacy. Crucial is Charles Garside's discovery that Zwingli used Karlstadt's fifty-three theses *De cantu gregoriano disputatio*, although Garside – who did not put the theses in Karlstadt's own context – underestimated the radical nature of his own discovery.[14]

The Zentralbibliothek of Zurich and its archival Simmler Collection possess 4, 14 (2 copies), 29 (2 copies), 32, 40, 43, 44, 48 (2 copies), 52, 54, 55, 56, 59, 60, 63, 68, 71, 73, 78, 81, 86, 90 (2 copies), 92, 95 (3 copies), 97, 102 (2 copies), 107, 111, 115, 116, 120 (3 copies), 121, 122, 126, 129, 131 (2 copies), 135 (2 copies), 138 (2 copies), 139, 142, 143, 145, 147 (3 copies).

The Stadtbibliothek of Schaffhausen has 73, 134.

The Stadtbibliothek of St Gallen owns 13, 29, 51, 52, 60, 63, 73, 76, 78, 81, 86, 87, 90, 103, 105, 124, 131. These came from the library of Joachim von Watt (Vadianus), teacher and friend of Konrad Grebel, whose sister Dorothea he married.

 9 Köhler, 'Huldrych Zwinglis Bibliothek.'

10 Köhler, 'Aus Zwinglis Bibliothek,' ZKG 40, 41f; 42, 4f; 45, 243f.

11 Köhler, 'Huldrych Zwinglis Bibliothek,' *13, no. 89.

12 Ibid, *22. nos. 176–7; these are *Dialogus* (126) and *Sacrament* (149). See also *41, no. 377, which is *Messen* (131).

13 In his Letter to Matthäus Alber, Zwingli refers to *Missbrauch* (135) as a booklet, printed on three sheets (*trium paginarum*), entitled *De exsecrabili abusu eucharistiae*. See z 3, 335:14–17.

14 Garside, *Zwingli and the Arts*, 28f, 54f. On some points my interpretation differs from Garside's. Although Karlstadt argued mostly from history and Zwingli mostly from Scripture when dealing with music, this does not express a basic difference. We shall see that on celi-

The *Disputatio* was printed only once, in the third Basel collection of Karlstadt's theses entitled: *LUTHERI. MELANCH. CAROLOSTADII &c. PROPOSITIONES VVITTEMBERGAE* ... This collection covers much more than Karlstadt's theses on Gregorian chant, for, besides some of Luther's and Melanchthon's theses, it includes virtually all of Karlstadt's theses from 1520 to 1521.[15] In them Karlstadt discusses papal authority, natural and divine law, prayers for the dead, eschatology, celibacy, the Lord's Supper, perfectionism, the primacy of God's Word over works and ritual, the ritual of the mass, silent prayer, psalm-singing, the mandatory use of the vernacular, the fall of the church, tithes and almsgiving, public fasting, pilgrimages, and additions to the baptismal water, in the order cited.

The only major issue in the Zurich Reformation from 1521 to the end of 1523 which is not treated in Karlstadt's theses is iconoclasm. But Zwingli knew Ludwig Hätzer's *Ein Urteil gottes*, for, as censor, he permitted its publication by Christoph Froschauer, and in a publication of his own he summarized it.[16] Finally, although Zwingli had some reservations about them, he urged the people to read Karlstadt's works even after the Council of Zurich had forbidden their public distribution.[17] Andreas Castelberger is the most likely person to have supplied Zwingli with Karlstadt's writings. Castelberger initially sought contact with Karlstadt in 1524. Probably he was also involved in having Karlstadt's treatises printed in Basel, and he had been Zwingli's personal bookseller since 1516.[18] Karlstadt's influence may also explain Zwingli's opposition to the 'adoration,' though not the 'imploration,' of the saints as early as 1519.

bacy Karlstadt argued primarily from Scripture and that Zwingli introduced a number of historical examples. Karlstadt had in fact already done more in terms of Scripture than Zwingli. I also disagree with Garside when he sees Karlstadt as arguing purely from a single 'fall of the church.' Finally, I think that one should not compare Karlstadt's theses of *1521* with Zwingli's work of *1523* to conclude that 'Whereas Karlstadt was a reformer, Zwingli was a revolutionary' (Garside, 56).

15 BARGE 1, *Exkurs* V. This includes the following sets of theses: nos. 5–7, 9–12, 14, 15, 17, 18, 20–2. No. 19 has been attributed to Melanchthon by Bubenheimer, 'Scandalum et ius divinum,' 314f. There Bubenheimer also ascribes to Karlstadt the ten theses *De iubileo et anno remissionis* (p 33f).

16 See Z 2, 654, n 14.

17 The protocols of the council for this period are lost, but Rudolf Wirth (Hospinian) relates in *Historiae sacramentariae (pars altera)* (1602), 32v: 'Provocatus hoc modo ad certamen, Carolostadius libellos aliquot de Coena Basileae edidit, qui longe lateque sparsi sunt. Eius tamen expositio verborum Coenae plerisque displicebat Senatus quoque Tigurinus rei novitate turbatus, cavebat ne publice hi libelli in urbe sua venderentur. Zwinglius autem, etsi ne ipse quidem Carolostadianam istam expositionem probaret, hortabatur tamen pro suggestu Senatum, ut libellos illos sicuti alios quoque, ab omnibus legi pateretur, totamque ecclesiam ad lectionem eorum incitabat, ut eo magis esset ingenua veritatis victoria.'

18 Goeters, 'Die Vorgeschichte,' 244.

A year earlier than Zwingli, Karlstadt addresses this same issue, arguing: 'no wonder [the scholastics and Capreolus] spin such nonsense, for in their pestiferous servility they fashion humans into gods, to bless them, whether [the saints] want it or not. The devils!' Then he concludes:

> In sum, I teach you the proper adoration, which is to pray according to the law of God, as the Lord directs the way according to his Word, that you may be neither proud nor exceedingly humble, that is mistaken, being robbers of God's honour, transferring what is owed to God to the honour of a saint – not according to the proper manner, but illicitly ... [Acts 14:10–17].[19]

Thus in 1518 Karlstadt distinguishes between proper and illicit honouring of a saint. In 1521 he becomes the first reformer to denounce the invocation of the saints. He exclaims:

> Therefore all reputed Christians who love the saints as if they were gods, [and] call on them and vow to them, commit adultery with their gods and they kill themselves spiritually.
>   It is against God and divine Scripture that one, in times of need and struggle, implores anyone other than God. Therefore Scripture says: 'In the day of your troubles and sorrow, you must call on me, and I shall deliver you (Ps. 50(49 Vulg.):15). The saints sing daily: 'Not to us O Lord, but thine be the glory.' Therefore we pray: 'hallowed be thy name,' and the saints respond: 'It is not we who aid you, but faith in God, in the name of Jesus Christ' [Acts 3; 15].[20]

Karlstadt treated the subject of the invocation and intercession of the saints *before* Luther and Zwingli, and late in 1523 he completed his attack on Mary's intercession in the work entitled *Fürbit Marie* (108).

---

19 KÄHLER, 97:4–6: 'Non est mirum, quod similia fingunt, cum homines "pestifera adulatione" faciant deos, ut illos beant, quando volunt, quando nolunt. Cacodaemones'; 98:1–5: 'Redeundo, moneo vos legittime adorationis, hoc est, quae est secundum legem dei, orantes, ut dominus dirigat secundum verbum suum, ne altum sapiatis, ne nimium humiles, hoc est ignorantes, piratae sitis honorem dei, transferentes a deo debito ad aliquem sanctorum honorem, non modo indebitum, sed illicitum.' For Zwingli's remark see z 7, 181.
20 *Gelubden* (50), A3: 'Alsso seind alle gesagte Christen, so die heyligen wie gotter lieben, anruffen und yhnen geloben, mit gottern unkeusch und ertodten sich ym geyst'; A3v–[4]: '[Es ist] wider gott und gottliche schrifft das eyner in noten und anfechten ymands anders dan gott anrüffet. Die schriefft sagt alsso. "Du solt mich in dem tag deynes umtreybens und elendes anrufen, sso wil ich dir ausshelffen [Ps 50:15]." ... Die heylige singen teglich: "Non nobis domine, sed nomini tuo da gloriam." Sso bitten wir: "sanctificetur nomen tuum," und sagen uns die heyligen: "Wir seind nicht die euch helffen sonder der glaub zu got, durch den nomen Jhesu Christi [Actu. 3; 15]."'

Zwingli's Reformation Treatises of 1522

The influence of Erasmus on the young Zwingli is the theme of Pipkin's work. This study and the tradition for which it stands deserve to be considered.[21] Erasmus's critical edition of the New Testament and his editions of the church Fathers gave greater access to the traditions of the early church, and thus humanism stimulated the Reformation. Zwingli's first reformatory act derived from his studies of the Fathers. When Zwingli discovered that Augustine and Chrysostom often preached serially, he introduced the practice in 'the German lands,' when he began to preach in Zurich in January 1519.

Yet Zwingli became a reformer because he went *beyond* the Fathers and humanism, and in 1523 he still praised Luther as 'an accomplished fighter of God.'[22] In fact, Zwingli had followed developments in Wittenberg for several years. The humanist Ulrich Zasius had written to Zwingli as early as 1519, giving details about the Leipzig Debate between Karlstadt, Luther, and Eck.[23] The Zurich Reformation was not born in isolation, and Erasmian humanism prepared Zwingli for the Reformation in Wittenberg.

The first public clash with tradition was provoked by the 'sausage-eaters.' The printer Christoph Froschauer instigated the first defiance of the Lenten regulations on 9 March 1522 when he and his friends ate sausages for dinner and supper. The act was veiled in ambiguity. Zwingli himself had already preached a sermon on fasting.[24] Froschauer defended Zwingli as a preacher 'unexcelled in the whole of Germany,'[25] and he was to become a faithful Zwinglian. Others who were involved in this matter became critical of Zwingli at a later date, when they became Baptists.[26] Zwingli himself did not join the fast-breakers when he was asked to partake of the sausages,[27] but he defended the act in his first reformatory treatise: *On Choice and Freedom of Foods.*[28]

---

21 Pipkin, 'Zwinglian Reformation to August, 1524.' Pipkin errs in treating the Swiss Reformation almost independently of Wittenberg, but his work as such is solid. However, one must take into account Zwingli's decisive turn away from Erasmianism when he began his reformatory programme. See e.g. Neuser, *Die reformatorische Wende*, esp 114–25; to be qualified by Locher, *Die Zwinglische Reformation*, 116, n 228.

22 z 2, 145:21–5, 147:14–16: 'Luther ist, als mich bedunckt, so ein treffenlicher stryter gottes, der da mit so grossem ernst die gschrifft durchfüntelet, als in tusend jaren uff erden in zin ist.'

23 See BARGE 1, 149.

24 Cf Goeters, 'Die Vorgeschichte,' 241f.

25 Egli, *Aktensammlung*, 74, no. 234.

26 Ibid, 72–4, no. 233. Involved were Heini Aberli, Barthlime Pur [Pfister], Simon Stumpf, Hans Ockenfuss, and Wolf Ininger. Perhaps [Klaus?] Hottinger and [Lorenz] Hochrütiner must be added. Leo Jud and Zwingli were present.

27 Ibid, 73: 'Das essint si all, usgenommen M. Uolrich Zwingli, lütpriester zum Grossen Münster.'

28 z 1, 88–136.

Others had anticipated Zwingli's attack on fasting. In 1520 Luther exposed abuses connected with fasting as well as popular superstitions, aimed at heightening its effect. Ultimately, Luther leaves proper fasting to the individual conscience.[29] A year later Karlstadt puts theory into practice, granting communion to those who have not fasted, but also telling the abstinent that it is 'worse than a sin' to prepare oneself with fasting for one's encounter with God.[30] The title and theme of Zwingli's On Choice and Freedom of Foods may have been inspired by Karlstadt's thesis: 'No Christian should be forced to observe a work contrary to Scripture, like celibacy, choice of foods, and other works of this type, so Christian freedom is not robbed and man does not become a slave of man' (italics mine).[31]

We cannot prove that Zwingli was influenced by Karlstadt's and Luther's remarks on fasting, but Zurich followed the events in Wittenberg, and there may have been a causal connection. In agreement with Karlstadt and Luther, Zwingli's treatise makes a simple appeal to freedom, but Zwingli also appeals to the exclusive principle, already employed by Karlstadt and decisive for Zwingli later, of not adding to Scripture.[32]

The primary difference between Karlstadt and Zwingli lies in the political realm. Zwingli accepts the right of a Christian to break the Lenten fast, but he does not participate in the decision to do so – probably because this also infringes on civil law. Robert Walton, in his work Zwingli's Theocracy, has established that Zwingli did not accept a theocracy in the modern sense of a state with ecclesiastical control over political matters. Instead, Zwingli's viewpoint resembles early medieval Gelasianism.[33]

I accept Walton's basic thesis and therefore question the theory of John Yoder who sees Zwingli forsaking Konrad Grebel in 1523, when he abides by the decision of the Zurich Council.[34] Yoder has no more than one verbal threat by Zwingli to draw upon, whereas Walton demonstrates a pattern of consistent action in which Zwingli accepts the freedom to preach and to exhort the Zurich Council, but leaves to the magistrates the implementation of reform.

The next issue agitating Zurich is not provoked by lay action. Zwingli discusses celibacy in two treatises, the Supplicatio (2 July 1522) and Bitt (13 July

---

29 WA 6, 245–7.
30 Messe (71), F2v: 'Etliche fasten. Etliche steuppen sich. Etliche thund andere ding, dero doch keines den menschen geschickt macht: ja sie hindern mehr dan sunde.'
31 BARGE 1, 479, th 57–9: 'Ad opus autem, quod praeter scripturam statuitur, non debet Christianus obstringi. Ut est caelibatus, ciborum delectus et alia id genus opera. Ne videlicet adempta libertate christiana, fiat servus hominum.' Zwingli knew the theses as part of the third Basel collection.
32 Z 1, 133:10–136:32.
33 Walton, Zwingli's Theocracy, 15–29, 225–6.
34 Yoder, Täufertum, 20–8.

1522). *Bitt* is little more than an expansion in the vernacular of *Supplicatio*. The basic argument in *Supplicatio* revolves around eight scriptural passages, of which the first (Matthew 19) is called the 'anchor' passage. The 'anchor' is linked to a chain that reaches back to Wittenberg. Four of Zwingli's texts are derived from Luther.[35]

Luther makes the first public attack on celibacy. Zwingli is dependent on Luther, and the Baptists are to share in this general heritage of the Reformation. Zwingli's *Bitt* appeals to the 'Lords of Switzerland,' just as Luther has appealed to the rulers of the German nation in *Nobility*. Both Luther and Zwingli combine 1 Timothy 3:1–2 and Titus 1:5–6 to argue for a married priesthood, and incidentally – in connection with both texts – Luther and Zwingli also appeal to Jerome to unify the offices of bishops and elders.[36] Similarly, Luther and Zwingli claim that the law of matrimony takes precedence over other laws.[37]

The appeal to freedom as applied to celibacy is also common to both Luther and Zwingli, as is the argument that the 'vow of chastity' had been made in so far as human frailty permits.[38] Both mention that, on the question of celibacy, the Greek church is preferable to the Roman church.[39]

Some minor points of correspondence may seem speculative or irrelevant. For example, Zwingli refers to priests who study in Rome in order to discover the pretty prostitutes in the *Campo di Fiori*. Earlier Luther makes a more oblique reference to the same locality as one of the places where indulgence money is spent.[40]

Luther raises the issue of celibacy before Zwingli does, and Luther's scriptural texts as well as his secondary arguments have a tangible effect on Zwingli. Luther's earlier attack on celibacy is all the more remarkable since it rests on theoretical affirmations, whereas Zwingli honestly concedes that fornication was one of his own problems. Zwingli's debt to Wittenberg does not stop with Luther. Three of Zwingli's basic texts stem from Karlstadt's *Apologia* for Bartholomäus Bernhardi von Feldkirch – the first of Karlstadt's students to be married.[41] A fourth text from Hebrews, cited only in *Bitt*, had already been cited in Karlstadt's *Eheweÿber*, the German version of the *Apologia*.[42] We have already noted that copies of both treatises were owned by friends of Zwingli.

35 These are Matt. 19 (z 1, 201:13, 203:31–3, 227:9f); 1 Tim. 3:1f (z 1, 205:1f, 231:20f); Titus 1:5–6 (z 1, 205:15f, 239:22f); and 1 Tim. 4:1–3 (z 1, 205:19f, 233:1f) They appear in Luther's *Nobility* (WA 6, 440–1).
36 WA 6, 440:26–8; z 1, 231:24f.
37 WA 6, 443:4–9; z 1, 229:5–15.
38 WA 6, 441:31–442:2; z 1, 202:21–5.
39 WA 6, 440:35–6; z 1, 241:6–9.
40 WA 6, 427:10–12; z 1, 240:5–6.
41 1 Cor. 7:7, 7:28, 7:35 appear in *Apologia*, A3.
42 *Eheweÿber*, B2v, where this text is mistakenly cited as Eph. 13. Zwingli silently corrects this, z 1, 205:33–4, 241:4–6.

As we have seen in relation to Luther, Karlstadt's influence does not extend only to scriptural references but also to Zwingli's argumentation. Ignoring similar arguments that merely restate the contents of the texts Zwingli takes from Karlstadt, we find other correspondences that are striking. On behalf of Feldkirch Karlstadt appeals to Albert, Bishop of Mainz. Zwingli's *Supplicatio* is an unusual appeal to his own bishop. Both note that celibacy has become a stumbling-block, and this contravenes Christ, who commands concern for 'the little ones.'[43]

Zwingli follows Karlstadt in arguing that there are two types of chastity: one, a gift from above; the other, a 'feigned chastity' from below.[44] Both Karlstadt and Zwingli are quite candid about abuses connected with celibacy, whereas Luther takes a more delicate stance on this issue. Against Luther, Zwingli accepts Karlstadt's argument (based on 1 Cor. 7:9) that those who 'burn' have been *commanded* to get married.[45]

Karlstadt notes that Hilary [of Poitiers] was married. Zwingli expands on this idea with a long list of married priests and of clergymen, including popes, who were the sons of priests; however, his list begins with Hilary.[46] Finally, Karlstadt is the first reformer to absolve monks from their vows, whereas Luther at first felt that only the secular clergy could be married.[47] Ultimately, Luther retracts his previous restriction in *On Monastic Vows*, which was written after Karlstadt's *Apologia* and other treatises on celibacy, and its publication delayed until February 1522. When he publishes his two treatises, Zwingli has not yet consulted this work on vows, for he ignores all of Luther's new texts, except for Titus 1:5–6, which Luther has derived from Karlstadt's *Apologia*.[48] Even so, Luther's *On Monastic Vows* would have influenced Zwingli later. Zwingli's colleague Leo Jud translated it into German, to be printed by Froschauer in Zurich.

Zwingli does not engage in the simple plagiarism that we shall find in Manz's adaptation of Karlstadt's dialogue. He adds several rhetorical sections to defend the Wittenberg interpretation of Scripture. His style is humanistic and his Latin is more classical than that of Luther or Karlstadt. Nevertheless, without the texts

---

43 *Apologia*, A4v; z 1, 206:5–6, 242:27–31.

44 *Apologia*, A3: 'Docet autem duo genera esse castitatis. Alterum, ubi cum flammis carnis simulatur castitatis. Alterum, divinitus datur, cui nihil cum isto solito furore.'

45 *Apologia*, A2–3; see also the German title: 'Das die prister eheweÿber nemen mögen und sollen.' For Zwingli see z 1, 205:5–7, 207:20, 244:14. Luther had attacked Karlstadt on this point (BARGE 1, 476–7).

46 *Apologia*, A3v; z 1, 242:18f.

47 See WA 6, 441:22–4. Karlstadt first rejected monastic vows in *Coelibatu*, a copy of which Erasmus Schmid possessed, or Zwingli could have known the theses from the third Basel collection: LVTHERI ... [D6], th 1: 'Sicut viduas reicimus iuniores, sic monachos et iuvenes presbyteros caelibes.' For Zwingli see z 1, 204:19–20: 'Qui dixit "quisque" neminem except, non sacerdotem, non monachem, non vulgarem.'

48 *Apologia*, A2; z 1, 239:22f.

and arguments he derives from Luther and Karlstadt, Zwingli's writings on celibacy would be devoid of substance. Here is one of many issues where all reformers, Baptists included, profited from the reformers in Wittenberg.

Zwingli's Discontent with Luther

Zwingli's praise for Luther was modified by criticism in 1523. He commends Luther as 'an admirable warrior for God,' but he 'does not want to bear the name of Luther.'[49] The point of friction is the same as that which alienated Karlstadt from Luther: 'I also know that [Luther] yields much to the weak on several points, though he would prefer to act differently. Here I do not agree with him. Not that he says too much; rather, he does not say enough.'[50]

Wilhelm Neuser has argued that Luther influenced Zwingli during an inner struggle over the meaning of the fifth petition of the Lord's Prayer ('Forgive us our debts, as we likewise forgive our debtors'). This led Zwingli to a new experience of the forgiveness of sin. Crucial in Zwingli's elaboration of this text are three points: 1 / God has a twofold will: he is holy and demanding on the one hand; on the other his *real* will is gracious and forgiving. 2 / Each person must admit his perdition 'so that God can liberate him from his disobedience.' 3 / 'Since the recognition of sin and grace comes only from God, his fearful and liberating Word is of central significance.'[51]

This scheme, in fact, reflects *Karlstadt's* teaching concerning predestination (discussed in chapter 2). There is no reason to pass over Luther's contributions, but Karlstadt's influence tends to be ignored. For instance, Arthur Rich lists the eight (ten) works of Luther with which Zwingli was conversant during his early reformatory period.[52] Neuser complains that Rich ignores the fact that the Luther volume published by Froben contains *several* writings of Luther's, and thus adds another six works.[53] My complaint is that both Rich and Neuser pass over Karlstadt's theses against Eck in the *Ad Leonem X* volume, where Karlstadt discusses predestination. Thus I maintain that the particular 'reformatory turn' that Neuser highlighted must be explained with reference to Karlstadt as well as to Luther.

Zwingli and Karlstadt had more in common with each other than either of them had with Luther. Though Zwingli began as a more thorough Erasmian than

---

49 z 2, 147:14–15, 27–8.
50 z 2, 148:3–6: 'Ich weyss ouch, das er vil nachgibt in etlichen dingen den blöden, das er vil anderst handlen möcht, in dem ich nit seiner meinung bin, nit das er ze vil, sunder ze wenig gredt hat.'
51 Neuser, *Die reformatorische Wende*, 142–7.
52 Rich, *Die Anfänge der Theologie Zwinglis*, 80–1.
53 Neuser, *Die reformatorische Wende*, 86–7.

Karlstadt, the latter was much more open towards *noster Erasmus* than Luther.[54] Though Karlstadt was better trained as a theologian than Zwingli, both were trained in the works of Thomas and Scotus, whereas Luther's background was nominalistic.[55] Both Karlstadt and Zwingli were secular clerics, while Luther began his career as a monk. Luther's reformation was concerned with practical life, but he insisted above all on pure doctrine. More than Luther, Zwingli and Karlstadt were aroused by the excesses of popular piety. Karlstadt could not escape from the popular superstition at the Cathedral Church of All Saints which housed Frederick's relics, and Zwingli had spent nearly three years at the pilgrimage centre of Einsiedeln. Such similarities in background and experience made Zwingli receptive towards Karlstadt's views. Zwingli's liturgical views, which Garside has shown to be influenced by Karlstadt, are best understood as a reaction against popular abuses. Even Karlstadt did not object to images *per se*, for example, but popular ideas had to be considered, and this induced him to apply a strict biblical principle. The difference between Zwingli and Karlstadt was mainly political. No matter how much Zwingli sympathized with taking a stronger course versus the weak, he saw that radical reform had failed in Wittenberg because Karlstadt had not reckoned with the weaknesses of the rulers. Thus Zwingli's course tended to mediate between Karlstadt's and Luther's.

Others moved even closer towards Karlstadt. Although the origins of Swiss radicalism are not identical with the origins of the Swiss Baptists, we now turn to an evaluation of Karlstadt's influence on the proposals of radical Zwinglians.

Early Swiss Radicalism

The tithes controversy

The controversy over tithes endured as a central concern of the Swiss radicals. The earliest incident in which tithes were questioned in Zurich occurred in February 1520. Zwingli claims that tithes are not anchored in divine law (*ius divinum*). He does not seem to have belaboured this point in a practical way; in

---

54   For Zwingli's Erasmian phase we have noted Pipkin's contribution. See also Rich, *Die Anfänge der Theologie Zwinglis*, 1–72, 151–64. This must be compared with Neuser, *Die reformatorische Wende*, esp 49–52, 56–9, 76–84, 90–9. For the literature on Erasmus's influence from 1885 to 1969 see Goeters, 'Zwinglis Werdegang als Erasmianer,' 255, n 3. For Goeters's own contribution see 263–71.

55   Goeters, ibid, 255–62, stresses the impact of Scotism at the expense of Thomism (259, n 28). Goeters's arguments on Scotist influence are convincing; nevertheless, they do not preclude the influence of Thomas. Zwingli's introduction to the *via antiqua* in Vienna would have ensured a knowledge of Thomas. Cf Pollet, *Huldrych Zwingli et la Réforme en Suisse*, 15, n 4. Also Farner, *Huldrych Zwingli 1*, 213–27, and Locher, *Die Zwinglische Reformation*, 49, 63 including n 48, 204.

fact, he makes his remarks in Latin for the benefit of the clergy.[56] A more thoroughgoing attack on tithing occurred in September 1522 when Simon Stumpf, priest of Höngg and later a Baptist, preached in Affoltern on the subject 'that one does not owe tithes.'[57] (Stumpf, like Karlstadt, was a native of Franconia.) From then on the agitation over tithes intensified and, since the Zurich Councils reaffirmed the practice, this factor fed the alienation of the radicals from the Zwinglian Reformation. The strongest centre of opposition to tithes was Witikon, but tithes were an irritant in several areas. The tithes theme is picked up by the Baptists; for example, Johannes Brötli, who, when he was in Zollikon before his expulsion, worked with his hands, renouncing tithes for his services.[58]

The controversy remains problematic because the primary documents do not allow one to gauge the motivations of those who originally opposed tithes. The subject has been almost exhausted by both Goeters and Stayer.[59] The only point they do not consider is whether Stumpf's criticism was original. Since only the fact of his opposition to tithes is known, one cannot answer this question with certainty. However, Johannes Brötli's attitude may well implicate Karlstadt, who likewise tried to work with his hands. But what about the tithes issue as such? In 1522 the third Basel collection of Karlstadt's theses appeared in print. Most of the theses can be dated with precision, with the last set belonging to October to November 1521. The theses on tithes contain, as Barge has noted, an anticipatory reference to the legislation for the poor which was established in Wittenberg in January 1522. The tithes theses were probably composed from late December 1521 to early January 1522.[60] Karlstadt argues as follows against the greater (the 'tenths') and the lesser (the 'elevenths') tithes:

1 Tithes are not based on the New Law [i.e. Testament].
2 An argument from the Old Law to the New is invalid.
3 The priests who continually vex the Christian flock with the payment of tithes err gravely.
4 Even if they are to be rendered [on the basis of civil regulations?], the customary tithes are more of a hindrance than a potential benefit, for they quietly supply bandages for much moral turpitude.
5 Concerning tithes, not one word can be found in the New Law, except when Christ was dealing with the Pharisees.
6 He who collects from the altar the tithes of those whom he does not serve offends gravely. Indeed, he eats and drinks hell.

56 Neuser, Die reformatorische Wende, 108–9.
57 Egli, Aktensammlung, 93, no. 267.
58 TQ SCHWEIZ 1, 37.
59 Goeters, 'Die Vorgeschichte,' 246, 249, 256–9, 268, 273; Stayer, 'Anfänge,' UT, 27–33.
60 BARGE 1, 385–6, 494.

7 Of all things, the liability of the altar particularly demands the dispensation of the Divine Word.

8 Hence, he who does not preach cannot receive tithes without sinning ...

10 Decimation that is later alienated (i.e. to the thief and to the brigand), whether for charity or for necessity, is objectionable.

11 Therefore it is to be abolished with confidence, and to be used for the poor in our community.

12 The one who cultivates it eats of the field, and he who plants drinks from the vine, even if one talks about tenths or elevenths.

13 Laymen have not been taught either by Christ or by the apostles to support the servants [ministris] of their churches with the necessities of life, in order that they might pay, in addition, the penalty of tithes.

14 Therefore: Any community which, in accordance with divine law, has its own bishop [episcopum], that is elder [presbyterum], who works in conversation [sermone] and doctrine – the latter is worthy of double honour.

15 One who thinks otherwise concerning tithes tramples Christ and Paul alike.[61]

The radicals were disappointed when the magistrates of Zurich confirmed existing laws making tithes mandatory on 22 September 1522.[62] Goeters has shown that this issue survives the mandate, and he was the first to press for a link between the tithes controversy and the origins of the radical Zwinglians and the Baptists.[63] Since Goeters can establish a connection only in retrospect – for he ignores Karlstadt – he limits himself to the 1523 publications of Zwingli, Mathis Wurm, and Karlstadt's student Jakob Strauss.[64]

I agree that many contributed to the tithes controversy simply by keeping the issue alive. Nevertheless, only the influence of Karlstadt best explains the emergence of the Swiss controversy during the summer of 1522. Karlstadt's theses on tithes were part of the same collection which, as Garside has shown, was consulted by Zwingli.

Ludwig Hätzer and iconoclastic incidents in Zurich, 1523

Garside must be credited, not only with exhibiting the link between Zwingli's and Karlstadt's liturgical reforms, but also with showing that Ludwig Hätzer's pamphlet Ein urteil gottes was based on Karlstadt's pamphlet Bylder. Hätzer's work in turn shaped Zwingli's attitude towards images.[65] Garside's article is very persuasive. He considers Hätzer's pamphlet even more impressive than Karl-

61 BARGE 1, 494, th 1–8, 10–15.
62 Egli, Aktensammlung, 97–8, nos. 273–4.
63 See Goeters, Ludwig Hätzer, 31–3.
64 Ibid, 33–4.
65 Garside, 'Haetzer's Pamphlet,' 20–36.

stadt's *Bylder* because of its terse style and simple quotation of scriptural texts – this is an excellent *modern* judgment.[66] But I accept without caveat Garside's statement that 'the substance of Hätzer's pages is not original.'[67]

A single point of originality should not be obscured, however, for it seems later to have caused friction between Karlstadt and Hätzer. Hätzer had augmented Karlstadt's iconoclastic texts with a citation from Wisdom, whereas Karlstadt had written two treatises against the canonicity of the Apocrypha in 1520.[68] Zwingli must have favoured Karlstadt's position because he cited all of Hätzer's other texts but omitted Wisdom.[69] Karlstadt may have confronted Hätzer on this matter later in 1524, when he came to Zurich. At least Karlstadt's allusion to Hätzer's pamphlets is rather caustic: 'There is also one, not unknown to me, who – in plagiarizing – is accustomed to add what is his, to my books.'[70] Afterwards Hätzer translated several of the Apocrypha, and he included an oblique attack on Karlstadt:

All of the learned say that the [Apocrypha] are not in the canon – that is they are not rightly or truly biblical; the church has not accepted them; they are not supposed to be of Hebrew origin. Thus one can accomplish nothing with them, neither use them for a claim, nor preserve them. To this I say the following: The canon is neither here nor there. The books have no defect, and they give a righteous testimony of how one can and must return into the One, just as with the other books, even if they do not agree everywhere with the other books, for that often happens in the biblical books as well.[71]

The attack on acceptance by the church is odd, unless one recalls that Karlstadt had not only argued that the canon determines itself[72] but also appealed to a criterion of universal usage.[73] Hätzer's statement therefore fits an attack on

66 In *Urteil* Hätzer himself added an introduction, several comments, and four arguments, together with four counter-arguments, thus adding to the scriptural texts.

67 Garside, 'Haetzer's Pamphlet,' 34–5.

68 Hätzer, *Urteil*, [A4–v]; Karlstadt, *Scripturis* (35) and *Bucher* (46–8).

69 z 2, 654.

70 wa 18, 465:21–2: 'eyner ist mir nicht unbekandt, der das seyn ynn meyne bücher pflegt klicken.'

71 Hätzer, preface to *Baruch*, 2v–3.

72 *Bucher* (46), [C4]: 'mercke das die biblische bucher krichisch canonici, lateynisch regulares, zu deutsch regeln geheyssen werden. Derhalben, das sie form, massen, und regeln des rechten glaubens seint, und das wir keynes menschen wort sollen fur ein regel und richtmass christliches glaubens achten, sonder allein gottis wort das er in die propheten und aposteln geredt und gegeben uns zusagenn.'

73 Ibid, A3: 'Alle bucher, die unsser bucher dem alten gesetz zuschreyben, und seint nicht in obgemelten ordenungen begriffen, die seint nit von allen gleubigen angenommen, und fur gotliche odder biblische schrifft gerechnet.'

Karlstadt's *Bücher*.[74] Garside regrets that the evidence for Hätzer's dependence on Karlstadt is entirely literary and internal.[75] I think that this exchange gives *external* corroboration, even though Hätzer was fair enough to respond to an indirect attack in a similarly oblique fashion.

Hätzer's dependence on Karlstadt deserves further investigation, especially for the period before he came under the influence of Hans Denck. Goeters has noted many points of similarity between Hätzer and Karlstadt, and Garside has refuted Goeters's argument that Hätzer remained independent. A renewed investigation would probably establish Hätzer's dependence. His shifting viewpoints seem derived from Karlstadt and Denck (and Hut) with a secondary influence by Zwingli and Oecolampadius.

Hätzer must have known more than just Karlstadt's pamphlet on images. On the title page of Hätzer's edition of *Ein urteil gottes* in Zurich there appears the motto that graces most of Hätzer's later publications: 'O God deliver the Captives!'[76] Karlstadt's *Willen gottes* (102) ends with a dramatic peroration that includes the exclamation: 'O God deliver Thy Captive People!'[77] Karlstadt had attacked Hätzer for having plagiarized more than one book. It is consistent with Hätzer's condensation of Karlstadt's *Bylder* to assume that Hätzer was so moved by Karlstadt's exclamation that he adopted it as the device proclaiming the mission of his own life. Nevertheless, I accept Goeters's evaluation of Hätzer as a marginal Baptist as long as it is recognized that even marginal Baptists can be central figures in a historical process of transmission, crucial for both Baptist and Reformed theology.

Hätzer's arguments for removing images clearly reflect what Karlstadt had written in *Von abtuhung der Bylder*. Goeters mentions that images were removed from altars, that Lorenz Meyer maintained that precious objects should be sold to benefit the poor, and that votive lamps were attacked.[78] In *Bylder* Karlstadt *especially* objects to images placed on altars.[79] He argues that the unnecessary wealth of the church should support the poor.[80] For the removal of votive lights Karlstadt cites the terrible precedent of Nadab and Abihu, who offered illicit fire before the Lord (Num. 26:60–1).[81]

---

74 *Bucher* (48) was printed by Adam Petri in Basel.
75 Garside, 'Haetzer's Pamphlet,' 33.
76 Hätzer, *Ein urteil*, [A]: 'O Got erlöss die gfangnen.'
77 *Willen gottes* (102), 13v: 'O Got erlöss deyn gefangen volck! Lass synckenn deynen ausgestreckten arm. Dryff sye, das sie deynen namen nicht lenger verkleynen. Hilf Gott es ist itzt tzeyt! Lere unss deynen wyllenn, unnd mach das wir wellen unnd mögen thun, das du wilt, es sey tod oder leben. Amen.'
78 Goeters, 'Die Vorgeschichte,' 261.
79 KT 74, 4:23–4, 8:17–29.
80 KT 74, 28:1–5.
81 KT 74, 5:34–5, 7:33–4, 14:11–13, 15:36–7, 30:4–5.

One of the violent features of Swiss radicalism is the smashing of crucifixes. Klaus Hottinger and Lorenz Hochrütiner instigated such an incident in Stadelhofen. Karlstadt's *Bylder* vilifies crucifixes for revealing Christ's flesh which, according to John 6:63, 'profits nothing.'[82] When Luther mounted the pulpit in Kahla, one of Karlstadt's zealots had placed a smashed crucifix on the lectern.[83] There is a connection between the Baptists and these earlier religiously inspired acts of vandalism. Felix Manz expressed his sympathy for Hottinger,[84] and Grebel, as Goeters has noted, commends 'the brother from God and Christ' Lorenz Hochrütiner, when the latter was also expelled.[85] The difference in attitude between Grebel and Zwingli is pertinent. Zwingli endorses Karlstadt's and Hätzer's attitude towards images but, unlike Grebel, he has reservations about Hochrütiner's impulsive course of action.[86] Two years later Karlstadt, Westerburg, Manz, and Castelberger stayed at Hochrütiner's house in Basel, while they arranged the printing of Karlstadt's tracts on the Lord's Supper.[87] Locher regards the image-breaking outbursts as spontaneous events,[88] but, in view of the evidence cited above, this is unlikely. One must also resist Locher's attempt to drive a wedge between Leo Jud and Ludwig Hätzer.[89]

I accept Locher's argument that Leo Jud confined himself to the Ten Commandments and used New Testament texts, and on one point his answer is 'pneumatological' rather than biblicistic. However, in *Ein urteil gottes* Hätzer himself addresses the question of the use of Old Testament texts. He justifies them because the New Testament confirms the Old Testament position, and he specifically emphasizes the Ten Commandments. For the New Testament Hätzer appeals to Paul in 1 Cor. 5[:9–11], 8[:4], 10[:7], translating 'idolaters' ($\epsilon\iota\delta\omega\lambda o\lambda\acute{\alpha}\tau\rho\alpha\iota$) as 'image worshippers,' deriving the meaning from the root $\epsilon\iota\delta\omega\lambda o\nu$ (image). Similarly, Hätzer appeals to Galatians 5:19, 20; 1 Peter 4:3; and 1 John 5:21.[90] These arguments are further supported with secondary arguments drawn from the gospels and Acts.

Again, like Jud and Hätzer, Karlstadt favours the Ten Commandments.[91] In addition to his other New Testament references, all of Hätzer's references to 1 Corinthians stem from Karlstadt.[92] Hätzer does add the references to Galatians

82 For Hottinger see Egli, *Aktensammlung*, 163, no. 421. For Karlstadt see KT 74, 10:10–21.
83 BARGE 2, 130.
84 TQ SCHWEIZ 1, 27, n 21.
85 Goeters, *Ludwig Hätzer*, 31.
86 See R.C. Walton's discussion in 'Turning Point?' MQR 32 (1958), 53. Zwingli was consistent; see Z 2, 655:4–8.
87 See below, Appendix II, 293, n 12.
88 Locher, *Die Zwinglische Reformation*, 130.
89 Ibid, 132.
90 Hätzer, *Urteil*, B3v–[4v].
91 KT 74, 6:26–34, 7:17–23, 8:20–3, 14:29–33, 18:23–5.
92 KT 74, 9:32–10.5.

5, 1 Peter 4, and 1 John 5, but these merely confirm the arguments based on 1 Corinthians 5, 8, and 10.

If one compares only Jud and Hätzer, Jud's pneumatological argument may seem to clash with Hätzer's biblicism. However, this seems to imply that Jud knew Karlstadt's as well as Hätzer's work, for just as Hätzer has quarried virtually all of his arguments from Karlstadt, so Jud's references to images that obstruct prayer 'in spirit and in truth' come from Karlstadt's *Bylder*.[93] Thus Karlstadt provides a significant link between the early Zwinglians and the future Baptists.

The mass

The first recorded criticism of Zwingli by Balthasar Hubmaier and Konrad Grebel dates from 28 October 1523. No precise explanations are given, but the disagreement centres on Zwingli's proposed revision of the canon of the mass, the singing of hymns, and the use of vestments by the clergy. There is also controversy over Zwingli's tactic of allowing the magistracy to implement reform at its own pace.[94] We note that Karlstadt had dropped the canon from the mass on Christmas Day 1521, that he had administered the Lord's Supper in ordinary clothing, and that in a sense the act defied the electoral commission which had forbidden the introduction of novelty in the 'new year,' since Christmas inaugurates the new year in the church calendar. The remarkable number of parallels between ideas current among the Zurich reformers and views that were earlier expressed in Karlstadt's writings – writings that are known to have circulated in Switzerland – makes it likely that Karlstadt was quite influential among the radicals in Zurich.

The Emergence of the Zurich Baptists: Konrad Grebel

More is known about Konrad Grebel (1498?–1526) than the other Swiss radicals. Harold Bender, in his biography of Grebel, regards him as the central figure responsible for the rise of the Swiss Baptists. The Baptists in Zurich are simply referred to as the 'Grebel Circle.' More recently Goeters has challenged the centrality of Grebel, preferring to see Andreas Castelberger's Bible School as the centre of the Zurich Baptists. James Stayer follows Goeters in reminding us that there were other radicals besides Grebel, and that Zurich did not exist in a vacuum.[95] This is a reasonable corrective to the traditional preoccupation with

---

93 KT 74, 16:15–16: 'Got hat bilder verboten. Item Christus spricht dass got ein geist ist. Alle die got wahrhafftig anbeten, die beten got ym geist an Joan. iiii.'
94 Yoder, *Täufertum*, 20–8.
95 Stayer, 'Die Anfänge,' 27–9.

Grebel, but Stayer, perhaps in reaction to Walton, seems to favour too late a date (1526) for the emergence of the Swiss Baptists.[96]

I accept Walton's argument that radicalism surfaced in Zurich as early as 1522.[97] Nevertheless, even the radicals shared many points with Zwingli. As we have seen, Zwingli defended the reading of Karlstadt's tracts in late 1524, even though the council frowned on them and even though Zwingli would have known that the tracts were made available by Felix Manz and his friends. Thus I would suggest that the roots of the Zurich Baptists lie in the radical movement identified by Walton, but the movement cannot be considered as independent as Walton implies.

John Yoder's date for the break between Grebel and Zwingli is also too early. His statements about Zwingli's 'somersault' are largely indefensible.[98] The last date when it can still be established that Grebel pondered bowing to political pressure is 14 January 1525. He writes to his brother-in-law, Joachim von Watt (Vadian): 'A week before yesterday, that is Friday, my wife was delivered. The child is a daughter, called Rachel. She has not yet been baptized and [has not yet] swum in the Romish water bath.'[99]

Here Grebel follows Karlstadt's preference for postponing baptism to adulthood without as yet contemplating adult baptism for those baptized in infancy. He even calls baptism a 'water bath' as Karlstadt did as early as 1520. Grebel

96 Stayer agrees with Deppermann in seeing Michael Sattler as a 'separatist' in 1526 ('Die Anfänge,' 20, n 5). I consider the baptisms of 1525 a separatist act, for I interpret later approaches to Zwingli as an attempt, not to establish a radically reformed church, but rather to gain converts for the new sect. I accept Stayer's insight ('Die Anfänge,' 20) that Schleitheim is 'the birth-date of the Swiss Brethren,' but in the restrictive sense rather than in Yoder's comprehensive sense of Schleitheim as the birth of the Swiss Baptists. Baptism of adults who had been baptized in infancy is of course not a separatist act per se. The mass baptisms at Zollikon, Witikon, Hallau, St Gallen, and Waldshut included most of the adult population. Thus the context determines the implications of such an act.

97 Walton, Zwingli's Theocracy, 58–69.

98 Yoder, Täufertum, 20–8. Yoder's own volte-face occurs on pp 29–33. He dramatizes a single rash remark by Zwingli by first exploiting the differences and afterwards considering the common ground that still exists. Such a procedure seems artificial.

One difference between Grebel and Zwingli should be considered. Yoder rightly emphasizes that Grebel was a theocrat (p 30). Walton has shown that Zwingli was not a genuine theocrat. Though theocratic ideas were too common to establish dependence, Grebel may have been influenced by Karlstadt's reform programme, appended to Bylder, which, as we saw with Hätzer and Zwingli, circulated in Zurich. Hätzer, at any rate, was influenced by Karlstadt's theocratic principles in Bylder. Thus he copied Karlstadt again when his Acta of the Second Zürich Disputation appeared with the legend: 'Getruckt in der Christlichen statt Zürich,' for Karlstadt's Bylder had announced on the title page: 'Carolstatt in der Christlichen statt Wittenberg.'

99 TQ SCHWEIZ 1, 33: 'Min frow ist gnesen gester, dass ist fritag, acht tag. Dass kind ist ein tochter, heisst Rachel, ist noch nit in dem Römschen wasserbad getoufft und geschwemmt.'

would have known the new mandate of the council on baptism.[100] His remark that Rachel has not yet been baptized suggests that he plans to comply under pressure.

The theoretical alienation from Zwingli was already a fact, though it happened gradually. The point at which the cleavage takes place in practice is especially obvious. It occurs when the Zurich Baptists begin to celebrate the Supper on their own (as Karlstadt recommends, even for laypeople, in October 1521),[101] and when the first adult baptisms occur late in 21 January 1525 (as not foreseen by Karlstadt).[102]

John Howard Yoder discusses several dates for the 'crystallization' of the Swiss Baptist movement, noting both positive and negative aspects of each position.[103] He favours an early date: the 'brotherly agreement of Schleitheim' in 1527. He also claims that the Schleitheim agreement is aimed only at Bucer and Capito, and does not refer to an antinomian wing of the Baptists.[104] Yoder fails to support this latter point, however, and thus I accept Meihuizen's meticulous argument that the position formulated at Schleitheim combats Denck, Hut, and Hubmaier, as well as Capito and Bucer.[105] Further evidence from the context of the Strassburg Reformation has been presented by Deppermann.[106]

Stayer finds that the adult baptisms of Zurich were unduly dramatized by Ernst Troeltsch as the emergence of the 'sect type' in contrast to the 'church type,' even though the Zurich Baptists defended a 'non-separating congregationalism.'[107] Stayer and Yoder tend to ignore the ecclesiastical ramifications of a separately celebrated Lord's Supper and the performance of a baptism of initiation (by laypeople!) in direct opposition to the established church. Despite this, I agree with Stayer, Yoder, and Haas that what Grebel believes does not yet apply to the radical movement in the Swiss countryside. The theocratic perspective of Grebel and his friends may harden into sectarianism (as happened at Schleitheim), but Troeltsch's 'types' should not be regarded as inflexible.

Nevertheless, the acts of celebrating the Lord's Supper and adult baptism are sectarian. In 1525 both Zwingli and the Baptists of Zurich were aware of the

100 TQ SCHWEIZ 1, 32–3, no. 21.
101 BARGE 1, 489, th 112–13.
102 TQ SCHWEIZ 1, 38–43.
103 Yoder, 'Kristallisationspunkt,' 35–47.
104 Ibid, 42–4.
105 Meihuizen, 'False Brethren,' 200–22. In one paragraph Yoder shows his unwillingness to discuss Meihuizen, responding with a series of catchwords and rhetorical questions ('Kristallisationspunkt,' 43).
106 Deppermann, 'Die Strassburger Reformatoren,' 24–41. See also the exchange of letters between Yoder and Deppermann in MG 30, nf 25 (1973), 42–52.
107 Stayer, 'Die Anfänge,' 20–1.

split. According to Zwingli, he admonished Simon Stumpf against trying to 'set up a special people and a church.'[108] Grebel had approached Zwingli for the same purpose, but Zwingli warned him also. 'None the less,' Zwingli says, 'they have proceeded, and they held nightly gatherings in New City [Street], [being] of the opinion they were founding a new church.'[109] Of course, from Zwingli's viewpoint they are *not* founding a new church. Therefore he contests their action in principle, but the practical fact of separation is obvious – even to him. Zwingli also met Felix Manz in Hans Hujuff's workshop, and Manz demanded a new church of all 'who knew themselves to be without sin.'[110] Zwingli's account must be taken literally – even the idea of sinlessness – for, although Karlstadt did not teach literal perfectionism, he had demanded holiness and, for a while, sinlessness, in the sense that unintentional sin is not sin. When Krajewski, Davis, and others do not accept Zwingli's statement, they also reject Balthasar Hubmaier, who admitted that some recipients of the true baptism claimed freedom from sin.[111] Zwingli's observations do not establish, but in fact corroborate, what Manz and Grebel were putting into practice.

Grebel's break with Zwingli went through several phases. Goeters has underlined Grebel's intellectual alienation from Zwingli during and following the Second Zurich Disputation of October 1523.[112] The ecclesiological break occurred in January 1525. This does not imply that Castelberger's Karlstadt Circle took a hardened sectarian stance such as was found in 1527 at Schleitheim.

Grebel naturally prefers to be part of a mass movement that will lead to reformation. When the majority proves 'weak,' Grebel insists on a biblically determined theocracy that proceeds without tarrying. When these preferred options fail, he becomes a separatist. This thoroughly consistent pattern is to repeat itself many times among the Swiss Baptists. The pattern does *not* represent a purely opportunistic response, nor is it a merely passive adaptation to circumstances; it reflects, in fact, the consistent vision of a theocracy on as large a scale *as is possible*.

---

108 z 4, 169.1–7.
109 z 4, 168:11–14: 'Und über sölichs sigind sy nudt dester minder fürgefarenn, und nechtlich zesamennkommungenn ghebt inn der Nüwenn statt, der meinung, ein besonndere kilchenn uffzurichtenn.'
110 z 4, 171:11–172:2.
111 For Karlstadt see *Willen gottes* (102), A2v. Davis, *Anabaptism*, 76, asserts that Zwingli 'insincerely' charged the Baptists with perfectionism. Davis cannot prove his point, and thus he merely establishes his own hostility towards Zwingli. See Balthasar Hubmaier, *Schriften*, TQ 9, 120: 'Ob aber ye durch ettlich torechtig menschen gleich solch reden beschehen (als mögen wir nach dem tauff nymmer sünden), soll mans den selben undersagen und sye rechtweysen, unnd nit von irer einfeltiger red wegen den gantzen christenlichen tauff hessig machen und vernichtigen.'
112 Goeters, 'Die Vorgeschichte,' 264–81. However, cf Stayer, 'Reublin and Brötli,' 85.

All these twists and turns that have been so well documented by Haas for the movement at large[113] had been anticipated by Karlstadt's development. He moved great crowds in Wittenberg with his Protestant liturgy in December 1521 and January 1522. He wanted the magistrates to be Christian, that is, to enact social legislation to protect the poor and change the patterns of worship. But Karlstadt withdrew to Orlamünde when most of his reforms in Wittenberg had been crushed by Frederick the Elector and Luther. The sectarian features of Karlstadt's reforms in Orlamünde were nevertheless implemented by the town council. Again, the elector intervened, as did Luther, and Karlstadt was banned from Saxony. His view of the church now shrinks to that of a small, persecuted remnant. This reluctant type of sectarianism, brought about by social pressure, has often been misunderstood. The Bender school has taken it as a firm defence of the separation of church and state, but one should avoid the application of a modern perspective to the sixteenth century.

One's theocratic convictions will seem to change quite radically depending on whether one expects success (then the rulers are provisionally Christian) or whether one is thwarted (then the rulers are antichristian). The thwarted theocrat will harden his stance and become sectarian. Thus in the *Brotherly Agreement* of Schleitheim biblical categories are used to assess the rulers: they are 'worldly,' 'fleshly' individuals who 'walk in darkness.' The positive theocratic impulse persists in a remnant, sealed off from the world and the powers of darkness. Soon the argument for toleration will emerge, as it had in the case of Balthasar Hubmaier, but it cannot be tested or taken seriously because it is first proposed by members of an unpopular minority.[114] True toleration, however, is achieved only when the *majority* allows freedom for dissenters. Even Erasmus did not favour toleration in that sense – in the first half of the sixteenth century such a position was virtually unknown in Europe. A possible exception was the Swabian reformer Johannes Brenz and some of his friends, but even Brenz's tolerance was not unlimited.[115]

In summation, I accept Walton's date (1522) for the emergence of radicalism in Zurich, though I do not opt for a rigid separation between radicals and reformers at this point, and the differences that emerge at first are mainly politi-

---

113 Haas, 'Der Weg der Täufer,' 50–78.
114 Hubmaier's *Uon ketzern* (Hubmaier, *Schriften*, TQ 9, 96–100) used two basic arguments. Like Karlstadt, Hubmaier argues that in religious matters one fights only with the spiritual sword. Hubmaier also makes an impressive appeal to Matt. 13:29–30 and similar texts that caution against separating the tares from the wheat. However, in *Uon ketzern* Hubmaier bitterly indicts the Catholic priests for heresy (art 2), calls the inquisitors arch-heretics (art 13), and – what seems more problematic – Hubmaier is not simply affirming the rights of others in a disinterested way, but he is writing in self-defence. Finally, there are theocratic tendencies in Hubmaier's theology.
115 See Estes, *Johannes Brenz*, 123–41.

cal. Goeters has made it clear that the intellectual break for Grebel occurred in October 1523. The first attempt at a comprehensive formulation of the radical programme appears in Grebel's letters and the *Protestation* [*Appeal*] of Felix Manz in the autumn of 1524. The public divorce between the Zurich group and Zwingli occurs on 21 January 1525. The narrowing of the larger Swiss movement into the Swiss Brethren is best traced to the agreement of Schleitheim in 1527.[116]

Thus, Grebel's letters are central in documenting the emergence of the Baptists in Zurich. He did not stand alone, as Goeters points out, but to examine the doctrines of the emerging Swiss Baptists one must turn to Grebel. Castelberger's letter to Karlstadt has been lost, as has an earlier communication to Karlstadt by Grebel. Therefore Grebel's letters to Müntzer must be examined, not to establish Grebel's eminence as the single leader, but because they remain the best witness to the doctrines of the Zurich Baptists just prior to their public break with Zwinglianism.[117]

Grebel's relationship to the Reformation

In Grebel's letters to Thomas Müntzer Luther is the target of scathing criticism. The ceremonies of Müntzer that Grebel abhors are either Müntzer's idea or they are derived from Luther. Wittenberg is the home of 'negligent scribes and doctors.'[118] Luther's liturgy on infant baptism [1523] is 'senseless and slanders God.'[119] Grebel plans 'to admonish [Luther] for sparing the weak, an attitude which he brought into the world without [the warrant of] Scripture.'[120]

Müntzer should defend the scriptural points of his doctrine if he falls into the hands of the duke and Luther. Luther has turned the Bible to *bubel* [knavery] and *babel* [babble].[121] Thus Grebel had read how Luther taunted Müntzer, and he reciprocates.[122] The Wittenbergers twist the Scriptures and fall from blindness

---

116 I use the term 'Swiss Brethren' to designate the Sattlerite wing of the Swiss Baptists, after it produced the *Brotherly Agreement* of Schleitheim in 1527. Prior to Schleitheim, and for those Baptists rejected by Sattler, I use the comprehensive term 'Swiss Baptists.' Historically, the title 'brethren' had already been used by Karlstadt and his 'brethren in Orlamünde.'
117 The best edition of Grebel's letters is that of Wenger, ed, *Conrad Grebel's Programmatic Letters of 1524*. Because it is more accessible, I use the edition in 'Thomas Müntzer: Schriften und Briefe,' QFRG 33 [1968], 437–47, hereafter cited as MS. For other editions of Grebel's letter see MS, 437. An English translation of Grebel's second letter is found in Siggins, *Luther*, 109–11. Minor deviations in my transcription are based on my reading of the photographic reproduction of the original manuscript found in Wenger's edition, 49–69.
118 MS, 439:34, 441:24–5. See Müntzer's comment, 238:29.
119 MS, 444:2–6. For Luther's liturgy see WA 12, 42–8.
120 MS, 445:4–6.
121 MS, 446:1–5.
122 WA 15, 211, n 3, 28–9: 'Es ist nichts mit der schrifft, Ja Bibel Bubel Babel, etc.'

into worse blindness, wanting to become papists and pope.[123] Luther has just issued a 'shameful booklet.'[124] Grebel is so proud of his admonition to Luther that he plans to send a copy to Müntzer, and it must have been sharp, because Grebel doubts whether he will receive an answer.[125] A few days earlier, when Grebel anticipates writing to Luther, he observes how, 'provoked by confidence in the divine Word, I shall perhaps call Luther to an accounting.'[126] In view of these statements it is difficult to credit Martin Brecht's argument that the Swiss Baptists were influenced by Luther in formulating their views on baptism![127]

For the emergence of the Swiss Baptists their attitude towards Zwingli and Leo Jud would be determinative. Grebel is deeply mistrustful of them. He attacks 'the papal word, and the words of the antipapal preachers.'[128] The preachers Grebel hears are deceivers who respect persons more than the truth, leading their followers 'into greater and more damaging error than has ever occurred since the beginning of the world.'[129] In all major articles the preachers spare the weak, and they follow their own inclinations and the Antichrist, whom they place above God.[130] The feelings of distrust are mutual, since the learned shepherds have rejected Grebel and his friends.[131] Grebel envisages separation, and he urges Müntzer to 'make a Christian church with the help of Christ and his rule, as we find it instituted in Matthew 18.'[132] Jud's baptismal liturgy is just as blasphemous as Luther's, and Grebel plans to write against all who pervert baptism. He also anticipates persecution, particularly from the learned.[133] The situation is tense: 'For our shepherds too, are just as furious, and they rage against us, decrying us as boys in the public pulpit and [as] Satans acting as angels of light. We too shall experience their persecution moving over us in the future. Therefore, do pray to God for us.'[134]

Intellectually Grebel has cut himself loose from Zwingli, but he does not yet move on his own; let Müntzer establish the new church. Others whom Grebel admires are Michael Stiefel, who published a few popular sermons, and Karlstadt's former student Jakob Strauss, whom Luther labelled as a follower of a 'total

---

123 MS, 446:29–32.
124 MS, 445:16–19. This alludes to Luther's *Brief an die Fürsten zu Sachsen* (WA 15, 216, n 1).
125 MS, 447:3–5.
126 TQ SCHWEIZ 1, 12: 'forsitan et Lutherum compellabo, fiducia verbi divini percitus.'
127 Brecht, 'Herkunft,' 147–65. I shall discuss this later.
128 MS, 438:20–1.
129 MS, 438:22–3.
130 MS, 439:3–6.
131 MS, 441:25–6: 'Wir sind ouch also verworfen gegen und von unseren gelerten hirten.'
132 MS, 442:15–17: 'Züch mit dem wort und mach ein Christenliche gmein mit hilf Christi und siner Regel, wie wir sy ingesetzt findend Mathei im xviii und gebrucht in den Epistlen.'
133 MS, 444:2–6.
134 MS, 446:15–18.

Karlstadtian.'[135] Fine accolades are bestowed on Karlstadt; he and Müntzer are 'the purest heralds and preachers of the purest Divine Word.'[136] Karlstadt and Müntzer are placed on equal pedestals, but this is because of Grebel's special pleading with Müntzer. In this letter there is no reason to plead with Karlstadt, and, as we shall see, Grebel's critique of Müntzer is thoroughly Karlstadtian. Grebel expresses the hope that Müntzer and Karlstadt are of one mind.[137] He implicitly holds up Karlstadt as the model for Müntzer, for, although he criticizes Müntzer, he does *not* find fault with Karlstadt. A letter has already been delivered to Karlstadt,[138] and a reply has been received, since Grebel notes that a new letter has been written by Castelberger.[139] Earlier Grebel wrote to Joachim von Watt (Vadian) that he himself is replying to Karlstadt.[140]

The two undelivered letters to Müntzer still exist, and thus they are much more impressive than the two or three letters to Karlstadt as well as Karlstadt's reply, all of which have been lost. If he had just received Müntzer's doubtless honest reply to his queries, Grebel would not have praised him as much as Karlstadt. Thus, Karlstadt's influence must be examined, but we shall first consider the impact of Müntzer.

Thomas Müntzer's influence

The editors of Müntzer's letters list five tracts that Grebel must have read,[141] but John Wenger reduces these to two.[142] We agree that Grebel refers to two booklets that induced him to write to Müntzer.[143] However, Grebel did know other writings that would not have induced him to write, but Wenger tends to belittle Müntzer's influence.[144] Actually, Grebel alludes to at least one more of Müntzer's writings when he says: 'We understand and have seen [*und han gesehen*] that you have translated the mass into German, and have established new German hymns.'[145] Wenger's translation of *gesehen* as 'noted' is tendentious,

135 MS, 441:23, 446:27. For Luther see BR 3, no. 854: '[Jakob Strauss] qui rusticum illum seditiosum [i.e. the 'Peasant from Wöhrd'] totum Carlstadiensem nobis longe praefert.'
136 MS, 441:14–15: 'und dass du mitsampt Carolostadio by unss für die reinisten usskünder und prediger dess reinisten götlichen wortes geacht sind.'
137 MS, 444:23–4: 'So du und Carolostadius einess gemütess sind, begerend wir ouch bericht werden. Wir hoffends und gloubends.'
138 MS, 444:25–6: 'Diser bott so ouch dem lieben unserem bruder Carolostadio brief gebracht hat von unss sye dir befolet.'
139 MS, 445:15: 'Der Andress Castelberg hat Carolostadio geschriben.'
140 TQ SCHWEIZ 1, 12: 'Rescribo Andreae Carolostadio.'
141 See MS, 438, n 4, 439, n 10. Bender has accepted this (*Conrad Grebel*, 110).
142 *Grebel's Letters*, ed Wenger, 10b.
143 MS, 438:3–5. These are *Getichten glawben* (MS, 217–24) and *Protestation* (MS, 225–40).
144 *Grebel's Letters*, ed Wenger, 10b.
145 MS, 439:14–15.

for Grebel had examined Müntzer's *Messe*. On behalf of his liturgy Luther appeals to 1 Corinthians 14.[146] Using the same text, Muntzer defends hymns in the preface to his mass.[147] This was, in fact, a defensive rejoinder to Karlstadt's criticism.[148] Without referring to Müntzer's *Messe*, Grebel suddenly retorts to Müntzer that 'Paul scolds the learned Corinthians for mumbling (just as if they were singing) more than he praises them.'[149] Thus Grebel must have questioned Müntzer's use of 1 Corinthians 14 in *Messe*.[150] Grebel knows Müntzer's *Messe*, but he also refers to Müntzer's German hymns, which had appeared in *Deutzsch kirchen ampt*. Nevertheless, Grebel may not have known this work, and he may have been alluding to a few hymns within the *Messe* itself, or he may have known of *Kirchen ampt* indirectly through Müntzer's defence of his previous hymns (*lobgesänge*) in the preface to the *Messe*.

It is doubtful whether Grebel knew *Kirchen ampt*, and we cannot support the conjecture of the editors of Müntzer's letters that Grebel knew the *Ordnung und berechunge*, for this contains a section on infant baptism that would have been deplored by Grebel.[151] Thus Grebel knew three, perhaps four, of Müntzer's tracts.

Müntzer's arguments on 'faked faith' (*getichten glawben*) impressed Grebel, for he notes that Müntzer's two treatises on this subject induced him to write. Müntzer had tried to attack Luther's *sola fide*, and his comments about Luther were about as fair as Luther's comments about him. Yet Grebel accepts Müntzer's criticism, which alienates him further from the Wittenberg reformers.

Grebel contrasts 'true faith' with the 'hypocritical faith' which does not bear fruit, which does not lead to trials, which is stressed at the expense of love and hope.[152] Müntzer's contrast between the 'honey-sweet Christ' and the 'bitter Christ' is echoed in Grebel's comment on the 'sinfully sweet Christ.'[153]

Grebel believes that the ancient forefathers fell away from God and Christ into unprofitable rites, a theme which also occurs in Müntzer's *Protestation*.[154] Grebel also attacks the 'learned,' as did Müntzer.[155]

146 WA 12:35–7.
147 MS, 163:1–17.
148 See below, Appendix I, 282, n 16.
149 MS, 439:16–18.
150 MS, 437:18–19.
151 MS, 214:11–215:6. Grebel knows only Müntzer's 'protestations against infant baptism' (MS, 443:34–6), and he expresses positive approval (MS, 443.1): 'Dess Touffs halb gfallt unss din schriben wol.'
152 MS, 438:15–17.
153 MS, 221–2, 441:26–7.
154 MS, 438:8–18, 225f.
155 For Grebel see MS, 441:6, 24, 443:10, 444:8, 446:6, etc. For Müntzer see e.g. MS, 223:27, 238:27–239:3.

Müntzer may well have influenced Grebel's views on persecution and martyrdom. Zwingli can characterize the Christian life as one that involves suffering and persecution, but he also adds the positive Erasmian stress on the triumphant Christian.[156] Karlstadt suggests that suffering and martyrdom are the marks of the Christian life.[157] Müntzer's view of the Christian life as one of persecution and suffering had been developed *after* Karlstadt, and Müntzer abandons it with alacrity in 1524. Nevertheless, Grebel had clearly read *Von dem getichten glawben*, including the following paragraph:

> To deliver wretched and stupid Christendom from such offensive horrors one must first of all give ear to an earnest preacher. With John the Baptist he should cry out with compassion and tears into the wilderness of the crazed and raving hearts of people. Thus they may learn the manner of God's work and become sensitive to the manifold movement of the Word of God which points to the well of salvation, the Son of God. He was a mild lamb who opened not his mouth when he was slaughtered and thus he bore the sins of the world. This he did, so we as sheep with him are to experience our [own] slaughter thoroughly, and in such suffering we should not mumble and grumble like groaning dogs, but like the sheep of his pasture that he holds up before us, granting the salt of his wisdom in suffering and nothing else.[158]

Finally, Grebel opposes infant baptism; although he does not reiterate Müntzer's arguments on this subject, they could have heightened his own feelings on this point. Karlstadt, however, had undermined the traditional interpretation of baptism by 'water and the Spirit' (John 3:5) two years before Müntzer. For Karlstadt, at that time, Scripture is the source from which flows the water of the Spirit, which he identifies with persecution. Müntzer emphasizes the independent role of the Spirit. What Grebel did with Müntzer's interpretation is not known for he merely says that he is considering it. However, Balthasar Hubmaier is close to Karlstadt when he discusses this text in his *Von der Freyhait des Willens* in 1527.[159]

---

156 Neuser, *Die reformatorische Wende*, 116–17.
157 *Ausslegung* (15), B3v. *Gewaldt* (63), B3: 'Das yst das sie alle sagen das wort gottis muss vorvolgung haben. Das reden sie von den die gotis wort leren oder lernen, und werden vorvolgt.' Cf B3v–[C4v].
158 MS, 221:23–222:5.
159 Karlstadt's passage in *Gewaldt* (63), B3v, has been discussed. Müntzer refers to John 3:5 in MS, 228:16f. Müntzer is independent in so far as he connects this text with John 7:37 (Vulg.) and stresses the Spirit. Yet, at the same time he notes that 'the knowledge of God must be attested from Holy Scripture' (MS 228:20–1). Müntzer says that John 3:5 has been misunder-

Müntzer, in effect, attacks every rite of outer baptism, and yet he practises infant baptism, showing what Gritsch considers characteristic pragmatism and nonchalance,[160] which must be contrasted with the attitude of the Baptists, including Karlstadt. Hostility towards 'the learned' is also expressed in Karlstadt's writings, and this reverberates in Müntzer. In addition, Karlstadt anticipates Grebel in linking faith with love and hope.[161]

Evidently Grebel has only recently read Müntzer, and that in a rather superficial way.[162] We have already referred to Grebel's consideration of Müntzer's interpretation of John 3:5, which reveals that the idea is new to him, and that he has not yet made up his mind. There is also Grebel's exhortation to Müntzer not to worry 'for God's sake' that he addresses him without using titles.[163] Had Grebel digested Müntzer's allusion to titles as 'shit,'[164] he would have omitted this precatory overture.

In summary, we credit Müntzer with deepening Grebel's alienation from the established reformers. He influenced Grebel's remarks on 'faked faith,' and he may well have confirmed, if not formed, Grebel's attitude towards non-resistance and martyrdom. His impact cannot be dismissed as marginal.[165]

Grebel and Karlstadt

In his letter to Müntzer Grebel summarizes the points which he considers essential, that is, strict adherence to the Word of God apart from tradition or human notions, the establishment of the rule of Christ in the church through discipline, the observance of biblical ceremonies: undiluted baptism and the Lord's Supper.[166] We add to these Grebel's defence of non-resistance. If Grebel had known Müntzer's position better, he would have dissented from him on these five major issues.

stood in the whole of Christendom. Karlstadt had made the same point with respect to Matt. 11:12 in *Gewaldt*. Müntzer probably knew this treatise for, at least through 1519, he systematically collected Luther's and Karlstadt's writings (MS, 554–60). There are no later orders extant, but that, of course, does not prove that Müntzer ceased collecting. Since Müntzer was, at first, a friend of Karlstadt, their relationship deserves further exploration. For Hubmaier see TQ 9, 383–4. Like the younger Karlstadt, he emphasizes that the living Spirit is mediated through the Word. Grebel's comment is found in MS, 445:25–6.

160 Gritsch, *Reformer*, 176.
161 *Gewaldt* (63), [A4v].
162 TQ SCHWEIZ 1, 12: 'Thomae Münzero, cuius libellum geminum de ficta fide nuper nactus legi.'
163 MS, 437:15–18.
164 MS, 238:5–6.
165 Bender, *Conrad Grebel*, 110–11. See also Bender, 'Zwickauer Propheten,' 262–78. Krajewski devotes his fifth chapter to this question (*Felix Mantz*, 48–59).
166 MS, 446:23–6: 'und wellist allein götlichs claress wort und brüch, mitsampt der regel Christi unvermischtem touff und unvermischtem nachtmal ... uffrichten und leren etc.'

Karlstadt has already urged physical non-resistance in his treatise *Gewaldt* (63), printed in July 1521. Grebel seems to have known this tract, for only *there* does Karlstadt offer an unusual argument that recurs in Grebel's letter. Grebel makes an obscure remark about Luther when he notes that Luther has tied his gospel to the duke, just 'as Aaron had to have Moses for a god.'[167] This allusion to Moses as Aaron's 'god' is rather cryptic, but it can be amplified with *Gewaldt*, where Karlstadt contrasts Aaron, the priestly type, with Moses, the prophetic type. In this comparison, discussed above, page 55, Aaron is worsted. The central argument involves Exodus 4:14–16. Karlstadt explains that the prophet Moses receives his inspiration directly from God, whereas the priest Aaron has to depend on the tradition of others.[168] Thus Grebel accuses Luther of being inspired by a worldly ruler, rather than by God. We have already twice used *Gewaldt* to show that some of Müntzer's ideas, found also in Grebel, could have come from Karlstadt.

Grebel asserts that followers of the gospel avoid protection with the physical sword.[169] The excommunicated are heathen, to be left alone, without persecution.[170] Christians are like sheep among wolves. They must be baptized with fear and suffering unto death, to be tested by fire. They do not slay their physical enemies, but they struggle with their spiritual foes.[171]

Karlstadt similarly resists at the spiritual level only. The church of the persecuted fights by means of the Word of God rather than a physical sword.[172] No Christian seizes the kingdom of God through violence, and Matthew 11:12 has all along been misinterpreted.[173] Those who seize the kingdom do not belong to the church, for they persecute it.[174] Karlstadt does exhort the church to purify itself from within, without violence but through banning and shunning, that is, holding without esteem and ignoring the existence of false brethren.[175] However, though the church shuns evildoers, it does not follow the Old Testament in killing outsiders, for *Christ* is the sword, cutting believers loose from false brethren.[176]

Grebel has given some thought to the nature of the church, but he is not yet engaged in positive reconstruction. The church contains *botten* (messengers) and

---

167 MS, 445:19–22.
168 *Gewaldt* (63), Cv–2.
169 MS, 442:27–9: 'man soll ouch dass evangelium und sine ann nemer nit schirmen mit dem schwert oder sy sich selbs, alss wir durch unseren bucher [!] vernommen hand dich also meinen und halten.'
170 MS, 442:22–6.
171 MS, 442:29–37.
172 *Gewaldt* (63), C3v.
173 Ibid, A–B.
174 Ibid, Bv–[C4v].
175 *Was bann*, (119), B3v; KS 1, 84:8–10.
176 *Was bann* (119), A2v.

gesandten (heralds) as well as *usskünder* (proclaimers). Grebel's loose usage implies that there is no rigid distinction of offices and that the functions may overlap. We have seen that Karlstadt uses the same, or similar, names for the people of God who are his messengers (*botten*). Whether Grebel knew *Malachiam* (93) and *Engeln* (123), where Karlstadt discusses his new biblical titles, is a moot point since Grebel does not explain his terms. Dependence is plausible if Karlstadt discussed the functions of his church in the letter that had already reached Grebel.

Typical of Grebel's letter and of the later Swiss Baptists is the exclusivistic appeal to Scripture. Grebel argues that one may not add to God's own ceremonies;[177] such additions are 'antichristian.' Thus hymnody and chanting must be excluded from the services.[178]

We have seen that Karlstadt stresses such an exclusivistic Scripture principle against Luther, as for example in his theses *On Celibacy* of July 1521. Anyone who adds to or subtracts from God's word is automatically excommunicated. Human additions are evil, and one may not even change a precept into a counsel or a counsel into a precept.[179] With these basic points out of the way we shall now turn in the next two sections to Grebel's beliefs concerning baptism and the Lord's Supper.

Grebel on baptism

In his *Explanation of the Sixty-Seven Articles* Zwingli refers to infants who die unbaptized, noting that it is more probable that they are saved rather than damned.[180] Several years later Zwingli notes that the Baptists first argued, on the basis of salvation by faith, that inarticulate infants were damned, but, says Zwingli, later they made an about-turn, believing that children were born in a state of innocence.[181] There is here a fascinating parallel with Karlstadt, who first taught the possibility of infant damnation in 1518; late in 1523, however, he reversed himself on the basis of Matthew 18, now stating that believing infants are innocent.[182]

Although we do not know when the Baptists in Zurich switched, or whether in 1523 Zwingli already intended to prove infants innocent, Brecht offers the plausible suggestion that the belief in the innocence of infants reveals Zwingli's influence. Brecht has written a stimulating article on the baptismal view espoused

---

177 MS, 438:8–14.
178 MS, 439:14–36.
179 BARGE 1, 477, th 5–9.
180 Z 2, 455:18–19.
181 Z 4, 315:26–32.
182 Cf LÖSCHER 2, 92–3, th 264–76 with KS 1, 19:15–17.

in Grebel's letters, which, he argues, is based on a *systematic* understanding of this subject. Bender has considered Grebel a biblicist, not a systematician, but Brecht rejoins: 'But this does not apply to the letter to Müntzer and the *Protestation* of Felix Manz.'[183] Brecht's article confirms this judgment, and he rightly probes for the historical antecedents of Grebel's and Manz's baptismal theology. Meanwhile, we also endorse Bender's judgment that Grebel was not a systematic theologian, and even Brecht concedes this when he *excepts* Grebel's letters and Manz's *Protestation* (*Appeal*). This renders the problem of Grebel's (and Manz's) viewpoint especially acute, for when a biblicist suddenly becomes systematic, one must consider dependence before one accepts a temporary aberration, based on the highly improbable assumption that an able systematician did not apply his knowledge most of the time. Brecht resolves the problem of dependence with his conclusion that both Luther and Zwingli influenced Grebel, who nevertheless arrives at his own construction. He briefly considers Karlstadt:

Naturally [*Selbstverständlich*] there is common property in the rejection of infant baptism and in the placement of faith before the reception of baptism. To the proper reception of baptism belongs, for both Karlstadt and the Zurich [Baptists], repentance, the leaving of the old and the taking on of the new life. However, Karlstadt also emphasizes that the water bath is an external thing or sign, and is no more than water. At any rate Grebel was aware that neither Müntzer nor Karlstadt had developed an extensive theology of baptism.[184]

When Brecht observes that Grebel knows that Karlstadt and Müntzer had not developed an extensive theology of baptism, he misinterprets Grebel. Grebel claims that Müntzer and Karlstadt had not *written* (we assume this means published)[185] enough against infant baptism and its practices,[186] but Grebel does not imply that their theological understanding of baptism is incomplete or deficient.

Grebel rightly notes that Karlstadt did not publish a single treatise that integrates his scattered observations on baptism, but this does not prove that Karlstadt lacked an extensive baptismal theology. Karlstadt's statements on baptism embrace virtually everything written by Grebel and Manz on the subject. The lack of a baptismal treatise by Karlstadt was caused by obstacles in the way of publication; for example, within a month after Grebel wrote to Müntzer, Felix

183 Brecht, 'Herkunft,' 154. For Bender see Brecht's reference, ibid, 148, n 5.
184 Ibid, 151.
185 See Grebel's parallel usage of 'schriben' for 'publication' (MS, 443:1–2).
186 MS, 443:38f.

Manz failed to have Karlstadt's baptismal dialogue published in Basel.[187] Thus Karlstadt inserts what may seem to be merely occasional remarks on baptism in his treatises, but together they reveal a systematic wrestling with the major issues.

Brecht notes that Grebel had consulted other views on baptism, and thus his examination of Luther's influence gains credence, but Brecht skips the one 'senseless and blasphemous' (unsinnig gotzlesterich) baptismal liturgy of Luther that Grebel claimed to have read.[188] Grebel also alludes to the writings 'by some [etliche] who have treated [baptism] even more shamefully.'[189] Thus Grebel himself reveals that the other writings which he had read were even worse. In fact, it is the differences between Luther's baptismal views in 1523 and those of Grebel in 1524 which are interesting. Even the point where, in Brecht's view, Grebel is most dependent on Luther may be better understood with reference to Karlstadt. Brecht excludes Karlstadt's influence on Grebel's conception of the baptismal sign because Karlstadt can separate the external act from what it represents. Brecht bases his whole argument for Luther's influence on Grebel on the integration between sign (signum) and thing (res) which he considers peculiar to Luther and Grebel. However, a true integration of sign and thing occurs only in an ex opere operato doctrine that is not balanced by an ex opere operantis view – a view that was rejected by most of the Schoolmen and all of the reformers. Brecht rightly claims that Luther is more successful than the other reformers in integrating sign and thing, but this is because of Luther's partial acceptance of ex opere operato, in the sense that the baptismal sign of itself strengthens faith, and so on. Yet this is precisely the point that Grebel contests.[190] Any other integration without inherent power in the sign, whether based on faith or God's command, etc, must remain coincidental.

Now let us return to Karlstadt. Brecht slights Karlstadt's influence on Grebel because Karlstadt can treat even the baptismal sign as a 'water bath.' Nevertheless, Grebel also refuses to confer any inherent power on 'the water': 'Thus the water does not confirm and increase faith – as the learned in Wittenberg say – and how it comforts very strongly, and is supposed to be the ultimate comfort on one's deathbed.'[191] Here Grebel clearly adheres to Karlstadt, disdaining the view of Melanchthon who, in his Loci communes, declares that the baptismal sign increases faith and gives refuge to the dying.[192] Since Grebel does not mention Melanchthon, his criticism may not even be original.

187 See below, Appendix II, 290–4.
188 MS, 444:3–5.
189 MS, 444:5–6.
190 MS, 443:9–11.
191 MS, 443:9–11: 'also dass dass wasser den glouben nit befeste und mere, wie die glerten zu Wittemberg sagend, und wie er ser fast tröste, und die letst zuflucht in dem todbett sye.'
192 See Karlstadt in Messe (71), C3: 'Nit das [sie] mogten krefftiger und grossers glaubens machen. Sondern unsserm unglauben tzu neid und hass, gibt uns got seine tzeichen.' This is a criticism of Melanchthon, CR 21, 212:11–22.

Brecht maintains that it is 'self-evident' (*selbstverständlich*) for Grebel and Karlstadt to stress faith *before* the baptism of dying and rising with Christ, but when Brecht notes that both Grebel and Luther refer to baptismal dying and rising, this is not 'self-evident,' for he assumes Grebel's dependence.[193] Karlstadt must be taken more seriously if one wishes to place Grebel's views in their natural context. In Zurich there were already some who refused to have their infants baptized, but this action had been anticipated at least six months earlier in Orlamünde. Thus a systematic comparison between Grebel's and Karlstadt's views on baptism is needed.

Grebel discusses two 'rites' (*brüch*) in the church: baptism and the Lord's Supper. His conception is legalistic. One must insist on 'proper Christian rites' (*rechte Christenliche brüch*), 'God's rites' (*brüch gottes*), and 'divine rites' (*götliche brüch*).[194] There is no freedom to move beyond Scripture: additions make the rite 'antichristian.'[195] Grebel exhorts Müntzer 'to act in everything only according to the Word and to advance and establish the rites of the apostles with the Word.'[196] Although Grebel uses the word 'rite' (*brüch*) to describe baptism and the Supper, this is not a technical term. Grebel prohibits unbiblical terms: terms such as 'sacraments, mass, signs' indicate the 'old antichristian rites.'[197]

Since the wrong rites are antichristian, and since the proper rites are unessential for salvation, Grebel counsels abstention from improper rites, which are to be denounced in preaching that does not spare the weak.[198] Grebel applies this admonition specifically to the Lord's Supper, but it is just as applicable to baptism. In Zurich the traditional additions to the baptismal water were optional (Leo Jud, 1523). Clearly, one was not hedged in by explicit biblical direction, and this is even truer of Luther's ceremonies, observed by all to spare the weak. Grebel does not spare the weak.

What Grebel says about the rites reflects Karlstadt's viewpoint. Karlstadt claims he follows Paul in opposing the weak.[199] Even minor additions to the biblical commands are 'a great sin.'[200] Karlstadt exclaims:

> And I want it said to the world, that the devil introduced no greater hidden damage into Christendom than you have introduced through the papistic sacrament! You should prefer to learn from Paul that neither with

193 Brecht, 'Herkunft,' 158–9.
194 MS, 438:17, 32, 439:10.
195 MS, 438:17–20.
196 MS, 440:38–441:1.
197 MS, 444:8–10.
198 MS, 440:36–441:10.
199 KS 1, 20–3.
200 KS 2, 37:39–40.

baptism nor with the bread should we act differently from what God has commanded.[201]

Karlstadt has already spurned the word 'sacrament' as unbiblical.[202] In *Messen* (131) he renounces the word 'mass.' The term 'eucharist' he also deems inappropriate.[203] Where evil practices interfere with proper observance, Karlstadt also counsels abstention.[204]

Only once does Grebel deviate from Karlstadt, who does not object to the word 'sign,' provided it is understood properly.[205] Yet, Brecht notes, despite Grebel's verbal objection his baptismal theology implies the presence of a sign.[206] Thus when Grebel extrapolates a Zwinglian element,[207] he becomes inconsistent, which is surely another indication of his dependence elsewhere.

As we have seen in his remarks about the 'water,' Grebel does not bond the sign to the significance of baptism. When Grebel discusses the fundamentals for salvation that are ignored by the 'evangelical preachers,' he slashes at their 'faked faith without the fruits of faith, without the baptism of trial and testing, without love and hope, without proper Christian rites.'[208]

The 'baptism of trial and testing' is mentioned apart from the 'rites,' or, to continue a more accurate usage, but one foreign to Grebel, the 'signs.' Karlstadt has separated 'the baptism of tribulation' from the external rite by citing Mark 10:38, where the future baptism of Christ refers to suffering. This is unrelated to the baptism of John, which Jesus had already accepted in the River Jordan.[209] Against Zwingli, Balthasar Hubmaier would similarly distinguish between the baptisms of John and Jesus.[210]

201 *Leyb* (129), Dv, D2.
202 KS 2, 10:32–6. Independently Zwingli has criticized the traditional connotations of the word 'sacrament,' but he continues its usage in the sense of 'sign' (z 2, 120:23–122:10).
203 *Christus* (124), [A4].
204 Ibid, A3v; KS 2, 33:2–5.
205 KS 2, 11:22–5.
206 Brecht, 'Herkunft,' 155f.
207 Zwingli emphasizes 'bruch und übung' in the sacrament (z 2, 150:16–22). See also the title of his later tract *Action oder Bruch des Nachtmals* (z 4, 13–24). Thus Grebel is in a sense dependent on Zwingli here, but, unlike Grebel, Zwingli continued to use the word 'sign.'
208 MS, 438:15–17.
209 *Leyb* (129), C–v: 'Demnach müssen die gegenwertige wort als zükünfftige verstanden werden. Ein ander exempel von Christo. Christus spricht zu den kindern Zebedei, "Ir werdet mit der tauff getaufft werden mit welcher ich getaufft." Matth. 20. Mar. 10. Das aber redet Christus nicht von der tauff welche er von Joanne zuvor in dem Jordan entpfangen hett, sonder von seinem leyden, dar in Christus noch künfftiglich solt getaufft werden, und redet dannest von solcher tauff durch ein wort das einen gegenwertigen tauff bedeütet, nemlich baptizor.'
210 Steinmetz, 'The Baptism of John and the Baptism of Jesus,' esp 173–80.

Like Karlstadt, Grebel can divorce the baptism of tribulation from the rites and yet proclaim the need for rites. Thus, signs (rites, brüch) are ideally integrated with the experience. Brecht rightly takes this attempted integration of sign and significance to mean that Grebel was not a spiritualist.[211] Neither was Karlstadt a spiritualist, and his fierce battle with Luther over baptism and the Lord's Supper is foreign to spiritualism. Nevertheless, the sign does not channel God's grace; it is inferior to what it represents: 'The external acts are merely signs between God and man, and they signify that God alone makes a man holy, and not our works, and what is signified through the external [sign] is true for both angels and men.'[212]

For Karlstadt the significance is internal and eternal, whereas the temporary outward sign may or may not be an expression of what it ideally represents. Sign and significance are related for the believer. One can, if need be, abstain from the outward sign; but the reality which it signifies is essential for salvation.

Grebel likewise lays stress on the significance, not the sign. The water of baptism does not add to faith, nor does it confer salvation.[213] Inward baptism is the saving reality.[214] Because Luther ascribes some positive power to the sacrament of holy baptism and considers it essential in all but the most extreme circumstances, he has integrated sign and significance more successfully than either Grebel or Karlstadt. However, Grebel and Karlstadt press for an integration of outward and inward baptism at the level of its New Testament meaning which refers to adult life. There Luther and the other magisterial reformers fail, because they cling to infant baptism.

Since faith becomes the crux of integration between sign and significance, we now consider Grebel's conception of faith. Unlike Luther, Grebel ignores infant faith (fides infantium) or the godparents' substitute faith (fides aliena). Children have no faith; besides they are not liable.[215] Faith is required of those who have gained 'discernment' between good and evil.[216] Then comes the call to repent and believe with the offer of God's grace, but some resist God's Word and movement.[217]

True faith may not be divorced from its fruits like the 'baptism of trial and testing,' love, hope, and 'proper Christian rites.'[218] Those rites are secondary to the fruit of trials, love, and hope, for later Grebel speaks of 'true faith' and 'rites.'[219]

211 Brecht, 'Herkunft,' 160.
212 KS 1, 25:31–5.
213 MS, 443:9–15.
214 MS, 443:8–9.
215 MS, 443:15–27.
216 Note the restriction (MS, 443:17–18).
217 MS, 442:22–3.
218 MS 138:15–19 (double negative eliminated).
219 MS, 438:31–2.

Grebel keeps up a similar scheme when he refers to 'faith, walking in virtues, rites.'[220] Once he joins 'faith and love,' and thus a special relationship seems to obtain between them.[221] Grebel's references to faith are skeletal, but they are consistent with Karlstadt's view of faith.

In *Gelaub* (139) Karlstadt asserts that true faith (or true unbelief) does not exist in the stage of confusion, known as the 'intermediate state,' when one is neither damned nor saved.[222] Trial and persecution (that is the baptism of tribulation) determine whether one responds with true faith. For Karlstadt such faith flows from God; it is a 'love-filled discernment (*erkantnüs*) of God, and it is called the knowledge (*kunst*) and the revelation of God.'[223] Grebel uses *unterscheid*, rather than *erkantnüs*, but both terms mean 'discernment.'[224] Karlstadt connects true discernment with a 'love-filled faith,' and we have seen that Grebel also links faith and love on one occasion.

True faith or true unbelief arises freely at the time of discernment, for Grebel refers to an unbeliever who 'resists God's Word and action.'[225] In an anti-predestinarian theology God's grace is resistible, and Karlstadt holds that the elect 'want to accept God's justice' whereas the damned reject it.[226] With faith based on a conscious and free decision, the question of means must now be considered. For Luther there is only one way: faith comes through hearing (*fides ex auditu*). According to Grebel, God moves through his Word but also through direct action (*hendlen*). On the basis of Genesis 1 Karlstadt speaks of God's Spirit which moves over, agitates, stirs, (*schweben, bewegen, rühren*) the waters of the soul. Then one chooses to accept or resist this movement, which occurs directly through the movement of the Spirit, and indirectly through God's Word.[227] Although Karlstadt first discusses the Spirit's movement, he then describes the process in terms of God's Word: 'God's Word has not vainly been compared to many things which move all men, who are touched by it. ... It reveals the thoughts of one who hears it, and it touches the heart so it is upset, and [the Word] casts many upon their faces.'[228] Consequently Word and Spirit are in harmony. As with Grebel, faith arises in turmoil produced by God's direct action and the Word. Although they do not use this terminology, Grebel's and Karlstadt's faith comes from hearing and

220 MS, 441:9.
221 MS, 442:18.
222 *Gelaub* (139), B2v.
223 Ibid, C2.
224 The use of different terms does not need to indicate differences of substance. Grebel wrote in Swiss German, Karlstadt in High German.
225 MS, 442:22.
226 *Gelaub* (139), D3v.
227 Ibid, D3v.
228 Ibid, B4.

the spirit (*ex auditu et spiritu*). Moreover, Grebel's fruits of faith have already been discussed by Karlstadt: 'Behold, the apostle John [ch 3] teaches us that faith and love keep God's commandments, and [John] shows that through the keeping of God's commandments, we are to understand faith and love, just as we discern a tree by its fruits.'[229]

This still leaves us with Karlstadt's references to faith arising out of tribulation, whereas Grebel treats tribulation as one of the fruits of faith. However, Grebel sometimes places repentance before faith,[230] and Karlstadt also knows of a faith which is tested in the storms of God's judgments, in the midst of which it stands like 'a firm mountain of iron' (*ein fester stehelin berg*).[231] Finally, the Pauline conjunction of 'faith, hope, and love,' which must have induced Grebel to place hope among the fruits of faith, had been taught by Karlstadt several years earlier.[232]

Grebel has accepted Karlstadt's, not Luther's, conception of sign and faith. However, Brecht argues that Grebel integrates sign and significance through faith in a way which reminds one of Luther's baptismal tract of 1519.[233] We cite the appropriate passage in Grebel:

For us Scripture describes baptism which, through faith and the blood of Christ, signifies to one who has been baptized and who believes before and afterwards the change of heart [*gmüt*] and the fact that the sins have been washed away. It signifies that one has died and must die to sin and walk in newness of life and spirit, and that one will certainly be saved by the inner baptism, the faith, if one lives according to its significance [*bedütnis*] in such a way that water does not confirm and increase faith, as the learned in Wittenberg say.[234]

Brecht shows clearly that in the latter part of 1519 Luther uses faith to integrate meaning and sign in baptism. In January 1519 Karlstadt, in harmony with Luther,

229 ks 1, 53:5–9: 'Sihe der Apostel Johannes leret uns das glaube und liebe gottes gebott halten, und zyget das wir auss volbringung götlicher gebotten verstehn sollen, glauben und liebe, als wir einen baum auss seinen früchten erkennen.'
230 ms, 442:22.
231 *Gelaub* (139), A3v.
232 *Gewaldt* (63), [A4v].
233 Brecht, 'Herkunft,' 156–9.
234 ms, 443:4–10: 'Den touff beschribt unss die gschrift, dass er bedütte durch den glouben und dass blut Christi (dem getoufften dass gmüt enderendem und dem gloubenden vor und nach) die sünd abgewäschen sin; dass er bedütte, dass man abgstorben sie und sölle der sünd und wandlen in nüwe dess läbens und geist, und dass man gwüss selig werd, so man durch den inneren touff den glouben nach der bedütnuss läbe, also dass dass wasser den glouben nit befeste und mere wie die glerten zu Wittenberg sagend.'

upholds justification by faith: 'Faith is not of ourselves, it is the gift of God. By faith Christ dwells in the heart of the interior man. Therefore we are justified through faith; we live by faith.'[235] Nevertheless, Karlstadt's view of justification involves more than a divine declaration, for it embraces mortification, perdition, and dying and rising with Christ, in correspondence with Christ's life. Karlstadt also connects the meaning of baptism (that is the imitation of Christ in one's life) to the baptismal rite:

Indeed, the Christian life must be fashioned after the deeds of Christ and whatever Christ has done on the cross, in his burial, resurrection, and ascension, should be related to the life of one who is justified. Just as Christ has been crucified, so it is necessary to affix the old man with the sinful inclinations [concupiscentiis] to the cross, and in the same way that Christ has been buried, so a Christian man is buried with him through baptism in death [Rom. 6].[236]

Thus, already in 1519 Karlstadt bases justification on faith, but justification itself embraces the meaning and reality of baptism. In other words, what can be called sanctification based on faith integrates the baptismal rite. Thus Grebel may have derived the idea of faith linking the act and meaning of baptism from Karlstadt as well as from Luther. Unlike Luther in 1519, however, Grebel speaks, not only of the subjective precondition of faith, but also of the objective integrating power of Christ's blood-baptism. We have seen earlier that Karlstadt has linked faith to the blood-baptism of Christ to establish the salvation of infants.[237]

In the quotation from Grebel faith is not conditioned by outward baptism; faith must be present before and after the rite. Karlstadt argues that one must have certainty *before* participating in the Lord's Supper, for the 'sacrament' is not a pledge.[238] Although he does not apply this argument to baptism, he offers in this context another argument that involves baptism as well as the Lord's Supper. For Karlstadt *Christ* is the believer's certainty, and whoever derives assurance from the 'sacrament' steals from Christ. He is a thief and robber who does not enter through Christ, the only door.[239]

---

235 *Iustificatione* (13), [A4–v].
236 Ibid, A3: 'Nempe, vita Christiana gestis Christi configuratur, et quicquid Christus in cruce, morte, sepultura, resurrectione, ascensione ad coelum egit, iustificati vita referre debent. Nimirum, quemadmodum Christus crucifixus est, ita hominem veterem cum concupiscentiis cruci oportet adfigi, et quemadmodum Christus sepultus est, ita homo Christianus consepelitur illi per baptismum in mortem. R. vi.'
237 WA 6, 26, th 8; Gerdes, ed, *Scrinium*, 326, ep 35.
238 *Missbrauch* (135), Cv.
239 Ibid, C2–3.

Karlstadt and Grebel share other deviations from Luther. Brecht notes Grebel's emphasis on dying and rising with Christ. It is human decision that requires moral transformation rather than a promise, as in Luther, that is central. Brecht states: '[Grebel] understands baptism more punctually.'[240] In discussing the Lord's Supper Karlstadt is also impatient with Luther's concept of 'promise':

What Christ, with futuristic words, mentions to the disciples as a promise, namely that Christ was to give his body for us, that the apostles proclaim as something which has been accomplished, as a fulfilled promise [Acts 13:32–3]. Moreover, the new and crafty papists have, in this matter, gone way out of bounds, when they speak every day about this promise.[241]

Thus both Grebel and Karlstadt accentuate the fulfilment rather than the promise. Finally, Brecht points out that the concept of inner and outer baptism in Luther is also found in Grebel.[242] Yet the connection is tenuous, for Luther refers only once to 'spiritual' baptism, whereas Karlstadt uses the phrase 'inner and outer baptism' as Grebel does.[243]

Grebel devotes one sentence to the subject of baptism and discipline, which, he admits, is not original with him: 'We have received a message, that even an adult must not be baptized without the rule of Christ regarding binding and loosing.'[244]

This single sentence does not reveal much, but Brecht is right in suggesting that the person to be baptized accepts brotherly discipline according to Matthew 18 as part of his baptismal obligation.[245] Karlstadt considers discipline a prerequisite for the Lord's Supper in his sermon of Christmas 1521. Confession before communion is useless; its neglect cannot bar anyone from participation. Only God's discipline as found in 1 Corinthians 5 and Matthew 18 is pertinent.[246]

Discipline is newly scrutinized in Karlstadt's treatise of January 1524, On Shunning (119). Since we have already seen how baptism ultimately absorbs characteristics earlier associated with the Lord's Supper, it is probable that Karlstadt had written to Grebel about the requirement of church discipline before baptism and the Supper.

240 Brecht, 'Herkunft,' 158.
241 Leyb (129), [A4], B3.
242 Brecht, 'Herkunft,' 160, n 83. Cf MS, 443:8–9.
243 Coelibatu (62), C.
244 MS, 443:2–3: 'wir werdend bericht dass man on die regel Christi dess bindens und entbindens ouch ein erwachsner nit gtoufft solte werden.'
245 Brecht, 'Herkunft,' 153.
246 Emphahung (76), Bv.

When one considers these correspondences between Karlstadt's and Grebel's baptismal theology, and the fact that Karlstadt's views can be documented only by means of more writings than Grebel would probably have possessed, Grebel's references to baptism must have been based on the now-lost letter from Karlstadt. In his earlier letter Grebel must have asked Karlstadt to explain his view of baptism, and this must have provoked an extensive reply. Grebel's reference to a message he received (*wir werdend bericht*)[247] should now be taken as an allusion to Karlstadt's letter.

My interpretation of the Karlstadtian nature of Grebel's theology is confirmed by one source. When Grebel wrote to Müntzer, he also wrote to Luther. Luther left the chore of replying to a Swiss student in Wittenberg, Erhart Hegenwald, whose letter has been preserved. Harold Bender has this to say about Hegenwald's response:

> It is clear from Hegenwalt's letter that he reckons the Grebel group with Carlstadt, for four times he refers to a new booklet which Luther was writing against Carlstadt, and which was soon to be published [*Heavenly Prophets*]. He [Hegenwalt] says in fact, at the close, that they will probably find in this booklet Luther's answer to their own letter.[248]

Only Luther would have authorized Hegenwald to write a reply, and only he could have told Hegenwald about his own still unprinted answer to Karlstadt in *Heavenly Prophets*. Thus, when Luther read Grebel's letter, he saw the author as a disciple of Karlstadt.

Grebel on the Lord's Supper

The parallels between Karlstadt's and Grebel's interpretation of the Lord's Supper appear to go back to Karlstadt's earlier writings. Therefore, it seems likely that Karlstadt's reply to Grebel had baptism as its main topic. This makes sense, since Castelberger and Grebel must have found Karlstadt's earlier works congenial; otherwise they would scarcely have written him in the summer of 1524. Since Karlstadt had been able to publish his views on the Lord's Supper, his baptismal stance would have elicited more curiosity. Grebel even mentioned to Müntzer that he felt the need for publications on baptism.

Grebel's view that the Supper is a supper of unity, not of consecration, is influenced by Zwingli.[249] Grebel's demand for ordinary bread could reflect Karl-

---

247 MS, 443:2.
248 Bender, *Conrad Grebel*, 109.
249 MS, 439:37, 440:3. Brecht has noted this link between Grebel and Zwingli ('Herkunft,' 149).

stadt's exclusivistic scriptural principle and his claim that Christ used common bread.[250] Karlstadt had recently attacked Christ's image on 'the idol bread' of the oblations.[251] The references to 'the love meal' may be peculiar to Grebel,[252] as is the demand for frequent observance.[253] The use of ordinary vessels[254] had been implied by Karlstadt. It is consistent with his reversion to apostolic practice and his scornful references to 'silver and golden monstrances.'[255]

Grebel also discusses whether the Supper should always be celebrated as a *supper*, but he does not fix a specific time.[256] Long before Grebel, Karlstadt had protected the more perfect (*perfectiores*) from the imperfect (*imperfectis*) who disapproved of the eating of the Supper 'at supper-time or after other foods.'[257] Thus Karlstadt did not insist on a supper either, but he did consider it 'more perfect' to reject fasting. Grebel could not have known this from Karlstadt's writings, for the argument occurred in Karlstadt's *Reply to Emser*, which had been confiscated by the Wittenberg censors. Karlstadt also conceded that there were accidental events, such as the fact that only thirteen ate at the original Supper.[258]

Grebel's main arguments are reminiscent of Karlstadt's early views on the nature of the Lord's Supper. He reiterates Karlstadt's statement that the bread remains bread, but 'in faith' it is to the communicant the body of Christ.[259] Both also hold bread and wine to signify the already accomplished incorporation of believers in the body of Christ.[260]

250 *Messe* (71), [A4]: 'Dan Christus nam naturlich und gemein brot in seine hende.'
251 KS 2, 46:14–20.
252 MS, 440:9, 11, 16. However, Karlstadt calls the Lord's Supper a meal, based on 'intense love and remembrance': 'und darnach zu essen (auss grosser lieb und gedechtnüss) des hern brodt' (KS 2, 28:15–16).
253 MS, 440:27–8: 'Ess solt offt und fil gebrucht werden.'
254 MS, 440:5: 'Ess sol ouch ein gmein trinckgschirr sin.'
255 KS 2, 16:8–9, 30:37.
256 MS, 440:33–5. Grebel first raises this issue in 1523. See Yoder, *Täufertum*, 24–5.
257 BARGE 2, 563–4. Did a Wittenberg student take the argument back to Zurich? Or is this a genuine parallel development? But why then do such parallels surface in Zurich *after* they develop in Wittenberg?
258 BARGE 1, 489, th 106.
259 MS, 440:7–8: 'die wil dass brott nüt anderss ist dann brot, *im glouben, der lib Christi* und ein inlibung mit Christo und den brüderen.' Cf BARGE 1, 485, th 34: 'Ita hoc thema, Panis est corpus, verum esse contendo, quia credo extrema eadem.'
260 MS, 440:13–14: 'solt ess unss antzeigen dass wir warlich ein brott und lib und ware brüder mitt einander werind und sin weltind etc.' Cf *Anbettung* (68), B2v–3: 'Demnach spricht Paulus auch, "Wir seind alle ein brot, die von eynem brott essen" [1 Cor. 10:17], allso ist uns der herr genent, oder tzu eynem namen, das wir ein brott, ein leyb, ein Christlicher hauff seind. Darauss volget, weil Christus ein zeichen ist [Matt. 24:30], das auch brott und wein tzwey tzeychen woll mogen genent werden, und das die sso tzeychen brauchen und genissen yhre name erlangen, mogen brot genant werden.'

Grebel and Karlstadt agree that the outward sign may distract one from the inner meaning.[261] Opposing Luther, both apply the passage on the 'heavenly bread' in John 6 to the Supper.[262] Both regard the Supper as a joyous celebration.[263] As Karlstadt had done in 1521, Grebel wants the administrator of the Supper to wear ordinary clothing.[264] The bread must not be displayed in 'temples.'[265] It is not to be administered outside of Christ's rule of 'binding and loosing' (Matthew 18).[266] We have seen that Karlstadt discussed this rule as the substitute for the traditional requirement of confession in one of his earliest treatises on the Supper.[267]

Grebel argues against private celebration.[268] In harmony with Luther, Karlstadt had opposed private celebration too, but then he conceded it on one occasion so that laity or clergy could observe the Supper in the form established by Christ.[269] That issue becomes obsolete when Karlstadt introduces what he considers the apostolic norm in Orlamünde. Grebel's reference to the meal of the Spirit and love also has its antecedents in Karlstadt, who contrasts the meal of Christ's Spirit with the fleshly meal of the Mass, calling it a meal of 'powerful *love*, unity, peace and hearty fellowship.'[270]

With minor shifts in emphasis, which are not contradictory, Grebel shares Karlstadt's view of the Lord's Supper. The systematic approach is consistent with Grebel's view of baptism, even with respect to the attempted integration of *signum* and *res* at an objective as well as a subjective level. The evident symmetry reveals a systematic perspective.

Hymnody

Grebel – unlike the later Baptists – condemns hymnody. The church did not sing in New Testament times. Chanting in Latin is also objectionable and translation

---

261 MS, 440:5–11. *Anbettung* (68), B3: 'Nun soll auch niemant anfencklich und endlich in dem brott und wein, mit anbetten oder glauben fuessen, dan sie seind jhe creaturen.'

262 MS, 440:8–10, 441:4–5. Cf BARGE 1, 486, th 48, where Karlstadt applies John 6 in opposition to Luther. See also *Messe* (71), C2v–3. After arguing that the signs do not justify as such, Karlstadt cites John 6:64: 'Caro nihil prodest.'

263 MS, 440:12: 'sol ess mit freud genomen werden.' Cf *Empfahern* (54), A2–v, and [C5v]: the sacrament is *freudenreich*.

264 MS, 440:32: 'on pfäffische kleidung und messgewand.'

265 MS, 440:25–6: 'Ess sol ouch nit gebrucht werden in templen.' Cf *Coelibatu* (61), [E2], th 1–4.

266 MS, 440:28.

267 *Emphahung* (76), B3v–4.

268 MS, 440:20–5.

269 *Coelibatu* (61), [E2], th 3, argues against private participation. For the concession see BARGE 1, 489.

270 MS, 440: 8–9. Cf *Messe* (71), C2v–3; *Leyb* (129), D3v.

cannot change this. True singing comes from the heart, not from the mouth. Christ did not command singing; therefore it has been prohibited. Poor singers are unhappy; good singers are proud.[271]

Some of Grebel's arguments recall Zwingli, and, as Garside has shown, Zwingli had drawn upon Karlstadt's theses to arrive at his own position. Karlstadt had been tempted to forbid singing.[272] He also used the argument that good singers become proud and poor singers vexed.[273] Again, if singing is inevitable, Karlstadt prefers singing in unison in the native tongue.[274] He condemns choirs and polyphonic chanting.

As it was, later Baptists were somewhat closer to Karlstadt than to Grebel in the matter of hymnody. However, both Grebel and Karlstadt would have accused their spiritual descendants of ignoring the fundamental Baptist principle of exclusive adherence to Scripture. Baptist hymns were not even limited to versified scriptural passages, but it is understandable that the Baptists wanted to recall their own martyrs in hymns, despite the inconsistency in doing so.

Felix Manz and Karlstadt

Karlstadt's *Von dem Tauff*

Grebel's correspondence reveals that he and Castelberger had written to Karlstadt in the summer of 1524. Their letters must have reached Orlamünde when Karlstadt's expulsion seemed imminent. Gerhard Westerburg, Karlstadt's brother-in-law, had been present at Jena in August when Luther, at the Inn of the Black Bear, challenged Karlstadt to write against him. Thus, Westerburg was sent to Zurich, where he arrived early in October. For six days Westerburg read to the Zurich radicals seven of Karlstadt's works, namely *Christus* (124), *Dialogus* (126), *Leyb* (129), *Messen* (131), *Missbrauch* (135), and *Gemach* (135), as well as the baptismal dialogue *Von dem Tauff*.[275]

The Zurich radicals were so closely attuned to Karlstadt that they raised most of the money needed to have the treatises printed. When Westerburg left Zurich, he was accompanied by the bookseller Andreas Castelberger and Felix Manz, a fervent Karlstadtian who, for his Baptist convictions, was to be executed by drowning in January 1527. Westerburg, Castelberger, and Manz rode on horseback to Basel, where they stayed with Lorenz Hochrütiner, who had been driven from Zurich on 23 November 1523 for having smashed a crucifix. Manz and

271 MS, 439:14–36.
272 *33 Concl.*, th 25.
273 BARGE 1, th 9–10.
274 Ibid, th 36, 53.
275 See below, Appendix II, 290–4.

Westerburg now persuaded Johannes Bebel and Thomas Wolf to print Karlstadt's seven treatises. This happened in late October or early November 1524. Karlstadt joined them secretly, but he and Westerburg left Basel before the printing was accomplished.

According to the printers, Westerburg arrived in Basel in early August[276] and the treatises were printed before mid-August, but a motive for perjury by the printers is evident. By claiming that they had printed Karlstadt's works to be sold at the Frankfurt Fair, which opened on 15 August, the printers could call Westerburg an 'evil schemer,' thus deflecting responsibility for the distribution of Karlstadt's booklets in the Swiss Confederacy. But the evidence shows that the presence of Westerburg in Basel, early in August, is impossible. Since Westerburg was present in Jena on 22 August during the debate between Karlstadt and Luther,[277] he could not have been in Basel in early August and have attended the Frankfurt Fair later in August. Moreover, none of the reformers knew of Karlstadt's new publications until November.

Barge claims that all the Basel treatises were written after Luther challenged Karlstadt to write against him openly during their bout in Jena,[278] but circumstances militate against this supposition. After settling his own affairs Karlstadt was driven out of Orlamünde towards the end of September. Subsequently Karlstadt, with his family, visited Heidelberg and then Strassburg early in October. The printers in Basel mention Karlstadt's presence there towards the end of October. Travel itself would have consumed most of Karlstadt's time during this period.

Barge argues that Luther was unaware of Karlstadt's polemical works when the two combatants tilted in Jena: 'The fact that Karlstadt published his treatises on the Lord's Supper only during his exile is an important corrective to the customary psychological judgment – not only of Karlstadt, but also of Luther.'[279] But this does not mean that the manuscripts had not yet been written. There is ample internal evidence which shows that, although the publications appeared after the two combatants tilted in Jena, they were actually composed during more peaceful times in Orlamünde.

The *Dialogus*, which often disguises attacks on Luther as clashes with the 'papists,' is the most humorous work Karlstadt ever published. But in September his mood must have been grim: he had been exiled from Saxony with his pregnant wife and eldest son, and his second son, Andreas III, had died in the previous month. In *Gemach* (138) Karlstadt discusses 'some changes which have happened here'[280] – 'here' alludes to Orlamünde. He also says that he is 'without a care'

---

276 See below, Appendix II, 290, n 2.
277 WA 15, 341:1: 'Es was auch do bey doctor Gerhart Westerburg vonn Cöln.'
278 FB, 325; BARGE 2, 126, n 88.
279 BARGE 2, 152, n 9.
280 KS 1, 74:10–11.

(*unbekommert*) in the defence of the truth.[281] Again, he obliquely dissents from Luther by belittling a non-existent *concilium* of the church.[282] Karlstadt also mentions how Moses covenanted with God *and the people*,[283] which, after Karlstadt's reply to Müntzer in July, is inconceivable without a disclaimer regarding covenants made with men.[284] One also doubts whether Karlstadt would have charged the high princes (*grossen fürsten*) with ravenous violence (*wüterey*)[285] after he became alarmed at Müntzer's league.

Karlstadt's arguments about capitalization and punctuation in the Greek and Latin were directed at the people of Orlamünde as a shortcut defence of what he accepted on exegetical grounds but could not disclose to a lay audience. Karlstadt would never have told Luther that 'A big letter *Hoc* means the beginning of a sentence.'[286]

Messen (131), which is a copy of a letter (!), contains the offer: 'If you are not content, write me your objections, for I am willing to serve you.'[287] This presumes a stable situation in which Karlstadt can be reached without difficulty. Karlstadt's expulsion from Saxony goes unmentioned in any of the Basel publications, except for *Leyb* (129), but even the bulk of *Leyb* would have been written earlier. There Karlstadt illustrates Luther's intolerance with reference to the Waldensians.[288] Karlstadt's exile is mentioned only in the *Beschluss*,[289] which was added after Karlstadt finished the original treatise with the 'Amen' that appears just above the *Beschluss* heading.

Even Barge may have known that the Basel publications had taken more than a month to be written. The most moderate booklets are listed first in his bibliography and, with one exception, Barge's sequence is reasonable. Towards the end of the *Dialogus* Karlstadt lists the titles of some of his other works, but this does not establish precedence. Just as in *Leyb*, there is a clear break here, with an appendix after the 'Amen' ending of the original composition.[290] Thus, Barge's sequence should be amended in the case of *Gemach* (138), since it responds to Luther's 'Invocavit Sermons' and the suppression of Karlstadt's pamphlet against Emser in 1522. Hertzsch has already implied that *Gemach* is earlier by placing it before the *Dialogus*.[291]

281 ks 1, 75:19.
282 ks 1, 76:5–6.
283 ks 1, 81:13–18.
284 See below, Appendix i, 285.
285 ks 1, 77:38, 78:2–3.
286 ks 2, 14:3–5. A similar argument occurs in *Christus* (124), C3v, F.
287 *Messen* (131), 4v.
288 *Leyb* (129), 2v.
289 *Leyb* (129), D3v–[5v].
290 ks 2, 23.
291 See *Gemach* (ks 1, 73f) and *Dialogus* (ks 2, 5f). For the other treatises Hertzsch follows Barge's chronology.

After Karlstadt's exile Westerburg took the eight writings to Zurich where they were read with approval by Grebel and his friends in early October. Grebel defends Karlstadt from Luther in a letter to Joachim von Watt (Vadian):

> Because we wrote something to Karlstadt ... , a letter has recently been returned by him. Besides, approximately eight books have been shown to us by the messenger. He showed what happened between Karlstadt and Luther; how, after they met less than a month and a half ago, they separated from one another; how Karlstadt accepted the golden coin from Luther to write against him and he explained and read, conferring with us for six days in Zurich. The name of the messenger is Gerhard Westerburg, and you may perchance have read his booklet *On the Sleep of Souls* ...
> What is happening here is also happening in Wittenberg, but a fair reader will conclude from the books of the Karlstadtians in what reactionary fashion Luther behaves himself, and how he is a prominent temporizer and valiant defender of his own scandal.[292]

Westerburg's primary aim, besides training Karlstadt's converts, was to raise money for publication. His hope of receiving such support would have been pinned on previous correspondence that probably included an encouragement to have more materials printed.[293] Manz and his friends responded generously; Manz and Castelberger departed from Basel with at least 5,300 of Karlstadt's booklets.[294]

The most salient point that the oaths of the printers in Basel establish is Manz's possession of the manuscript of Karlstadt's baptismal treatise, *Von dem Tauff*, after Westerburg and Karlstadt had left Basel. Manz badgered the two printers to publish it. However, the printers were fearful of scandal and thwarted Manz, returning the manuscript to him nearly a week before they themselves were arrested by the Basel authorities.[295] Thus, clearly the magistrates did not confiscate *Von dem Tauff*.[296] Although the printers could perjure themselves over the date of Westerburg's arrival, they would not have argued that they returned the manuscript after refusing to print it if the authorities had caught them in the act of printing. This is of decisive importance for my argument that the *Protestation*, a personal appeal that Manz presented to the Zurich authorities within a month after he left Basel, was based on Karlstadt's manuscript.

---

292 TQ SCHWEIZ 1, no 15 (Grebel to Joachim von Watt (Vadian), 14 October 1524), 21–2.
293 See the parallel prodding of Müntzer (MS, 443:38–444:1).
294 z 4, 464. See below, Appendix II, 291, n 6.
295 See below, Appendix II, 292, n 10; 294.
296 BARGE 2, 176, assumes that the treatise was confiscated.

The Writing of the *Protestation*[297]

The *Protestation*, which discusses baptism, is written in a mishmash of High German and Swiss German that cries out for source-critical analysis. Walter Schmid has discussed certain features of the work.[298] The slightly more than three sheets of writing contain seventy-nine corrections. There is a fairly consistent pattern of diphthongization, but in the final section Swiss German is dominant, yet throughout several words appear in both Swiss- and High-German forms. Schmid notes the presence of *nicht* and *nichts*, which were not yet current in Zurich. Diphthongization was used in the Zurich Bible in 1527, but in Swiss documents the traditional forms persisted well into the seventeenth century.[299] Schmid suggests that the presence of High German can best be accounted for by Manz's adoption of Luther's style,[300] yet surely, if Manz had consciously used High German, he would have been more consistent.

This problem is best resolved with an examination of the Swiss-German section towards the end of the work, which Manz could not have copied, for there he discusses the Zurich situation. There are also numerous corrections in which Swiss-German forms predominate. This implies that the *Protestation* was closely copied from a High-German document that had to be adapted to the needs of Manz, at which points he introduced Swiss German. This is the basic pattern, but there are exceptions. These may indicate that Manz had occasional problems in deciphering his original text, which must then have been written down; in addition, it is possible that the High-German text was not always suitable for Manz's purpose, which would have been true if the original document had been cast in an unusual form (e.g. a dialogue).

Manz makes the rather curious claim that he has been accused of rebellion and that there may be bloodshed. Schmid tries to explain this comment by referring to Grebel's remark that persecution will probably come.[301] It is true that Grebel and his friends expected persecution, which, according to Karlstadt, was one of the marks of the church. Nevertheless, accusations of rebellion and the threat of bloodshed go well beyond the generalized expectation of persecution. This claim could not have been copied from a work by Luther, but it does fit Karlstadt's situation. At first Karlstadt was convinced that Luther wanted to see him executed, because he had charged Karlstadt with violence and tied him to

297 In z 3, 368–72 the text has been attributed to Grebel. A reprint is found in TQ SCHWEIZ 1,
     23–8. I use the latter, emending errors of transcription on the basis of the manuscript (Zürich,
     Staatsarchiv, E II 340, 8–9v).
298 Schmid, 'Der Author,' 139–49.
299 Ibid, 139.
300 Ibid, 146.
301 Ibid, 148–9.

Müntzer, despite Karlstadt's public disavowal of Müntzer's League of the Elect.[302]

If we grant that Manz is copying Karlstadt's appendix to *Von dem Tauff* when he refers to persecution, we can explain the accusations. Karlstadt's and Manz's problems had enough similarity for Manz to copy or slightly revise some of Karlstadt's own observations on this subject. At one point, however, Manz appeals in impeccable High German to 'all with whom I have ever been involved' *(alle die, mit denen ich je zu schaffen gehaben)*.[303] Of course, Manz could appeal to others, but this statement, which refers to broken relationships that occurred in the past, makes better sense when applied to Karlstadt's situation. Manz also speaks of wrongs already inflicted on him,[304] again a statement which is more appropriate to Karlstadt.

Manz did not suffer from an intense persecution complex, for his *Protestation* indicates that he still hopes to persuade the council in his favour. On one occasion Manz shows that he is aware of the differences between his and Karlstadt's situation; he strikes out 'by many' in the following statement: 'Since I am also considered [a rebel] by many *(von mencklichem)*, but untruthfully.'[305] The phrase 'by many' fits Karlstadt's ominous situation only too well, but after Manz copies it, he must realize that others might think him guilty of exaggeration. Thus, in striking this phrase Manz concedes that his situation is not yet serious.

There is a whole series of errors that can only have been caused by accidents in copying. For example, once Manz enters *Derhalben* in his text, but then he strikes it, and he begins a new sentence.[306] Four lines later *Derhalben* reappears, and this time Manz finishes the sentence. This illuminates Manz's procedure, for there are altogether twenty-two errors of this type (including instances of pure haplography), as well as three corrections of dittography – all found in the primarily High-German section.[307]

This seemingly clumsy procedure of copying, correcting, and occasional adding has been preserved because Manz submitted the first draft to the council. Manz uses almost all the space available; his margins are rather small and often used for additional comments. Clearly, Manz tried to preserve paper and he did not pay an official scrivener to present as neat a protestation as possible.

302 See Karlstadt's reply (KS 2, 53, 71–2).
303 TQ SCHWEIZ 1, 23.
304 Ibid, 27.
305 Ibid, 23, n *f*.
306 TQ SCHWEIZ 1, 23, n *b*. The manuscript has a capitalized *Derhalben*.
307 TQ SCHWEIZ 1, 23, nn *b*, *g*, *h*; 24, nn *m*, *n*, *o*, *p-p*, *s-s*, *w*, *y*, *dd*; 25, nn *ee*, *mm*, *uu*, *vv-vv* (for the struck clause refers to Rom. 6, not Rom. 5!); 26, nn *xx*, *yy*, *zz*, *ac*, *af*, (*das* rather than *was* has been struck here), *ag*; 27, n *av*. For clear errors of dittography see 24, n *v*; 25, *hh*; 28, n *bf*. Manz must have been impatient.

One of Manz's mistakes shows that he was copying a manuscript rather than an unknown printed source. The original would have discussed dying in Christ's death and rising in his resurrection. Thus a High-German clause that Manz copies should read: 'mit im begraben im [!] todt, widerumb mit im auferstanden in newerung des lebens.'[308] Manz misreads todt and introduces touff, undercutting the parallel for baptism. Now touff has no diphthong, which confirms that Manz does not aim for a belletristic effect. When he makes a mistake, the Swiss form appears, while elsewhere he often copies Karlstadt's diphthongic tauff, tauffen, getaufft.

In a few instances Manz tries to correct the original. He changes the clause 'after the death of Christ' to 'after the ascension [uffart: Swiss German!] of Christ.'[309] Having tried this correction, Manz realizes that the original was right after all, and so he adds 'previously' (vorhin). The effect is ludicrous. Fortunately, Manz's aggregative result allows one to rescue the contents of Karlstadt's baptismal tract from oblivion, because Manz's minor additions and corrections can be traced through the Swiss-German forms, embedded in the High German.

It must be noted, however, that in Manz's brief letter of 18 February 1525[310] there is indeed a seemingly irrational co-existence of Swiss- and High-German forms. This mixture must have been deliberate, and Manz had no model to copy here. I would suggest that the High German of the Protestation had elicited a favourable comment, and that Manz was human enough not to admit to plagiarism. He now had a reputation to uphold; thus in his letter he also uses both Swiss- and High-German forms. He again strikes a few errors, but here they are not caused by copying.

As for content, the Protestation reflects Karlstadt's view of baptism, as also found in Grebel's letters to Müntzer. Rather than submit the Protestation to an analysis in which Karlstadt's ideas appear for the third time, we summarize the main points. The Protestation contains several appeals to Scripture, based on a strict biblicism, and inspired by what Christ has commanded (befolhen),[311] without additions or subtractions.[312] Karlstadt's favourite text (Galatians 1:8) is also cited. Manz refutes the opinion that externals do not matter. Like Karlstadt, he places baptism among the 'outward commands' (eusserlichen gebotten), and he adds that even such commands need to be heeded, for 'the two sons of Aaron'

---

308 TQ SCHWEIZ 1, 26.
309 Ibid, 24.
310 Ibid, no. 42a, 49–50. Another letter attributed to Felix Manz (no. 201, 218–19) is probably a pious forgery. If it is based on a now lost original, it was paraphrased later in High German. The vagueness of the letter is itself enough reason for caution.
311 Ibid, 24.
312 Ibid, 27. This feature has been stressed by Krajewski, 'The Theology of Felix Mantz,' 77–80. All attempts to arrive at an independent theology for Manz will have to be abandoned.

were consumed by fire, precisely because they transgressed such an outward command. As the editor notes, Manz alludes to the incident in Leviticus 10:1.

In a treatise on the Lord's Supper Karlstadt has raised the same problem in the same way. Someone argues that the bread of the Lord's Supper is ordinary (schlecht) bread and that therefore observance does not matter. Karlstadt retorts that God must be feared 'in all his precepts,' and he cites Leviticus 10 to show that Nadab and Abihu were slain for introducing strange fire into God's tabernacle.[313] Karlstadt then relates this text to baptism and 'the bread.' Manz confines the theology of baptism to basic details. Romans 6:4 is central. It describes baptism as dying and rising with Christ. This text 'shows clearly how one has died to the old life, has been circumcised of the heart, and has died to offences with Christ, is buried with him in baptism, and has again been resurrected with him unto newness of life.'[314] We repeat a quotation from Karlstadt (1523):

This is what it means to be a baptized Christian: one who has come to the life of Christ and has died in Christ's death and is dead and redeemed with respect to his sins, enters upon a new life in righteousness, in truth, and he says: 'I do not live, but Christ who lives in me.' Rom. 6.[315]

As we have noted, the Romans text first appeared in Iustificatione (13) in Karlstadt's discussion of repentance, and it remains central to his conception of baptism. Only one of Manz's ideas is not found in the passage from Karlstadt cited above, and that is Manz's reference to 'circumcision of the heart.' This theme is often discussed by Karlstadt, and he covertly links it to baptism when he cites Mark 16[:16] to maintain that only faith or circumcision of the heart establishes a Christian people.[316] Elsewhere, he explains circumcision of the heart as a 'whole-hearted love [of God].'[317]

Because love, faith, and repentance precede baptism, Karlstadt can accept a rite only for adults, but how does he regard infant baptism? Manz calls infant baptism 'evil, false, and of the antichrist: the pope and his followers.'[318] If, with Hertzsch, we accept Gemach (138) as the earliest of Karlstadt's Basel tracts, we find the first reference to the 'new papists' there.[319] Subsequently Karlstadt wrote the tract entitled Against the Anti-Christian Misuse of the Lord's Bread and Cup.

313 Leyb (129), Dv.
314 TQ SCHWEIZ 1, 24; cf 26.
315 Willen Gottes (102), F.
316 Ibid, G2.
317 KS 1, 61:34–5.
318 TQ SCHWEIZ 1, 23.
319 KS 1, 90:8–12.

Thus Manz's argument against anti-Christian rites, which even when used by Protestants are papistic, also echoes Karlstadt.

Discussing baptism, Manz cites passages that Karlstadt used previously.[320] A few texts appear later in one of Karlstadt's tracts of 1525.[321] Although the ideas of the *Protestation* are not new, Manz does expand on Acts 22:14–16.[322] In addition, we have seen that the reference to Acts 10:40 occurs only in Karlstadt's *Hauptartickeln* in 1525. Karlstadt could have had this last text brought to his attention during his encounter with Manz and Grebel in 1524. Earlier in 1524, however, Karlstadt preached serially on Acts during the weekday services in Orlamünde, and no doubt he seized on every reference to baptism he found there. Moreover Karlstadt probably never knew of the one copy of Manz's *Protestation*, and in his later writings he may just have been recalling a few texts from his unpublished *Von dem Tauff*, for Manz's discussion in the *Protestation* of the two passages in Acts appears in nearly impeccable High German.

The Aftermath

The Zurich Baptists sold over five thousand copies of Karlstadt's Basel treatises which they 'spread everywhere' in Switzerland.[323] 'Everywhere' included Waldshut at the German-Swiss border, for Balthasar Hubmaier merely echoed Karlstadt's views of the Lord's Supper in *Unterricht der Messe*.[324] The Zurich Baptists also were immersed in Karlstadt's theology, and within two months after Karlstadt's visit to Zurich, during which he discussed his ideas with the Baptists and snubbed Zwingli, the first adult baptisms took place in Zurich. Nevertheless, Karlstadt suffered the fate of many Baptist reformers. He was soon forgotten, in spite of his formative influence on the primitive Baptists.

Why did this happen? Karlstadt himself scorned the personality cult of early Lutheranism. Konrad Grebel criticized similar adulation conferred on the Zwinglian preachers in Zurich.[325] Thus there was no incentive to remember Karlstadt, who wished to re-establish the New Testament church, not to found a Karlstadtian church. The Swiss Baptists tried to circumvent the church of history, to return to the New Testament church. One looked mostly back to Christ (Karl-

---

320 See e.g. Matt. 28:19; John 4:29 (*Willen gottes* [102], G2v); Mark 16:16 (*Wasser* [30], A3–v; *Coelibatu* [62], C], and the already mentioned reference to Rom. 6.

321 Acts 10:40; Eph. 4:22. See KS 2, 90:1f, 17.

322 TQ SCHWEIZ 1, 25–6.

323 Z 4, 464.

324 Hubmaier, *Schriften*, TQ 9, [101]–4. Cf Sachsse, *D. Balthasar Hubmaier*, 88–9, 154–7. Sachsse concludes (p 157): 'Karlstadt hat ihm den Weg gewiesen von der Messe zum Abendmahl.'

325 MS, 438:22–3.

stadt, Zurich Baptists) or forward to Christ (Melchiorites) for inspiration. The rest of history was an interim when a few believers traversed a hostile world, and the lives of those saints could not add to the already perfect example of Christ. Menno[!]nite church history is a (sound) deviation from the Baptists' primitivism.

Karlstadt's writings were still considered precious by the Swiss Baptists in 1525. When Johannes Brötli wrote to his brethren in Zollikon, where the first Swiss Baptist congregation was established, he begged for two essentials: 'Send to my wife her black petticoat, and to me the booklets of Karlstadt.'[326] It would not be long, however, until the Swiss Baptists would have known of Karlstadt's unheroic course when he, for the sake of his family, accepted a unilateral cease-fire with Luther. In 1529 Karlstadt again agitated for more radical reform when he joined Melchior Hoffman in Holstein. However, he was induced to sue for peace with Zwingli, and he ended his life as a Reformed professor of Hebrew in Basel.

Felix Manz and his fellow Baptists would have been bitterly disappointed in Karlstadt's shirking of martyrdom and backsliding into witting unbelief after having attained discernment between good and evil, and they would have preferred to forget that their theological system originated with one who ended among the damned.

Even if Karlstadt had been willing to face martyrdom, his wife would probably have resisted. Two of her children had never been baptized; only those two died in infancy. Did she ascribe these disasters to chance or to the finger of God? We cannot be sure, but after Karlstadt died in Basel, Anna Bodenstein did write one letter to Luther, filled with complaints. She – who had married Karlstadt at the zenith of his Wittenberg career – may have become embittered.

In 1525 even the one surviving son must have suffered from ill health. In his letter to the Elector of Saxony Karlstadt pointed to the condition of his wife and child.[327] His family was also his main concern in his letter to Luther.[328] Had Karlstadt chosen martyrdom and had he left his family desolate, one of his proudest achievements would also have been trampled on. In Basel Karlstadt's tombstone refers with deserved pride to his rejection of celibacy.[329] The Roman Catholic apologist Thomas Murner saw clearly what had happened to Karlstadt: 'Karlstadt, who made a baked bread out of the venerable Sacrament of the true body and blood of Christ, has recanted. However, not sincerely, but out of love for

---

326 Egli, ed, *Aktensamlung*, 302: 'Schicken dem wib die schwarz underjüppen, und mir des Carolstatts büchli.'
327 BARGE 2, 580.
328 BR 3, 529:3–5.
329 BARGE 2, 520.

his wife, who very much wanted to return to Wittenberg.'[330] Karlstadt chose in favour of his family, and against some of his own convictions. We saw that he had changed his attitude towards original sin and the salvation of children when he became a father. Karlstadt made his peace with Zwingli in 1530, again for the sake of his family. In spite of this he still criticized the Magisterial Reformers for their greed, contrasting them with the Baptists: 'It is clear how great the damage is which this causes. Because of this offence, many are set up against and are alienated from the gospel. In the virtue contrary to this vice, the Baptists walk off as the victors.'[331]

In Basel Karlstadt became more conciliatory towards Luther's view of the Lord's Supper, and he was also accused of harbouring Baptists and Catholics in his own Reformed congregation.[332] Ultimately, Karlstadt must have concluded that persons mattered more than ideas.

Adam Bodenstein became a physician in Basel. He was a friend, follower, and publisher of the ideas of Paracelsus. Paracelsus, who is now considered 'the father of modern medicine,' was quite controversial in his own age. For his radical ideas Adam Bodenstein was ousted from the Basel medical association and barred from practising medicine.

The Baptists remained faithful to Karlstadt's earlier vision. They probably considered Karlstadt another victim of the damnable status of being 'learned,' even of one who had realized that only children enter the kingdom of heaven. Karlstadt could have countered that he and his family had already been victimized enough. The Baptists were also victims – of wrong ideas, some might say, or of wrong circumstances, or of both. But even right ideas can unleash terrible consequences and, once let loose, they cannot be recalled. Yet, Karlstadt himself did not desire to see the train of martyrs produced by the Baptist movements.

330 Ibid, 373.
331 Ibid, 452.
332 Ibid, 476f, 492.

Weissagung vß heiliger götlicher geschrifft.

Von den trübsalen diser letsten zeit.

Von der schweren hand vnd straff gottes über alles
gottloß wesen.

Von der zükunfft des Türckischen Thirannen / vnd
seines gantzē anhangs.

Wie er sein reiß thün/vnnd volbringen wirt/ vns zü
einer straff/vnnd rütten.

Wie er durch Gottes gwalt sein niderlegung vnnd
straff entpfahē wirt.ꝛc.

Melchior Hoffman.

Anno.   M.   D.   ?

Title-page of Hoffman's *Weissagung*,
which was published in 1529 or 1530 by Balthasar Beck in Strassburg.
Here Hoffman predicts the outcome of 'the troubles of these latter days,'
including the downfall of the 'Turkish tyrant.'
By courtesy of Universitätsbibliothek, Freiburg im Breisgau

Part Three

Karlstadt and Hoffman

Hoffman in his cell in Strassburg.
Copperplate engraving, 20.9 × 26.9 cm.
This fictitious portrait was engraved and published by Christoffel van Sichem
in *Iconica et historica descriptio præcipuorum Hæresiarcharum*, 1609.
By courtesy of Universiteits-Bibliotheek, Amsterdam

6

Hoffman in Livonia

In the chapters that follow, Hoffman's formative years, before he arrived in Strassburg, will be examined in detail, but since no biography of Hoffman exists in English, an introductory overview of his life follows here.

Of his origins only this is known firmly: Melchior Hoffman was born in Schwäbisch Hall and became a furrier by trade and a lay preacher by vocation. No doubt his trade contacts led him to establish himself in Livonia. Hoffman's earliest exhortatory activities are summarized in the following comments by Karlstadt:

> The furrier spent some time in Livonia. He was visited by God with grace, and his eyes were opened unto him with the recognition of the Word of divine truth and of Christ. Thus he began to preach the Word of God in a town called Wolmar [now Valmiera, Latvian SSR] under the jurisdiction as they call it of the master of the Teutonic Order. There he suffered much persecution until, at last, he was expelled at the lord master's command for the sake of truth.[1]

After the controversy in Wolmar Hoffman moved to Dorpat [Tartu, Estonian SSR], where he won over a large number of the people to the new religion. When the castellan of the bishop of Dorpat sent his guards to arrest Hoffman, the populace rose against the clerics; several church buildings were sacked, and four or five persons perished. Hoffman was made to leave, but he was promised a future role in Dorpat if he secured a recommendation from Luther. Hoffman never was a Lutheran; his iconoclastic activities would have prevented that. He clung to traditional exegesis, opposed even voluntary confession, and supplemented Luther's form of the doctrine of *sola scriptura* with a demand for good works as

1 *Dialogus* [1529], Av–2.

proposed in James. The fact that Hoffman was neither educated nor ordained would also become a barrier between him and the Lutheran pastors. At this time, however, Hoffman concealed his differences from Luther, and was granted the required certification to preach. Luther generously published Hoffman's letter, along with his own and Bugenhagen's missive to the Livonians.[2] No doubt Hoffman felt grateful to Luther, whose commendation he could now flourish before the eyes of his Livonian detractors.

Back in Dorpat, Hoffman was allowed to resume his preaching until he humiliated the daughter of one of the burgomasters during a sermon. Hoffman was expelled once again, but 'God led him to a city called Reval [now Tallinn, Estonian SSR], where he became a comforter of the sick, and, at the instigation of false brethren who pretend to be evangelical, he was once again sent into exile.'[3]

Hoffman now went to Stockholm, where his first two independently published treatises appeared in print (Gelöfigen and Daniel 12), late in 1526. They show a unique blend of apocalypticism and the ideas of Karlstadt, modified by some ideas drawn from the young Luther. Early in 1527 King Gustaf I wrote to his representative in Stockholm, cautioning him against Hoffman's careless preaching. An iconoclastic riot which Hoffman seems to have provoked may have contributed to his imprisonment and expulsion from Sweden. After a brush with the old believers in Lübeck, he 'with wife and child came to Holstein, where Frederik, king of Denmark, ordered him to appear before him, for he wanted to hear [Hoffman's] sermons. Since he taught God's Word aright, the king accepted him as his servant and granted him a sealed letter, permitting him to preach all over the land of Holstein, and appointed him specifically to Kiel as a preacher.'[4] Before this happened, however, Frederik urged Hoffman to apply to Wittenberg once again for approval, but by now the complaints from Livonia and Sweden proved effective. Hoffman's request for an updated preaching licence was rebuffed, and he retreated in haste.[5] Hoffman's account of his second stay in Wittenberg shows that he felt insulted after a sharp exchange over his exegesis: 'When I revealed such an explanation to my teachers in Wittenberg and clearly wanted to follow Scripture, I – poor worm – was considered a great sinner and a dreamer, and thus I was terribly mistreated, maligned, and despised.'[6] Luther felt

2   WA 18, 417f (Luther), 421f (Bugenhagen), 426f (Hoffman).
3   Dialogus [1529], A2.
4   Dialogus [1529], A2–v.
5   BR 4, 412 (no. 1239, Luther to Pravest, 14 March 1528). Hoffman's secret flight is mentioned in a now lost letter of Luther and Bugenhagen to Prince Christian, referred to by Weidensee, Underricht (1529), A3v: 'Wath hefft doch Doctor Martin und her Johan Bugenhagen an dussem Hoffman geschaffet, welkere so se öhn wolden christliken vormanen, toch he heymelick wech van Wittenberge, unnd wolde öhres vormanendes nicht affwachten, wo den öhrer beyder hantschrifft, welke J[uwer] F[örstliken] G[naden] noch by syck hefft vormelden.'
6   Hoffman, Matt. 1, 445.

embarrassed by his earlier endorsement of Hoffman: 'I gave it to him, being foolishly deceived.'[7] King Frederik was pleased with Hoffman, however, and allowed him to preach in Kiel. There Hoffman got embroiled in a pamphlet war with several Lutheran pastors, including Nikolaus von Amsdorf, the church superintendent of Magdeburg. In 1527 Luther had written to Amsdorf and alluded to Hoffman as 'that Livonian Prophet.' He therefore regarded Hoffman as an 'enthusiast' for, as Karlstadt had already learned, Wittenberg would no longer harbour more than one prophet. As a result of this, and of the shabby treatment already meted out to him by Amsdorf at Luther's instigation,[8] Hoffman grew to dislike Luther. In a printed blast at Hoffman Amsdorf bragged of clinging to common opinion and the doctrine of the 'worthy and in God dearly beloved lord and father: Doctor Martin.'[9] Hoffman showed no respect for such credentials: 'The other point about which this fine instigator writes is this, that Martin is his father. I didn't know this fine hero was the son of a monk and a bastard.'[10] Hoffman then addressed the self-styled son of Luther as 'son of a whore,' and his resolve against Luther stiffened into overt doctrinal repudiation.

As was customary, the rulers regarded religious pluralism as an attack on the established order. Thus Hoffman was accused of sedition: in fact a charge of treason was the usual way of disposing of dissenters. Whether King Frederik believed such accusations is not known, but he did not wish to take any chances, and he knew that only the ejection of Hoffman would prevent religious turmoil. This he planned by placing Hoffman on trial in Flensburg for his doctrinal views. Since the king asked Prince Christian – an ardent Lutheran – to preside over the trial and to report back to him, the outcome was preordained. Hoffman would not recant; his possessions were confiscated, and he was ousted from Holstein.

Joining Karlstadt, Hoffman found refuge with Chief Ulrich von Dornum in East Friesland. Hoffman stayed for two months, and then left for Strassburg. He had related some of the events of his life and given a detailed account of the Flensburg Disputation. This information Karlstadt turned into a dialogue. At this time Karlstadt may have had renewed impact on Hoffman, for after their encounter in Holstein Hoffman revised his view of baptism, repudiated predestination, and began to teach the typically Karlstadtian combination of a universal offer of salva-

---

7 BR 4, 202 (no. 1105, Luther to Amsdorf, 17 May 1527).

8 BR 4, 202: 'Melchiorem illum prophetam Livoniensem si venerit, ne suscipias amice nec familiariter.'

9 Amsdorf, Nicht ein Wort (1528), A2: 'Die weil ich mich keiner neuen und eigen lere understehe, sonder bey gemeiner lere und gemeinem geist, so ich von andern und sonderlich von meim erwirdigen ynn got lieben herrn und vater Doctori Martino gelernt und geschept habe.'

10 Hoffman, Dat Nicolaus Amsdorff (1528), [Av]: 'Den anderen punct den de fyne dreper schrifft, ys de wo Martinus syn vader sy. Ick hebbe nicht geweten, dat de fyne heldt eines mönnekes söne was, unde unecht.' Amsdorf also argues according to 'de arth der huren kinder.'

tion by God, with unbelievers choosing to be damned. Since Karlstadt had already shaped Hoffman's thinking with regard to images, confession, the Lord's Supper, and above all his doctrine of the church, Hoffman was deeply influenced by Karlstadt.

Hoffman's doctrines were once again in flux, however, and he accepted a heavenly-flesh Christology in Strassburg. His apocalypticism also set Hoffman off from Karlstadt. Ironically, this apocalypticism, which made Hoffman believe that the end of the world was near, fanned his ardour all the more: he began to proclaim Strassburg as the New Jerusalem from which the 144,000 apostolic messengers of Revelation 14 would go forth to prepare the way of the Lord's return in 1533. The enormous crowds Hoffman drew on the streets of Strassburg compared favourably with the handful who listened to Martin Bucer. This may have emboldened Hoffman to demand that a church building be reserved for the Baptists. Because of this, and because Hoffman had published his conclusion that the Emperor Charles v equalled the dragon of Revelation 12, an order was issued for Hoffman's arrest, but he escaped.

Hoffman returned to East Friesland, where he was allowed to baptize in the Great Church of Emden, gaining four hundred converts. As always for Hoffman, opposition followed initial success, and he decided to leave in November. His converts carried on his work, however, and Emden became the primary centre from which the Baptist movement radiated into the northern Lowlands. Hoffman himself appeared in Amsterdam in the summer of 1531. In December ten of Hoffman's followers were executed in The Hague. Hoffman was by then again in hiding in Strassburg, but hearing of the executions he tried to forestall further martyrdoms by suspending baptism for two years, by which time the world was to end anyway. Hoffman seems to have spent a good part of 1532 in the northern Lowlands,[11] and Melchiorites appeared from Holland to Zeeland and from Groningen to Limburg. They formed a mass movement from which the Dutch Baptists (Doopsgezinden) developed. Many of their descendants were absorbed later by the Reformed churches.

Hoffman spent most of the winter of 1532 to 1533 in Emden. An old man prophesied that Hoffman would be arrested in Strassburg and be imprisoned for half a year, after which Christ would return. Hoffman believed the report, but the end of his world did not come as speedily as he expected. Returning to Strassburg in secret, Hoffman barred the bigamist Claus Frey from receiving the Lord's Supper of the Baptists. Frey then accused Hoffman of planning a revolution and revealed Hoffman's whereabouts to the magistrates. When Hoffman was arrested, he took this as a sign that the old man's prophecy was being fulfilled. In a state of spiritual exaltation he removed his shoes and cut off his stockings at the ankle, evidently following the example of Moses before the burning bush. Frey later withdrew his accusation; nevertheless, Hoffman was kept in prison.

Hoffman fasted for half a year in anticipation of Christ's return. This event kept being delayed, however, so Hoffman continued to postpone the date a year or two at a time. Some of the Melchiorites had captured the city of Münster in Westphalia in an attempt to establish the New Jerusalem there. During this episode the Strassburg magistrates, worried that an attempt might be made to capture Strassburg as well, had Hoffman cast into a dungeon. He was removed when he became seriously ill, but it was feared that he might escape. A minor recantation, in which Hoffman retracted his objections to infant baptism, did not materially improve his condition. His cell was walled in as a security measure, and he was fed through a trapdoor. He died, probably in 1543 of pneumonia.

As we have seen, Hoffman underwent a religious conversion in Livonia; yet he did not really become a Lutheran. What then was the religious and cultural context in which Hoffman moved and which explains so much about him, not only in Livonia, but also during his subsequent career?

The Radical Reformation in Livonia

Sixteenth-century Livonia embraced the southern two-thirds of present-day Estonia and the northern half of what is now Latvia. German was spoken in the Baltic harbours and the inland towns, which belonged to the commercial network of the Hanseatic League. Estonian or Latvian was current in the hinterland and even in the German towns among the lower classes, who were denied political power.[12] Thus Hoffman had to learn only Low German in order to preach in Livonia; a weaver interpreted Hoffman's sermons to the Estonians.[13]

Supreme legislative power in the Livonian Confederation was vested in the *Landtag*, which had representatives from the Teutonic Order, the landed gentry, the town councils, as well as the church with its own political privileges.[14] Livonia's premier churchman was Johannes Blankenfeld who, by papal dispensation, held plural offices. He was coadjutor to Archbishop Jasper Linde in Riga, as well as bishop of Reval and Dorpat. The towns vied with their political rivals, and Riga

---

12 For the composition of the population in the major towns see DEPPERMANN, 41–3.

13 Amelung, 'Melchior Hoffmann in Livland,' 206f. It also appears that two Estonian followers of Hoffman were killed in the Dorpat riot; see 'Sylvester Tegetmeier's Tagebuch,' 503: 'dat van der borger syden iiii doth bleven, ii Dudeschken und ii Undudeschken.'

14 A useful introduction to German expansion in the Baltic is Rörig, *The Medieval Town*, 30–47, with additional materials on 198. The political struggle is described by Pohrt, 'Reformationsgeschichte Livlands,' 45f. See also the summary in DEPPERMANN, 38–42. An Estonian viewpoint is represented by Vööbus, *Studies in the History of the Estonian People* 2, 1–78. For Archbishop Blankenfeld see Berendts, 'Johann von Blankenfeld,' 29–60; and Schnöring, 'Johannes Blankenfeld,' 1–115.

declined to inaugurate Blankenfeld after he succeeded to the archbishopric upon the death of Jasper Linde on 29 June 1524.[15] In 1525 the political aggression of Riga and Dorpat became obvious at the *Landtag* in Wolmar (2 July), when Dorpat urged Wolter von Plettenberg, master of the Teutonic Order, to oust Blankenfeld and claim sovereignty over Dorpat. Meanwhile the town of Riga felt it had already progressed enough along these lines to suggest that the master secularize his order.

Despite the threat posed by the towns the feudal powers (Teutonic Order, landed gentry, Catholic church) failed to unite because their interests clashed. Finally, in December 1525, Plettenberg imprisoned Blankenfeld for negotiating with the Russians. Thus, when Hoffman entered Livonia, the old power structure still prevailed, but it would swiftly be transformed as a direct result of the Reformation.

The Reformation invaded Livonia from the Baltic port of Riga, an important centre of the fur trade.[16] Since the hinterland was productive of hides, bookbinding thrived in Riga. Thus, although it still lacked a printing press, and despite its geographic eccentricity, Riga was exposed to the latest religious currents from the German mainland.

Andreas Knopken

The Reformation became officially entrenched in Riga with the installation of Andreas Knopken as archdeacon of the Church of Saint Peter in October 1522, a year after Knopken's expulsion from the City School in Treptow, Pomerania (Trzebiatów, Poland). In Treptow Knopken had taught with his friend Johannes Bugenhagen, and both were fascinated by the progress of the Reformation. At their instigation the Treptow clergy, during a procession, were met with a hail of filth, and the Church of the Holy Ghost was broken into and its images cast into a well. As a result the Treptow school was closed and Bugenhagen and Knopken had to flee.[17] Bugenhagen went to Wittenberg while Luther lived at the Wartburg, and he was swept along by Melanchthon and Karlstadt until the Wittenberg movement collapsed in 1522. Meanwhile, Bugenhagen sent some of the latest Wittenberg publications to his friend Knopken, who, before being promoted, had already been agitating for reform as assistant priest at the Church of Saint Peter.[18]

Although he at first kept abreast of the Reformation, Knopken ignored Luther's later development.[19] Knopken had corresponded with Erasmus, but he

---

15 ARBUSOW, 332.
16 For a traditionalistic English introduction to the Estonian Reformation see Laantee, 'The Beginnings of the Reformation in Estonia,' 269–78.
17 Brachmann, 'Die Reformation in Livland,' 17.
18 ARBUSOW, 183–4.
19 Ruhtenberg, 'Beziehungen,' 57.

did not try to correspond with Luther, despite opportunities to do so when the Rigan syndic, Johann Lohmüller, dispatched his own letters to Luther in Wittenberg.[20] When Knopken wrote to have his commentary on Romans published in Wittenberg, he addressed Melanchthon and Bugenhagen but not Luther.

Knopken's *Romans* lacks volatile matter, and minor points smack of Melanchthon, who had originally recommended Knopken for his post in Riga.[21] The sober tone of the Knopken commentary may be due to caution and the fact that it was published in Wittenberg. Knopken had granted Bugenhagen censorship rights as the price of publication.[22] This chore may even have been handled by Melanchthon.

However, the theses that Knopken debated at the Church of Saint Peter on 12 June 1522 are absolutely frank.[23] They reveal that Knopken accepts the principle of *sola fide*, but that he also insists on good works that are not meant to contribute to one's own salvation.[24] This position shows Luther's impact in an area that became the common property of many Protestants. Knopken also inveighs against the scholastic notion of infused grace (th 13) and works of supererogation (th 16), and he declines to sunder faith from good works on the basis of James 2:19: 'The devils also believe and they tremble.' Unlike demonic faith, genuine faith produces love and works that are crucial at the final judgment (th 14). The law, though fulfilled through Christ, must steadfastly be preached.[25] There is no tension between law and gospel, as there is in Luther. On predestination Knopken is less strict than Luther. Man's natural will is tied to sin, but Knopken accepts some free will in the *believer* if it is 'borne by the divine work.'[26]

---

20 BR 2, no. 532 (20 Aug. 1522); BR 3, no. 684 (11 Nov. 1523). Arbusow, 230, has noted this. For Lohmüller's efforts to translate Lutheran piety into magisterially inspired political action see Quednau, 'Johannes Lohmüller,' 51–67, 253–69.

21 ARBUSOW, 244–50; Ruhtenberg, 'Beziehungen,' 61f.

22 ARBUSOW, 249.

23 Reprinted in Pohrt, 'Reformationsgeschichte Livlands,' 114–25. I cite the numbers of the theses rather than the pagination.

24 Th 1: 'Verae fidei in Christum reluctantur operarii, qui suis meritis regnum dei expugnare volunt.' Th 6: 'Scriptura non iuxta externum specimen, sed operantis affectum meritur opera, quo nemo potest bonum facere, nisi ipse prior sit bonus ... Et ita opera non faciunt bonum, sed bonus facit bona opera.' Th 12: 'Idcirco iustificanti fide non ideo faciunt bona opera, ut deum sibi concilient aut iustiores evadant, id enim fide consecuti sunt, sed ut per bona opera iustos se esse factos declarent et fidem vivam in se esse ... non mortuam opinionem ostendant alioquin et daemones credunt et contremiscunt. Opera igitur quae post fidem sequuntur non augent iustitiam, sed sunt eius fructus.'

25 Th 9: 'Labia sacerdotis custodient scientiam et legem requirent ex ore eius quia angelus exercituum est.'

26 Th 5: 'Liberum, quod aiunt arbitrium nisi ope divina fulciatur, peccat et in omne turpitudinis genus prolabitur.'

Knopken purges the traditional liturgy. He contrasts Moses with Christ – not to oppose law and gospel, but to distinguish the man of tradition from the one who breaks with it.[27] Tradition equals damnation:

At the last judgment Christ will not [heed] any pious works: no superstitious fasting, no everlasting chanting, not the Olympus of the intercessors, no memorials, no sodalities, no participation in [traditional] good works, no indulgences, no foundation of vicarages, no building of churches and altars, no pilgrimages, but he will acknowledge works of charity that proceed from faith. Paul teaches good works that are quite different from those of our babblers who know not how to proclaim anything except regulations, rosaries, votive masses, sweet benedictions, [and] mouthed prayers – with which they redeem the souls from purgatory, i.e. they deliver themselves up to hell.[28]

Knopken disparages those who 'pray to their little gods and believe images are vessels of divine grace.'[29] He mocks the Roman priests who claim clerical immunity to exploit the faithful, to gamble, to drink, and to serve their bellies.[30] They claim political power which the true church renounces. There is only one kind of clergy, the *ministri*, who serve rather than rule.[31] Knopken is no copyist, but sources for his ideas suggest themselves. On the subject of predestination one is reminded of the first careful treatment to have come out of Wittenberg – the debate between Karlstadt and Eck at Leipzig (1519). Karlstadt's disagreements with Luther on the canonicity of James and the relation of law and gospel had surfaced a year later with Karlstadt's *Booklet on the Canon*.[32] If Knopken knew it, he tacitly backed Karlstadt. Karlstadt's opposition to images could also have been known in Livonia. For the attack on sodalities Knopken may have been

27 Th 24: 'Spermologi hodie Mosen Christo miscent, sal infusum reddentes, i.e. evangelicae doctrinae energiam humanis traditionibus et artibus vitiantes.'
28 Th 14: 'In extremo examine Christus nullam pietatem, nulla superstitiosa ieiunia, non perpetuas cantiones [corrected for *cautiones*], non praecularum Olympum, non memorias, non fraternitates, non participitationes bonorum operum, non indulgentias, non vicariarum fundationes, non templorum et altarium erectiones, non peregrinationes, sed caritatis opera ex fide prodeuntia agnoscet.' Th 17: 'Paulus longe diversa bona opera docet quam nostri spermologi, qui praeter regulas, rosaria, missas votivas, dulces benedictiones et orales orationes, quibus animas ex purgatorio redimant, i.e. se ipso inferis devoveant, nihil norunt sonare.'
29 Th 3: 'Magna amentia hodie coepit eos, qui in diversis locis divulos invocant et mortuas imaginunculas credunt divinae gratiae capaces.'
30 Th 9, 15, 16, 19, 20.
31 Th 20: 'Non enim agnoscit Christus successores apostolorum nisi ministros, qui reges et principos eos esse vetuit.'
32 *De canonicis scripturis* (34–5) and *Bücher* (46–8).

inspired by the version of the Wittenberg Ordinance published with Karlstadt's tract *On the Removal of Images*. Luther had first attacked sodalities in 1520, but the combined attack on sodalities and images may point to Karlstadt's tract.

Knopken adopts Karlstadt's anticlericalism, and he spurns externals in worship. From a Lutheran standpoint Knopken and Karlstadt are legalists. A year later Knopken uses Karlstadt's theses, printed in Basel.[33] That they already underlie his first set of theses seems to be indicated by his attack on 'mouthed prayers.'[34]

The second set of Knopken's theses survives as an enclosure with a letter to Luther by Lohmüller, the syndic of Riga. It is clear that the sentences were composed by a clergyman, and with the editor of the theses I would assign them to Knopken.[35] These theses resemble those of 1522, showing a comparable blending of Karlstadt and the young Luther.

In the theses Knopken delineates his view of the Lord's Supper. Ancient rites add to the Bible and hence are 'nothing,' or they defy Scripture and are 'exceedingly impious.'[36] The command to fast before communion is impious, for the disciples ate before Christ distributed bread and wine.[37] Christ's Supper is a testament, which means nothing may be added to it.[38] The Lord gave *bread*, and this undermines transubstantiation.[39] How the bread becomes Christ's body has not been revealed, and it is forbidden to pry into God's secrets.[40] The bread is the body of Christ, for Christ says 'this *is* my body.' It is Christ's body at the time of fraction, for Paul links fraction and the communication of the body of Christ.[41] Christ said, 'take' the bread, that is, take it with one's hands. To deny the laity this right is to countermand Christ's practice and injunctions.[42] Knopken uses the term 'laity' for convenience, but he challenges its pejorative connotations. As a minister Knopken notes that 'laity' is a term which 'we nowadays apply to the people of God, who in many things are better than we.'[43] The communion bread must not be borne aloft in procession or be displayed. Candles, songs, mouthed

---

33 *Articuli* (67).
34 Th 17. Cf BARGE 1, 492.
35 BR 3, 190, n 3.
36 BR 3, 190:22–3.
37 BR 3, 190:25–7.
38 BR 3, 191:30–4.
39 BR 3, 191:35–7.
40 BR 3, 191:42–3.
41 BR 3, 191:44–5. Karlstadt rejects this view in 1524 (KS 2, 26).
42 BR 3, 191:48–54.
43 BR 3, 191:50–1. Cf Karlstadt's reference to the clergy as *ministris* in BARGE 1, 494, th 13. This was not intended as a new title, however. Knopken's sentiment that the laity is better than the clergy can be found in Karlstadt's earlier tract *Fürbit Marie* (108), B3: 'Ich wayss das vil handtwercker in gottes leer meer wissen dann pfaffen, so die bosskugel und kegel werffen. Gott leret die layen, das sy den gekrönten doctorn und maystern vorgant.'

prayers, and the adoration of the bread deflect the aim of Christ who gave the bread to be eaten.[44] One must receive Christ worthily, that is only in faith. One partakes unworthily with preparations and vestments not commanded in Scripture.[45]

The Lord's Supper is in remembrance of Christ alone. 'Our testator [Christ] wants nothing more than that all other additions should perish.'[46] One remembers Christ, that is, his teachings:

> Here Christ is truly placed before your eyes, not as they depict him nowadays, but rather his word and doctrine, for which he suffered death. For his doctrine is the New Testament, and Christ calls this sacrament a new testament, i.e. a lesser sign [signaculum] and a seal [sigillum] of the New Testament, confirmed in the death of Christ. Therefore the gospel is to be preached here to the people. Thus Paul says: 'Ye shall proclaim the Lord's death until he comes, whenever ye shall eat this bread and drink of this cup.'[47]

Only in this manner is the Lord eaten worthily, and Knopken argues against participation at set times. The gospel must be preached at each communion service. Finally, Knopken argues for communion under both species. The cup may not be withheld from Christians (Knopken's substitute for 'laity'). He taunts the Catholics: 'But you say there is danger in this. You know what Christ did not know? You are the fools who have said in their hearts, "there is no God." Thus they trembled with fear where there was no fear.'[48]

Christ's body is not dead but alive when eaten by God's people. Christ's death and his blood shed on the cross are signified by the cup. Both bread and wine are essential because the two signs refer to separate promises. Christ gives both food *and* drink.[49] In what seems to be a thrust at reserving the bread and wine Knopken asserts that the elements should not be feared.[50]

It is obvious that Knopken knew the *Babylonian Captivity* (1520), where Luther reduces the number of the sacraments, disavows transubstantiation, and fights against the sacrificial aspects of the mass. Positively faith is required for a

---

44 BR 3, 191:60–4.
45 BR 3, 191:66–8: 'Dignus accedis, si fide integra accedis; quam si non habeas, indigne manducas, et impius es cum omnibus tuis praeparationibus et vestibus pontificalibus, quae hic non legis.'
46 BR 3, 391:72: 'Nihil aliud vult testator noster, ut pereant omnia alia additamenta.'
47 BR 3, 191:73–8.
48 BR 3, 192:89–90.
49 BR 3, 192:91–7.
50 BR 3, 192:98–101.

worthy reception of the elements, which are a testament and a sign and seal of Christ's promises. Luther also claims the cup for the laity, and theoretically he affirms the priesthood of all believers. Such themes became the common heritage of Protestantism, and here *all* reformers owed a debt to Luther.[51]

Even so, Knopken does not simply imitate Luther. For example, Knopken expresses revulsion at unbiblical ceremonies, which Luther regards as unessential options.[52] Like Karlstadt, Knopken is biblicistic.

From the traditional viewpoint Luther devalues the sacrifice of the mass into a sign and seal of Christ's promises. Knopken is more extreme in calling the sacrament a 'lesser sign,' employing a medieval distinction, also found in Thomas Aquinas. On the basis of Romans 4:11 Thomas places circumcision among the 'lesser signs,' the 'declarations of faith,' on whose basis the benefits of Christ's grace were showered upon the patriarchs. Such a *signaculum* does not have the full power of a sacrament like baptism, as it does not confer enabling power (*characterem*).[53] Of course, Thomas never applied this distinction to communion, and Knopken has detracted from its value, perhaps because Karlstadt subordinates the sign under the promise, and the promise under faith, in effect inverting the relationship between the declarations of faith and the sign.[54] Karlstadt also draws a parallel between Christ as a sign on the cross and the brazen serpent in the wilderness.[55]

Still, Knopken would have detected development in Karlstadt's theses. At first Karlstadt allows the adoration of the New Testament sacrament because, in this respect, he still distinguishes Old from New Testament signs.[56] Soon thereafter Karlstadt abandons such adoration.[57]

Both Luther and Knopken call the sacrament a testament, but from this Knopken deduces that one may not add to or subtract from it. The younger Luther once makes the same observation, but on this point he changed his mind.[58] Knopken does not select from tradition but rejects it.

Regarding the words of institution, Luther claims that the bread *is* the body of Christ, but even in his early writings Luther is speculative. Christ's body is 'under the bread.'[59] At one point Karlstadt accepts this argument,[60] but it clashes

51 Karlstadt at first follows Luther's use of signs and seals. Because of the trust one derives from the signs, they may be called seals (*Gestaldten* (71), Cv–3v).
52 WA 6, 355; WA 8, 511. Also see WA 10/3, 1–64 *passim*.
53 *Summa theologiae*, 3, q. 62 a. 6.
54 BARGE 1, 283–4, 413, th 12–13.
55 BARGE 1, 490, th 120.
56 BARGE 1, 486, th 49.
57 *Anbettung* (68), A3.
58 WA 8, 490–1.
59 WA 2, 749; WA 6, 359, 508.
60 BARGE 1, 486, th 38.

with his own earlier identification of the *unchanged* bread with Christ's body: a miracle, not susceptible to rational explanation.[61] Knopken irons out the inconsistency with Karlstadt's rather than Luther's argument.

Knopken's insistence that the laity receive the cup as well as the bread is derived from Karlstadt. Luther calls the practice of withholding the cup 'monstrous,'[62] yet to him communion with both species is inessential.[63] When Karlstadt insists on both, Luther, upon returning from the Wartburg, defiantly restores communion with bread alone.[64] Knopken also adopts Karlstadt's early theory that bread and wine signify distinct promises. To Karlstadt the bread is the living body of Christ. He bases this conclusion on John 6:51.[65] Luther dismisses this passage as unrelated to the Lord's Supper.[66] Karlstadt rejoins that the verse is futuristic ('the bread which I *shall* give is my flesh'), and therefore it makes sense only when applied to the sacrament.[67] Knopken also uses John 6:51, attaching a separate promise to the wine.

For Karlstadt in the period from 1521 to 1522 the bread is Christ's crucified and living body which prefigures the believer's resurrection. The wine signifies the remission of sin, brought about by the shedding of Christ's blood on the cross.[68] Communion in both species is essential.

Knopken's *insistence* on taking the bread in one's hand also deviates from Luther. Luther favours the idea, but he does not insist on it, and he restores oral reception for the laity after Karlstadt has prohibited it.[69] Knopken's cautious admonition against reserving the elements may be inspired by Karlstadt's bolder statement that the sacrament must not be reserved in a pyx.[70] If Knopken possessed the theses that appeared in the Viennese edition of Karlstadt's *On Celibacy*, he would have read: 'Just as the images of Christ, of the glorious Virgin and other saints should be levelled in Christian temples, so also the festive pomp with

61   BARGE 1, 485, th 34. For Luther *only* see Sasse, *This Is My Body*, 99f.
62   WA 6, 504.
63   WA 2, 742; WA 6, 507.
64   WA 10/3, 45–7.
65   BARGE 1, 485, th 27. The application of John 6 to the Supper can be traced back to Tauler, whose sermons Karlstadt read in 1517. For references to Tauler, Erasmus, and Zwingli see Baring's note in TQ 6/2, 25, n 20.
66   WA 6, 502: 'Primum, c. vi Ioannis in totum est seponendum ut quod nec syllaba quidem de sacramento loquitur.'
67   BARGE 1, 486, th 48: 'Non obstabit, quod illic non agit de sacramento, quia praefatur Christus de pane, quem ipse postea fuit daturus, dicens, quem ego dabo. Non dixit quem do, sed quem dabo.'
68   *Emphahung* (76), B–v, refers to the promise of resurrection. BARGE 1, 488, th 75, refers to the promise of forgiveness.
69   WA 10/3, 42.
70   BARGE 1, 292, n 123, th 9.

which the venerable sacrament is carried to and fro.'[71] Knopken must have consulted several of the tracts Karlstadt published from 1521 to 1522. Essential is his possession of the theses debated on 17 October 1521.[72]

Sylvester Tegetmeier

We have seen that Riga was a centre of the book trade, and that Bugenhagen sent Knopken letters and tracts from Wittenberg. Another mediator of Karlstadt's ideas in Livonia was Sylvester Tegetmeier. Tegetmeier entered Riga a month after Knopken's installation as minister. He was an activist, who has been called a 'firebrand.'[73] Some bits of information come from his diary, which was mutilated, presumably by a Lutheran (the older Tegetmeier?) ashamed of the radical origins of Livonian Lutheranism.[74] The fragments retain some value for assessing Tegetmeier's Karlstadtian phase. Arbusow, in the standard work on the Livonian Reformation, had tagged Tegetmeier as a Karlstadtian, even before Baerent-Arrasch referred him to the *Album* of the University of Wittenberg, where Tegetmeier appears as an immatriculant on 4 September 1521.[75]

Tegetmeier came from Hamburg and he studied in Rostock, obtaining the MA degree on 20 February 1519.[76] Academic success led to ecclesiastical promotion, and on Easter, 8 April 1520, Tegetmeier became chaplain at the cathedral in Rostock. Rostock still clung to the old faith, but Tegetmeier or one of his colleagues collected Hussite works which were read by one of Karlstadt's friends.[77]

---

71 BARGE 1, 293, n 123, th 12: 'Sicut Christi, gloriosae virginis, et aliorum sanctorum imagines in christianorum templis subvertendas, ita etiam solemnes pompas, quibus venerabile sacramentum hinc inde circumfertur, abrogandas arbitror.'

72 *Articuli* (67), Wittenberg, 17 Oct. 1521. For the reprint in Basel (1522) see also WA 1, 629.

73 Brachmann, 'Die Reformation in Livland,' 22, calls him a *Feuerkopf*. See also ARBUSOW, 236.

74 'Sylvester Tegetmeier's Tagebuch,' 502.

75 ARBUSOW, 832, regarding p 237. The entry for 4 Sept. 1521 reads: 'Silvester Deggenmeyher, Hamburgensis.' This is the same Tegetmeier, for Lohmüller refers to him as one who came *ex civitate Hamburgensi* (BR 2, 593, interpolation q). Ruhtenberg, 'Die Beziehungen,' 62, neglects Arbusow's addition. He assumes that Tegetmeier remained in Rostock and did not meet Karlstadt. Yet, he concludes: 'Zweifelsohne ist er aber stark von Karlstadt beeinflusst worden.'

76 *Matrikel Rostock* 2, 73.

77 Martin Reinhart, who befriended Karlstadt and his brother-in-law Gerhard Westerburg, read Hussite works in Rostock, shown him by an innkeeper named Hans Kaffmeister. They were part of a library left in Kaffmeister's keeping by a priest who had left Rostock. This happened in 1521, during Reinhart's second journey to Denmark. Since he had come back to Wittenberg after his first journey in March 1521, he probably returned to Denmark during the latter half of 1521, when Tegetmeier had left Rostock to study in Wittenberg. Tegetmeier may well have referred Reinhart to Kaffmeister. Thus Reinhart used the personal library of Tegetmeier or one of his colleagues. Cf Reinhart, *Anzaygung*, A2v. The Hussite works that Reinhart

The first entry in Tegetmeier's diary refers to Karlstadt's debate in Leipzig (Luther and Eck are not even mentioned).[78]

When Tegetmeier matriculated in Wittenberg, Luther was at the Wartburg and Karlstadt wielded considerable influence, although he was never a leader like Luther. Others could have had an impact on Tegetmeier, for example Melanchthon, the Augustinian monk Gabriel Zwilling, and perhaps the Zwickau Prophets. The Prophets did not tarry in Wittenberg; Melanchthon made an about-turn in January 1522; Zwilling recanted upon Luther's return. Karlstadt was not swayed, however, and steadfastly upheld his principles, until they culminated in a Baptist position.

The ideas Tegetmeier encountered were basically Karlstadtian, even though Karlstadt – like Luther – did not exert his influence unaided. The Wittenberg *Album* contains no records of when a student left, but travel conditions alone would have induced Tegetmeier to spend the winter in Wittenberg. He stayed at least through March 1522, for on 18 February Karlstadt began his lectures on Malachi. Tegetmeier lectured on Malachi in Latin while he was in Dorpat in February 1525, and he presumably used Karlstadt's notes.[79]

Early in March 1522 Luther delivered his *Eight Invocavit Sermons*, directed against Karlstadt's reforms.[80] Tegetmeier, however, was not persuaded to let the weak set the pace for a while. He returned to Rostock, assailing the 'Pelagianism' of the old believers, and they, in turn, decried him as an iconoclast.[81] Soon Tegetmeier left to settle his brother's estate in Riga.[82] Knopken's reforms there were congenial to Tegetmeier, and conflict in Rostock would have made him eager to look for a change. He secured an appointment to the Church of Saint James in

copied and reprinted do not show a mutual dependence of Tegetmeier and Karlstadt on those tracts. Nevertheless, such writings could have predisposed Tegetmeier to Karlstadt's radicalism. Hussite influence in Rostock can be traced back to Nikolaus Rutze; cf Hoyer, 'Nikolaus Rutze,' [157]–70. For Reinhart's later propagation of Hussite articles see Hoyer, 'Martin Reinhart,' [1595]–1615.

78 'Sylvester Tegetmeier's Tagebuch,' 503: 'Int jhar xviii up Paschken toch ick wedder na Rostock, als Carlstadt syne positiones tho Lipsick disputerde.' This is a reminiscence, for the date is wrong.

79 Karlstadt announced his lectures on Malachi in his preface to *Malachiam* (93), Av, that is, 18 Feb. 1522; he finished them before 19 March, for it was then reported: 'doctor Carolstadt [liest] Zachariam' (Kawerau, ed, *Der Briefwechsel des Justus Jonas* vol 1, p 85, n 1). Tegetmeier's report of his Malachi lectures comes from 'Sylvester Tegetmeier's Tagebuch,' 504: 'Anno 25 [quam ick tho Dorpt] am avende lichtmissen [1 Feb.] ... Was dar even iiii weken, predigte alle dage unde lass Malachiam latine, beth up den dingesdag vor asscherdage [28 Feb.].'

80 WA 10/3, 1–64.

81 Hoffman, *Gelöfigen* (1526), A5v: 'Datt [Tegetmeier] vörsakt de heilsamen lere Christi, sy pellaganisch [!] und serrenisch schilt, ist nicht wunder, dann he hefft idt vor hen ock tho Rostock gedon.' Interested in drawing a parallel, Hoffman twists his sentence.

82 Arndt, ed, *Liefländische Chronik* 2 (1753), 185f.

Riga, for which he gathered his own congregation. For his inauguration on 30 November 1522 he preached on Zacchaeus, who 'made haste' to receive Jesus (Luke 19:6).[83]

Knopken and Tegetmeier founded the Livonian Reformation. They denounced celibacy, and under their influence Father Rehberg left the cloister, grew long hair, and discarded his clerical attire for lay clothing.[84] After two years their labour bore tempestuous fruit. Knopken and Tegetmeier were influential beyond their pulpits, for they also served as vicars to the Brotherhood of the Blackheads (Kompagnie der Schwarzen Häupter), the guild of the Hanseatic traders.[85] The Brotherhood had earlier endowed Knopken's church with an altar on which an intricately carved triptych had been mounted, but it had to be removed since its use involved 'a slanderous abuse of the Holy Testament of Jesus Christ.'[86] When the altar was sent back to the house of the Brotherhood, a riot caused its destruction. This first iconoclastic incident in Riga (10 March) was no doubt also fuelled by public anger at Bishop Blankenfeld's appeal to the pope to have Riga laid under interdict for fostering the Reformation.[87] In swift succession two more riots erupted, both involving Knopken's church again as well as Tegetmeier's congregation. Thus the reformers' own churches were purged, and they fretted over the cathedral until 8 August, when the last offending vestiges of medieval piety were smashed. The civil authorities were pleased, because they accepted Reformation doctrine[88] and also wished to deliver a political blow to Blankenfeld. On 16 March

83 Pohrt, 'Reformationsgeschichte Livlands,' 30.

84 ARBUSOW, 258–9.

85 Founded in the fourteenth century, the Brotherhood of the Blackheads represented the unmarried Hanseatic traders and was named after its patron St Maurice, whose black head, flanked by a golden cross and sword, was depicted on the Blackheads' ensign. St Eucherius, bishop of Lyons 435–50 first recorded the double decimation and subsequent extermination of the Theban Legion that St Maurice served as primicerius. As Christians the legionaries declined to offer sacrifice, made compulsory during the persecutions of the Emperor Diocletian (ruled 284–305). From Agaunum, now St Maurice en Valais, where the executions took place, the cult of the Theban martyrs (celebrated on 22 September) spread via the Rhine Valley into Germany. The primary source on St Maurice in the late Middle Ages was James of Voragine's account in the very popular Legenda aurea. As an alternative explanation the Legenda derives Maurice's name from 'mauron, which in Greek means black according to Isidore [of Seville's Etymologiae] for Maurice was bitter because he was taken from his own country.' What James of Voragine had taken figuratively, the iconographers, who depicted him as a Moor, took literally; no doubt the reference to Maurice's Theban origins encouraged this. The uprooted traders would have identified with Maurice's bitterness at being far from home. After the Reformation the Brotherhood was secularized, and thus it survived until 1940. For the coat of arms of the Blackheads, see The Dom Cathedral in Riga, ed Yuri Vasilyev, illustrations 104–7.

86 ARBUSOW, 293–5.

87 DEPPERMANN, 45–6. Nothing was done on the papal side.

88 BR 3, 192f.

1523 the statue of the Virgin was burned as a witch. This act suggests a link with the Treptow riot of 1521, when images were drowned in a well. By dint of contagious magic the Virgin of tradition was executed through the ordeals of water and fire, respectively. Knopken probably held that popular veneration endowed the Virgin with the charms of a witch. The statue of the Mother of God was an ideal target for the reformers, since a strong current of Marian devotion had characterized Livonian Catholicism. Tegetmeier led the charge on 16 March – the third tumult within a week in Riga. This riot is described as follows in the Brother-book of the Estonian Beer-Carriers' Guild:

> Moreover, in 1524, during Lent, on Wednesday after Judica [16 March] the Lutherans performed a miracle in Riga. The blind received their sight; the dumb began to speak; the lame started to walk; wood was turned into people. This should be understood as follows. They broke into both churches, that is Saint Peter's and Saint James's, and they wrecked all the images, crosses, statues of Mary, and whatever was there. Moreover, the relics of the saints, immured in the altars, they pried out and they smashed them and cast out what was to be found in the churches. At night, when all of this had taken place, they sang 'On This Day of Easter' and some psalms. Following this [Tegetmeier] began his sermon approving of this righteous course, which would prevent idolatry.[89]

However one gauges the iconoclastic fever of the Livonians, the riots which spread to Wolmar, Reval, Dorpat, Felling (Viljandi, Estonian SSR), and Pernau (Pärnu, Estonian SSR) settled the struggle for religious supremacy.[90]

Knopken's attack on sodalities suggests that he knew the version of the Wittenberg Ordinance that was appended to Karlstadt's tract *On the Removal of Images*. In the same document it is argued that offensive church furniture should be sold to support the poor and the local community chest. This idea was aborted in Wittenberg, but it lived in Livonia.[91]

To regard the Livonian Reformation as initially Lutheran is an anachronism. In his mammoth work on the Livonian Reformation Arbusow has this to say:

> For some time the Reformation in Livonia had its own colouring. In part its origins were hardly Lutheran; at least not with a clear awareness of its teachings. [Towards the person of Luther] one was originally quite indiffer-

---

89 Böthführ, 'Bemerkungen,' 66–7.
90 Pohrt, 'Reformationsgeschichte Livlands,' 67–8, lists ten outbursts. Since we conclude that a similar riot also took place in Wolmar, this gives a minimum of eleven.
91 ARBUSOW, 300f, 599f.

ent; with his teachings, sometimes more than unimpressed. Towards a common and deliberately made connection with Wittenberg, the Livonians would only move under the leadership of their magistrates.[92]

However, Arbusow has exaggerated on one point, for Knopken and Tegetmeier indeed knew that they differed from Luther.

Hoffman the Iconoclast

Since, as we have seen, Hoffman became a radical in Livonia, he must originally have lived in Riga, unless he was converted when Tegetmeier came to Wolmar. Knopken's defence of Hoffman in 1525 and the fact that Hoffman knew of Teget-meier's last days in Rostock imply that Hoffman knew both firebrand preachers personally. Hoffman's view of the Lord's Supper shows traces of Karlstadt's early theses; since Hoffman knew no Latin, however, he may have learned of Karl-stadt's teachings through the sermons of Knopken and Tegetmeier.

Hoffman began to preach in Wolmar in 1523 and was expelled in 1524 after an imprisonment. Besides the statement cited earlier, Hoffman penned this enig-matic passage:

Further, [I ask] the dearest friends in Wolmar not to be led into error on account of such lies, so as not to turn away from the teaching. For you know that I was imprisoned at the time for the sake of God, when an offence [unrat] took place among you, and while I was imprisoned, the spirit who taught among you cast upon himself the judgment that he was a cause of the matter.[93]

The allusion to 'the spirit' implicates Tegetmeier, for in this context there are several references that apply only to him. Thus, the 'offence' for which Hoffman was confined in Wolmar also involved Tegetmeier. Hoffman can hardly be absolved from complicity in the offence (probably an iconoclastic outburst), how-ever, for both he and Tegetmeier were expelled in the autumn of 1524. Naturally, Hoffman tries to conceal this in a letter that was, after all, printed on the royal press of Stockholm.[94] Hoffman now went to Dorpat where his work was to be

92 ARBUSOW, 627. See also Vööbus, Estonian People 2, 56: 'During the formative years, Luther's personal influence in the reformation movement in Livonia is practically very small.' Kuhles interprets the Livonian Reformation from a Marxist perspective. Not surprisingly he regards the Livonian Reformation as a popular revolt that was suppressed by the magistrates who established Lutheranism; see 'Die Unterdrückung,' [171]–91.

93 Hoffman, Gelöfigen, A5v.

94 LINDEN (46f) drew a similar conclusion.

interrupted by the iconoclastic riot of 10 January 1525, a riot which took the lives of four or five persons, left twenty wounded, and involved the storming of six churches and chapels of which three were gutted. It was an extraordinarily violent riot, even for Livonia. The burning of the Dorpat archives at the behest of Czar Ivan IV ('the Terrible') in 1558 led to the loss of what may have been the most valuable primary documents on the events of 10 January. Four accounts of the riot remain, but one suffers from brevity.[95] A succinct account comes from Tegetmeier's diary; most detailed are the sombre reflections of Doctor Philipp Olmen in Tilmann Bredenbach's *Belli livonici*; and a few points are clarified by the annals of the Livonian *Ständetage*.

Tegetmeier's diary account of the riot shows Hoffman in a favourable light. Because Hoffman preached the gospel, Peter Stackelberg, castellan of Bishop Blankenfeld, sent his cohorts to arrest the furrier. When Hoffman's converts tried to block Stackelberg's soldiers, the soldiers killed two Germans and two 'non-Germans' (Estonians). In retaliation the people then stormed the churches. Aided by mercenaries from Reval, they finally seized Blankenfeld's castle.

Philipp Olmen paints a gloomier picture. He was not an eyewitness, but Olmen had served the then still Catholic Dorpat Church of Saints Peter and Paul for a period beginning in 1551. Bredenbach published Olmen's version of the riot, and though he did not quite succeed in writing *sub specie aeternitatis*, his dates are unreliable, and he adds miracles that illustrate how the Livonian Reformation aroused the wrath of God. These failed to thwart the Reformation, but, with Russian aid and other supernatural calamities, the Almighty wrought manifold pestilences upon the Livonians in the three decades following Hoffman's appearance in Dorpat.

With musty eloquence Olmen describes how Hoffman's fanatic preaching incited the riot which surged from the (Estonian) Church of the Virgin to the Church of Saint John, and from thence to the monasteries of the Dominicans and the Franciscan Minorites. Next the rabble invaded the Convent of the Poor Clares, who knelt before their tormentors and begged to be left in peace for the common name of Christians which they bore. Their prayers unheeded, the nuns were dragged by the hair out of their cells, and forced 'to embrace *coniugium*.' Three churches were damaged beyond repair: the Dominican church was turned into an armoury; the Franciscan church was converted into a lime kiln; the

95 Hildebrand has edited and modernized the text on the basis of the *Conceptbuch* of the Teutonic Order. It is found in LEENDERTZ, 24, n 1, and LINDEN, 51. It reads: 'Im Herbst 1524 war hier Melchior Hofmann als Verkünder der neuen Lehre erschienen und seinetwegen kam es am 10 Jan. 1525 zu jenem Auflauf zwischen Bürgern und Leuten des Stiftsvoigts. Als man in der Stadt Sturm läutete, die Waffen ergriff und das Geschütz gegen das Schloss richtete, ward es vom Voigt geräumt und von Gliedern der Ritterschaft, des Capitels, und Raths in Verwaltung genommen.'

Russian church did further service as a public latrine.[96] These churches having been gutted, the episcopal guard shielded the Cathedral Church of Saints Peter and Paul, heroically resisting the armed mob, which was egged on by Hoffman. The bells tolled until most townsmen climbed the hill to storm the cathedral. Movable art treasures had been transferred to the castle, but the rabble smashed a splendid baptistry and sculptures of the Saviour and his disciples. With swords and lances the mob pierced the images of the saints and the crucifixes.[97] Then the populace beleaguered the episcopal fortress, which peacefully surrendered after mercenaries arrived from Reval.

Hoffman's biographers have impugned Olmen's version of the riot. Leendertz, who could not obtain a copy, casts aspersions on Olmen's veracity, which, to be sure, is not difficult.[98] Linden concedes that Olmen's description of the progress of the riot appears accurate,[99] but he considers 'Bredenbach a fanatic Catholic and as such highly partisan.'[100] Linden opts for Tegetmeier's version; so does Deppermann.[101]

Tegetmeier, however, was no less fanatic and partisan than Olmen and Bredenbach. If they were our only sources for information about the riot, Hoffman's role in the affair could be ignored, but there is other damning evidence against him. Tegetmeier first favoured Hoffman, for he then advocated image-breaking, and, following the riot, Tegetmeier recommended Hoffman to the Dorpat authorities. However, after spending the next month in Dorpat, Tegetmeier charged Hoffman with manslaughter (todtslagh).[102] It follows, then, that the entry in Tegetmeier's Tagebuch was written before Tegetmeier visited Dorpat, and thus the notation could only have been based on Hoffman's own account. If Tegetmeier added new evidence to his diary, it was deleted later. Hence Tegetmeier's (i.e. Hoffman's) version is partisan, and there was a remarkable change in Tegetmeier's view of Hoffman once he visited Dorpat.

Since the political authorities were anti-Catholic, they eagerly exploited the situation. When mercenaries were called in from Reval, the episcopal castle sur-

96 Bredenbach, Belli, C3v–4: 'Et paene a fundamentis universam aedificii molem subvertunt. Porro ne dirutarum basilicarum nullus omnino usus esset, Dominicanorum ecclesiam tormentis bellicis adservandis destinant et in publicum armarium convertunt. Franciscanam aedem calci coquendae deputant. Rutenorum templum in foricam conversum, excipiendis foetoribus, sordibus, et excrementis humanis mancipant.'

97 Ibid, C5v: 'Erat in eadem Torpatensi basilica baptisterium summo artificio et magnis impensis exstructum. Inter caetera ornamenta, sculpta erant salvatoris et duodecim apostolorum imagines, has magno impetu invadit sacrilega iconoclastarum cohors.'

98 LEENDERTZ, 26.

99 LINDEN, 52.

100 Ibid, 51.

101 Deppermann, 'Melchior Hoffmans Weg,' 175–6; DEPPERMANN, 48–51.

102 Hoffman, Gelöfigen, A5v: 'ock datt he miner lere tho lecht todtslagh.'

rendered. This action implicates the council, for a mob could not have called in the soldiers. Moreover, the council favoured radical religion, having already tolerated the preaching of Hermann Marsow and Hoffman. After the riot the authorities dispatched the town secretary, Joachim Sasse, to Riga to obtain the services of Tegetmeier, who was not known for his moderation. Nevertheless, in spite of their sympathies with the radical movement, they now wanted to be rid of Hoffman, and required him to be certified by the preachers of Riga and Luther. We assume that this leniency towards Hoffman arose from a desire to salvage the Reformation, yet his presence was now an embarrassment.

Furthermore, even Bredenbach makes concessions. Although he says the soldiers acted in self-defence, he mentions the disconcerting fact that 'five' persons were killed in the riot. Bredenbach also notes that Hoffman 'was placed' in the pulpit of the Church of the Virgin by the throng.[103] Though he was eager to stress Hoffman's aggression, here he may have thought him literally carried away by the multitude. The riot then raged on towards confrontation with Stackelberg's cohorts at the cathedral. When asked why the mob was armed, Hoffman retorted that they came to strike the canons to the ground,[104] provoking the skirmish in which 'five' persons perished.

Olmen's version clarifies why Tegetmeier later accused Hoffman of manslaughter and why the Dorpat authorities turned on Hoffman as well as the bishop, for the killings were provoked by Hoffman's inflammatory rhetoric as well as by miscalculation on the part of Stackelberg.[105]

We have seen that Bredenbach's account of the riot rested on the findings of Olmen, who lived in Dorpat twenty-six years after the event. Olmen may have had access to the town archives which at that time still existed.[106] He is at his strongest in assessing the physical damage the riot caused, the kind of evidence which can be ascertained years later. The flowery account of the reactions of the monks and nuns has apologetic ends, but it is obvious that the regulars would have been aroused when their world collapsed.

---

103 Bredenbach, *Belli*, C–v: 'pellio ... in civitate Torpato clancularias conciones in aedibus quorundam incolarum habere coepit, plurimus e iunioribus mercatoribus, novis dogmatibus, a catholicismo seducens, usque adeo, ut vehementer adaucto factiosorum numero ... seditiose ac magno cum tumultu in basilicam divae virgini sacram irruerent, suumque illum concionatorem violenter in suggestum collocarent.'

104 Ibid, C4v: 'Pellio ... consilium de invadenda cathedrali ecclesia proponit ... [Satrapes] eos compellans, quaerit quid moliantur, qua de causa armati accedant? Respondet pellio, se canonicos profligatorum.'

105 For a contrary view see DEPPERMANN, 77.

106 This is a likely source for the incident with the chain (Bredenbach, *Belli*, D2) or the killing of *five* persons. The earlier account of Tegetmeier (Hoffman) mentions four dead; the fifth may have died later from his injuries.

Bredenbach is too complex, however, to be a mere chronicler. He is a clever propagandist and a verbal artist. We have seen that the iconoclasts were said to perform the impossible feat of *piercing* the crucifixes – Hoffman and his mob were re-enacting the drama of Golgotha. The scene of the nuns dragged out by the hair recalls the rape of the Sabines. The artificial date of the riot can also be explained – since Olmen disremembered the exact year, Bredenbach's artificial precision appears to enhance the credibility of his report. Then by staging Hoffman's riot and Ivan's attack a quarter century later on the same day of the church calendar Bredenbach cements a purely literary relationship.

Although such artistic and apologetic motifs can be sifted out, the comment on the 'conjugation' of the nuns remains ambiguous. Perhaps this is just Bredenbach's way of expressing the later marriages of some of the nuns, but it is possible that some of the rioters committed acts of rape.

The records of the Livonian *Ständetage* uphold Hoffman's account on one crucial point: Stackelberg provoked the original riot by sending his cohorts to arrest Hoffman.[107] No doubt Hoffman was emboldened by the incarceration of Bishop Blankenfeld in December, and it was probably Hoffman's invasion of the pulpit of the Church of the Virgin which provoked the attempt to arrest him. Thus, Hoffman was left in peace as long as he preached in private homes, but his occupation of a pulpit was a radical challenge.

Deppermann stresses that Stackelberg wanted to imprison Hoffman 'illegally' and 'without authorization.'[108] This is technically correct, though one must caution against a modern bias. Hoffman had been driven from Wolmar by the master of the Teutonic Order. Moreover, Bishop Blankenfeld claimed the legal right of vetoing the presence of undesirable preachers, and, reluctantly, the Dorpat Council had still honoured this right in 1523 with the expulsion of Hermann Marsow.[109] From a purely legal standpoint Stackelberg's case for intervention seems as strong as Hoffman's case for preaching in Dorpat. Thus the burgomasters of Dorpat refused to press charges against Stackelberg, a defensive manoeuvre designed to prevent him from defending himself before the *Landtag*.[110]

---

107 *Akten und Rezesse der livländischen Ständetage* 3, 475: 'alhir binnen Dorpte dorch dem erbarn stifftsvagede ein uproer und schermutzell erwecket.'
108 Deppermann, 'Melchior Hoffmans Weg,' 175; DEPPERMANN, 49.
109 Hausmann, 'Monstranz,' 189: 'der Rath hatte den Prediger Hermann Marsow, der aus Riga stammte und in Wittenberg studirt hatte, berufen, der Bischof erzwang dessen Entlassung.'
110 *Akten und Rezesse der livländischen Ständetage* 3, 524: '22. Dar boneffen de stichtvageth Peter Stakelberch sick yrbaden tho vorantwerden. Welker de her borgermester van Darpth yrweret, yndeme he van ene nicht yrklaget nach boschuldiget, se ene und he wedderumb he sze tho yegenwardigem landesdaghe nicht bodaget.'

It is, of course, impossible to determine how many were killed at first in defence of Hoffman, or how many were killed when Hoffman sparked the storming of the cathedral. Even by Tegetmeier's standards, however, Hoffman could not be absolved from blame. Yet, Hoffman's case was not exceptional for others had anticipated his iconoclastic activity and fulgurant sermons. He did not attempt to gain personally from his convictions, and he suffered many deprivations for the gospel as he construed it.

One event remains to be considered. Bredenbach claims that the mob demolished the organ of the Church of Saint John.[111] If this act was rational at all, Hoffman must also have condemned musical instruments – a further indication of Karlstadt's imprint on Livonia.[112]

---

111 Bredenbach, *Belli*, Cv: 'Consimili modo in aedem D. Ioannis velut homines fanatici se proripiunt, aras subvertunt, imagines confringunt, organa demoliuntur, omnemque templi ornatum in foro congestum, ignibus et flammis subiiciunt.'

112 For Karlstadt's rejection of organs see BARGE 1, 492, th 18: 'organa, tubas et tibias in theatra chorearum et ad principum aulas relegamus.' Knopken knew these theses.

7

From Wittenberg to the Stockholm Riot

Hoffman in Wittenberg, 1525

Hoffman's future in Dorpat depended on his ability to secure a recommendation from Luther. In Wittenberg his efforts were successful, and there Hoffman penned the *Letter to the Christian Congregation in Dorpat* (1525), his first extant work. He begins by stressing apocalyptic Scriptures. Fully opened for the first time, the gospel can now be preached throughout the world, preparing the way for Christ's imminent return. One must hark to the Word, and Christ the vine, from which every fruitless branch will be lopped off to be cast into the fire. Hoffman introduces an attribute overlooked in traditional theologies: the furrierhood of God. The animal God slew for Adam and Eve to cover their nakedness with a furry skirt is a type of Christ, the lamb strangled for our sake.

Hoffman states that faith in Christ, as gracious gift from God, washes away sin. Believers must practise love and intercede for the unenlightened, who should learn to pray at the altar, which is Christ. Where Christ, the sun (Rev. 1:16), shines,

> the fruits of the Spirit are manifested, which are love, joy, peace, long-suffering, friendliness, goodness, faith, meekness, [and] chastity, Gal. 5:22–3. The law is not against those who practise this, as Saint Paul himself says.[1]

Hoffman notes that unfortunately enthusiasts (*schwyrmgeister*) plot to devour the flesh of the rulers, like the Teacher who stood in the Sun (Ezek. 29; Rev. 19). This teacher commands the birds under heaven, and his birds are found in Livonia: 'They are the reckless ones ... who carry Christ and faith in their mouths – O

---

1 WA 18, 428:3–6.

God, I wish he'd crept into their hearts.'[2] Such birds are false prophets. Hoffman says that, having been on the left, he and his followers were led to the middle, but now some push them to the right.[3] But the church does not counter with violence:

> For though the wrath of God is upon the rulers, and lords, and those who are unspiritual – that their sins may be punished with sin – those who are instrumental in this are not Christian. In short: 'He who fights with the sword, will perish by the sword.' 'For vengeance is mine says the Lord.'[4]

Hoffman believes that he is now living in the empire (reich) of the devil, and therefore he prays: 'Thy kingdom come.' The two witnesses, Knopken and Tegetmeier, sent their letters along with Hoffman. Hoffman had also been slandered in Riga, but the devil is a liar who needs no refutation. Hoffman then expresses the wish soon to return to Dorpat, and he commends his converts to Christ.

Hoffman had been chastened by the Dorpat riot, and his longing for peace may also have been quickened by the debacle of the Peasant Revolt. Significantly, he had kept news of the riot from the Wittenbergers, for neither Luther nor Bugenhagen refers to it. In their letters they urge uniform liturgical practice. Bugenhagen also discusses confession (even auricular confession is useful, if it is not compulsory), and he faults the Livonians for drunkenness and gluttony. Hoffman makes the same complaint in Daniel 12.[5] He must have told Luther and Bugenhagen the truth, but not the whole truth. One would expect Luther to be ill-informed about the situation in Livonia.[6] Perhaps Tegetmeier, sympathetic to Hoffman before going to Dorpat, had cautioned him to ignore the riot; from his own Wittenberg experience Tegetmeier knew Luther's stance on iconoclasm. Although Luther and Bugenhagen were not informed of the riot, they may still have had some doubts: though they published their letters with Hoffman's missive, they cautiously neglect to mention him.[7]

Hoffman's letter has been harmonized with Luther's views by his interpreters,[8] and certainly Hoffman would have mapped out the common ground

2 WA 18, 428:24–6.
3 WA 18, 429:1–3.
4 WA 18, 429:12–19, with omissions.
5 Hoffman, Daniel 12 (1526), 3v, L2.
6 Ruhtenberg, 'Beziehungen,' 56, 59.
7 Strodach observes this already: LW 53, 43. For a different interpretation see LEENDERTZ, 34. Leendertz thinks Luther was confident enough about Hoffman but did not want to become embroiled in the Livonian controversy.
8 LEENDERTZ, 39: 'In die dagen was hij nog werkelijk volgeling van Luther.' LINDEN, 39: 'Da erscheint er uns denn in den Hauptpunkten durchaus als Anhänger Luthers.' Noll, 'Luther Defends Melchior Hofmann,' 49: 'Hofmann's letter to Livonia reveals his theological compatibility with Luther.' DEPPERMANN, 57: 'Die wichtigsten Positionen Luthers ... wurden deutlich in Hoffmans Schreiben hervorgehoben.'

between them in order to secure the necessary recommendation.[9] He had a fairly good understanding of the gap between himself and Luther. Luther may have made available his two-volume work against Karlstadt (which would imply suspicion!), or else Hoffman had procured it for himself. Hoffman's references to *schwyrmgeister* indicate that he knows it, as does his avowal to steer a middle course between the left (Rome) and the right wing (Karlstadt and Müntzer), a position that echoes Luther.[10] In *Heavenly Prophets* Luther states as his primary concern the proper relation between faith and works, and Hoffman also discusses this issue.[11]

Luther's diatribe must have been offensive to Hoffman. There are slighting references to 'the populace,' 'the common herd,' 'the rabble,' 'Mr Everyman,' and the like: a far cry from Luther's earlier writings. On images and liturgy Hoffman has accepted Karlstadt's view. On other issues, like the controversy over the Lord's Supper, he would have delved more deeply into Karlstadt's views, even though Luther distorts them. Luther's attacks on the 'uncalled' Karlstadt must have had a painfully familiar ring.

In delineating common ground between himself and Luther Hoffman engaged in curious posturing. His attack on the *schwyrmgeister*, for example, carries one message for Luther, another for the Livonians. Hoffman fights an 'enthusiast' and 'false prophet' who was a teacher. Luther would have identified this figure as Karlstadt, but Hoffman refers to one who rules the birds in Livonia. He is a Judas: 'May another take his bishopric.'

To break Hoffman's code one can use the method he applies to Scripture. The key to the passage is the reference to 'the birds' (which is Hoffman's own idea), rather than the reference to the *schwyrmgeister* (a concept of Luther's which Hoffman uses in order to cloak the real message).[12] Birds of diverse plumage appear in Hoffman's *Daniel 12*. The ravens and night owls are said to have ruled before Christ, the sun, began to dawn. Such epithets depict the old Catholic clergy.[13] The ruler of these 'birds' must be a highly placed cleric. Another clue is the reference to him as a Judas, allowing Hoffman to apply Acts 1:20: 'May

---

9 Hoffman, *Gelöfigen* (1526), A5: 'tho der sulven tijdt dat ick tüchnis hollen muste van den lerern tho Wittenberg.'

10 WA 18, 111–12.

11 WA 18, 63–5.

12 Hoffman did not use the epithet *schwärmer* in a technical sense; Amsdorf is a *schwermer-him*, for example (Hoffman, *Nasengeist*, 13[C]).

13 Hoffman, *Daniel 12*, B2v: 'O wie viel tausend pfaffen schreien ytzt uber das liecht und lieber hetten die finsternus. Joan. i. Dann in der finsternus waren sie herren erkant, und grosse helghe geystliche leut. So aber nun die sunn ist auff gangen sieht man wie sie so greulich nachtraben zu huhu und eulen seindt.' See also [B4]. In KS 2, 12:35 Karlstadt has Victus reply to Gemser, the cleric: 'Du singest deinen gesang wie en rab.' 'Raven' or 'grackle' was a common epithet for clerics and schoolmasters. The theme of the Reformation as the dawn which scatters the creatures of the night had been popularized in Hans Sach's poem 'Die Wittembergisch Nachtigall.'

another take his bishopric.' Judas's 'bishopric' occurs in Luther's New Testament as well as the Vulgate, where it is a literal rendition of $\dot{\epsilon}\pi\iota\sigma\kappa o\pi\acute{\eta}\nu$, which does not have the technical meaning it acquires later.[14] Hoffman did not know this, and he understood the reference to 'bishopric' anachronistically. Thus he alludes to a bishop who foments revolt and who must be replaced. This figure is Johannes Blankenfeld, leader of Livonia's Catholics and bishop of Dorpat, who instigated the iconoclastic riot.

Even to the Livonians the allusions to the birds would have seemed complex, for some birds 'carry faith on their tongues' but do not have it in their hearts. Here Hoffman is alluding to Tegetmeier, who now dislikes him. To have known about Tegetmeier's changed opinions Hoffman must have tarried in Riga after leaving Dorpat in January of 1525 – this is likely, since he could not travel to Wittenberg until late spring when the weather was more favourable. Thus, he must have quarrelled with Tegetmeier upon the latter's return to Riga from Dorpat in early March 1525.

Knopken and Tegetmeier had supported Hoffman on the basis of his own version of the riot. After Tegetmeier's return only Knopken shielded Hoffman. Thus the 'enthusiasts' are Hoffman's opposition in Livonia, both the Catholic 'left' wing, headed by Blankenfeld, and the Protestant 'right' wing, represented by Tegetmeier.[15] Hoffman made his visit to Luther under formidable pressure in order to cajole him, and his playing with the word 'enthusiasts' misled later interpreters.[16]

Had Hoffman really been arrayed against Luther's enthusiasts, he would not have eschewed ideas like spiritualism, the Lord's Supper, images, and the pace of reform. His preoccupation with apocalyptic writings portends an even greater alienation from Luther. Hoffman's view that rulers are governed by Satan is striking. Luther could make similar pronouncements on occasion, but Hoffman is less balanced.[17]

Hoffman's observation that the law does not accuse believers contradicts Luther, for whom the law is *ever accusing*. Hoffman's *sola fide* position also differs from Luther's. Luther accepts no faith without works as its natural fruit, but Karlstadt and Knopken are more sceptical. They retain the law for believers, insisting that *Christian* morality is essential, whereas Luther regards morality as part of the natural law engraved on the hearts of all. For Hoffman, Knopken, and Karlstadt the canonicity of James is secure.

14 Already noted by Noll, 'Melchior Hofmann,' 65, n 55.
15 Hoffman's indiscriminate allusions to both Catholic and Protestant clerics as 'birds' may have been influenced by Karlstadt's deliberately indiscriminate designation of both Catholics and Lutherans as 'papists.' On Knopken as Hoffman's sole supporter see Hoffman, *Gelöfigen*, A5v.
16 Krohn, *Wiedertäufer* (1758), began this tradition. He chides Hoffman's love of the Old Testament, Revelation, and allegorizing (49–50), but says that his tract contains many 'good' (read 'Lutheran') points, 47–9.
17 WA 18, 417:24–5.

Luther probably was not the sole reformer Hoffman met in Wittenberg. Leendertz has withdrawn his suggestion that Hoffman met Karlstadt in 1525 because he thinks that Karlstadt did not return to Wittenberg until November 1525,[18] and because he believes that, if Hoffman had met Karlstadt, he would have mentioned the meeting in his writings. Ultimately Leendertz contends that Hoffman first met Karlstadt in 1527.[19] But it is unlikely that Hoffman would have mentioned meeting Karlstadt precisely *because* this would have embroiled him further in the radical cause. In addition, Hoffman is not given to reminiscing about whom he met.

There seems to be some circumstantial evidence for a personal relationship between Hoffman and Karlstadt at this time. Hoffman was stimulated not only by the younger Karlstadt, as mediated to him via Knopken and Tegetmeier, but also by later developments in Karlstadt's theology. In 1526 Hoffman condemns oaths.[20] Unless this view is derived from the reformers of Riga (whose views are not known), or is dependent on Karlstadt's 1522 tract *Gelubden*, Hoffman may have discussed this concept with Karlstadt himself.[21] Karlstadt no longer advertises his opposition to oaths, presumably in order not to furnish Luther with ammunition implicating him as a rebel.

Linden has tried to trace Hoffman's rejection of oaths to the Swiss Brethren, but he cannot find specific evidence.[22] Antje Brons has suggested that Hoffman visited Zurich in 1523, on the basis of a conjectural letter in which Zwingli alludes to Hoffman. However, at this time Hoffman lived in Livonia; the letter of Zwingli has never been located; and 1523 does not fit the development of the Swiss Baptist movement. On this matter Kawerau disagrees with Brons,[23] and in a later edition of her book Brons has ignored the letter of Zwingli.[24] In fact, direct Swiss Baptist influence is not evident until 1530, when Hoffman lives in Strassburg. Thus Hoffman's rejection of oaths seems best explained by a personal encounter with Karlstadt.

In 1529 Hoffman invited Karlstadt to the Flensburg Disputation;[25] and Karlstadt rushed to Holstein. True, Karlstadt's position in Saxony was precarious

18 LEENDERTZ, 42.
19 Ibid, 100.
20 Hoffman, *Daniel 12*, [E2v] (not dijv]–3v.
21 BARGE 1, 478, th 44; *Gelubden* (50], B3v, C2.
22 LINDEN, 92
23 Kawerau, *Melchior Hoffman*, 1.
24 I could not obtain Kawerau's edition for comparison, and thus I cannot indicate where the omission occurs.
25 Cornelius, *Geschichte des Münsterischen Aufruhrs* 2, 292: 'Carolostadius relinquens Saxoniam disputationi interesse cupiebat, vocatus a Melchiore cum suis, sed a duce Holsatiae indictum illi erat, ne urbem disputationi ordinatam intraret. Tandem Melchior cum suis urbem exire iussus est. At Carolostadius et Melchior ad comitem Emdensem, ubi Rhodius noster apostolum agit, devenerunt.'

after he spurned Luther's appeal for a common front against Zwingli,[26] but he could have fled elsewhere, as he did a year later. Why did Hoffman correspond with Karlstadt? Why did Karlstadt respond at once, even leaving his family behind for a while? If we assume that they were friends, it was Hoffman who had come to Karlstadt, since the latter was confined to Saxony. Hoffman visited Saxony in 1525 and 1527, and – as we have seen – Leendertz assigns Karlstadt 'a preponderant influence' by 1526. Thus 1525 is the preferred date for a first meeting.

Hoffman had arrived in Wittenberg by 12 June 1525.[27] Ten days later his letter to the Livonians was ready. In it Hoffman expresses the hope of returning soon, but this statement may already indicate he had his doubts. Hoffman had to tarry until the tracts were printed. Both Luther and Bugenhagen also wanted to see their letters distributed in Livonia, but often the printing presses in Wittenberg were taxed to capacity. If Luther had to complain about delays, so did Hoffman. When Hoffman finished his letter, Karlstadt was probably living at Luther's home. Karlstadt completed his *Endschuldigung* on 24 June. Two days after that Melanchthon wrote to Camerarius that Karlstadt's family was expected in the evening.[28]

Karlstadt enjoyed Luther's hospitality for about eight weeks.[29] He now lived under the same roof as Hoffman. Though his visit was shrouded with secrecy (Karlstadt was still banned from Saxony), the arrival of Karlstadt and his family would have been noticed by other boarders at the former Black Cloister. In *Endschuldigung* Karlstadt had offered an ambiguous recantation,[30] and Luther wrote to Briessmann that Karlstadt clung to his old position.[31]

Since they were both staying at the Black Cloister, Karlstadt and Hoffman must have been inexorably drawn together. Hoffman was an almost perfect incarnation of Karlstadt's ideals. Moreover, Hoffman was a layman by birthright, Karlstadt merely by adoption. A first meeting in 1525 also makes more probable the 1527 meeting proposed by Krohn and Leendertz.

At last Hoffman returned to Livonia, and though he did not fully meet the demand of the Dorpat Council (Tegetmeier's recommendation was now worthless), he was allowed to resume preaching. The authorities no longer feared another riot, for the episcopal castle had surrendered and the churches of Dorpat were now devoid of smashable items, except for the people.

---

26 BARGE 2, 386f.
27 I assume that the 'Franciscus Weiss de Terbato' who registered at the University of Wittenberg on that day (*Album academiae Vitebergensis*, 126) had travelled with Hoffman.
28 KS 2, 118:13: 'Dat. Ioannis Baptistae [24 Jun.] Anno xxv.' For Melanchthon see CR 1, col 751.
29 TR 2, no. 2064.
30 BARGE 2, 364f.
31 BR 3, 355.

Hoffman was finally expelled from Dorpat after an incident in which he publicly humiliated the daughter of one of the burgomasters.[32] Like Karlstadt, Hoffman demanded that goods alienated from the churches should benefit the poor; again like Karlstadt, Hoffman exemplified apostolic simplicity, wearing only one simple coat. The burgomaster's wife and daughter met the first requirement because they possessed a stolen monstrance, the value of which they had donated to the poor. They failed to meet the second condition, however, for the vessel had been forged into two golden chains which they wore. When the daughter arrived late in church, Hoffman halted the service, ordering all the women and girls to kneel before her, 'just as the papists did when the golden coat of Jesus was carried in.' One understands why Hoffman baited the wealthy, but one can also understand why they retaliated. The time of egalitarianism was still to come, and the basic question is at what level such an ideal should be accomplished.

After being ousted from Dorpat, Hoffman went to Reval as comforter of the sick. Linden praises Hoffman's disinterested efforts on behalf of the poor, but too little is known about Hoffman's work in Reval to judge the virtue of his course; did Hoffman desire to play such a subordinate role, or did he simply choose what was left for the time being? Moreover, did the 'false brethren who pretend to follow the gospel' exile Hoffman simply for having consoled the afflicted?[33] From Reval Hoffman embarked for Stockholm.

Hoffman's own ideas left no lasting imprint on Livonia. The Lutheran magistrates and their clerical acolytes were able to displace the foremost lay shock-trooper of the Livonian Reformation. Some of Hoffman's followers may have continued their efforts, but all that is known about them is a single anecdote. Hoffman had commissioned a weaver to proselytize among the Latvians. This weaver offered absolution on the basis of a very light penance. He administered the Lord's Supper to a crowd, but when he ran out of oblations, he substituted radish slices. According to the *Livonian Chronicle*, the communicants were heard to sigh: 'Ah, sweet Jesus, why have you become so pungent?'

Politics and Religion in Sweden

The birth of the Swedish state and the attendant religious shift to Lutheranism have been described more fully elsewhere.[34] The Union of Kalmar in 1397 had

32 Bredenbach, *Belli*, D2.
33 *Dialogus* [1529], A2: 'Da ist er [in Revell] der krancken diener worden, und durch falscher brüder anschefftung die da wöllen evangelisch sein, ist er aber eins des lands verwisen worden.' The reason why Hoffman was expelled, however, may have been his preaching, e.g. the following warning, *Gelöfigen* (40), [A6]: 'Gy Revelschen wacht jw ock dat jw de düfel nicht inn strick zieh, dann richt nach der schrifft, lot jw menschen ler nicht vorfören.'
34 Bergendoff, *Olavus Petri*.

inaugurated a troubled and not unchallenged history of Danish hegemony in Scandinavia. In November 1520 King Christian II of Denmark ordered the beheading of ninety Swedish leaders, including two bishops, for treason against the pope. This Stockholm massacre failed to cow the remaining nobles, who revolted under Gustaf Vasa. The Union of Kalmar was a dead letter in 1523 after Gustaf ousted the Danes from Stockholm. The Diet of Strangnäs elected Gustaf king in June 1523, though the coronation was postponed until 12 January 1528.

Gustaf's brilliant political strategy led to the subjugation of the church. His reform programme consisted of the confiscation of church tithes, the stabling of horses in the monasteries, and the unilateral appointment of church leaders. Olaus Petri and Lars Andreae implemented the king's policy for the church without sacrificing their integrity on what they deemed to be the basic religious issues. Their position led to friction with the king, who waited for a decade to dismiss Petri and Andreae for a period of two years. At the Örebro Council of 1540 Gustaf claimed kingship by divine right, and the council submitted, adjuring its traditional electoral rights.

When Hoffman arrived in Sweden (late in 1525 or early in 1526), the king's power was still somewhat shaky and the religious situation was fluid. Petri and Andreae had only recently begun to proclaim the new faith in Stockholm: a faith that circumvented Luther's political ethic in order to justify Gustaf's revolution. This state of affairs would have looked tempting to Hoffman the radical preacher; moreover, Stockholm was the centre where furs from the eastern Baltic were transshipped, an attraction for Hoffman the furrier.

In Stockholm Hoffman styled himself 'the German preacher.'[35] A letter from King Gustaf reveals that Hoffman was not appointed by the crown, but beyond doubt he served as 'German preacher' in an unofficial capacity. Hoffman preached on Daniel 12 and Luke 21:25–8 during regular church services. The passage from Luke was the lectionary reading for the Second Sunday in Advent, and Hoffman's conclusion of the reading of Daniel 12 with *Laus Deo* does not bespeak delivery in the market place. Daniel 12 was, in fact, the Old Testament reading for Michaelmas.

The Church of Saint Gertrude had not yet been established, but a German congregation worshipped at Saint Nicholas Church, where Olaus Petri preached in Swedish. Hoffman preached in Low German both inside and outside the church. He knew Jörgen Richolff, printer for the royal press of Stockholm from 1525 to 1529. Richolff printed Hoffman's sermons, but later he must have regretted his audacity; he avenged himself in 1529 when he set up his own press in Hamburg and printed Schuldorp's, Weidensee's, and Bugenhagen's attacks on Hoffman.

---

35 *Dialogus* [1529], A2: 'Also hatt gott seinen weg gefertiget in Schweden, das er ist kummen in ein grosse kauffstatt Stockholm genant, da selbst ist er teüschen prediger worden ein zeytlang.'

Hoffman's first Stockholm publication is the *Brief Admonition to the Believing Congregation in Livonia*, a work that reminds one of the Wittenberg letter. There are renewed charges against those who preach but do not practise faith, yet the need for faith is reaffirmed. The rulers are still in compact with the unjust.[36] The language of this work is no longer conciliatory. Rebuking the Livonian ministers, Hoffman changes his former emphasis on the need for peace: 'God will straighten it out, for Christ speaks: "I have come to bring not peace but the sword."'[37]

From the first page on, Hoffman denounces the New Devil. This New Devil lives in Riga, and once he praised Hoffman, but then he gave the lie to his former endorsement. This 'servant of his own belly' came to Dorpat. He knows three languages and he hails from Rostock. Obviously Tegetmeier is the target of Hoffman's attack. Only one man in Riga – Knopken – is still a 'faithful shepherd' (*trwen herden*).[38]

The Reformation has conquered Livonia with new clerics worse than the pope:

> The pope is a terrible devil and antichrist, but, on some points, he never acted in such an unchristian manner as the belly servants ... You don't have to worry about the pope's bunch. They will arise from among us, but they will not be of us.[39]

The haughty 'belly servants' deny Hoffman's call:

> They openly prepare their tangles and their snares, and they think freely: 'We alone have right and power. What we impose is law.' What would they think when I say that not one minister in Livonia has been rightly chosen, in accordance with the Scriptures? I would not rebuke them for this though, if they saw that you shouldn't put Hagar above her mistress Sarah.[40]

However, their behaviour is to be expected. If the Pharisees call the father (Christ) Beelzebub, they will not spare the rest of the household (Matt. 10:25).

There are other areas of friction. Tegetmeier has accused Hoffman of manslaughter; if that charge were true, Hoffman parries, then Christ slew the Holy Innocents, and Stephen and the other martyrs were not guiltless of suicide.[41]

---

36 Hoffman, *Gelöfigen*, A2v.
37 Ibid, A5v.
38 Ibid, A4v–5v.
39 Ibid, A4v.
40 Ibid, A4. Hoffman's shifts from the singular (Tegetmeier) to the plural (the ministers in Livonia) have been eliminated for clarity.
41 Ibid, A5v.

Next Hoffman examines diverse ministries in the New Testament. Believers are kings and priests, who serve as prophets, apostles, and evangelists.[42] Hoffman ranks himself among the prophets, for in their human wisdom the Livonian ministers are said to quench the spirit of the prophets.[43]

Tegetmeier considers Hoffman *pellaganisch* [!] *und serrenisch*.[44] The charge of Pelagianism seems strange, for in *Believing Congregation* Hoffman attacks those 'who preach freedom, where there is no freedom.'[45] This statement presumes a form of predestination, unless it is a legalistic attack on Luther. In *Daniel 12* Hoffman divulges an extreme doctrine of double predestination. However, Hoffman's attacks on the lack of spiritual fruit in the lives of the Livonian ministers ('we all preach Christ, but with the deed we forsake him') may have seemed to be a return to righteousness based on works.[46] In that case Hoffman is fending off the same misconception that Luther had about Karlstadt.[47]

When Tegetmeier reviled Hoffman for being *serrenisch*, he was alluding to Hoffman's iconoclasm.[48] This is a *volte-face* for Tegetmeier. In Dorpat he realized that the burnt offerings of others seem less savoury than one's own. Tegetmeier had learned from the Dorpat experience, but to Hoffman he must have appeared inconsistent. Finally, Tegetmeier had tackled Hoffman's fascination with apocalyptic literature. Hoffman responds at length, noting the consistency with what he taught in Dorpat.[49] Hoffman's apocalyptic obsession is old-fashioned. Since Hoffman does not use the medieval exegetical terminology, he follows ancient tradition and borrows biblical images. Using the four beasts of Ezekiel 1 for illustration, he argues that the lion equals the law, and the calf is the figures of the Old Testament. The human face is Christ's parables. It conceals the eagle, that is the spiritual meaning felt by God's children in their hearts.[50] Hoffman did not modify this type of exegesis until 1530, when he went to Strass-

---

42 Ibid, [Av].
43 Ibid, A4,5.
44 Ibid, A5v.
45 Ibid, A2v.
46 Ibid, A4v.
47 WA 18, 63:5–22.
48 The *Serrenisch* refers to Serenus of Marseille who was reprimanded by Pope Gregory I ('The Great') for having removed the images in his church when the people venerated them. See Gregorius I, *Epistolarum*, liber xi, indictio iv, epistola xiii (PL 77, 1128–30).
49 Hoffman, *Gelöfigen*, [Av]–2.
50 Ibid, [Av]–2. I do not know on whom Hoffman depended, but the basic idea is ancient. Irenaeus, Bishop of Lyons (ca 140–ca 202), identified the four figures with the evangelists, and he also held that the lion is God's direct revelation before Moses; that the Mosaic laws are represented by the calf (used for sacrifice); that the human face symbolizes the incarnation of Christ; and that the eagle signifies the gift of the Spirit. See *Adversus Haereses* 2.11.8 (*Sources chrétiennes* 34, 192:23–202:8). Although different, this idea was a precursor of the medieval *quadriga* or fourfold sense of Scripture. The four beasts were also connected with the four

burg. There he can speak like Thomas Müntzer about the Key of David,[51] which he also calls the doctrine of the cloven hoof. By then he accepts genuine tensions in Scripture, as do the central German Baptists. Sometimes Hoffman's exegesis appears more arbitrary than it is because he tends to rush along without explaining his identifications. The fourfold scheme is little more than the Augustinian principle of the Spirit and the Letter, applied in different ways to the Old and the New Testament. Karlstadt accepts the doctrine of the Spirit and the Letter, but Luther has abandoned it. Hoffman uses metaphors to explain the apocalyptic writings: here Hoffman's approach simply continues medieval tradition.

Why does Hoffman seize on apocalyptic literature? Unlike Melanchthon, Hoffman wants to provide an antidote to pagan astrology. One who wants to know the future should consult Scripture.[52] Like most of his contemporaries, Hoffman is convinced that he is living in the latter days.[53] Here Hoffman is independent of Karlstadt, who almost removed Revelation from the canon.

Luther never quite overcame his original scruples regarding Revelation either, but his New Testament, which Hoffman owned, contains woodcuts inspired by Dürer's *Apocalypse*. Thus Lukas Cranach and his school may have fanned Hoffman's apocalyptic inclinations. However, there is also a progression from Dürer to Cranach to Hoffman. Let us illustrate this with the woodcut based on Revelation 17:1f, the theme of which is the rulers' fornication with the Whore of Babylon. Dürer depicts the whore, mounted on the seven-headed dragon, in harmless fashion. Soldiers and commoners adore her, but no rulers are represented, for the original text is too subversive.[54] In the version of Cranach's school the whore is crowned with the papal tiara, and one monk and a ruler venerate her.[55] The ruler's crown is of indifferent make, so he cannot be identified. In the title frame of Hoffman's *Explanation of the Secret Revelation* and the *Visions to Ursula Jost* (1530) the whore's crown bears little resemblance to the papal tiara. Striking is the figure who bows before the whore, for he holds the sceptre and wears the imperial crown, and a beard covers his protrusive jaws. This figure bespeaks Charles V, both physiognomically and through the insignia of his office.

evangelists by Victorinus, bishop of Pettau (d 303 or 304), in his *Commentarii in Apocalypsin* (*Corpus scriptorum ecclesiasticorum latinorum* 49, 48:12–54:4). There Victorinus made still another connection, with the four rivers in paradise, a view we shall encounter in Hoffman's *Matt. 1*. Since the four beasts became universally connected with the evangelists, Hoffman's audience would have been familiar with these symbols, which graced many cathedral doors.

51 MS, 208:3f.
52 Hoffman, *Daniel 12*, 3v. Cf *Weissagung* (1530), A2.
53 For Luther see Deppermann, 'Melchior Hoffmans Weg,' 179, n 13.
54 Dürer, *Complete Woodcuts*, 119.
55 DB 7, 515.

Luther's contribution to Hoffman's doctrine of the latter days should not be ignored. Hoffman was influenced by Luther's *Kirchenpostille* for the Second Sunday in Advent.[56] There Hoffman parts company with Karlstadt. Perhaps it is typical that Hoffman also differs from Luther in several respects, but in the main he is dependent on him.[57] In Hoffman's scheme Elijah precedes Christ's return (Mal. 4:5; Matt. 17:10f.). Many Swedes regarded Luther as the New Elijah.[58] That he did not identify Luther with Elijah underscores Hoffman's initial ambivalence towards Luther, and Hoffman's appropriation of the title of Elijah for himself is indicative of his final break with Lutheranism in 1529.

In 1526 Hoffman also declares that some aspects of Luther's eschatology are inept. When he preached his sermon on Daniel in Stockholm on the Second Sunday in Advent, he consulted the postil where Luther points to changes in the weather and other signs to establish that the end is near. Hoffman turns to the Bible 'on account of the inept explanation of some and of others who point to astronomers and to strange signs. Therefore I wish to serve with a brief explanation, to declare such things from Holy Writ.'[59] Hoffman's political attitude was shaped by Revelation and Daniel. The role Hoffman assigns the rulers, of shielding the wicked and crushing the righteous, must have made an unfavourable impression on the governing authorities, and thus Hoffman saw experiential verification of the truth of his predictions.

Since this subject is not relevant for Hoffman's relationship with Karlstadt, and since apocalyptic enthusiasm waned considerably after the Münster episode, we bypass the apocalyptic schemes,[60] but Linden, Leendertz, Kawerau, and Deppermann have treated them at length. It should be noted that the basis for Hoffman's apocalypticism had already been laid in Livonia and Sweden, even though he revised some of his expectations in Strassburg.

In December 1526 Hoffman published two sermons in *Daniel 12*. Besides refining his apocalyptic schemes Hoffman overreacts to Tegetmeier's charge of Pelagianism. Hoffman begins with an address 'to the elect saints of God in Livonia.' He rejects free will, for the natural man is evil. Salvation is ordered by God alone, who elects and reprobates. Hoffman outdoes Luther's *On the Bondage of the Will* (1525) when he undermines even certitude of salvation, stabbing at the

---

56 WA 10-I-2, 93–120. See also Luther's preface in O. Albrecht, 'Luthers Arbeiten,' ARG *Texte* 23 (1926), 6f.

57 See DEPPERMANN, 67f.

58 Sandblad, *De eskatologiska föreställningarna i Sverige*, 42.

59 Hoffman, *Daniel 12*, 3v.

60 In contrast Karlstadt's eschatology is confined to expectations concerning personal immortality and the resurrection. See Kleiner, 'Karlstadt's Eschatology.' For Karlstadt's Basel period see also Schmidt, 'Karlstadt als Theologe und Prediger zu Basel,' 155–68.

heart of Luther's form of the Reformation experience.[61] After his 'union with God' a 'deified man' who has renounced his will will praise God at the final judgment even if he has been classified among the damned:

> What a great and marvellous picture it is, when a completely deified man, who stands in complete self-surrender (gelassenheit), is indifferent about whether God has made him ... for the kingdom of life or of death. It is all the same to him. He does not say to his Creator: 'make me this or that way' ... but if such a deified man knew that God wanted to damn him and had created him for this purpose, he would still esteem and praise [God] above all. Even if he cannot praise [God] in yonder age, he will still have praised him, when he still belonged to his Creator.[62]

Not Lutheran predestination but the medieval mystical notion of resignation unto hell has surfaced. Hoffman recants this idea in his *Romans* (1530) as due to 'a satanic lying spirit and the impulses of a fantastic fool.'[63] Since Hoffman was not referring to himself, he probably had another reformer in mind. He may have misunderstood Karlstadt's intention in *Willen Gottes*, where Karlstadt argues that hell may be turned to heaven if the believer enters it in full *gelassenheit*.[64] In the same work the crassest form of predestination is proposed in an attempt to caricature it. This is followed by weak questioning that took a much stronger form in later tracts.[65] Karlstadt had inherited the scholastic habit of first advancing his opponents' arguments and then presenting his rebuttal, but his rejoinders in this work are weak because, before his ejection from Saxony, he strove to avoid a public collision with Luther. It is understandable that this method of argument perplexed Hoffman, who did not understand that Karlstadt's weak questions had to be read in conjunction with his caricature of predestination in order to discover his true sympathies. Thus Hoffman, upset when he realized later that Karlstadt rejected predestination, probably identifies Karlstadt in 1530 as the 'fool' who had led him astray. Hoffman also blends in material from the German translation of

---

61 WA 18, 600f. LINDEN, 86f, thinks that Hoffman's view is more extreme than Luther's, but their predestinarian ideas are compatible.

62 Hoffman, *Daniel 12*, C3–v. Cf [2], C2v, H3–v.

63 Hoffman, *Romeren*, M3: 'Het leeren zommige, indien godt den mensche verdoemen wil, dat si geerne verdoemt sullen willen zijn. Ende derselfder leeringe spelen zommige na ... Mer ghi doet een sulcke gelatene wenschinge wt eenen sathanischen logen geest ende wt eener fantasyigen ghecx drijvinge, want het is niet gods natuer ende aert dat hi ooc van aenbegin der werlt tot op den joncksten dach eenen mensche verdoemen soude.'

64 *Willen gottes* (102), H. Luther may be alluding to this, above, 27, n 10.

65 Hoffman could have derived this from the *Theologia Deutsch*, but then the reference to the 'fool' (gheck) does not make sense.

Luther's *On the Bondage of the Will*. Three passages in *Daniel 12* echo Luther on predestination.[66]

In Stockholm Hoffman begins to work out his views on the ministry. He admonishes the fruitless 'belly servants' who exalt persons above Scripture. They are the third of the ministers who will lapse, for the Dragon sweeps away one third of the stars (Rev. 14:4).[67] This means that two-thirds of the paid ministers will remain constant; they are the faithful 'belly servants.'[68]

Most valuable are Hoffman's positive ideas about the church and the ministry. Hoffman wants to reconstruct the church on the basis of New Testament practice. He refers to 1 Timothy 3:2–7 and Titus 1:6–8. There are teachers, apostles, bishops, and deacons, whose functions are not made explicit,[69] probably because distinct callings do not give rise to new titles. Only Christ rules the church, and 'it is all the work of brothers and sisters.'[70] Hoffman is paraphrasing Matthew 23:1–8, the passage with which Karlstadt also opposes clerical titles. Without explanation Karlstadt styles himself in his tracts as 'Brother Andreas,' 'the new layman.'[71] He argues that laypersons are messengers and angels from God, and Hoffman echoes the same idea.[72]

Hoffman assigns to the individual minister only the power of the Word, but even this is shared with the laity. The power of the keys lies only with the congregation. This is Karlstadt's position as well.[73] Hoffman does not wish to curtail excommunication with this stricture, for there should be more excommunications – again he reflects Karlstadt.[74]

The minister must be elected from the congregation rather than from the outside. Ironically, this idea may be derived from Luther's *Nobility*.[75] The minister works with the people, encouraging them to prophesy. As Leendertz has shown, here Hoffman regurgitates Karlstadt's interpretation of 1 Corinthians 14.[76] Hoffman also rejects the Pauline and Lutheran argument to remain in one's original calling (1 Cor. 7:20–4). Hoffman asserts his right to preach without official

---

66 Hoffman, *Daniel 12*, C2v–3, D, H3.
67 Ibid, [I4v], D2v.
68 Ibid, 3v–[4].
69 Ibid, L3v, M3v–4.
70 Ibid, Cv.
71 Beginning with *Willen gottes* (102).
72 Hoffman, *Daniel 12*, A2v. For Karlstadt see his treatises *Malachiam* (93) and *Engeln* (122) passim.
73 Hoffman, *Daniel 12*, Bv, Cv. For Karlstadt see *Emphahung* (76), B3v–[4].
74 Hoffman, *Daniel 12*, [N4v]–0. For Karlstadt see *Emphahung* (76), [B4]; *Was bann* (119), passim.
75 WA 6, 440. Luther, however, demands learning besides piety.
76 Hoffman, *Daniel 12*, [L4]. See LEENDERTZ, 44–5.

training or a knowledge of Latin because many types of builders help to erect Christ's temple.[77]

The preacher should be more than theologian, for the Bible rather than theology is the original source. The church needs people of the Spirit, not of the Letter. People of the Letter resemble the scribes who pointed the magi to Bethlehem without going there themselves. Hoffman marks off his position against the pope, the emperor, and the university theologians (Wittenberg is not excepted).[78] The preacher must be called by God rather than by a human agency. Of course, one's calling is a public event, because one does not hide one's light under a bushel.[79] Against Luther Karlstadt also maintained his spiritual call to Orlamünde. To identify with his church he accepted citizenship there and served there as a layman. Karlstadt and Hoffman also regard persecution as an essential mark of the Church.[80] The minister of God's little remnant prefers the living waters of Christ to the theology of the universities.[81] Such a minister is humble and encourages others to prophesy.[82] In 1526 Hoffman's doctrine of the church is already Karlstadtian.

Hoffman shares Karlstadt's view on church decoration as well. Ministers should wear no vestments.[83] Churches should be devoid of images, which, following Karlstadt, Hoffman calls ölgötzen.[84] On the Lord's Supper Hoffman uses some arguments that are found in Karlstadt's Latin theses, probably mediated to him by Karlstadt personally. The words of institution are interpreted literally; thus, bread and wine are the body and blood of Christ, and Hoffman adds that the eating of them is mutual. As Christ eats believers in the Supper, so they eat him. Obviously such eating is spiritual. By eating believers, Christ assimilates them in his mystical body, the church, but Christ remains the head and the garment. Believers are united with Christ through faith, just as drops of quicksilver become one fluid. Hoffman follows Luther, the younger Karlstadt, and Knopken in calling the Supper a sacrament, seal, and sign. It is a memorial for believers who receive the sign of Christ. Hoffman comes close to Karlstadt when he says that unbelievers receive the sign of Judas, that is, the devil enters into them.[85] Since no

77 Hoffman, *Daniel 12*, D2v, [D4], E2, F2.
78 Ibid, [F4v]–G.
79 Ibid, Dv–2.
80 Ibid, H2v. For Karlstadt see *Ausslegung* (15), [B4]; *Gewaldt* (63), [B4]; KS 2, 56, etc.
81 KS 2, 7.
82 *Fürbit Marie* (108).
83 Hoffman, *Daniel 12*, B3.
84 Ibid, B3, G. Only once does Hoffman use ölgötzen in the more usual sense of 'blockheads,' K2.
85 Ibid, [M4]. Karlstadt refers to unbelievers who outwardly eat the Lord's bread but actually (i.e. internally) eat the food of the devil (*Christus* (129), C2). He refers to drinking the devil's cup in *1 Cor. 10* (142), [C4]. In 1521 Karlstadt spoke of an unworthy priest who 'eats and drinks hell' (BARGE 1, 494, th 6).

objective change occurs in the Supper, Hoffman follows Karlstadt and Knopken in arguing against reserving the elements:

for the bread which you eat in faith and in the power of the Word, that is to you the body of Christ, and the drink is [to you] his blood, but what remains is no sacrament or testament, neither is it the body of Christ, nor his blood.[86]

Like Karlstadt, Hoffman discards all tradition apart from Scripture. One may not, for example, reserve the elements, for this has not been enjoined in Scripture.[87] This position Luther had already censured in Karlstadt, whose prohibitions were said to limit freedom as much as the papacy's commandments.[88]

Like Karlstadt, Hoffman categorically prohibits the adoration of the sacrament.[89] In this connection Hoffman stresses a relationship with spiritual prayer. Karlstadt emphasizes spiritual prayer (e.g. Hannah) in 1521.[90] Hoffman and Karlstadt also apply John 6 to the Lord's Supper,[91] and they agree that the elements are not essential for communion.[92] Hoffman does not use Karlstadt's *touto* argument (he may not have understood it), but he accepts Karlstadt's earlier position of identifying the elements and Christ's body and blood in a spiritual sense. Hoffman has updated Karlstadt's earlier argument to produce a viewpoint similar to the later Karlstadt. Luther's influence must also be noted – if specifically Lutheran arguments are few, there is the common ground between the younger Karlstadt and Luther of what is increasingly called the Wittenberg theology. Specifically, one is reminded of Luther when Hoffman notes that the superstitious use of the sacrament has given genuine offence to the Jews.[93] Although this argument is hardly central, Hoffman does show he has been reading Luther.

One argument seems close to Luther, but it actually comes from Karlstadt. Hoffman refers to the Supper as a memorial and a feast of inner union of Christ and the believers. Linden claims this idea for Luther,[94] but Luther tries to achieve a genuine parallelism between the inner eating and the outward act, whereas Hoffman and Karlstadt ultimately divorce the outward sign from the inward

---

86 Hoffman, *Daniel 12*, N.
87 Ibid, N.
88 WA 18, 110–13, 122–3.
89 Hoffman, *Daniel 12*, N–v. For Karlstadt see *Anbettung* (68), A3; *Messen* (131), 2v–[3].
90 BARGE 1, 492, th 1–4.
91 Hoffman, *Daniel 12*, Nv. This is derived from Karlstadt (BARGE 1, 485, th 25f).
92 Hoffman, *Daniel 12*, Nv–2v. See KS 2, 24: 'Das sacrament ist nit von nöten; das erkänt-nüss Christi ist von nöten.'
93 Hoffman, *Daniel 12*, Mv. For Luther see WA 2, 752.
94 LINDEN, 88.

experience. Only mystical eating is required, for 'we do not know Christ according to the flesh.'[95] Thus Karlstadt's thesis that 'the flesh profiteth nothing'
triumphs.[96]

For his terminology Hoffman is deeply indebted to Karlstadt. We have
already mentioned the use of ölgötzen. Hoffman also says that Christ cannot
be contained in a stone church – this type of polemic originated with Karlstadt
five years earlier.[97] The slurs on preachers as 'belly servants' (pfaffen) and
'smeared ones' (geschmierten) are foreshadowed in Karlstadt.[98] Mystical references to the man who is gelassen (self-surrendered), müssich (empty), vergottet
(deified), or a child of God recall Karlstadt.[99] Ultimately this position goes back to
Tauler or the Theologia Deutsch, but, like Karlstadt, Hoffman borrows useful
mystical terms without advancing a mystical system.[100] We have seen, for
example, that even the 'deified man' can be condemned. Thus, predestination at
this point undercuts the language of the mystics.

Hoffman is a biblicist, but he accepts prophecy along with Scripture. As a
youth Hoffman heard an otherwise unidentified prophecy of green geese and
piebald birds that would perish before the end of the world.[101] This he applies to
the Roman clergy, as a prophecy that is now being fulfilled. Thus, Hoffman grew
up in an environment of medieval piety, rife with speculations about the end of
the world, and the voice of prophecy. Karlstadt is averse to apocalyptical forecasts,
but he does maintain that God inspires simple laypeople to prophesy and hear his
voice.[102]

In Daniel 12 Hoffman also illustrates the thwarted theocratic aspect of Karlstadt's political theology. Hoffman classifies earthly rulers with Satan and the
devils. God battles the world and those who govern it. The pope, bishops,
emperor, kings, and rulers try to drown the church. George, duke of Saxony, and
the Polish tyrant are 'bloodhounds.'[103] Hoffman circumvents Romans 13. He first

95 Hoffman, Daniel 12, N2.
96 BARGE 1, 489, th 95.
97 Hoffman, Daniel 12, Nv. For Karstadt see Gelubden (50), D3v.
98 This may merely be traditional anti-clericalism, but the attack on geschmierten (Daniel 12, C,
  N3) does recall Karlstadt, who distinguishes between those who have been anointed (gesalbten)
  after a call from God and those who are without a divine call and have been 'smeared' like
  unbelieving papists (Priesterthum (113), A3–v). Linden has noted this connection already
  (LINDEN, 92, n 1). Ultimately Karlstadt spurns all forms of anointing in ordination; then
  'gesalbten' equals 'geschmirdten' (KS 1, 76:13–15).
99 Hoffman, Daniel 12, C3–v, D, H2v, N2v.
100 Leendertz first notes Hoffman's use of Karlstadt's Gelassen (104) (LEENDERTZ, 43–4).
101 Hoffman, Daniel 12, Cv.
102 KS 2, 17.
103 Hoffman, Daniel 12, [1v], [4v], A3v–4v, B2, B4, Kv–2v, L2v. For Sigismund I Hoffman must
  have had in mind his role in crushing the Reformation in Danzig (Gdańsk). See Williams,
  The Radical Reformation, 406.

agrees with Paul, but Paul's rulers punished evildoers and protected the good, whereas present rulers do the opposite. Of course, the sword is useful, for not all are Christian. This confirms Paul, but since the rulers are now evil, 'we must obey God, rather than men' (Acts 5:29). Thus we fight tyranny with the sword of God's Word.[104] This is also a favourite theme in Karlstadt.

Not all rulers are evil, however, and then the positive theocratic aspect emerges. There are two kingdoms symbolized by the wings that sprout from the head of the eagle, wings which bear the church to safety (Rev. 12:14).[105] Hoffman must be alluding here to Scandinavia. The eagle symbolizes the Holy Roman Empire and the two wings sprouted when Denmark lost control over Sweden. Thus Hoffman makes a (theo-)logical move in going to Holstein (then part of Denmark) after being chased out of Sweden. Even after his ejection from Holstein Hoffman remains positive towards the Danish king and his son, Duke Christian.[106]

There are three references to Luther. Hoffman refers to Luther's *Commentary on Psalm 22*.[107] He identifies himself with Luther when he says that the truth is being repudiated as 'Lutheran and heretical.'[108] He refers again to Luther when he says:

> One points to the Almanac, a second here, a third there. If you instruct them with clear Scriptures, they are stiff-necked and some say: 'Martin has explained it this way,' and they certainly know a lot. Martin does not point you to himself, but to the Scriptures. At first he had to be weak with those who are of the flesh, but if you'd hear him now, you'd find the power much better explained.[109]

On one point it is uncertain whether Hoffman is influenced by Luther or by Karlstadt. In 1521 Karlstadt proposes that the traditional form of confession is 'useless' (*unnutz*), but he advocates a substitute:

> Note also ye housewives ... that your husbands can give you more certain counsel – even when they have but little learning – than the pope, the bishops, priests, and monks. With that collapses the main reason why

---

104 Hoffman, *Daniel 12*, A4–v. For a different interpretation see Stayer, *Anabaptists and the Sword*, 211–26.
105 Hoffman, *Daniel 12*, G2.
106 *Dialogus* [1529], B2v.
107 Hoffman, *Daniel 12*, D. For a different evaluation of the three passages see Krohn, *Wiedertäufer*, 83–4.
108 Hoffman, *Daniel 12*, H4.
109 Ibid, I2.

many people go to confession, i.e. to visit the priests for counsel ... If the husband can give godly counsel, they should be satisfied and not inquire further. If he is a *Nabal* (fool), they should ask their *pastor* or preacher – if the latter know the Scriptures at all. These burdens do not belong to confession, which is useless at any rate.[110]

Karlstadt never rejects personal confession of one's sins to God. Thus one confesses to God, to a relative, or to someone who knows the Scriptures. Hoffman uses a similar scheme in *Daniel 12*. One first confesses one's sins to God or to another person, or, in order to obtain understanding, one takes counsel from a 'learned man.'[111] Linden has noted a parallel line of argument in one of Luther's sermons (1524) to show Hoffman's dependence on Luther,[112] but Luther's influence is often asserted in areas where there is common ground between him and Karlstadt. Where there are differences, however, Hoffman frequently betrays Karlstadt's influence. This is true of Hoffman's attitude towards confession. Karlstadt denounces traditional confession.[113] Through Bugenhagen's letter to the Livonians Hoffman knew Luther's position that even auricular confession is good as long as it is voluntary.[114] Hoffman stigmatizes this concept:

Where has more treachery been committed than through confession? Where did more harlotry, adultery, and violation of virgins occur than during confession? The priests and the monks never went awhoring as much as during confession.[115]

In Dorpat Hoffman had already faced dissent over confession. The controversial matters are lay absolution and the dropping of confession as a requirement for communion.[116] Hoffman may have received these concepts from Knopken, who had assimilated Karlstadt's Latin theses.[117] Karlstadt also argues, even more sharply than Hoffman, that confession detracts from the forgiveness to be sought in communion.[118]

---

110 *Gelubden* (50), Hv–2. For my translation of *anderss* see A. Götze, *Frühneuhochdeutsches Glossar* (7th ed).
111 Hoffman, *Daniel 12*, I2.
112 LINDEN, 87.
113 In April 1522 Karlstadt rejects auricular confession. His attack on Emser so scandalized Luther that it was destroyed by the Wittenberg censors. Among the offensive passages is the following: 'Diabolus est confessionis pater, in qua nihil boni' (BARGE 2, 664, G2).
114 WA 18, 423:33f.
115 Hoffman, *Daniel 12*, N4.
116 Ibid, N3–v.
117 See BARGE 1, 286.
118 *Emphahung* (76) passim.

Finally, Hoffman mentions a counter-trinity, consisting of pope, emperor, and erring teachers.[119] Karlstadt does not develop a complete triad, but he does refer to the pope as 'the first begotten son of the devil,' and he contrasts believers with the 'unbelieving sons of the devils.'[120]

To sum up, Karlstadt exerted 'a preponderant influence' on Hoffman in 1526, as Leendertz has noted.[121] Influential are Karlstadt's attitudes towards ecclesiology, liturgy, and Scripture, not to mention Karlstadt's ascetic tendencies and his demand for faith, rooted in works of love, performed in obedience to God's law. Luther still modifies Hoffman's view of the Lord's Supper, and he influences some of Hoffman's statements on predestination. Hoffman's concern with apocalyptic writings clearly distinguishes him from Karlstadt. Although Hoffman's doctrinal *pot-pourri* is unique, it is primarily derivative – Hoffman does not yet seem to create *new* doctrines.

Hoffman's Expulsion from Sweden

The records of King Gustaf I contain an answer to a query from Master Lars Andreae (a colleague of Olaus Petri) about Hoffman's preaching. In January 1527 King Gustaf replied from Enköping: 'We have heard something from others who have heard his [Hoffman's] sermons, that he fascinates great crowds and that he is rather careless with his words. Therefore, it seems inadvisable to employ him for any public sermons before the populace.'[122]

Hoffman was silenced, but new problems were plaguing him before the king made his mild assessment. In *Daniel 12* Hoffman urges his Livonian followers to take his sermon to heart, 'because I am worried that where I am now, I shall no longer be able to send you something.' He fears his road will turn 'to a hard place,' a euphemism for imprisonment, for he thinks he will be handed over like Samson.[123] New disaster had struck, and probably not just because of his preaching, since King Gustaf used the new religion to attain his own political ends. In the *Chronicles of King Gustaf I* Peder Swart reports an iconoclastic riot in Stockholm, which was sparked by an apocalyptic sermon of a 'really desperate fanatic:

119 Hoffman, *Daniel 12*, F4v.
120 KS 1, 44:32–5; *Gelaub* (139), [C4v].
121 LEENDERTZ, 41: '[de] man, die omstreeks dezen tijd een overwegenden invloed op Hofmann heeft gehad: Andreas Carlstadt.'
122 *Konung Gustaf den förstes registratur* 4, 25: 'Som i mesther Larss oss tiilscriffwe om Melchior etc wij haffwe nogoth forfarit utaff andre som hans predican hörth haffwa ath han phanteserar stor hoopp och aer noghot owarlich i sin ordh. Ther före ticker oss icke rad vara ath han brwkar naghon oppenbårligh prediken för menighe hopen. Som wi wårth sinne och meningh ther om haffwe oss elskeligh mesther Hans borgmestere i Stockholm ytermera til kienne giffwet etc.'
123 Hoffman, *Daniel 12*, [4].

a Baptist called Melchior the furrier.'[124] Later Hoffman was arrested, threatened with execution, and forced out of Sweden. Swart wrote this down long after the event. The date he gives (1525) is wrong, and what he says about Hoffman's later career is mistaken. Linden criticizes some aspects of Swart's story and Leendertz's critique is massive.[125] Although I accept most of their arguments, two points remain: first, three unrelated sources report a riot in Stockholm; and, second, in December 1526 Hoffman was expecting incarceration.

Other documents also implicate Olaus Petri and Lars Andreae in the riot. Before the Diet of Örebro (1534) King Gustaf charged Petri and Andreae with iconoclastic activity while the king resided in Småland during the spring of 1526.[126] Hoffman's fears of imprisonment were justified if he had this image-breaking episode in mind. Thus I contest Leendertz's view that Swart merely predated an event that probably occurred in 1529.

The riot is also reported in a text dealing with church plunder. Petri and Andreae are mentioned, as is 'the preacher or furrier Balthasar' (then predikanten eller skinneren Baltzar).[127] Hoffman was the only furrier who acted as a preacher, and Knut Westman explains the confusion in the name by pointing out that Balthasar, like Melchior, was one of the Three Kings.[128] I accept Westman's hypothesis, and add that Melchior himself may have contributed to this confusion, for he seems to have enjoyed bantering with others named after the Three Kings.[129]

But would Petri, the founder of the Lutheran Reformation in Sweden, have participated in an iconoclastic riot? Certainly, for, as we saw in Livonia, Luther was not considered the only Reformer worthy of note during the first decade of the Baltic Reformation. The younger Petri was not as Lutheran in his beliefs as has been supposed. He had studied in Wittenberg from 1516 to 1518 when Karlstadt and Melanchthon were influential along with Luther.

Westman documents radical tendencies in the younger Petri: some regard boards and stones as the bride of Christ; God's laws are set up against the laws of men; and Petri spurns 'church decoration with altars, images, and votive lights.'[130] Moreover Petri had to justify at least one political revolution. Linden has already sensed the influence of Karlstadt on Petri's doctrines of the Lord's Supper and the

124 Swart, Konung Gustaf den förstes krönika, 87–9.
125 LINDEN, 96–8; LEENDERTZ, 59–63.
126 Westman, Reformationens genombrottsår, 320.
127 Ibid, 321–2.
128 Ibid, 321, n 3.
129 In Strassburg Hoffman chose for one of his tracts – Michael Wachter (27) – the pseudonym Caspar Beck, no doubt a joke on Balthasar Beck, who had printed the original edition of Hoffman's Dialogus, but who did not print Hoffman's later writings.
130 Westman, Reformationens genombrottsår, 323.

priesthood.[131] In a recent and thorough study Sven Ingebrand supports Westman's view of the riot, and he thinks Petri experienced a phase that reflects Karlstadt and Melanchthon.[132]

Unlike Westman and Ingebrand, however, I do not place the Stockholm riot in the spring of 1526. True, Gustaf I's accusation at Örebro refers to his stay in Småland, which was in the spring of 1526, since he resided in Enköping towards the end of 1526. However, the letter of Lars Andreae, which the king answered on 13 January 1527, shows Hoffman's presence had only recently become problematic, and the choice of Hoffman's texts (Dan. 12; Luke 21) in *Daniel 12* establishes that he preached in Petri's church on the Second Sunday in Advent (9 December 1526). King Gustaf's measured reply to Andreae shows that he was unaware of a riot, and when he learned the truth, it may have been presented to him as having occurred much earlier. That would have softened the impact. Therefore, the king's reference to his stay in Småland is probably his own reasonable – but wrong – conjecture of the date, based on an unreliable report.

I offer the following reconstruction of the riot and subsequent events. The riot may have taken place as early as 9 December, when Hoffman, while preaching, made inflammatory digressions about images and liturgical objects. The riot involved Hoffman, Petri, and Andreae, among others. Since all the preachers of the new faith were implicated, news of the riot was kept from the king: hence his calm reply of 13 January 1527 to Andreae. Nevertheless, Andreae had discreetly brought up the problem of Hoffman's preaching. He, and perhaps Petri, wanted Hoffman out of the way before King Gustaf uncovered the truth. A silenced Hoffman could be induced to leave Sweden, making him *in absentia* an ideal scapegoat. Thus the riot is best placed somewhere in the month of December.

The attempt to hush up the riot also accounts for the confused dates of later chroniclers. Ultimately the king had to be told about it, since the reports refer to considerable damage.[133] When King Gustaf learned about the riot, he ignored it as politically inexpedient. Petri and Andreae helped to draw a cloak of legitimacy over his revolution and his alienation of church properties and tithes. Meanwhile, the king played Andreae's game of making Hoffman the scapegoat. Finally, when there were new tensions with the reformers in 1534, the king, whose position was now secure, thought it expedient to accuse Petri and Andreae of what he himself admitted had happened eight years earlier.

131 LINDEN, 95.
132 Ingebrand, *Olavus Petris reformatoriska åskådning*, 323.
133 Here the reports (Westman, *Reformationens genombrottsår*, 319–21) are unanimous. Swart says: 'They broke some [images], burned others, mutilated heads and noses.' King Gustaf accused Andreae and Petri of storming altars, churches, and cloisters. The report on church pillage refers to the storming of altars and plunder of church goods.

Hoffman was an extremist, but he lived among radicals like Knopken and Tegetmeier in Livonia, and Petri and Andreae in Stockholm. Mutual influence seems to have existed, but, significant as Stockholm was to Hoffman as the place of his first major publications, Hoffman's ultimate impact on the Swedish Reformation was negligible. Sandblad concludes: 'Thus, on the whole, Hoffman's appearance in Stockholm was merely an episode'; and then he adds: '[But it is] an extremely interesting phenomenon.'[134]

134 Sandblad, *De eskatologiska föreställningarna i Sverige*, 56.

8

Hoffman in Denmark

Hoffman's path from a Stockholm dungeon to the Flensburg court of King Frederik I of Denmark was not smooth. After Hoffman was ousted from Sweden with his wife and child, he embarked with them for Lübeck, but that city harboured powerful friends of Bishop Blankenfeld. Not surprisingly Hoffman was invited to leave, most likely in May 1527. Karlstadt offers a cryptic report: 'Next, the high rulers of Lübeck were really after his neck, blood, body, and life, but God helped the furrier to escape from all his enemies.'[1]

Since one of the Scandinavian wings of the eagle of Revelation had failed him, Hoffman was determined to try the other. He visited King Frederik I, charming him and his spouse with a sermon.[2] Ill-treatment by the Swedes was an asset in Denmark, and Hoffman might have been authorized to preach, but Luther's endorsement of him was by now dated. Thus Hoffman went off to Wittenberg together with the Danish royal chaplain, travelling by way of Magdeburg, where he stopped to confront Nikolaus Amsdorf.[3] As Hoffman has it later, he was very civil, addressing Amsdorf 'only once' as a 'bloated windbag.'[4] Amsdorf had already received a letter from Luther who, as we have seen, advised rough treatment of Hoffman. Hoffman may not have known this, as he vainly tried to renew Luther's recommendation. The stops on Hoffman's journey show that he followed the Hanseatic trade route, and thus he must have come within a league of Karlstadt's domicile in Kemberg – a tempting opportunity to renew their friendship.

1 *Dialogus* [1529], A2.
2 For the progress of the Reformation under King Frederik, see Dunkley, *The Reformation in Denmark*, 37–66.
3 The Hanseatic trade routes are mapped out in Bruns and Weczerka, 'Hansiche Handelsstrassen,' *Quellen und Darstellungen zur hansischen Geschichte*, no 13, pt 1 [1962]. For Hoffman part A, chart 6, and part B, chart 8, are useful.
4 For Amsdorf's life see Kolb, *Nikolaus von Amsdorf*, 27–61.

Since Hoffman was now also rebuffed by Luther, it is likely that he was drawn even closer to Karlstadt.

When Hoffman stopped in Magdeburg on his return to Holstein, he was arrested and robbed. He blamed Amsdorf for causing his arrest. Although Amsdorf denied the charge,[5] Hoffman claimed he had four witnesses: an 'employee of the town' (prison warden?), a colleague of Amsdorf (prison chaplain?), a woman who had gossiped with Amsdorf's 'girl-friend,' and finally Amsdorf himself, who had threatened Hoffman when he first went to Magdeburg.[6] Bidden to leave Magdeburg, Hoffman had to beg for alms.[7] He moved on, returning to Flensburg, where King Frederik now endorsed him. Soon Hoffman was preaching at Saint Nicholas Church in Kiel,[8] where great crowds were held spellbound as Hoffman explained the prefiguration of Christ's life in the furniture of Moses' tabernacle. He preached serially on Daniel, Revelation, and the Song of Songs.

Hoffman became embroiled in another controversy. Wilhelm Pravest, the head pastor of Kiel, wrote to Luther to disparage Hoffman, and Luther was sympathetic. Pravest, who was a crypto-Catholic, now circulated a lampoon on Luther which reached Wittenberg. Luther angrily penned three letters to Kiel, noting that Hoffman was not as bad as Pravest. Soon after, Pravest withdrew to the cloister of Bordesholm.[9] Buoyed by this reversal, Hoffman may now have vilified the magistrates of Kiel as thieves who deserved a hanging.[10]

A week after Hoffman appeared in Magdeburg Amsdorf penned a tract against Hoffman. Amsdorf was on the defensive, because, apparently, the Magdeburgers were comparing Hoffman's personality and life to the detriment of Amsdorf. Amsdorf warns that, instead, one should heed sound doctrine:

It does not matter whether the person appears to others to be eloquent, learned, bright, just, and holy. In every respect it does matter, however, whether the teaching is sound according to the simple intent of Christ ... Do not regard [Melchior's] personality, how he is dapper, learned, and elo-

5 Amsdorf, *Falscher Prophet* (1528), B2v.
6 Hoffman, *Nasengeist*, [15].
7 Bugenhagen, *Acta* (1530), Nv: 'der doch dahin kam als ein vorjageter betteler, den Sankt Niclas Pfarher zu Hamburg einen zehr pfenning gab.'
8 The king granted Hoffman the right to preach anywhere in Holstein. However, Hoffman did not have a definite position at St Nicholas Church, since the permanent positions were under the jurisdiction of the cloister of Bordesholm and the magistrates of Kiel (Volbehr, *Kieler Prediger-Geschichte*, 6–11).
9 LEENDERTZ, 106–9; LINDEN, 117–20.
10 If Schuldorp (*Breef an de Glövigen* (1528), B3v) can be trusted.

quent, for the devil is also eloquent and he can disguise himself as an angel of light.[11]

A year earlier a good friend, who may have been Petri or Andreae in Stockholm, had asked Amsdorf to comment on Hoffman's *Daniel 12*.[12] Amsdorf's comments must have been negative, for Hoffman reproached him for causing him 'to experience great suffering.' Amsdorf now claims that he is not responsible for how others treat Hoffman, but he has the right to vent his own opinions.

Hoffman's teaching is too 'dark,' Amsdorf says. According to Hoffman two prophets will prophesy for three and a half years, and there will follow another three and a half years of persecution; then the end of the world is to come. Hoffman has *not* shown when the seven years begin, nor has he identified the prophets; thus his scheme is too vague to have been inspired by the Holy Ghost and too clear to have been inspired by Christ.[13]

Amsdorf now deals with Hoffman's claim to be a prophet. Hoffman has not had a regular call; therefore, if Hoffman preaches faith, love, and the cross, he has *no* call from God, because others, who have been properly called, are already engaged in preaching this message. If Hoffman claims that he has the Spirit of prophecy, he has not been called by God. Christ himself had such a Spirit, but he did not preach until he was baptized and ordained by his Father. Should Hoffman claim that he is called directly by God, without human means, he must attest this with a *new* message. Then he must preach *essential* truths, not known hitherto, or he should charge and convict the Lutheran ministers of error or heresy. Clearly Amsdorf tried to undermine Hoffman's ministry by stipulating unreasonable conditions.

Finally Amsdorf resumes his attack on Hoffman's scheme for the end of the world, which, he claims, proves Hoffman has been sent by the devil rather than by God. Amsdorf snarls at Hoffman in conclusion: 'Oh, you black devil, I know you well ... The devil can also sneak in and act humbly. Believe me.'

Perhaps weary of strife, Hoffman tried silence, but Amsdorf was not satisfied and decided to bait Hoffman once again. In the title of his second tract Amsdorf celebrates the fact that 'Melchior Hoffman has not responded to my booklet with a single word.' Amsdorf boasts of his dependence on Luther. He offers no new criticisms of Hoffman, merely repeating the old charges: Hoffman has a 'lying, grubby, and nosy spirit'; he cannot prove his teaching from Scripture; therefore he tells lies about the end of the world to please the common rabble.[14] Hoffman

11 Amsdorf, *Vormanung*, A2, 3.
12 Ibid, A2–v.
13 Ibid, A2v: 'Der heilige geist redet nicht so tunckel und unverstendig, sonder klar ... Christus [und] die Aposteln ... lassen die zal der jar ungewis bleiben.'
14 Amsdorf, *Nicht ein Wort*, A2v.

should prove when the last seven years begin; otherwise 'this prophet and his prophecy will lie down in shit.'[15]

Marquard Schuldorp, a former colleague of Hoffman, aided Amsdorf by personally distributing the broadsides against Hoffman in Kiel.[16] Schuldorp had been opposing Hoffman for over a year,[17] and Hoffman was exposed to gibes and ridicule for not responding. Consequently he now purchased from Hans Arndt in Lübeck two printing presses with accessories, a planer, five chests with letters, several moulds, and a kettle for boiling ink.[18] Hoffman also received King Frederik's permission to print copies of the Old and New Testament and other religious books.[19] Soon he knew how to print. Though he did reverse the signatures on his tract *Nasengeist*, that happened only once. In response to Amsdorf Hoffman flooded Holstein with pamphlets – and no doubt Magdeburg as well.[20]

Freely paying back Amsdorf with his own invective, Hoffman nevertheless indicates that he is not eager to become embroiled in further controversy. He complains:

If you [Amsdorf] and Schuldorp had kept the peace and had left me alone, that would have been fine with me. But he who wants to be top knight has to down the other in a fight. That means he will have to suspect straightaway that he could just as well wind up lying underneath as on top.[21]

Amsdorf's credentials as a 'son of Luther' do not impress Hoffman. Moreover, Amsdorf's claim that only Christ and the Apostles teach significant doctrine is firmly rejected; the doctrine of the end of the world is found scattered through the entire Scriptures: Daniel 12, Joel 3, Matthew 24, Luke 17, 2 Thessalonians 2, and Revelation 11–12. Hoffman adamantly opposes Amsdorf's truncated canon:

Was it not the Apostle John who wrote the Apocalypse on the island of Patmos at the time indicated? Was not Daniel apostolic? Christ referred to Daniel in three of the gospels. Have the Old Testament and Moses been

---

15 Ibid, A3v.
16 Hoffman, *Nasengeist*, 19–20.
17 In *Nasengeist* (1528), [19], Hoffman says Schuldorp had opposed him for a year. In the fall of 1527 Schuldorp had already complained to Luther about Hoffman (BR 4, no. 1190).
18 See Benzing, *Die Buchdrucker*, 284. For the inventory of Hoffman's press see Volbehr, *Kieler Prediger-Geschichte*, 11, n 1.
19 Dunkley, *The Reformation in Denmark*, 51.
20 See Bugenhagen, *Acta*, A4v, where Hermann Tast refers to Hoffman's 'buchern die durch die welt gefurt sind.'
21 Hoffman, *Dat Nicolaus Amsdorff*, Av–2

done away with? Ah, you wretched bloody devil, you must be raving, or [else] during your days you've never even made a beginning with Scripture. You haven't understood it in your heart, nor have you received it. The holy Paul speaks clearly in Romans 15:[4, 8–12] that all Scripture is for us one teaching.[22]

Hoffman also sees through Amsdorf's tactic of trying to commit him to a more specific date for the end of the world. If Amsdorf claims that Hoffman's scheme leads to the end of the world in 1533, he is wrong.[23]

Hoffman argues that Amsdorf's ridicule of his apocalyptic claims is purely partisan. Luther himself must be credited with numerous unfulfilled prophecies about the end of the world. When Michael Stiefel was imprisoned for stating that the end of the world would occur at 8:00 a.m. on 19 October 1533, Luther and Melanchthon interceded for him. Stiefel's caballistic *Arithmetical Booklet on the Antichrist* had been printed in Wittenberg in 1532, and he was still making predictions in 1553 when he published his *Very Wonderful Word Calculation, Together with a Remarkable Interpretation of Certain Numbers in Daniel and the Apocalypse of Saint John*. Since Stiefel was a Lutheran academic, his predictions are pardonable, but Hoffman's are not.

Amsdorf now replies to Hoffman with a counterblast, repeating his old charges. He claims that Hoffman's apocalyptic predictions rouse the rabble, and that he has not answered Amsdorf because the beginning of the seven last years has not yet been fixed. The two witnesses who are to be martyred have not been identified. Christ did not know the end: If only he had consulted Hoffman! Eschatology is not needed for salvation. The gospels and Saint Paul's epistles are sufficient. Amsdorf elaborates a somewhat more extreme view than Luther's 'canon within the canon' – only that which preaches Christ is valuable.[24]

Amsdorf's final tract includes a direct address to the people of Kiel. He – Nikolaus von Amsdorf – is a regularly called parson in Magdeburg who opposes Hoffman's apocalyptic scheme because of its shoddiness. As Hoffman explains it, Christ could return in 1533 or 1534. When Hoffman says that he preaches where there is need, he is a 'false prophet.' God calls his own preachers legally, and he does not need Hoffman.[25] Hoffman is a wolf in sheep's clothing.

Amsdorf's *Falscher Prophet* contained invective that was designed to wound Hoffman's religious sensibilities. Because Hoffman boasts that he knows the time of Christ's return, 'he certainly cannot belong to the disciples of Christ and the

22 Ibid, A2v.
23 Ibid, A2v. Hoffman silently retracts his earlier position in *Daniel 12*, G–2. See DEPPERMANN, 66–7.
24 Amsdorf, *Falscher Prophet*, [A3].
25 Ibid, B–2.

Christians.'[26] Hoffman is 'a devil and a scoundrel,' a 'wolf in sheep's clothing,' a 'false prophet,' a liar.

Hoffman responds to this charge like a follower of St Grobian, the mythical patron saint of coarse invective. To Amsdorf's factual charges Hoffman replies that his own apocalyptical scheme may be somewhat obscure, but that does not make him a liar because God's promises in Scripture are often just as vague.[27] As to being 'uncalled,' Hoffman preaches where there is need, following the example of Apollos and Stephen.[28] Moreover, if an outward call is needed, all papists qualify. Hoffman has been despised simply because he is not a cleric: 'If I had been anointed and knew Latin, and was not a leather dresser or furrier, I'd have been left in peace by you mocking spirits.'[29] One is easily distracted by Hoffman's invective in Nasengeist. More importantly, however, Hoffman is also grappling with questions of exegesis. He does not merely parrot Scripture, but he wrestles with its meaning:

For it is of no use to write piece by piece, but we must understand the context. For, before Christ told his disciples to be awake on the last day, he proclaimed to them all the signs until the end of the day which has no future. That's how the prophets write and the apostles and Christ in the three [synoptic] gospels. Therefore it does not matter that I want to cry: 'Christ says that you should watch for the end, every hour and season.' But what does matter is to understand the Word, what it refers to, and to recognize the way it is said, how and when such words were spoken. For Christ and the apostles are not against each other.[30]

Hoffman's spiritual exegesis is medieval, but he uses it to relate the Old and the New Testament to the past, present, and future:

Above all it is clear that the spiritual temple, which the spiritual Solomon (Christ our Saviour) built with his apostles, has been destroyed for us by the papal empire. Just as the [material] temple, which was a figure, was

26 Ibid, A3v.
27 Hoffman, Nasengeist, [6].
28 Ibid, [10].
29 Ibid, [11]: '[Nu weis ich] wenn ich ein gesmirter were, und latinisch künd, unnd nicht ein körssner odder peltzer, so wurd ich wol von euch larvengeistern frid haben.' Pravest had already complained to Luther about Hoffman's ignorance of Latin, and Schuldorp in his tract referred to himself as the 'geweyde Schuldorp' versus the 'ungheweyde Hoffman' (Breef an de Glövigen, B2). This type of arrogance drew forth Karlstadt's protest against the Lutheran clergy as the 'new papists.' However, Hoffman did ignore the doctrinal differences in the comment cited above.
30 Hoffman, Nasengeist, [9].

[destroyed] by the Babylonians, so the same with the spiritual Babylonians. From this Babylonian captivity we are now being redeemed through God's power, and now that the spiritual temple is being rebuilt through God's Word like the [rebuilt] figurative temple, so the spiritual temple follows the same pattern. And as the [rebuilt] physical temple was destroyed with the physical city, so our [rebuilt] spiritual temple will again be destroyed before the Day of the Lord. Not one stone will be left on another.[31]

It is clear from this quotation that Hoffman is denouncing Lutheranism. For as the first spiritual temple represents Catholicism, the second spiritual temple represents the Lutheran Reformation. Thus Hoffman claims that, after the first Babylonian captivity of the church (under Rome), there will be a second captivity, involving Lutheranism. Hoffman opposes the new clerics; now the interpretation of Scripture is the privilege of the laity as well as the clergy: 'No, dear lying-spirit, God's Word is a precious golden rock, on which we who are poor are now through God's grace also able to separate the foam from the gold and silver.'[32]

Hoffman's irritation with the way in which he had been treated had induced him to fight back; politically, however, Hoffman could still be a tactician.

Hoffman realized that Amsdorf's tracts and Luther's moves against him could have baneful consequences. Luther warned Crown Prince Christian to silence Hoffman.[33] To Wilhelm Pravest Luther had written that the enthusiasts were worse than the pope, but, when Luther discovered that Pravest was a secret Catholic, he preferred Hoffman. Hoffman knew that the letters now coming out of Wittenberg were more favourable to him. He responded by writing a commentary on Matthew 1 to pacify Luther further. Krafft, the last writer to have consulted the whole copy, notes Hoffman's meek style.[34]

A court official forwarded this tract to Luther with a covering letter stressing King Frederik's appreciation of Hoffman's modesty and honest life. After Luther read the preface, he wondered ironically whether Hoffman was also among the Doctors of the church.[35] Meanwhile, Hoffman continued with his sacramentarian sermons. This Janus-like posture galled Schuldorp, who wrote:

And although you, Melchior Hoffman, have issued your latest booklet so no one would suspect that you teach or believe such and such, because you worry you could be driven out of the land once again because of your enthusiasm [Schwarmerie] – nevertheless, your public sermons, which I

31 Ibid, [8–9].
32 Ibid, [10].
33 For the exchange of letters see Noll, 'Luther Defends Melchior Hofmann,' 47f.
34 Krafft, Jubel Gedächtnis (1723) (entered under Hoffman, Matt. 1), 106.
35 TR 5, 360 (no. 3797).

have heard in part and which I can confirm in part through other witnesses, prove that you have the same opinion as the enthusiasts, ... although
you look for verbal agreement with us.[36]

Hoffman's preface does not really deal with Matthew, but it is designed as a reply
to Luther, who in 1527 castigated Hoffman for using the figures of lion, calf,
human face, and eagle in his exegesis of Scripture. Thus, Luther must have
argued with Hoffman over the first two pages of *Gelöfigen*, where Hoffman
treated the four beasts of Ezekiel. We can assume that Luther did not know
Hoffman's *Daniel 12*, or his attack would have covered more than Hoffman's
exegesis.

Hoffman's interpretation shows both the best and the worst of his exegesis:

It is to be noted that the Old Testament spreads itself out with its wings
[like the cherub near God's throne] and with its power in the Word of the
Law, which Word is compared to the lion in Rev. 4. For, as a lion scares
with its voice and kills with its mouth, so did the Word of the Law. The
lion or Word of the Law is compared with the north wind, of which the
bride also sings in the Song of Songs, chapter 4, 'Arise, O north wind, and
come, O south wind, and blow upon my garden, that its spices may flow
out.' Thus is to be understood the yellow silk [of the tabernacle curtains]
and the brass [of the vessels] and the yellow colour on the peace sign [i.e.
the rainbow], as well as the head water which divides itself in Paradise,
through which the prophet waded up to his ankles. Ezek. 46.
    The other wing of the Old Testament refers to the Word of the figures,
and is likened unto a calf. Rev. 4. Just as a calf is altogether coarse and
ridiculous in its gait, so the figurative meaning appears to the wise of this
world ... , as [it] appeared to Nicodemus [John 3], when Christ confronted
him with the spiritual figure, that he should be born anew. And exactly
where the Israelites have used and understood the figure and the Law
according to the flesh, [being] moved by the literal sense, so we in the
New Testament should interpret it spiritually. Thus the figurative meaning is compared to the west wind and the red silk and the red colour in
the rainbow, as well as the tin of the booth of Moses and the river which
divides itself from Paradise, through which Ezekiel passed in the spirit up
to the knee. Furthermore, the Word of the Prophets, or the Word of the
New Testament, divides itself into the Word of sayings, riddles, com-
parisons, or parables, which Word is compared with the human face ...
which [in turn] refers to the spirit and courage ... with which the above-

36 Schuldorp, *Breef an de Glövigen* (1528), B2–v.

mentioned Word is proclaimed. This the Psalmist mentions in Ps. 78, regarding the person of Christ, where he says: 'I shall open my mouth with sayings, and divulge ancient matters, which we have heard and know, and which our fathers predicted.' That was the old, which had previously come to light in the Scriptures. Those are the roseate lips which the bride mentions in the Song of Songs, ch. 4. These are like the silver trumpets, Num. 5, and the silver vessels in the tabernacle, Exod. 26, and the roseate cord which Rahab had hanging from the window as a sign [Josh. 2]. Also in the Word of the sayings it is compared to a roseate silk, as well as to the south wind and the third river which divides itself in Paradise and through which the prophet waded up to his kidneys. It also refers to the rosy dawn and the rosy hue of the rainbow and the blood spilled at the time of the spiritual birth of the children of God. The Word of the New Testament spreads farther, namely in the fourth beast, which is the flying eagle, through which is revealed the clear Word ... Spirit, power, and life. This Word is compared with the spun-out silk, and also with the gold and the east wind and the fourth river, called Euphrates, which divides itself in the Paradise of God and through which Ezekiel the prophet could not wade in the spirit, neither could he fathom it. This Word is also compared to the white and the green colours of the rainbow ...

It is compared to a water flood, or to a flying eagle to [whose heights] no [other] bird can soar, neither can the human spirit rise up to the transparent, pure, clear Word, nor can it fathom it. For the higher the spirit rises, the eagle drifts still higher. Therefore, here one should be still and every spirit would fain look towards the sun and the eagle.[37]

This conventional interpretation reveals Hoffman's debt to medieval exegesis. A mystical meaning explaining a specific number is taken from a context where its meaning is clear and applied to other areas. Colours and metals are treated in the same way. Such schemes impose a static, non-historical principle of unity on certain parts of the Bible. Hoffman was therefore unable to accept Amsdorf's and Luther's dynamic conception of a canon within the canon.

Nevertheless, Hoffman senses the historical progress of divine revelation. There is a progression from law to the meaning of the law and from veiled prophecies to their fulfilment and meaning. Despite Hoffman's conviction that parts of Scripture are made plain in the end of days, certain matters remain to be viewed through a mirror dimly.

An aura of mystery enwraps the eagle, swooping against the sky, and the sun which reveals and blinds at the same time. The dynamics of revelation are also

---

37 Hoffman, *Matt. 1*, excerpts from Krafft, *Jubel Gedächtnis*, 443–5.

seen in the wading of Ezekiel. The literal law is easy to plumb; its meaning takes more effort. The prophecies go deeper, and their fulfilment cannot be fathomed by mere mortals.

Hoffman lacked the historical tools, and did not care, to investigate the development of the scriptural canon. Yet, willy-nilly, he grasped some essential principles, for he had moved beyond memorizing Scripture to penetrating its meaning. There are similarities between Karlstadt's and Hoffman's exegetical viewpoints. Both rejected Luther's canon within the canon. Both claimed that the New Testament played a role superior to the Old. Karlstadt applied medieval principles to Old Testament passages, interpreting with reference to Christ. When the Song of Songs says 'My dove is in the cleft of the rock,' the rock is Christ and the holes are his deep wounds laid on by human sin.[38] Karlstadt likewise assumed that the tabernacle prefigured Christ.[39]

The primary difference between Hoffman and Karlstadt resulted from Karlstadt's study of the canon of Scripture. Historical criteria settled for Karlstadt the questionable canonicity of Revelation and the excision of the Apocrypha. Hoffman could not have followed Karlstadt's arguments there. However, if Karlstadt had felt it necessary to unseal in the latter days the obscure passages of Scripture, his exegesis would have been similar to Hoffman's. Whether Hoffman was indebted to Karlstadt for his exegetical views is an open question. Karlstadt's *Von dem Newen und Alten Testament* (143) would clarify only some of Hoffman's exegetical views. Certainly Hoffman's use of the four figures was *not* anticipated by Karlstadt.

In the last two pages of *Nasengeist* Hoffman taunted Schuldorp to combat him openly. Schuldorp's distribution of Amsdorf's tracts in Kiel had been an irritant, and Schuldorp had also attacked Hoffman by name from the pulpit. In addition Schuldorp had married his own niece, a marriage which was forbidden under canon law, since Schuldorp had not purchased a dispensation. Protestant opinion on the degrees of consanguinity was, since 1520, indebted to Luther for its greater leniency. However, because Hoffman disliked Schuldorp, he now seemed to side with the old believers, though he lamely claimed that he opposed Schuldorp's marriage because nobody had married his niece in the New Testament. Hoffman's reference to Schuldorp as one who lives incestuously (*blutling*) precipitated the clash that led to Hoffman's expulsion from Holstein.

Schuldorp is quite polemical, but his targets are real issues. Hoffman's apocalyptic schemes are 'useless and empty bragging.'[40] Since 1527 Hoffman has dealt only with apocalyptic predictions and the abuse of the sacrament.[41] Hoff-

38 *Empfahern* (54), B.
39 Credner, par 52.
40 Schuldorp, *Breef an de Glövigen*, B2v.
41 Ibid, Bv.

man pretends to follow the apostles, but let him rather follow Paul, and preach faith and life in Christ Jesus, instead of empty figures of the tabernacle.

Schuldorp complains that Hoffman also names opponents from the pulpit. The organist in Hoffman's church has told him to be kinder, but Hoffman has replied: 'they must all be slaughtered.'[42] Hoffman abuses the regents of Kiel, calling them thieves (deve). Let him follow Paul rather than defame the sword of the magistrates:

> But when you preach before the regents, who have no power to exile you, and in the presence of the common people, then the Council of Kiel is full of scoundrels, worthy to be hanged from the trees, and to be replaced by a new council. That gospel – deep in their hearts – appeals to the rabble.[43]

Schuldorp shows that he is jealous of the multitudes Hoffman attracts, for he argues that, if Hoffman were to charge his hearers a penny each, he would be richer than many a juggler.[44] Hoffman's views have been spreading so fast that Schuldorp just has to denounce him from the pulpit.[45] Yet, Schuldorp does not want Hoffman's neck. If Hoffman had only wanted to be instructed, Luther and Amsdorf would have helped him.[46] Schuldorp then batters against a whole chain of arguments on the sacraments which Hoffman has borrowed from Karlstadt (see the notes for references to Karlstadt's influence).

Hoffman is an enthusiast, Schuldorp claims, and now people are beginning to ask where Christ's head and feet are in the eucharist. 'How can his body become bread? Wasn't the bread baked in the oven?'[47] Hoffman reasons against a miracle. In his Matthew Hoffman says that Christ is present in the mass, but this is a pretence, for on leaf 7 of the same work Hoffman applies John 6 to the sacrament.[48] Hoffman's orthodox language is deceptive, as his sermons prove. Schul-

---

42 Ibid, B2–v. Schuldorp's information is probably correct, yet, Hoffman was not as violent as he sounded. By 'slaughtering' he meant the preaching of Old Testament law. Through the law the people were to be 'slaughtered and devoured' by the preacher; thus, in repentance, they become part of the body of Christ (Hoffman, Cantica canticorum, 4:2). At any rate, Hoffman, like Karlstadt, preached law and gospel.

43 Schuldorp, Breef an de Glövigen, B3v.

44 Ibid, B4.

45 Ibid, Bv.

46 Ibid, Bv–2.

47 Ibid, C2–v: 'Nu vraghet eyn ider wor ys hyr hövet hende effte vöthe? Wo kan syn lyff brot werden, is id doch nicht ym aven gebacken?' See Karlstadt's attack on popular Lutheran and Catholic cannibalistic distortions of official doctrine: 'Ir eeret Christum als ein katze ir gefangene mäuss' (KS 2, 43:30–1). Karlstadt's first references to the 'baker's bread' occur in Anbettung (68), [A4v], B3.

48 Schuldorp, Breef an de Glövigen, C4v, 3v. Hoffman's use of John 6 came from Karlstadt, perhaps via Knopken.

dorp notes that he attended several of Hoffman's services during June and July 1528. On *Corpus Christi* (11 June) Schuldorp heard Hoffman say:

> If you want to commemorate the body given to you, then eat the bread, and if you want to commemorate the blood shed for you, then drink of the cup. He who teaches you otherwise about the sacrament teaches like a rascal and a scoundrel.[49]

Schuldorp upholds the simple (Lutheran) interpretation of the words of Christ: 'This is my Body.' The farmers of Holstein can do without a Swabian or Swiss hair-splitter to explain this matter. Schuldorp claims that on the feast of the Visitation of Mary (2 July) Hoffman failed to kneel before the host,[50] and that on the seventh Sunday after Trinity (26 July) Hoffman said:

> Christ was sitting with his disciples, gave them bread, and said 'Take, eat, this is my body.' With the Word of the Lord the disciples were fed. Therefore the disciples did not at all eat the visible body of Christ, which was sitting with them. But [they ate him] only in the Word.[51]

Schuldorp understands Hoffman when he observes: 'You also want that we eat Christ in the sacrament, namely that we believe in him.'[52] According to Hoffman the claim that Christ is bodily present, is made by 'papistic' deceivers who will come during the days of tribulation saying: 'Lo, here is Christ,' or 'There He is' (Matt. 24:23).[53]

Schuldorp charges that some of Hoffman's views in *Daniel 12* were reiterated in his sermon: Judas ate the devil, not Christ, at the Last Supper; Christ does not dwell in monstrances; he is present only when eaten (spiritually), not when elevated. Hoffman has again slighted the trappings of liturgy, for Schuldorp admonishes the regents and the congregation in Kiel to keep the simple command of Christ, 'together with the empty ceremonies, which *must* be used for the sake of the simple.'[54]

---

49 Schuldorp, *Breef an de Glövigen*, C3. Among the numerous passages where Karlstadt treats the Supper as a memorial see *Leyb* (129), D3; *Testament* (144), C2v, D.

50 Schuldorp, *Breef an de Glövigen*, D–v. Karlstadt's treatise *Anbettung* (68) already attacks the practice, and Knopken follows Karlstadt here.

51 Schuldorp, *Breef an de Glövigen*, C3v. Cf Karlstadt's *1 Cor. 10* (142), [C4v].

52 Schuldorp, *Breef an de Glövigen*, C3v. This is Karlstadt's position in 1521, mediated via Knopken. See BARGE 1, 485, th 34: 'Panis est corpus, verum esse contendo, quia credo extrema eadem.'

53 Schuldorp, *Breef an de Glövigen*, C4. Cf KS 2, 42: 28–9.

54 Schuldorp, *Breef an de Glövigen*, D3v.

Schuldorp deftly parries Hoffman's accusation of being a *blutling*. Now Hoffman attacks him, but formerly Hoffman lauded his marriage to his niece, saying: 'that's the way to smack the pope in the mouth.'[55] On the whole Schuldorp's tract is well reasoned. Compared to Amsdorf, Schuldorp is tranquil and he has analysed the theological issues with precision. The fact that Schuldorp had begun his studies in Wittenberg on 13 June 1521 would account for this, for Schuldorp must have sided with Luther in his struggle against Karlstadt during the following year.[56]

Hoffman's *blutling* attack on Schuldorp was indefensible; however, I doubt whether Schuldorp's attack on Hoffman, supposedly for denouncing the magistrates of Kiel as thieves 'who deserve a hanging,' stands on much firmer grounds. Hoffman was upset about the alienation of church funds, which he (and Karlstadt) believed should be used for the poor.[57] However, in his writings Hoffman never incites his followers to overthrow the government, and whether he did so in his sermons depends on whether one can believe the hostile report of a bitter opponent. At least in the case of Karlstadt such charges (made by Luther in *Heavenly Prophets*) were a total fabrication.

Schuldorp's attack on Hoffman's duplicity brought instant reaction. Hoffman now penned a circular letter to the ministers of Holstein, in which he threw off his mask and argued that 'he could not confess that a physical piece of bread is his God.' This confession aroused the ire of Crown Prince Christian, who ordered his chaplain, Eberhard Weidensee, to publish a rejoinder.[58]

Eberhard Weidensee (1486?–1547) had accepted reforming principles when he was an Augustinian canon and provost of Saint John's Church in Halberstadt.[59] Briefly imprisoned, he made good his escape to Magdeburg, where he began to preach in 1524. His first work, *Eyn tractetleyn von dem glauben* (1525), contained strong predestinarian arguments against sacramentalism. The presumptive regeneration of children who die baptized in infancy is *mere* presumption; it is God who determines their destiny from eternity. From 1526 Weidensee served as chaplain to Crown Prince Christian (later King Christian III) as a champion of Lutheran orthodoxy. In this capacity Weidensee was unleashed on Hoffman.

Hoffman's circular letter has been lost, but Weidensee makes reference to its contents. In the letter Hoffman calls the Lutheran preachers 'false prophets,' who would confine Christ in a special place.[60] In the same letter Hoffman charges Weidensee with defrauding the prince, presumably because Weidensee had tried

55 Ibid, D2v.
56 *Album Academiae Vitebergensis*, 126: 'Marquardus Schuldorff ex keyl dioc. Bremen 13 Junii [1521].'
57 For the alienation of ecclesiastical goods in Kiel see DEPPERMAN, 90, n 23.
58 Weidensee, *Eyn underricht* (3 Feb 1529), A2.
59 For Weidensee's career see Tschackert, *Dr. Eberhard Weidensee*, 1–46.
60 Weidensee, *Eyn underricht*, A3v, B2. Cf Bugenhagen, *Acta*, A4–v, 8.

to convene a trial to convict Hoffman of heresy. So far this plan had failed, for, although the crown prince was antagonistic towards Hoffman, King Frederik had not endorsed an attack on Hoffman.[61]

In his circular letter Hoffman openly repudiated Lutheran doctrine. He uses the image of the ring, given to the bride, as a parallel for the Lord's Supper;[62] Christ is not in the bread or wine, and only the false prophets cry out: 'Lo, here is Christ. Lo, there he is.'[63] In debating Hoffman Weidensee took Luther's attack on Karlstadt and Müntzer, *Heavenly Prophets*, for his model. Luther's fire-iron image for the sacrament of the altar, which appears there, is also used by Weidensee.[64] Hoffman is called a 'heavenly prophet, taught by God,' and an 'unlearned *swermer*.'[65]

Just as Luther made an unprovoked attack on Karlstadt's doctrine of Christ in *Heavenly Prophets*, Weidensee assails Hoffman's doctrine of Christ, but with a new twist. Hoffman will soon deny that Christ had a physical body, for, if Christ cannot be contained, he was not in the Virgin Mary either: 'And to sum it up, Christ did not take on humanity, for [humans] are all creatures, and if a creature cannot contain him, then he did not become a man.'[66] Weidensee's tactics may have backfired, making Hoffman receptive towards the 'heavenly flesh' doctrine he was to encounter in Strassburg.[67]

Hoffman's 'Lo, here is Christ; lo, he is there' recalls Karlstadt's argument in *Dialogus* (126), an argument that Zwingli also used for his part in editing the 'Letter of Cornelis Hoen.'[68] Weidensee's reply to Hoffman's argument parallels Luther's response to Karlstadt in *Heavenly Prophets*, with the demand that Matthew 24:23 be read in light of Luke 17:20 as a reference to Christ's kingdom.[69]

---

61 Weidensee, *Eyn underricht*, A2v.
62 Ibid, Cv. Hoffman's use of the ring image is similar to, but not identical with, the example given in Zwingli's *Letter of Cornelius Hoen*. Hoffman may have read the letter in a German translation (see Schottenloher, *Philipp Ulhart*, 126, no. 136), but his lack of precision seems to point to Zwinglian and Karlstadtian influence emanating from East Friesland, where Hinne Rhode, Karlstadt's former student, worked in Emden.
63 Weidensee, *Eyn underricht*, Bv, 3v.
64 Ibid, A4v–B. For Luther see WA 18, 186:10–26.
65 Weidensee, *Eyn underricht*, B2v.
66 Ibid, B3v. Cf Luther's attempt to impugn Karlstadt's Christology in WA 18, 206:10f.
67 Hoffman's heavenly-flesh Christology was not Valentinian or monophysitic; it reflected an early biblical understanding that predated Chalcedonian categories. Hoffman was influenced in Strassburg by the Karlstadtian Klemenz Ziegler, who had related his heavenly-flesh Christology to the doctrine of the Lord's Supper. Cf Oosterbaan, 'Een doperse christologie,' 32–47.
68 KS 2, 42:28f (the citation is based on Matt. 24:23). For Zwingli's contribution to the letter see *Avondmaalsbrief van Cornelis Hoen*, ed Eekhof, xviii–xxi; Cf Z 4, [507]–19.
69 For Karlstadt see KS 2, 42:28–9. Luther's reply is in WA 8, 210:32–211:30. Weidensee copies Luther's argument in *Eyn underricht*, A4. Since he takes Luther's reply to Karlstadt as his model, Weidensee sees in Hoffman another Karlstadt.

Wishing to shed the light of Christ, the sun, on certain obscure passages of Scripture that are to be unsealed in the last days, Hoffman published a commentary on the Song of Songs. A nascent interest in this subject had already surfaced in *Matthew 1*, but now the seals of the Song of Songs have been fully broken. In his self-conscious dedication of the commentary to Lady Sophia, the wife of Frederik I, Hoffman claims that his approach is new: 'I have thought it commendable to consider the same book and, opening it up, remove it from the hiddenness of God and explain it inasmuch as God permits his poor worm to do so through his grace and recognition.'[70] Whatever was new, it was not Hoffman's exegesis. Many of his figures were derived from the Lübeck Bible, printed in the previous century on the presses that Hoffman had purchased.[71] The Lübeck glosses were based in turn on the *Glossa ordinaria* and the biblical commentary of Nicholas of Lyra, who had Christianized Rashi and selected those Midrashic comments that appealed to him as being closest to the literal understanding of the text. We shall not ponder Hoffman's nuptial mysticism and his ideas about the lactation of milk, honey, and wine from the united breasts of bridegroom (Christ) and bride (church). For our purpose Hoffman's significant statements are only tangential to his discussion of the text of the Song of Songs.

In his commentary Hoffman elaborates his political ethic, which combines theocratic elements with a view of the church as seen from the catacombs. Lady Sophia is a 'Christian lady,' and her husband is a 'Christian lord and king.'[72] Such a positive assertion presumes Hoffman's identification of the two northern kingdoms with the wings of the church. The church, borne aloft by a Christian king in Denmark, escapes persecution from the world rulers who are among the 'once born.'[73] Persecution is the normal state of the church. Since Christ in his humiliation suffered with the church, Hoffman can interchange the characteristics of bride and groom. Thus when the bridegroom comes forth out of the desert in a column of smoke (Songs 3:6), Hoffman comments:

The desert is to be interpreted in a twofold way. But the desert of which the bridegroom speaks is to be understood as the world. The bride [!] moves forward out of it, and she renounces everything that belongs to the world and its rulers, and [she] turns to God in the true spiritual desert. There she follows after the cross and suffering, as Saint Paul says, 2 Timothy 3 [:12]: 'All who wish to lead a godly life must suffer persecution.' Christ, too, had to enter into glory through his cross and suffering. And God also refers to such persecution Zech. 13[:9] when he wants to

---

70 Hoffman, *Cantica canticorum*, 2.
71 Pater, 'Melchior Hoffman's Explication of the Songs [!] of Songs,' 177–80.
72 Hoffman, *Cantica canticorum*, 2.
73 Ibid, C2v–3.

lead his children through the fire, and test them like gold, and burn them like silver, and he will recognize them as his people, and they will call on him as their only Lord and Master. By means of such a hot fire, the bride of Christ must be thoroughly roasted, to become an abomination before the world, but before God and Christ, [she] is a noble odour of myrrh.[74]

Like Karlstadt, Hoffman can see the church in an active role, however, and then he can scarcely contain his spiritual violence:

The sword with which [the apostolic elders] have fought and fight is God's law and Word [Eph. 6; Heb. 4; Ps. 143]. All of God's teachers have taken up this sword, and they still take it up in their hands, that is, in their power.[75]

The slaughter takes place through God's law, with which one kills and strangles, and with the Gospel.[76]

Like Karlstadt, Hoffman maintains both law and gospel. The slaughter through the law explains Hoffman's comment to the organist, reported by Schuldorp. When Hoffman said that 'they must all be slaughtered,' he was not bent on physical violence, but he preached the law (the devouring lion) to prod the 'once-born' to repentance. In Strassburg Hoffman was exposed to the High German and Swiss Baptists. His view of Scripture developed further, for he then accepted certain *tensions* in Scripture, which he explained with his 'cloven hoof' doctrine. Some of Hoffman's followers in the Lowlands rejected the 'cloven hoof' or, as they called it, the 'two-paw' doctrine.[77] Thus, with one radical twist the Dutch Melchiorites externalized Hoffman's (and Karlstadt's) spiritual violence and thus brought about the brief triumph of the externalized, successfully theocratic aspect of Hoffman's thought with the founding of Christ's kingdom in Münster.

James Stayer no longer calls the Münsterites a 'bastard line' of the Melchiorite movement.[78] Nevertheless, the rejection of Hoffman's tensions between the New

74 Ibid, G3v. The idea of the exchange between bride and groom comes from Luther (wa 7, 25–6).
75 Ibid, [G4v]: 'Dat swerdt darmede se eren strydt gevöret hebben, unde vören, ys gades gesette unde wort: Ephesi. vi. Hebre. iiii. Psalmo. cxliii. Welckes swerdt alle gades lerer hebben gevöret, unde noch vören, in eren handen, dat ys, in erem gewalt.'
76 Ibid, [H4]: 'Dat slachtent geschut denn dorch Gades gesette, darmede me dödet, unde wör-get, unde mit dem Evangelio [se denn dorch de apostolischen lerer gegeten werden tho dem lychnam Christi unde der Gades gemene, unde tho dem ewigen ryke. Also ethen ock de duvels apostel de ungelövigen tho des duvels ryke, unde tho der ewigen vordömenisse.]'
77 Cornelius, *Die Niederländischen Wiedertäufer*, 64, 97, 99.
78 Stayer, *Anabaptists and the Sword*, 223: 'The line from Hoffman to Obbe and Menno is the legitimate one; that from Hoffman through Jan Matthijs, Jan of Leyden and Jan van Baten-burg is a bastard line.' But see Stayer, 'Reflections and Retractions,' 198, 209–12.

and the Old Testament by the Münster Baptists was a sharp departure. However, from the beginning Hoffman was more inclined towards iconoclastic and, perhaps, verbal violence than Karlstadt was, and the progression from Karlstadt to Hoffman to the Münsterites was not altogether illogical.

The tension between the law and the gospel was already foreshadowed by some of Hoffman's comments on the Song of Songs.[79] Nevertheless, Hoffman follows Karlstadt in affirming the continuing need for law to discipline the church. Ultimately the Old and New Testament have the same aim.[80]

Reminiscent of Karlstadt are Hoffman's comments about the mystical bridal union between Christ and the church. This union is total, and, just as Karlstadt continues to speak of the believers 'deification,' so Hoffman refers to the church's participation in Christ's deity.[81] However, this ultimate union is not consummated on earth. Like Karlstadt, Hoffman believes that the human body obstructs full union between Christ and the church, and this is the reason why in Song of Songs 2:9 the bridegroom stands behind the wall.[82]

When Hoffman finished his Song of Songs commentary, Karlstadt was living with him. It is known that Karlstadt avoided the Lutheran sacrament of the altar when he returned to Saxony. One can only infer Karlstadt's stance towards baptism during the period from 1525 to 1529, because circumstances forced his outward compliance with prevailing practice.[83] Karlstadt had stressed inward baptism more than the outward rite; however, he wanted to harmonize practice and theory, but this proved impossible. Thus one would expect Karlstadt to fall back on *inward baptism*, not as an ideal, but as a concession to circumstances beyond his control: a *Stillen im Lande* posture. Hoffman had never discussed baptism in his writings, but in the commentary on the Song of Songs he has this to say:

Through the washing and purification ... the teachers came to the true internal baptism [*de rechten ynnerliken Döpe*] which took place through fire and the Spirit. They have all been purified through the death and the shedding of the blood of Christ [Rev. 1]. Through this they have been born again [John 3] and came to true fruition since they were killed first

---

79 Hoffman, *Cantica canticorum*, F–v: 'De Israheliten synt ym winter unde in der nacht gewesen, dat ys, ym gesette unde schemen ... do Christus mit synen apostelen den sönnen glantz schynen leth, unde den warmen süden wind weihen, unde den kolden gesett regen wech nam.' See also Jv–2v.
80 Ibid, B2, Dv.
81 Ibid, D4.
82 Ibid, [E4v]. For Karlstadt see e.g. above, 50, n 25, and below, Appendix I, 280.
83 See the baptism of Andreas (II) Bodenstein, TR 2, no. 2667b.

and passed through the washing [*swemme*]. Thus is understood the true baptism which is signified by the figurative sign.[84]

Hoffman adheres to Karlstadt's doctrine of baptism as signifying regeneration, experienced through dying and rising with Christ. The objective basis of Christ's blood-baptism is stated, though the subjective response of the believer is not elaborated. The experience presupposed for baptism, however, is clearly that of an adult.[85] Within a year Hoffman accepted adult baptism in Strassburg, just as Karlstadt's followers did in Zurich within months after he left them, and as Gerhard Westerburg was to do in Münster. Had Karlstadt felt free to practise according to his own insights, he could not have objected to doing this himself. Nevertheless, Karlstadt maintained the same prudence which he at first observed in relation to the papacy, and which he observed for a while in relation to Luther: he would not court martyrdom for an ideal that remained non-essential.

Hoffman also expresses covenantal ideas. The kiss of bride and groom is the covenantal bond which Hoffman traces from God's dealings with Adam and Eve to Noah, to Abraham, and to Christ. Karlstadt had used a similar scheme, but the idea was common enough among most of the Reformers.[86]

Basically, the Song of Songs commentary is irenic, and it obviously falls into the 'olive branch' category of *Matthew 1*. Hoffman undoubtedly hoped to send the commentary to Lady Sophia to impress the court not to take action. When the tract was ready, however, Hoffman must have realized that the baptismal passage would provoke problems. Most of the copies of the tract on the Song of Songs would have been confiscated when Hoffman was harried out of Holstein; only one copy has survived, and it is now found in Prague.

---

84 Ibid, [H4–v]: 'Dat wasschen unde reinigen ys [den thenen unde] lerern dorch de rechten ynnerliken Döpe kamen, de dorch dat vuer unde geist beschehen ys. Unde synt solcke alle gereiniget ym dode unde blötvorgeten Christi. Apoca. i. dorch dat synt se nye gebaren. Johan. iii. unde denn recht in fruchtbarheit gestellet, so se vor gedödet, unde dorch de swemme gekamen synt, dar denn dat rechte döpent vorstan wert, dat ym figur teken bedudet wert.'
85 For Hoffman's mature view of baptism as developed in Strassburg see Armour, *Anabaptist Baptism*, 97–112.
86 Ibid, B–v, [C4]. Cf Karlstadt, *1 Cor. 10* (142), A3v–[4].

9

From Karlstadt to the Rise of the English Baptists

The Flensburg Trial

In January 1529 Hoffman invited Karlstadt to join him in Holstein. Karlstadt fled Kemberg in February and arrived in Holstein in March. For about five months Karlstadt and Hoffman laboured for the radical gospel in Holstein and East Friesland. Although Hoffman invited Karlstadt to join him, Karlstadt was eager to leave Saxony; he was being pressured by his Lutheran inquisitors, and his refusal to denounce Zwingli and Oecolampadius had strained relations even more.[1]

Aware of his dangerous plight, Karlstadt violated one of the terms Luther had imposed on him when he sought refuge in Saxony in 1525. To open a route of escape he corresponded with the Moravian Baptists at Nikolsburg who had been under the successful leadership of Balthasar Hubmaier. When a spy intercepted a letter from Karlstadt to Kaspar von Schwenckfeld and Valentin Krautwald, Luther was incensed. Luther wrote Chancellor Brück that Karlstadt was a problem *in* Saxony, that Karlstadt would be more of a problem *outside of* Saxony, and that some persons regarded life imprisonment to be the best solution. Karlstadt may have had spies of his own, for, as always, he escaped in good time. He now sped to Holstein, after taking the precaution of confiding to certain professed friends that he was travelling to join Zwingli in Zurich.

Karlstadt met a troubled Hoffman. With his frank abjuration of Luther's sacrament of the altar, and his view of the Lutheran clergy as 'false prophets' who claim to nail Christ down, pretending to conjure him into a piece of bread, Hoffman's future in Holstein was in jeopardy. Of course, Hoffman was merely responding in kind, for Amsdorf had already denounced him as a 'false prophet,' and Schuldorp had implied a comparison between Hoffman and a juggler. Unwilling to recant, Hoffman may already have despaired of maintaining his

---

1 BARGE 2, 386–93.

position in Holstein when he wrote his circular letter, but he preferred to fight to the end.

It seems that the circular letter finally induced King Frederik to order the Flensburg trial for 8 April 1529. Karlstadt wrote asking for permission to attend, but he was made to leave Holstein. However, the records of the debate at Flensburg show that Karlstadt had already helped Hoffman to prepare his defence. The Lutheran clergy regarded the situation in Holstein as critical, for during the dispute Hermann Tast claimed that Hoffman's books 'have been spread throughout the world, [and] as a result the [Lutheran clergy] are esteemed and derided as false prophets by many.'[2]

The disputation was an inquisitorial trial of Hoffman, not a colloquy. Except for three participants, Hoffman's followers were excluded. The primary Lutheran representative at Hoffman's trial in the Grey Cloister of Flensburg was Johannes Bugenhagen (1485–1558), who served in Wittenberg as the minister of the church Luther attended, but who then returned to northern Germany to help establish the Lutheran faith in Braunschweig (May–October 1528) and Hamburg (October 1528–June 1529), and served the Lutheran cause later in other parts of northern Germany and Scandinavia. Having arrived from Hamburg, Bugenhagen entered Flensburg in stately procession.[3] The debate was rigged so that several pastors examined Hoffman in turn, trying to exhaust him. Hoffman remained unflagged, and attempts to trap him verbally failed. However, Crown Prince Christian intervened four times on the Lutheran side,[4] and since he was to report his findings to King Frederik, the end was foreordained.[5] The trial concluded with one of Bugenhagen's long-winded sermons, rehashing twenty-one points in refutation of Hoffman.

Since the Acta of the trial were to be published, Bugenhagen at last issued a digest, and this document allows one to gauge Hoffman's view of the Lord's Supper with considerable accuracy. Six notaries recorded the proceedings. Hoffman begins on a conciliatory note, stating that the sacrament is a sign of a promise. He then points to some of God's promises in a covenantal context.[6] The fur coat is a sign for Adam and Eve; the rainbow for Noah; circumcision for Abraham, and the paschal lamb for the Israelites. When Christ gave the paschal lamb to his disciples, he called the bread his body and he called the wine his blood, because they were signs of a promise received in faith.

From this position Hoffman moved briskly towards confrontation. Christ simply cannot be contained in a monstrance, he says, and:

2 Bugenhagen, Acta, A4v.
3 Dialogus [1529], 505; Bugenhagen, Acta, Mv.
4 Bugenhagen, Acta, [B8], C, C4, [L6].
5 Ibid, [C8].
6 Ibid, [A8v].

The bread we receive is figuratively and sacramentally the body of Christ, but not *really* (*wahrhafftig*). Yet, I do not take it to be mere bread and wine, but it is to me a remembrance and I regard it as a seal, in such a way that I have received the promise that Christ has given himself in death for me. I do not esteem it any more than any other bread, since Saint Paul called it the Lord's Bread.[7]

The bread is figurative, not the Word which is Christ himself (John 1), for the Jews asked Christ who he was and he replied: 'I am he that speaks with you.'[8] Christ's words 'this is my body' and 'this is my blood' are not meant literally. Literalism frequently leads one astray. In John 19:26, for example, Christ says: 'Woman behold your son.' Mary also speaks to Jesus (Luke 2:48) and says: 'Your father and I have searched for you.' In conclusion: 'If we were to take the words the way they sound, we'd start some nice heresies!'[9]

Hoffman notes that Paul says in 1 Corinthians 11[:26]: 'Ye shall proclaim the Lord's death until he comes, as often as ye eat the *bread* and drink the cup,' and this spells out Hoffman's position. Christ is received with the heart and the bread with the mouth.[10] John records that Christ blew on his disciples and said: 'receive the Holy Spirit,'[11] but of course they did not receive the Holy Spirit until later at Pentecost. The words of Christ are similarly futuristic. The bread had already been broken, but Christ's body was still to be broken on the cross. Thus the bread points to Calvary, and Christ's body was not in the bread.[12]

If the bread is or contains the body of Christ, there are two bodies: Christ's body in the bread and the body with which Christ sat at table. But Hoffman

---

7 Ibid, B2: 'das brot das wir empfangen, ist figürlich und sacramentlich der leib Christi, nicht warhafftig. Doch halt ich es nicht fur schlecht brot und wein, sondern es ist mir ein gedechtnis, und halt es fur ein siegel, also, dar mir die zusage geschehen ist, das Christus sich fur mich inn den tod gegeben hat. Darumb achte ich es nicht mehr denn ein ander brot, weil es Sant Paul des Herrn brot nennet.' The 'nicht wahrhafftig' is obviously Bugenhagen's summary. Hoffman would no doubt have insisted that the spiritual presence of Christ is 'real,' and he would have considered the Lutheran idea of a physical presence an *unreal* superstition.

8 Bugenhagen, *Acta*, B2v.

9 Ibid, B3v.

10 Ibid, [B6v]. Spiritual eating and drinking are accepted by Luther and Karlstadt (*1 Cor. 10* (142), A3–v) alike, but Hoffman and Karlstadt in effect destroy Luther's parallelism between the inward and the outward eating. Karlstadt and Hoffman spiritually eat the body of Christ (which died on the cross) in the Word, not with the bread: *Leyb* (129), [C4v]. Luther's parallelism is also destroyed by Hoffman's observation that Mark claims the disciples drank the wine *before* Christ said 'This is the blood of the New Testament' (Bugenhagen, *Acta*, C2). Karlstadt has used this same argument in *Christus* (124), C3f.

11 Bugenhagen, *Acta*, B–v. This derives from Karlstadt's *Missbrauch* (135), C3.

12 Bugenhagen, *Acta*, Cv–2. Karlstadt similarly points to Christ's crucifixion as the real saving event. Christ is given on the cross, not in the sacrament: *Leyb* (129), C3.

serves only one Christ.[13] The bread of the Supper is a heavenly bread (John 6:32).[14] Hoffman appeals to the work of the young Luther for the notion that the physical eating of the elements parallels the spiritual eating of Christ.[15] The bread is the seal eaten with the mouth, but Christ is the Word appropriated with the heart in faith. Hoffman does not aim for genuine concomitance; thus there is tactical juxtaposition, not true parallelism.

When Hoffman is charged with trying to understand a miracle of God's power, he counters (according to Bugenhagen):

We do not want to argue here about God's power – whether or not this could happen. But we confess that Christ was born of Mary and conceived by the Holy Ghost, and [he] has given the body in the Word to his disciples and [he] has confirmed this with the seal of the bread. But you want to change the bread into the body of Christ and do not allow it to remain a memorial. On this article we have to come to an agreement, for, if not, much blood will be shed, just as it has already cost much blood. And who else would be guilty of this than you, who teach the people thus with your sermons.[16]

The argument from bloodshed may not be derived from Hoffman. True, Hoffman could get carried away (following Christ, who cleansed the temple?)

---

13 Bugenhagen, *Acta*, C2v, 3v–4. This is essentially Karlstadt's *touto* argument (KS 2, 14:29f) without the *touto*. Although Luther seized on this (weak) argument, Karlstadt's views can be explained without it. Karlstadt refused to concede the *touto* argument to Luther in 1527 (BARGE 2, 384), perhaps because he knew Luther would use it against him. Naturally, Karlstadt had no difficulty reaching agreement with Zwingli in 1530, for what Zwingli wanted was assurance that Karlstadt had not made a genuine recantation in Saxony. See the anonymous 'Lebens-Beschreibung Andreae Bodensteins, Carolostadii,' Zurich, Zentralbibliothek, Ms W26, 527v: 'Und als Zuinglius vernommen dass er seine vorige erzwungne meinung von dem H. Nachtmal verlassen, ist er von ihme auffgenommen, und zu einerm Diacono der kirchen gemacht worden.' It is possible that Karlstadt had already quietly dropped the *touto* argument by the time he joined Hoffman in Holstein.

14 Bugenhagen, *Acta*, C4v.

15 Ibid, C4v–5. We have already seen how Karlstadt has used the same tactic in *1 Cor. 10* (142), C3v.

16 Bugenhagen, *Acta*, C5v: 'Wir wollen hie nicht disputieren von Gottes macht, ob solches geschehen möge odder nicht. Sondern wir bekennen das Christus von Marien geboren, und vom heiligen geist empfangen sey, und habe den leib im wort seinen jüngern gegeben, und habe solchs mit dem siegel des brots befestiget. Ihr aber wollet das brot in den leib Christi verwandeln, und nicht ein gedechtnis lassen bleiben. In diesem artickel mussen wir uber ein komen. Wo aber nicht, so wird es viel blutvergiessens kosten, wie es geret viel bluts gekostet hat. Und wer ist des alles schuldig denn ihr, die ihr mit euerm predigen die leute also leret.' Karlstadt similarly appeals to his belief in Christ's virgin birth to prove that he is not a rationalist (KS 2, 12:14–19).

during iconoclastic riots, and Bugenhagen does give a basically honest account of Hoffman's views on the Lord's Supper. However, Bugenhagen, as we shall see, did not scruple at mendacity. Moreover, a radical threat of bloodshed hardly fits Hoffman's careful and guarded doctrinal statements. Hoffman refers to 'the sword of the Spirit' to vent his anger. Even if Hoffman had advocated hanging the magistrates of Kiel, he could have appealed to the punishment of the law. Therefore it is not necessary to take this threat of bloodshed seriously. Later Bugenhagen uses this remark as a reason for Hoffman's expulsion,[17] but Hoffman would have been expelled anyway, though a fabricated threat must have been helpful. Evidence for Hoffman's 'violence' can be found only in the writings of opponents, who use as a model Luther's *Heavenly Prophets*, in which Luther mendaciously connects Karlstadt to the violent schemes of Thomas Müntzer. Such sources are not historically credible. Hans Hillerbrand sums up the problem nicely: 'Though the charges against them [i.e. the radicals] often included one of political insurrection, their real crime was that they held to theological views different from those declared normative by their respective communities.'[18]

I am not claiming that Hoffman never indulged in visions of revenge. At a later stage Hoffman included violence in his scheme for the end of the world: the authorities are to slay the lying prophets, but this presumes the time when the seventh trumpet has blown (Rev. 16, 17).[19] None of these conditions is applicable here. Moreover, the slayers themselves are outside the pale of the church. Thus even the acute crisis at the end of the world does not see Hoffman or his followers involved in violence.

As the Flensburg trial continued, Hoffman argued that Christ is not eaten 'with feeling, with hair and bones in the sacrament.'[20] Hoffman returns to the theory of the 'two bodies of Christ,' coupling it with a spatial understanding of Christ's ascension: 'We say Christ ascended into heaven. If he ascended into heaven, then he cannot be in the sacrament, or else he has two bodies.'[21] The words of the Lord's Supper must be interpreted and should not be taken literally;

---

17 Bugenhagen, *Acta*, [L8]. Since Luther attributes his reformation to the sole power of the Word, but since he uses the magistrates to establish Lutheranism, the gap between theory and practice is bridged by charging the dissenters with violence. This is Luther's tactic in his *Heavenly Prophets*, for example.

18 Hillerbrand, 'Luther's "Deserting Disciples,"' 105.

19 DEPPERMANN, 228, 232.

20 Bugenhagen, *Acta*, [C6]. See Karlstadt's rhetorical question: 'Darumb frag ich ob Christus leib, arm, brust, schenckel und gebeyn ... in dem brodt seynd?' (KS 2, 12:2–4).

21 Bugenhagen, *Acta*, [C7]. Karlstadt also claims that, after the ascension, Christ's body was localized in heaven (KS 2, 32:27f, 36:40–37:4). Perhaps Karlstadt knew that, although Luther publicly taught the ascension because 'it is right,' he privately said 'I cannot believe it and I teach otherwise.' Luther therefore did consider his teachings on the sacrament of the altar to contradict the doctrine of the ascension (TR 4 (no. 4864)).

otherwise the evangelists contradict one another. For example, Mark [14:24] and Matthew [26:28] have 'this is my blood of the covenant,' but Luke [22:20] says: 'this is the cup: the New Testament in my blood.'[22]

Here the *Acta* end, but Bugenhagen has not used all the arguments in his excerpts of the notes. Some of Hoffman's statements suppressed in the *Acta* surface in Bugenhagen's sermon preached after others had examined Hoffman. Hoffman has again used the 'Lo, here is Christ; lo, there he is' argument of the false prophets.[23] Hoffman also claims that Christ is not received by the unworthy,[24] and he argues that elevating the host means having a 'baked God.'[25] In addition, Hoffman gives God the power of absolution, taking it from the Lutheran priests.[26]

Bugenhagen had been afraid to debate Karlstadt. Therefore, Karlstadt, in addition to being refused a safe-conduct to attend the debate, was expelled from Holstein. Then Bugenhagen spread the rumour that Karlstadt had run away from him like a coward.[27] But later Bugenhagen bragged to the ministers in Hamburg: 'What expelled Karlstadt – a man delivered to the judgment of God – from Holstein? God's mercy and our public request.'[28] The same hero who feared Karlstadt wanted to debate Hoffman, but King Frederik refused to grant permission; thus, others examined Hoffman at Flensburg. Bugenhagen offered this interpretation of the king's refusal: 'For His Royal Majesty did not want me to dispute, perhaps so

22 Bugenhagen, *Acta*, [C7v]. Karlstadt does not use this argument, but he frequently compares parallel texts to undermine a literalistic interpretation of the Supper. He plays off Matthew against Mark, for example: *Leyb* (129), Cv.

23 Bugenhagen, *Acta*, [G7]. We have already noted Hoffman's dependence on Karlstadt here.

24 Ibid, [I7]. Cf 1 *Cor. 10* (142), D3.

25 Bugenhagen, *Acta*, [K8v]–L. Karlstadt does not quite say the same thing. He frequently refers to the 'baker's bread,' and he rejects the elevation in the Lutheran mass, because elevation is related to sacrifice: *Messen* (131), 2v–[3].

26 Bugenhagen, *Acta*, F2v–3.

27 *Dialogus* [1529], 505: 'Der kürssner ist verschriben gewesst zum ersten von dem künig uss Dennmark, der selbig hat bey im Doctor Andreas Carolstat, dem warb er gleidt an den künig, kundt im aber kein gleid erlangen, wiewol man sagt, das er hab gericht und gerechtigkeit leiden künnen, und sich auch darzu erbotten, es sol aber alles nicht geholffen haben, müst wider zuruck auss dem land zu Holsten reysen, on allen verzug. Dann die Lutherischen triben solches alles, darumb villeicht dass sy sich vor dem selben doctor förchten.' Bugenhagen, *Acta*, M2: 'Er schreibt auch wie man sich fur Doctor Carlstad gefurchtet hat. Das ist spottisch. Was darfft ich mich fur dem furchten, der nicht küne war an den tag zukommen? Ich hörete wol das er da hin ins land gekommen were, der teuffel hatte ihm aber botten gesand, und der peltzer hatte ihm trostlich zugesagt, das er alda mit seiner tollen schwermerey mochte rhum uberkommen. Das bekenne ich aber, weil ich auch noch im fleische bin, das ich vileicht mich fur dem Carlstad furchten mochte, wenn ich zu ihm keme und er hatte bey sich die bauern an der Sale.'

28 Vogt, ed, *Dr. Johannes Bugenhagens Briefwechsel*, 90 (19 Feb. 1530): 'Quid eiecit Carlstadium, hominem iudicio Dei traditum ex Holstatia? Dei clementia et oratio nostra publica.'

no one could say that the furrier had been overwhelmed with words.'[29] Indeed, Hoffman was not vanquished with words. He was expelled from Holstein and his printing presses and materials were confiscated by those whom he may have called, by prolepsis as well as by observation, 'the thieves of Kiel.'[30] Karlstadt had attached himself to Hoffman, and when Bugenhagen, in his sermon, attacked the absent Karlstadt as the source of Hoffman's doctrine, Hoffman interrupted and quoted the proverb: 'Dislike leads to defamation.'[31] Soon Hoffman would be joining Karlstadt on the way to Emden. On Saturday afternoon, 10 April 1529, Johann Rantzow allowed Hoffman two nights and one day to leave Holstein. Then, as Karlstadt has it:

> The furrier, his wife, and child were driven out of the land, and his house was plundered, and about a thousand guilders' worth of books and printing materials were taken. The unbelievers were also really after his neck to kill him on his way, but God helped him to arise and delivered him out of the hands of murderers and tyrants.[32]

Hoffman had lost the political struggle. He was a victim of injustice, but he himself did not advocate true tolerance either. Could he have triumphed, the Lutherans may well have received similar treatment in Holstein. However, since they always suffered more than the clergy, the wealthy, and the scholars, Hoffman had the right to challenge injustice on behalf of the deprived classes.

Hoffman's Stay in East Friesland

Hoffman rejoined Karlstadt, and they travelled to Emden where they visited one of Karlstadt's former students, Hinne Rhode.[33] Thus Hoffman came for the first

29 Bugenhagen, *Acta*, [M6]: 'Denn K[önigliche] M[ajestät] wolt auch das ich nicht disputiren solte, vileicht darumb das niemand mochte sagen, man hette den peltzer mit worten uberweldiget.'

30 Hoffman's press was confiscated by the magistrates of Kiel. It stayed in Kiel until 3 March 1533, when the king demanded its surrender. Walter Brenner printed with it in Schleswig 1533–4, after which the press is lost to history. See Benzing, *Die Buchdrucker*, 84, 216, 380.

31 Bugenhagen, *Acta*, F4–v. As Hoffman quotes the proverb: '[Ja] dem man nicht gunstig ist, dem sagt man nichts gutes nach.'

32 *Dialogus* [1529], 521–2: '[Uff ein solch urteil des Pomers,] ist der kurssner mit weib und kind uss dem land verjaget, und im sein hauss geplündert, und sind im an bücher und an trucker zug, als gut als tusend gulden genommen, und stunden auch die unglaubigen hart nach seinem halss, das sye in wolten underwegen umb bringen, abert gott halff im, der im uff geholffen hat, und erlöset auss den henden der mörder und thirannen.'

33 Anonymous letter to Bucer [Amsterdam, 9 June 1529], cited in LEENDERTZ, 352: 'Carolostadius relinquens Saxoniam disputationi interesse cupiebat, vocatus a Melchiore cum suis; sed a duce Holsatiae indictum illi erat, ne urbem disputationi ordinatam intraret. Tandem omnia secun-

time to the city from which the Baptist movement was to penetrate the Lowlands.[34] At this point there is no evidence concerning Hoffman, but it is known that Karlstadt went to Oldersum and stayed with Chief Ulrich von Dornum. Karlstadt's relations with Ulrich remained cordial, and in 1531 Karlstadt dedicated his edition of Zwingli's commentary on Philippians to Chief Ulrich.[35] Capito considered Ulrich to be a patron of Karlstadt.[36]

Hoffman may have followed Karlstadt to Oldersum, for he refers to Ulrich later as a man with 'great zeal for the gospel.'[37] Since Hoffman dedicated two of his tracts to him, Ulrich may have financed their printing in Strassburg.[38] Ulrich's castle is also the most likely place for Karlstadt to have written the *Dialogus* of the Flensburg disputation on the basis of Hoffman's reminiscences.

Although the official *Acta* of the Flensburg disputation were to be published, Bugenhagen did not want to confuse his readers by giving them both sides of the issues. Thus he did not print the *Acta*, but in Hamburg he published his sermon as *Eynne rede vam sacramente*. Karlstadt then wrote down Hoffman's reminiscences in the *Dialogus*, a form he had used in his dialogue on the Lord's Supper, as well as in the dialogue on baptism which Felix Manz failed to have printed in Basel, whereas Hoffman had not written any dialogues.[39]

The *Dialogus* is valuable for reconstructing Hoffman's career, despite the terseness of Karlstadt's summary. Because of a feeling of modesty, perhaps, Hoffman had not told his readers anything directly about himself. Karlstadt's *Dialogus* also makes an invaluable contribution to our knowledge of the Flensburg trial. Bugenhagen did not publish the *Acta* until after he had received copies of the original Strassburg edition and the Augsburg reprint of the *Dia-*

dum votum Pomerani concludebantur ... Tandem Melchior cum suis urbem exire iussus est. At Carolostadius et Melchior ad comitem Emdensem, ubi Rhodius noster apostolum agit, devenerunt. Carolostadius et Melchior adversus disputationem et Pomerani argumenta librum edunt et prelo committent.'

34 Van der Zijpp, *Geschiedenis der Doopsgezinden* (1952), 25.

35 BARGE 2, 589, A2.

36 z 11, 506.

37 Hoffman, *Weissagung*, A2.

38 These are Hoffman, *Weissagung* (1529–30), Av–2; and Hoffman, *Prophecey* (1530), Av.

39 LEENDERTZ, 141, says Hoffman wrote it 'with the help of Karlstadt.' The anonymous writer to Bucer (above; cited in LEENDERTZ, 443, n 1) speaks of Karlstadt's and Hoffman's joint authorship. Bugenhagen (*Acta*, M2–v) attributed the sections by 'Erhart' to Karlstadt. However, Hyppolitus can also speak in the third person about 'the furrier.' The best analysis of the style and contents of the *Dialogus* was written by Faust, 'Einige Bemerkungen,' 96–8. He sees Karlstadt as the author, but believes that he based the *Dialogus* on Hoffman's report. Faust concludes (p. 98): 'Somit stellt sich der Dialogus als eine gegen Bugenhagen gerichtete, äusserst fein gearbeitete Tendenzschrift dar, deren Stoff bis ins einzelne Hoffman geliefert hat, die aber in der Form, wie sie uns vorliegt, Carlstadt zum Verfasser hat.'

logus; without the challenge of the *Dialogus* the *Acta* might never have been printed.[40]

There has been slight disagreement about the extent to which the *Dialogus* reflects Karlstadt's rather than Hoffman's views.[41] It is clear that the *Dialogus* must have been based on Hoffman's report, and that Hoffman could not have been opposed to its contents since he himself took it to Strassburg for publication. Beyond doubt Karlstadt had no qualms about furthering the views of one of his own disciples. If Hoffman sometimes used a novel argument, their basic positions were the same. Karlstadt had himself used scores of arguments against Luther, and a few more would have been welcome. Within sacramentarian limits Karlstadt was flexible.[42]

There are a few arguments in the *Dialogus* which are lacking in Bugenhagen's *Acta*. Karlstadt's favourite epithet for the communion meal, 'the Lord's Supper' (*des herren nachtmal*), is frequently used. According to Bugenhagen, Hoffman referred consistently to 'the sacrament.' Karlstadt preferred biblical usage, and tended to insist on it, but he sometimes used traditional words like 'sacrament' or 'eucharist' 'to speak with children.'[43] In the *Dialogus* the bread of heaven (John 6) is compared with the manna in the wilderness; Luther is called a new pope; and Bugenhagen is called a pompous 'papal legate.'[44]

In the summer of 1529 Hoffman was ready for new adventures; moreover, Oldersum was an inauspicious place for one who earned his living as a furrier. On 9 July Karlstadt wrote to Martin Bucer in Strassburg, recommending Hoffman to him, and three weeks later Hoffman had arrived in Strassburg, where Bucer welcomed him.[45]

---

40 According to Bugenhagen, *Acta* [L8], the *Acta* was already in press before he received the two editions of the *Dialogus*. Bugenhagen's own sermon, however, had been printed a year earlier, and even the second edition of the *Dialogus* had reached Wittenberg before Bugenhagen made this claim.

41 Kawerau, *Melchior Hoffman*, 7–8, basically accepts Faust's arguments, to which he adds a few of his own. He omits the *Dialogus* from the list of Hoffman's writings, 4–5. Noll, 'Luther Defends Melchior Hofmann,' 129, calls Faust's and Kawerau's judgment into question. He cites the *Dialogus* as Hoffman's own work. We agree with Faust that Karlstadt wrote the *Dialogus*, but, since there are no differences between Hoffman and Karlstadt on the Lord's Supper, Noll's approach presents no problems. Deppermann has opted for joint authorship (DEPPERMANN, 109f, 346).

42 WA 18, 455, n 1.

43 *Christus* (124), A2.

44 *Dialogus* [1529], 505, 509.

45 TQ 7 (Elsass 1), no. 188. Karlstadt's relations with Martin Bucer need further explication. Obviously Bucer was sympathetic towards Karlstadt, for on the basis of Karlstadt's recommendation Bucer accepted Hoffman and permitted him to publish the *Dialogus*. Perhaps Bucer also wanted to reciprocate a favour that Karlstadt had intended to grant to him. In 1521 Bucer had made arrangements for Otto Brunfels and Michael Herr to escape to Karlstadt in Denmark, in

Hoffman's Break with Karlstadt

Hoffman's and Karlstadt's paths crossed for the last time in Strassburg during March and April 1530. Leendertz assumes that Hoffman returned to East Friesland on the advice of Karlstadt.[46] This is possible, for they were still friends, and Karlstadt could have advised Hoffman about the political situation there. Soon, however, Hoffman was to denounce Karlstadt, and perhaps some tensions had already surfaced in Strassburg. Hoffman's new 'heavenly flesh' Christology would have repelled Karlstadt. Moreover, Karlstadt worried about his family. Even when he was a celibate, Karlstadt had a very strong view of one's marital obligation.[47] He had circumvented Luke 14:26 (on hating one's wife and children) by accepting three stages: first, one is selfish and one loves one's family for one's own sake; then comes *Gelassenheit*, the hatred of one's selfish love of family; finally there is *Gelassenheit in Gelassenheit*, when one no longer loves wife and children for one's own sake, but for God's sake.[48] Thus Karlstadt adjusted his differences with Zwingli in order to find a haven for his family. Having been advised to leave Strassburg and not being welcomed in Basel, they were poor and hunger-stricken, when he made his distraught move to Zurich. Afterwards Pierre Toussain wrote to Guillaume Farel about Karlstadt's situation:

I have found those of Zurich much more human and charitable, and if the good and saintly Karlstadt had told me how he had been treated in that town [Basel], I do not at all think that I would even have put foot in it. For that man appears to me as worthy as any man to receive works of charity. And, with his poor wife and children, he has been left here in the greatest need and starvation – worse than dogs. When the poor man saw that he had been left destitute here, without money, aid, and consolation, he took a morsel of bread to his breast and went to Zurich to see if he could find there a situation for nourishing his poor wife and children whom he had left here [in Basel] without butter, bread, and money. And while the poor man was there, settling matters with Zwingli and the

case they received no dispensation from their vows as Carthusians. See Brunfels's letter to the imperial councillor Jakob Spiegel (10 Jun. 1521): 'si aliunde tu potes extorquere aliquid ab Aleandro, fac, mercedem retribuet servator Christus, cuius gratia nunc quaerimus libertatem si non potes, fugiendum nobis ad Danos, regionem evangelicorum, nam illuc ire iussi sumus a Bucero ad Carolostadium, abunde illum nobis provisurum, stipendiis, desiderari enim ex omni regione doctos' (Friedensburg, 'Beiträge,' 492–3).

46 LEENDERTZ, 212.
47 A vow to go on a pilgrimage, and thus allow oneself 'to be drawn from the care of running one's own house,' makes one worse than an unbeliever: *Gelubden* (50), A3v.
48 *Gelassen* (104), [E4v].

brethren of Zurich, the poor wife with her children went without food for two or three days and, seeing that no one approached her, was compelled to send her three poor little children to beg in Little Basel, and thus to await her husband. What do we say to this? To pass over the papists, are we not worse than dogs, Turks, and devils?[49]

From Hoffman's viewpoint, however, Karlstadt's appeasement involved a return to being a 'belly servant' after having seen the light. In Strassburg Hoffman elaborated a scheme of salvation based on perseverance which had germinated as early as 1526.[50] In Gelaub (139) Karlstadt had argued that a rootless faith dies in persecution. A fall after one has been enlightened is final, for deliberate sinners are condemned eternally (John 3:36). God's forgiveness extends only to unintentional sin (1 Tim. 1:13).[51]

Hoffman took up this point and went slightly further than Karlstadt. True believers do not lapse. Some pagans (like Aristotle) can also be saved, if they

---

49 Herminjard, Correspondance des réformateurs 3, 5–8: 'J'ay trouvé ceulx de Zurich beaucoup plus humains et charitables, et si le bon et sainct Carolostade, m'eut dit comment il avoit esté traicté en ceste ville, je ne pense point que je y eusse jamais mys le pied, car cest homme me semble digne envers qui on exerce les œuvres de charité, sí quisquam alius. Et on l'a icy laissé long temps à plus grande nécessité et famine, avecque sa povre femme et enffans, que ne furent jamais chiens.

Quant le povre homme vit qu'il estoit icy destitué et d'argent et d'ayde et de consolation, [il] prent ung morseau de pain à son sein et s'en va à Zurich, pour veoir s'il trouveroit illecque quelque condition pour nourir ses povres femme et enffans, qu'ilz avoit icy laissé sans beure, sans pain, sans argent. Et ce pendant que ce povre homme estoit illecque, traitent ses affaires avecque Zuingle et les frères du dit Zurich, la povre femma avecque ses dicts enffans feut deux ou trois jours sans menger, et, voyant que nul ne la visitoit, feut contrainte envoyer ses trois petits enffans mendier à la petite Basle, et ainsy attendre son marry.

Quid hic dicemus? Ne sommes-nous point pires, je ne dis point que papistes, mais que chiens, que Turques, que diables?' [frequent underlinings omitted].

Herminjard questions the truth of this statement, referring to a letter of Oecolampadius that shows his solicitousness. Barge basically agrees (BARGE 2, 422), but he does think that Toussain is partially correct, for 'even nowadays the reserve of the people of Basel in dealing with strangers is proverbial.' When Toussain wrote, he lived in Basel and he must have heard an eyewitness of the begging episode. I draw the opposite conclusion from the evidence presented by Herminjard. Why was Oecolampadius so solicitous about Karlstadt's welfare? This can be better explained if something had gone wrong. Oecolampadius may not have known at first about Karlstadt's extreme poverty, and when he heard about it, he was no doubt helpful, and he also felt embarrassed. In the letter cited by Herminjard, Oecolampadius wrote: 'Nos iubet calamum sistere,' which I take as an allusion to Isa. 42:3. Thus Karlstadt appeared to Oecolampadius as 'a bruised reed,' and he and his family must have appeared to be in pitiful condition.

Already in Capito's recommendation of Karlstadt to Zwingli (Strassburg, 22 May 1530) there is the remark: '[Karlstadt] is destitute' (inops rerum est) (BARGE 2, 423, n 56).

50 See Hoffman, Daniel 12, D–v.

51 Gelaub (139), [A2v–4].

persevere in doing good. Those who fall deliberately are damned. Adam was such a person for whom there was no hope, and the church begins with Abel. Hoffman had to explain away the fall of the apostle Peter. He turned on Karlstadt with the criteria of *Gelaub*:

> As some have also experienced especially with Karlstadt, who, when he experienced bitterness, trod the truth underfoot. For such wanton and knowing violators of the Holy Spirit, one should not pray, but one should let them go to the one to whom they have delivered themselves.[52]

This denunciation notwithstanding, Hoffman admits in these same words that Karlstadt knew the truth. He made this assertion at a time when he had already petitioned the Strassburg authorities to reserve a church for the Baptists.[53]

Karlstadt's Abiding Influence

Hoffman's excommunication of Karlstadt does not alter the fact that Karlstadt's profound influence on the pre-Strassburg Hoffman continued to linger. The Strassburg experience cannot be seen as a radical turning-point for Hoffman, although it brought about several changes in his doctrine. Most of the new developments have been treated by Deppermann.[54]

On one significant point Hoffman moved even closer to Karlstadt, for he now rejected the doctrine of predestination. Two similarities between Hoffman's views on predestination and those of Hans Denck have been noted by Deppermann.[55] I doubt that Hoffman was influenced by Denck's *Was geredt sei* (1526), which would have seemed quite abstruse to Hoffman; however, Denck's *Ordnung Gottes* (1527) does appear to influence Hoffman's discussion of the reprobation of Esau in *Tuchenisse* (1532), [A5]. But that influence appears somewhat

---

52 Hoffman, *Ausslegung*, Q4: '[das sye im selben liecht darinn sy sünden, verblendet bleiben] als auch etlicher der ersten widerfaren ist am Carolstat, da die verbitterung empfangen, die warheit under die füss gedretten. Fur solche frevele, wissende schender des heyligen geists soll man nit bitten, sunder faren lassen, zum selben dem sye sich ergeben haben.'

53 TQ 8 (Elsass 2), 261–2.

54 DEPPERMANN, 194–235.

55 DEPPERMANN, 168–9, 195, n 9. Beachy, *The Concept of Grace*, 46–56, discusses the views of Denck, Hubmaier, and Hoffman. A comparison between them and Karlstadt makes it clear that all three of these authors were indebted to Karlstadt. Denck's claim that only good derives from God whereas evil derives from the self, as well as his assertion that God cannot be blamed for sin and that man voluntarily chooses for or against God after *recognition* – all this may well imitate Karlstadt. Hubmaier emphasizes two manifestations of God's will, which also seem derived from Karlstadt. Hoffman's basic viewpoint is similarly dependent on Karlstadt, although he adds several new illustrations drawn from the Bible.

later. In 1530 Hoffman's view of predestination shows primarily the influence of Karlstadt and of Balthasar Hubmaier.

Since Karlstadt was no longer publishing, his influence on Hoffman's rejection of predestination can be attributed to verbal communication during the time when they were in Kiel and East Friesland. Hoffman's references to God as light who wills no darkness, as well as to the divine intent that Satan be good, are themes from Karlstadt's *Teuffelischen falhs* (114), published in 1524. On the title-page of *Warhafftige erklerung* (1531) Hoffman cites Karlstadt's favourite text for undermining predestination, Hosea 13:9 (Vulg.): 'Perdition comes from you, O Israel; but from me comes your help.' Karlstadt may have cited this passage to clear up Hoffman's misunderstanding of his intentions in *Willen gottes*. Like Karlstadt, Hoffman also accepts the universality of salvation as divinely intended, yet limited in its effect, because of human free choice.[56] Hoffman also holds out the possibility of salvation to sincere heathens, though this is to be of instant effect, whereas Karlstadt first envisages a course through a heavenly university which he equates with purgatory.

Once Hoffman casts off predestination, he does borrow additional arguments against it. Hoffman must have read Balthasar Hubmaier's tract *Von der Freyhait des Willens*, which in turn shows traces of Karlstadt and Denck. Although this work is of minor significance for Hoffman's view of predestination, which Karlstadt had led Hoffman to reject in any case, Hubmaier's treatise has an impact on Hoffman's hermeneutics. Hubmaier discusses the tension in Scripture, which stands on 'two split hooves,' and which must be 'ruminated' to be understood. Since this theme occurs in Hoffman's writings of the Strassburg period, I accept George Huntston Williams's suggestion that Hoffman derives this point from Hubmaier. However, Hubmaier seems to be indebted to Luther's interpretation of the cloven hoof and rumination (see Luther's comments on Deut. 14:1).[57] Hoffman also refers to this principle as the 'key of David' (Isa. 22:22), a designation used earlier by Thomas Müntzer.[58]

South German influence appears to be the source of Hoffman's covenantal ideas. Walter Fellman identifies Denck's *Von der wahren Liebe* as influential, but I reject his statement that it is 'the cradle of this original Anabaptist idea.'[59] Covenantal ideas can be found in Luther, Melanchthon, and Karlstadt, but Müntzer is the first to develop a strong covenantal framework, and in Strassburg one thinks above all of Bucer.

56 For the universal offer of salvation in Hoffman see A. Pater, 'A Study of Selected Doctrines,' 64–72.
57 For Hoffman see Kawerau, *Melchior Hoffman*, 39–40. For Williams's comment see *Spiritual and Anabaptist Writers*, 134, n 14. For Luther see WA 14, 650–1.
58 For Hoffman see Kawerau, *Melchior Hoffman*, 38–9. For Müntzer see MS, 208:6–16.
59 *Hans Denck: Schriften*, in TQ 6/2, 81, n 2.

Hoffman disapproved of the sword in religious matters, but since his career had been punctuated with iconoclastic violence, his strong affirmations in Strassburg of physical non-resistance also brought him closer to Karlstadt. This is remarkable, since Hoffman believes that the battle of Armageddon is soon to be fought in Strassburg with physical engines of war. Even in this final drama, however, Hoffman's followers would desist from active combat, rendering only tactical support to the Reformed militia, who would fight alongside a legion of heavenly angels. For the Baptists, however, Hoffman firmly rejects the use of force, opening up the possibility of tolerance for outsiders. The 'Satanic Lutheran and Zwinglian congregations' use physical torture and execution to establish their blasphemies, but the Baptists should not requite their oppressors, for judgment is to be left to God.[60] With the violence of Münster Hoffman would not have sympathized, nor did he condone polygamy. When Münster was invaded, the Dutch Melchiorites had escaped Hoffman's control.

Hoffman and Menno Simons

Hoffman's and Karlstadt's work in East Friesland, as well as Hoffman's later travels, again to Emden and the Lowlands, laid the foundation of the northern Baptist movements. Krohn was the first to call Hoffman 'the father of Low German Anabaptism,'[61] and Cramer the first to call him 'the father of Dutch Anabaptism.'[62] I would call Hoffman 'the father of the northern Baptist movements,' recognizing Karlstadt's influence on him, and also on Westerburg's efforts around Cologne.

The influence of Hoffman on Menno has been controversial. Traditional *Doopsgezinde* historiography has treated the relationship between Hoffman and Menno in a manner analogous to Hoffman's view of the relation between Mary and Jesus. Hoffman was the historical oyster in which Menno the pearl was lodged for a season, but otherwise there is no connection.

To his credit Karel Vos broke with traditional *Doopsgezinde* historiography in 1914, when he argued that Menno came out of the Melchiorite tradition.[63] Of course, I also accept Vos's argument that this does not saddle the Dutch Baptists with the excesses of their forbears, nor – I would add – do the tales of martyrdom and persecution make modern Baptists inherently more pious. In spite of this, Kühler has not recognized Vos's honest concession,[64] and Krahn has followed

---

60 Hoffman, *Tuchenisse*, [A2–3].
61 Krohn, *Wiedertäufer*, 5: '[Hoffman] ist solcher gestalt einer der merkwürdigsten Personen unter den alten Widertäufern in Niederdeutschland, ja der Vater derselben geworden.'
62 Cramer, BRN 5, 127: 'In de "Bibliotheca" mogen enkele van de geschriften van Melchior Hoffman, den vader van het nederlandsch Anabaptisme, niet ontbreken.'
63 Vos, *Menno Simons*, 38–9.
64 Kühler, *Geschiedenis der Nederlandsche Doopsgezinden in de zestiende eeuw*, 169.

Kühler in asserting that Vos 'overestimated' the influence of the Melchiorites on Menno.[65]

Excepting Vos, I would concur with Mellink's appraisal of traditional *Doopsgezinde* historiography:

> Whereas the governmental authorities and opponents were unjust in identifying every form of the Baptist movements with Münster, ... the Mennonites themselves have always wanted to deny their Melchiorite and Münsterite origins, and they did violence to the historical truth.[66]

Krahn's argument that Menno attacked Jan van Leyden fails to disprove Menno's Melchiorite origins.[67]

An alternative Swiss connection must also be ruled out. Ubbo Emmius was unaware of any Swiss origins of the Baptist movements.[68] The *Brotherly Agreement* of Schleitheim did not appear in Dutch until 1560, well after the crystallization of the Dutch Baptist movements.[69] Several of Hoffman's major and some minor writings had been translated into Dutch from 1530 to 1533, and Hoffman's *Ordonnantie* was reprinted as late as 1611. Hoffman's Low German tracts would have been as intelligible to the Frisians and the Low Dutch-speaking inhabitants of the northeastern Lowlands as versions in High Dutch. In the imperial placards the terms Anabaptists, Baptists (*Wederdoopers, herdopers, An[n]abaptisten, dopers, baptisateurs*), and Melchiorites are used interchangeably.[70]

The theological pedigree of Menno Simons runs from Karlstadt to Hoffman, who baptized Jan Trypmaker in Emden in 1530. Trypmaker was left in charge of Hoffman's converts there, but he fled to Amsterdam, where he baptized many. Captured by the imperial authorities in The Hague, he was beheaded on 6

---

65 Krahn, *Menno Simons*, 32.

66 Mellink, *De Wederdopers in de Noordelijke Nederlanden*, 419: 'Terwijl de overheden en tegenstanders ieder doperdom ten onrechte met Munster bleven identificeren ... , hebben de Mennonieten zelf zich hun Melchiorietische en Munsterse oorsprong steeds willen ontvijnzen en de historische waarheid [vanaf van Braght tot Kühler] geweld aangedaan.

67 Krahn, *Dutch Anabaptism*, 152f. *The Blasphemy of Jan van Leyden* was published in the seventeenth century. It is stylistically rather different from Menno's genuine writings (continuous scriptural quotation; no piling up of adjectives or nouns; etc), and it assumes such a strong identification with the Anabaptists (while Menno was a priest) that it must be considered a pious seventeenth-century forgery. There was precedent for this: earlier a mixed collection had appeared which included excerpts of Menno's *Reply to Gellius Faber* (1554) but was predated to 1551. See Quiring-Unruh, 'Neues Licht,' 56f. An excellent survey of Menno's original and milder attitude towards the Münsterites is found in Bornhäuser, *Leben und Lehre Menno Simons*, 17–25.

68 Stupperich, 'Anfang und Fortgang,' 29–30.

69 BRN 5, 583f.

70 *Documenta anabaptistica neerlandica*, ed Mellink, 1, 10–39.

December 1531. Among Trypmaker's converts was Jan Matthijs, a baker from Haarlem, who in 1533 challenged Hoffman's moratorium on adult baptism, sending twelve apostles through the Lowlands. In December 1533 two apostles, Bartel Boeckbinder and Dirk Cuyper, passed through Leeuwarden on the way to the kingdom of Christ in Münster; there they baptized and appointed Obbe Philips as bishop (later: elder). The latter ordained Menno Simons (1505-61) in Groningen.

After Menno left the priesthood, he fled in 1536 to Oldersum, the scene of Karlstadt's labours from 1529 to 1530. There Menno performed his first adult baptism (of Peter Jans).[71] Vos also argues that Menno's family lived in Oldersum from 1536 to 1543 and he believes that Oldersum was the main base for Menno's excursions into the Lowlands, once or twice a year.[72] Here is another link between Menno and Karlstadt.

Menno claimed that he was first moved by the plight of the Baptists when he witnessed the beheading of the tailor Sicke Freerks in Leeuwarden on 20 March 1531. Sicke was a Melchiorite who, in December 1530, had been baptized in Emden by Trypmaker. As Menno's 'pedigree' suggests, the Dutch Baptists had a common Melchiorite origin. To try to distinguish 'Melchiorites' from 'Münsterites' or 'Obbenites' from 'Mennonites' is absurd before the late 1530s. The Melchiorites were a varied lot, but divisions did not occur and harden until later.

According to John Wenger, 'Menno zealously dissociates himself and his brethren from the Münsterites.'[73] However, this assertion holds only for the older Menno, who had been put on the defensive by the Münster episode. Menno's brother Peter was implicated in the Melchiorite insurrection at the Old Cloister between Bolsward and Sneek, and he was hanged with his fellow crusaders when the troops of the Frisian stadholder were victorious on 7 April 1535.[74]

Although Menno supposedly wrote against Jan van Leyden as early as 1535, he considered most of the Münsterites his 'dear brethren' as late as 1539, when he published the first edition of his *Foundation Book*:

> I do not doubt that our dear brethren formerly acted against the Lord in a minor way, since they wanted to protect their faith through resistance, but they have a merciful God, for I hope that they were not infected with these above-mentioned heresies. Moreover, they sought nothing but Christ Jesus and eternal life, and for this they forsook house, land, country, soil,

71 Vos, *Menno Simons*, 53, 243.
72 Ibid, [66, 67], 71. Cf Doornkaat Koolman, *Dirk Philips*, 17f.
73 Simons, Menno, *The Complete Writings*, 129, n 6.
74 Vos, *Menno Simons*, 1–2; Mellink, *De Wederdopers*, 247f. See also Stayer, 'Oldeklooster and Menno,' 51–77.

father, mother, wife, child, and their very own lives – even though they erred slightly.[75]

In the later edition of the *Foundation Book* this embarrassing passage was struck, and since that edition (1558) was used for the American translation, these sentences are lacking in Menno's *Complete Writings*. In this passage Menno also denounced the leaders of the Münsterites as unscrupulous. However, Menno had adopted from Hoffman Karlstadt's scheme on unintentional sin, and the reason why Menno forgave the Münsterites was precisely because he thought they erred *unintentionally*.

Menno was basically the heir of Hoffman. To avoid the unwitting sins of his predecessors, Menno filters out certain elements from Hoffman's theology. As a result, Hoffman's peculiar ideas tend to fade, whereas the Karlstadtian component survives in Menno. Especially durable is Karlstadt's biblicism, now without Hoffman's four beasts. In the same way Karlstadt also shapes Menno's rejection of reprobation by divine decree, Menno's doctrine of the church, and his reduction of the liturgy and the signs of the Lord's Supper and baptism. Karlstadt has a similar impact on Menno's political views, including the elimination of oaths and the advocacy of physical non-resistance. Karlstadt and Menno also agree in linking faith and works, and both insist on an ascetic lifestyle that includes such marks as simplicity of dress and avoidance of conformity with the 'world.'

Karlstadt's stay in Oldersum would have heralded the beginning of the Baptist congregation established there. Since Menno went there after his conversion, he must have been exposed to Karlstadt's lingering influence. This, and the collapse of the Münsterite movement, drove Menno in some ways closer to Karlstadt than to Hoffman. Although Menno's thought is more apocalyptically coloured than Karlstadt's, he resists Hoffman's chiliastic schemes. Menno and Karlstadt also tend to draw their message from more conventional parts of Scripture.

However, Hoffman did influence Menno's heavenly-flesh Christology.[76] On this point alone Menno and Hoffman would have excommunicated Karlstadt

---

75 Simons, Menno, *Dat Fundament des Christelycken Leers*, 202–3: 'Ick en twivel daer niet aen ofte onse lieven broeders, de en weinich tegen den Here voormaels mishandelt hebben, vermits sy met geweer wolden hoeren gelove beschermen, ofte die hebben een genadigen God, want sy hebben, hoop ick, met dese voorgemelde ketterien niet besmet weest, sochten oock niet dan Christum Jesum unde dat ewighe leven unde daervoor hebben si opgeset huys, hof, lant, zant, vader, moeder, wyf, kynt unde oock hoer eigen selves leven, hoewel sy nochtans in weinich gedoelt hebben.' This passage is cited to show that Menno felt a kinship towards the Münsterites. Menno, however, did reject their violence, which he blamed on bad leadership.

76 Unlike Hoffman, however, Menno argued that Christ took on human flesh in, but not from, Mary. Hoffman argued for the eternal existence of Christ's heavenly flesh. See Oosterbaan, 'Een doperse christologie,' 42.

even if he had not gone begging to Zwingli. However, on this same point Menno would have excommunicated also his modern Baptist and Mennonite descendants.

Some of the contrasts between the northern and the southern continental Baptists are related to Karlstadt's own development. Whereas the Swiss Baptists preserved Karlstadt's 1523 to 1525 stress on the importance of outward baptism, the northern Baptists preserved Karlstadt's earlier and later views that outward baptism is not crucial. Some of the northern Baptists, like Karlstadt, were flexible in their response to worldly rulers. The Swiss Brethren, however, adopted a hardened stance that reflects Karlstadt's thwarted theocratic pronouncements. Differences between the northern and the southern Baptists did not abate. The northern Baptists moved in a cultural milieu different from that of the southerners. Although the branches sensed their kinship, they never developed consensus.

Historically, the northern Baptists have been more significant. Though northern Baptists became respectable burghers and their number waned in Holland, their impact persists. It was felt in the seventeenth century in the national Dutch culture. It also helped to create the Baptists of the Anglo-Saxon world.

From the Dutch to the English Baptists

The Anglo-Saxon Baptists trace their lineage back to John Smyth (ca 1570–1612). In Cambridge Smyth was tutored by Francis Johnson, a Puritan and Separatist, who ultimately fled to Holland with his congregation, living first in Kampen and Naarden, before settling in Amsterdam. In Kampen or Naarden several members of Johnson's church became attracted to the *Doopsgezinden* (Dutch Baptists) and began to practise believers' baptism.[77]

Since the same pattern is observable later in the case of Smyth, one may well wonder what provoked such rapid assimilation. Smyth came out of a pattern of English Puritanism that failed to become fully established. In dissatisfaction the Separatists broke with the Church of England. Their outstanding leaders were Robert Browne (1550 to 1633), who in 1581 took his congregation to Middelburg in Zeeland, and Henry Barrow, who remained in England and was hanged for his views at Tyburn, London, in 1593. The chief difference between Browne ('the father of congregationalism,' at least in England) and Barrow was that Browne advocated democratic church government whereas Barrow clung to the Calvinist pattern of vesting power in the elders. Thus the historical evolution of thwarted theocrats led to a form of Congregationalism. In Holland Smyth was to encounter the Dutch Baptists, a heterogeneous collection of thwarted theocrats (e.g. the failure of the Münster kingdom). Some chose to become sectarian (the so-called

---

77 BURRAGE 1, 156.

'Mennists'], erecting their theocracy on a limited scale in their congregations, while insisting on the civil nature of the magistracy, and thus combining a rigid congregational life with a view of general toleration towards others in society at large. Others responded to the change from persecution to toleration by moving gradually towards toleration at the congregational level as well. These Waterlander Baptists came into contact with Smyth as the result of a remarkable convergence of interests.

The Separatists on English soil were inured to Calvinism and depended on Zwingli as well as Calvin for their covenantal theology. As it was, the Zwinglian tradition predominated. Thus, most Puritans stressed Zwingli's concept of mutuality in the covenant between God and the believer rather than Calvin's formulation of a covenant based solely on divine sovereignty. Smyth himself was a Zwinglian on this point, for he accepted the tradition of a twofold covenant.[78] The covenant concept deeply penetrated the consciousness of all Puritans, but was to be of even greater significance for the Separatists, because they had renounced the support of external structures, as found in the established church. Thus, their whole idea of the church had to be interiorized, with the covenant as its symbol. Since Separatism required considerable sacrifice and commitment on the part of its adherents, an even greater and experiential stress on mutuality became possible.

When the relationship between God and the believer moves from the paradigm of master and slave to a relationship between responsible persons, predestination may be undermined. When this new insight is then applied to baptism, which among Calvinists is justified in terms of covenant, the logical and symmetrically consistent outcome is a Baptist position. Of course, there may be historical and personal reasons that interfere with a logical development, but it remains a possibility.

Because of persecution and unstable conditions the early Separatists could not rely on lasting associations, and thus they became practically congregationalistic. This could be regarded as an unfortunate and temporary expedient, or the experience of government from below might be persuasive and lead to a congregationalism based on principle. The frequent imprisonment and occasional execution of Separatist leaders and the fact that many Separatist congregations were left leaderless in the traditional sense created a vacuum that had to be filled by lay participation. Lay theology, however, is characteristically less consistent and more pragmatic and experiential than a theological system such as Calvinism will allow. This explains the rapidity with which a complex structure of thought like Calvinism may disintegrate or reconstitute itself in a variety of simpler forms.

78 Møller, 'Puritan Covenant Theology,' 46–67. Cf SMYTH 1, 254.

Moreover, the continental Baptists had already contributed to the structure of Calvinism itself. Earlier we have examined the impact of Karlstadt on Zwingli in areas where Calvinists and Baptists alike are marked off from Lutheranism. Such areas of similarity include the conception of the Lord's Supper, liturgical simplicity, the idea of the church as a community of ascetic 'visible saints,' discipline, and relatively simple church structures that are responsive to pressure from below. One may, of course, note that these similarities rest on a piecemeal comparison of ideas without considering other factors and their conditioning effect. This is important when one compares the thought structures of systematic theologians. However, a piecemeal approach is mandatory when one considers lay theology. Lay people tend to absorb from doctrine only those teachings that address their lives (with their own inherent contradictions) and their situation (that is part of history with its own lack of symmetry). Lay theology is piecemeal theology. To hark back to only one example: we saw in chapter 5 how Konrad Grebel refused to call the Lord's Supper a sign, though his view of the Lord's Supper, which he appropriated from Karlstadt, rests on the assumption that it is a sign. This explains why, at the lay level, Calvinists and Baptists may feel mutually attracted, and the elaborate structures of the theologians, designed to ward off such interpenetration, are then dismissed as irrelevant. In *Calvin and the Anabaptist Radicals* Balke notes: 'One can speak of a "critical relationship" (S. van der Linde) between Calvin and the Anabaptist radicals. This explains why Calvinism has been able to absorb Anabaptism to a large extent.'[79] Balke is speaking from a Dutch perspective, but in the Anglo-Saxon world Baptists were mostly recruited from Calvinist ranks. There the debates benefited the Baptists especially. But even where Calvinism gained ground (as in Holland), it failed to dislodge the Baptists altogether. 'The result was that the Anabaptists survived only in the countries in which the Reformed Church had been established.'[80] Thus the notion of Baptists as disestablished Calvinists, or of Calvinists as established Baptists, often proves helpful.

Upon his arrival in Amsterdam, or soon thereafter, John Smyth refused to join the 'Old English Church' of Francis Johnson, his former tutor. In *The Differences of the Churches of the seperation* (1608) Smyth argues for 'spiritual worship,' i.e. direct interpretation of Scripture from the original text, and prayers and songs from the heart, that is without the aid of books.[81] Smyth also argues for a uniform ministry rather than the English Calvinist practice of distinguishing between pastors and elders who rule or teach.[82] Evidently Smyth prefers Brown-

---

79 Balke, *Calvin and the Anabaptist Radicals*, 329.
80 Krahn, *Dutch Anabaptism*, 250.
81 SMYTH 1, [274]–306.
82 Ibid, 307–15.

ism to Barrowism.[83] In other respects Smyth has no quarrels with the 'Old Church' Separatists of Francis Johnson and Henry Ainsworth. Ainsworth and Johnson had published their grievances against the Anglicans piecemeal, asserting that 'in other doctrines of the faith, we agree with the Church of England.'[84]

First of all Ainsworth and Johnson appeal to primitivism: 'Christ the Lord hath given to his church sufficient ordinary offices.' The 'true visible' church is:

> a company of people separated from the world by the word of God, and joyned together by voluntarie profession of the faith in Christ, in the fellowship of the Gospell. And that therfore no knowne Atheist, unbeliever, Heretique, or wicked liver, be received or reteined a member in the Church of Christ, which is his body; God having in all ages appointed and made a separation of his people from the world, before the Law, under the Law, and now in tyme of the Gospell.

This church must have ministers who 'carefully feed the flock of Christ, being not injoined or suffered to beare Civill offices.' The upkeep of church officers is based on 'free and voluntarie contribution,' and not on 'Popish Lordships and Livings, or Jewish Tithes and offerings.' The rule of the church rests on the 'lawes and rules, which Christ hath appointed in his Testament,' rather than 'Popish Canons, Courts, Classes, Customs, or any humane inventions.' Only the canonical Scriptures may be used in churches, and 'the Lord [must] be worshipped and called upon in spirit and in truth.' The sacraments should be administered only to the faithful. The church heeds no 'observation of dayes and tymes, Jewish or Popish, save only to sanctify the Lords Day.' Furthermore, 'all monuments of Idolatry in garments or any other things, all Temples, Altars, Chappels, ought by lawful aucthoritie to be rased and abolished.' All 'Popish degrees in Theologie, inforcement to single life in the Colledges, abuse of prophane heathen Writers, should be remooved and redressed.'[85] This programme of the Separatists could have been endorsed by any of the factions of the Dutch Baptists. The differences between the Dutch Baptists and the Separatists lay in their attitude towards the magistracy, their practice of believers' baptism, and predestination and related doctrines. Even in their general attitude towards the 'world' the Separatists and *Doopsgezinden* were of one accord. They both objected to 'godless' society, withdrew from 'worldly' amusements, and reproved fashionable clothing. Mrs Toma-

---

83 Smyth himself says he once walked 'in the waie of seperation called Brownisme' (SMYTH 2, 753). Smyth also described his career as moving from [non-Separatist] 'Puritanisme to Brownisme, and from Brownisme to true Christian baptisme' (SMYTH 2, 564).

84 [Ainsworth and Johnson], *An Apologie*, 36 or E2v.

85 Ibid, 36–8 or E2v–3v.

sine Johnson, wife of Francis Johnson, dressed in a worldly fashion. Francis's brother George could explain Francis's tolerance only by noting that he was 'blinded, bewitched, and besotted' with his wife.[86] The congregation censured her scandalous addictions:

> These things were reproved in Mris Tomison Johnson the Pastors wife touching apparel. First the wearing of a long busk after the fashion of the world contrary to Rom 12:2; 1 Tim 2:9–10. 2. Wearing of the long white brest after the fashion of yong dames, and so low she wore it, as the world call them kodpiece brests. Contrary to former places, and also to 1 Pet 3:3; 4:5. 3. Whalebones in the bodies of peticotes. Contrary to the former rules, as also against nature, being as the Phisitians affirme hinderers of conceiving or procreating children ... 10. The painted Hipocritical brest, shewing as if there were some special workes, and in truth nothing but a shadow. Contrary to modesty and sobriety.[87]

Such ascetic world-avoiding criticism would have been approved by the Dutch Baptists, who likewise insisted on simplicity of dress. Against such a background it seems clear that the losses that Johnson's congregation sustained and John Smyth's overtures to the Waterlander Baptists were not simply 'defections'; they were also reaffirmations of the Separatist tradition, now adjusted to a different cultural milieu. To what extent this Separatist tradition had been moulded not only by the inner logic of disestablished Calvinism but also by the presence of Dutch Baptists and Calvinists on English soil will probably remain a question of debate, in view of the lacunae that remain. Whether one stresses inner logic (Tolmie, *The Triumph of the Saints*) or whether one reconstructs the historical, if fragmentary, evidence (Horst, *The Radical Brethren*),[88] it seems unnecessary to choose sides.

The proponents of historical connections point to the many Dutch exiles who entered England while the northern Lowlands still suffered from Spanish occupation. These Dutch exiles, known in England as the 'Strangers,' were fervent enough to suffer exile for their faith; one doubts whether they would have declined to propagate their views among the English. In 1534 King Henry VIII

---

86 White, *The English Separatist Tradition*, 96–7.
87 BURRAGE 1, 160–1.
88 Whitley (*British Baptists*, 17f) argues that 'Baptists are to be sharply distinguished from the Anabaptists of the Continent.' See also Kliever, 'General Baptist Origins,' 291f, and 292, n 6. For the traditional literature on both sides see Torbet, *A History of the Baptists*, esp 17–18. For those who stress the links with the continent see Kliever, 'General Baptist Origins,' 292, n 5.

issued his first proclamation against the 'Anabaptists,' threatening them with execution. Bishop Jewel noted that 'the Anabaptists held private conventicles and perverted many.' Adriaan Haemstede, minister of the Dutch church at Austin Friars, was deposed for teaching a heavenly-flesh Christology.[89] Herriot argues: 'For no insignificant sect would ecclesiastical commisions composed of the most influential churchmen in the realm, armed with special powers, have been set in motion.'[90]

The Melchiorites of Holland made an impression on the dissenters in England. The king's general pardon of 1540 lists eight points characteristic of these English dissenters. Irvin Horst observes: 'The eight points listed above confirm the thesis that anabaptism in England was Melchiorite in persuasion and that it had much in common with that party in the Netherlands and elsewhere on the continent.'[91] I agree with Horst that the pardon of 1540 is directed at English followers of Melchior Hoffman. A few sweeping generalizations aside, Horst's evidence associates English radicalism with the Dutch Reformation.

For the Brownist and Barrowist traditions of dissent, from which Francis Johnson and John Smyth came, the Dutch may have been similarly significant. By 1583 the Mayor's Court Book of Norwich indicates that, out of the no more than 13,000 inhabitants of Norwich, 4,679 were Dutch. The 'Book of Orders' records the struggles of the Dutch Church to resist episcopal intervention by the Church of England. The membership of the church chose twelve deacons and twelve elders once a year. When their terms were finished a year later, they were renominated, together with forty-eight additional nominees, suggested by the leaders. Anyone in the congregation, who still felt the number of nominees to be restrictive, could make nominations from the floor. In June 1571 the congregation voted to bar its minister, Isebrandus Balke, from exercising his office. All episcopal efforts to have him reinstated were successfully blocked by the congregation. Slaughter concludes:

> Robert Browne 'harde saie' that the people in Norfolk were very forward in religion, and it may have been the presence of these Strangers that induced him to come to Norwich to teach. Some of them were reputed to hold Anabaptist views and Browne may have taken some of his more radical ideas from them. Be that as it may, the influence of the Strangers on religious beliefs in Norwich must have been considerable, and through

89 Herriot, 'Anabaptism in England,' 269.
90 Ibid, 268.
91 Horst, The Radical Brethren, 92. For additional connections see pp 54–8, 60–2, and esp 170–6. A similar study for the Elizabethan period and thereafter would be useful. For the years 1558–60 see Zerger, 'Dutch Anabaptism in Elizabethan England,' 19–24.

Robert Browne and his Norwich followers Congregationalism may owe more to these Strangers than it is aware of.[92]

When it is conceded that the Separatists had moved as far towards a continental Baptist position as they could without seriously impairing their Calvinism, there then arises the question of how open the Dutch would have been towards the English. Many of the Dutch Baptists demanded freedom of religion for all, so that each church could indulge in the stubbornness and pettiness with which the various factions fought and damned one another. However, from this generalization the Waterlander Baptists should be exempted, and it was to them that John Smyth ultimately applied for membership.

The Waterlander Baptists had revolted against Menno Simons when he and six other ministers and elders promulgated the Wismar Articles of 1554.[93] The Wismar Articles contained a rather strict interpretation of the shunning of 'unbelievers.' The Waterlanders were more liberal, and consequently they received into their fellowship many who had been excommunicated for minor deviations by the more conservative Baptists or 'Mennists.' The 'Mennists' in return referred to the Waterlanders as the *dreckwagen* ('cart of manure'). The Waterlanders might have remained without firm direction, were it not for the emergence of Hans de Ries as their generally benevolent though somewhat autocratic leader.

De Ries (1553–1638) was born in Antwerp of Catholic parents. As a youth he was attracted to the Reformed religion, but later he felt that the Reformed did not distribute their alms equitably; moreover, the Reformed tried to repel intolerant Catholics by carrying fire-arms to church. After De Ries witnessed the burning at the stake of several Baptists, he became attracted to their movement, but since they were 'Mennists,' De Ries objected to their practice of severe and rash discipline and shunning. A merchant from Holland then referred De Ries to the Waterlanders, and thus he travelled to De Rijp, where Simon Michiels baptized him. De Ries returned to Antwerp late in 1576 when he heard that his best friend Hans Bret was cast into a dungeon for his religious convictions. De Ries's efforts on Bret's behalf failed, Bret being executed by burning on 4 January 1577. Hans Bret's widowed mother was now left without support, and De Ries married her soon afterwards. Spies of the margrave charged them with being Baptists, however, and while the bailiffs kicked in the front door of their house, the recently wedded couple escaped through a postern gate. On the road they were overtaken on horseback by De Ries's former employer, a liberal Italian Catholic merchant, who gave them a handful of gold coins. 'Take these,' he said, 'and use them for

---

92 Slaughter, 'The Dutch Church in Norwich,' 31–2.
93 Simons, Menno, *The Complete Writings*, 1041–2.

your needs.'[94] At age 24 De Ries helped to provide the Waterlanders with a statement of faith: the Confession of 1577. In 1580 a new confession was published by De Ries in collaboration with Lubbert Gerrits.[95] De Ries served the Baptist Church of Alkmaar until his death.

After his experiences in Antwerp De Ries, moved by the arguments of the poet Dirk Volkerts Coornhert, became an apostle of toleration.[96] Even to the rather liberal Waterlanders, De Ries's friendship with Coornhert, a spiritualist who scorned the Baptists for their rigidity, seemed offensive. When Simon Jacobs reproached De Ries for befriending Coornhert, De Ries wrote to him: 'The Angel did not dare to pronounce a reviling judgment upon Satan, says the apostle [Jude 6]. Now, whether you who are not even an angel, have the right freely to judge a man who is not even a devil; that one would have to ponder carefully. I am not impressed.'[97]

Under De Ries's leadership the Waterlanders formed a tolerant community, ranging from the recently excommunicated but otherwise conservative 'Mennists' to those who had opposed the leadership of Menno Simons from the beginning. When other Baptists joined the Waterlanders, their baptism was held to be valid, even though their former communions did not reciprocate. The independent Baptist church of Emden rejected Hoffman's and Menno's heavenly-flesh Christology; it applied for membership with the Waterlanders and was accepted. Already in 1577 the Confession was not regarded as binding, since 'the Holy Scriptures contain all that is necessary [for] salvation.' The article on the incarnation was worded in such a way as to accommodate a heavenly-flesh or a traditional Christology. The Waterlanders were still trinitarian, however, for De Ries rejected all overtures from the Polish Baptist Christof Ostorodt. The Confession justified the practice of avoidance of the excommunicated, unless they were in need or unless the sharing of food might lead to their conversion. Rash and false oaths were forbidden, but the Waterlanders followed Melchior Hoffman (and Karlstadt) in asserting: 'We permit that one call upon God as witness to the truth of a statement, even as Paul did [1 Thess. 2:10].' Moreover, 'certain magisterial offices that did not involve them in the shedding of blood were acceptable.'[98]

The Waterlanders 'were the first [Baptists] who deliberately rejected the illusion of being the [only] true community of God.' They admitted Christians who were not of their persuasion to the Lord's Supper, accepting 'all who live in the

94 Kühler, *Nederlandsche Doopsgezinden*, 354–5.
95 See Dyck, 'The First Waterlandian Confession,' 5–13, and Lumpkin, *Baptist Confessions*, 44–66. For De Ries's life I relied on Kühler, *Nederlandsche Doopsgezinden*, 350–63.
96 Cf Dyck, 'The Middelburg Confession,' 154, n 24.
97 Kühler, *Nederlandsche Doopsgezinden*, 363.
98 Van der Zijpp, *Geschiedenis der Doopsgezinden*, 82.

love of Christ.'[99] From his Calvinistic period De Ries retained a predilection for the Psalms, and thus many of them were included in the *Liedtboeck* (*Songbook*) that he issued in 1582. He opposed the practice of loud individual praying in church and served the Lord's Supper at table rather than passing it around the congregation like the other Baptists. De Ries preferred the orderly practices of the Reformed to outright Congregationalism, and the congregational election of officers was replaced by a system of nomination by the existing leadership, to be followed by congregational acclamation. As Kühler notes, 'at the instigation of De Ries, the Waterlanders conducted their elections more in accordance with Reformed than with Baptist practice.'[100] Thus John Smyth, when he came to Amsterdam, needed to change his views only with respect to double predestination, the imputation of Adam's sin, the role of the magistracy, and believers' baptism to qualify for membership with the Waterlanders. Smyth did even more than that, for example, by accepting a heavenly-flesh Christology, which suggests that he also felt attracted towards the conservatives among the Waterlanders.

With this summary of Smyth's and the Waterlanders' background I now sketch Smyth's career. John Smyth was educated at Cambridge (1586–93) in medicine and divinity; at the conclusion of his programme he received the MA degree. In 1594 he was appointed a fellow, and thereafter he took orders in the Church of England, being then a non-separating Puritan. In 1600 he was appointed to the church in Lincoln, but he was deprived of this position in 1602 reportedly for having 'approved himself a factious man in this city by personal preaching, and that untruly against divers men of good place.'[101] In 1604 Smyth still considered himself 'far from the opinion of them which separate from our church,' but in 1606 he was elected minister of one of the two Congregational churches in Gainsborough on Trent. King James I grew increasingly severe towards dissenters, and when the future seemed bleak, 'by a joint consent they resolved to go into the Low Countries, where they heard was Freedom of Religion for all men.'[102]

After arriving in Amsterdam Smyth started a second Separatist church, late in 1607. In the winter of 1608–9 Smyth and his followers had been persuaded that believers' baptism was the scriptural norm, for infant baptism was not practised in the New Testament, and in the dominical mandate (Matt. 28:19–20) teaching preceded baptism.[103] Thus Smyth decided to administer baptism to himself (se-baptism) and then to the rest of his followers, including Thomas Helwys and John Murton. They lived and worshipped in the former Great Bakehouse of the

99 Ibid, 82.
100 Kühler, *Doopsgezinden in Nederland*, 19–20.
101 BURRAGE 1, 227.
102 Ibid, 231.
103 Torbet, *Baptists*, 35. See also SMYTH 2, 574.

Dutch East India Company, which was now in the possession of Jan Munter, a Waterlander Baptist. The first contacts with the Waterlanders must have preceded Smyth's baptism. Smyth implied as much when he defended his own actions, because, in order to receive baptism, 'ther was no church to whome wee could joyne *with a good conscience* [my italics].'[104] Thus Smyth already knew of the *practices* of the Dutch Baptists, but he did not yet approve of all their doctrines.

As for the baptisms themselves, they signalled a new departure for Smyth and his congregation. It is now known, if Henoch Clapham's partisan tract can be trusted, that another se-baptism occurred elsewhere, at least nine years earlier.[105] But Smyth does not seem to have known about this event, for he never referred to it as a precedent, even when the se-baptism embarrassed him later. Smyth's se-baptism is, of course, of far greater significance, for with it the English Baptist tradition began. Attempts to diminish its significance by assuming English Separatist precedent are unconvincing. Thus Estep, for example, claims: 'If believers' baptism had not actually been practiced in England, at least there appears to have been a desire for such action as early as 1590.'[106] Estep refers to Burrage, who cites an English churchman as follows: '[The Barrowists] hold it unlawfull to baptise Children emongst us [i.e. in the Church of England] but rather chewse to let them goe unbaptized.'[107]

This is probably a caricature of the Barrowist position by a hostile outsider, for (except for those Separatists who became Baptists in Holland) the Barrowists did not repudiate their own (infant) baptisms. The quotation may, however, reflect the decision of a few scattered radical dissenters, who did not have immediate access to the services of a Barrowist minister, not to have their children baptized. The quotation merely states that some oppose infant baptism 'emongst us,' that is in the Church of England. They did not oppose infant baptism as such. Smyth certainly did not carry his opposition to infant baptism over from his Separatist days. In *The Differences of the Churches of the seperation* (1608) Smyth does not fault Johnson and Ainsworth for their views on infant baptism; in fact all Smyth could do to justify his separation from Johnson's church was to use Brownist arguments against the Barrowists concerning church officers, and to advocate an extreme primitivism in respect of liturgy.

---

104 Cf SMYTH 2, 757, in contrast with Whitley, *British Baptists*, 21. The evidence for Smyth's baptism has been virtually exhausted in Dexter, *The England and Holland of the Pilgrims*, 453–8.

105 BURRAGE 1, 223. If one grants Burrage's interpretation, then this reveals Dutch Baptist influence. See the typically Mennonite views of these dissenters on p 224.

106 Estep, *The Anabaptist Story*, 216.

107 BURRAGE 1, 126–7.

Smyth was soon to adjust his views to the point where he became acceptable to those Waterlanders who knew him. Early in 1610 Smyth and his followers applied for Waterlander membership. They submitted, in succession, two confessions that reveal that they now shared the Waterlander opposition to predestination and original sin and adhered to the Waterlander views with respect to the civil magistracy and non-resistance.[108] There was urgency in Smyth's request that they be received 'as quickly as possible' by the Waterlanders, whom they addressed as the 'true church of Christ,' for by now Smyth had repudiated his se-baptism, and consequently he also regarded the other baptisms as invalid.[109] A few of his followers refused to budge, among them Thomas Helwys and John Murton. They left Smyth and his congregation, and for good measure accused them of the impardonable sin against the Holy Spirit, which they defined – like Karlstadt and Hoffman – as a deliberate rejection of the truth after one has received enlightenment.[110] On this basis Helwys excommunicated Smyth. In their rival address to the Waterlanders Helwys and his party proved their own baptism from the fact 'that John Baptist being unbaptized, preached the baptisme of repentance and they that beleeved and confessed their sinnes, he baptized.'[111] By implication Helwys too had concluded that Smyth's baptism of himself was invalid, though not his baptism of the others.

The Waterlanders rejected Helwys's overtures and were inclined to accept Smyth and his followers. Helwys's rash excommunication of Smyth made an unfavourable impression, because the Waterlanders all along opposed such rigour. Nevertheless, the Waterlanders seem to have accepted Helwys's argument on the validity of Smyth's baptisms, and the lack of validity of his se-baptism. The Waterlanders of Amsterdam took the precaution of informing the other congregations of their willingness to admit Smyth and his party. Their minister, Lubbert Gerrits, wrote as follows:

According to our feeling and preliminary insight these Englishmen should be accepted without another baptism. We find ourselves to be timid and

---

108 BURRAGE 2, 177. For the Latin and English confessions submitted see 178–9, 188–200. Cf Lumpkin, *Baptist Confessions*, 100–1.

109 SMYTH 2, 681: 'Nomina Anglorum qui hunc errorem suum agnoscunt eiusque paenitentiam agunt viz: quod incoeperint seipsos baptisare, contra ordinem a Christo constitutum: quique iam cupiunt hinc verae Christi ecclesiae uniri, ea qua fieri possit expeditione.' Photographically reproduced in Underwood, *English Baptists*, 40–1.

110 SMYTH 2, 756: 'Maister Helwys cast upon me certaine imputations as first the synne against the holy ghost, bicause I have denied some truth which once I acknowledged, and wher with I was inlightened.'

111 BURRAGE 2, 185.

do not dare to renew their baptism. Most of our congregation consents to this. For we know and have seen and experienced that no one dared to re-baptize those who were baptized by the [revolutionaries] in Münster, the *Naaktlopers* [Naked Runners] of Amsterdam, the people of Hazers-woude, and the [insurrectionists] of the Old Cloister. And what diverse baptisms do we not find nowadays; moreover, when we compare them, we regard the way these people performed their baptism as far better and more Christian, in our judgment on this matter, than those former baptisms that we tolerated and still tolerate.[112]

The responses to Lubbert's letter were predictable. All of the Frisian replies urged caution, and the congregation of Leeuwarden appealed to the opinions of the even more conservative Prussians and Germans.[113] Even on his death-bed Lubbert Gerrits continued to advocate the cause of John Smyth and his fellow English Baptists. From the leaders of the Waterlander Baptists, who were present as Lubbert Gerrits lay dying (17 January 1612), he 'earnestly desired that the cause of the English should not be forgotten, and that it be attended to as soon as possible. Regarding the baptism of Mr Smyth [the se-baptism] he had some reservations, since the Scriptures did not support it, but he would surely accept all the other Englishmen without baptizing them again.'[114]

In August 1612, several months after Gerrits died Smyth himself died of tuberculosis. Progress was slow until the Frisians were apparently placated; Smyth's followers were admitted to Waterlander membership on 20 January 1615.[115]

Smyth had not undergone a third attempt at baptism, but the Waterlanders had bestowed on him an even greater gift, namely religious toleration. The English Separatists stood in the vanguard of those who demanded tolerance for themselves only. That had also been Smyth's original position.[116] But the Dutch political rulers had become pragmatic advocates of toleration, while the Dutch Baptists stressed tolerance as an article of faith, even when all persecution had ceased. Ever since he applied to the Waterlanders for membership, Smyth moved

---

112 BURRAGE 2, 202.
113 BURRAGE 2, 203–13.
114 BURRAGE 2, 214: 'Heeft vorder oock ernstelick begeert dat men die saecke doch niet int vergen soude stellen vande Engelsche, maer metten eersten voltrecken soe het mogelick ware. Dan seijde inden doop van Mr Smid wat bedencken hadde, alsoe hij daer geen schriftuer toe en hadde, maer nu wel gerust alle die andere Engelschen, sonder weder te dopen op tenemen.'
115 BURRAGE 1, 250. The admission had been delayed, but it is misleading to claim that 'the Waterlanders rejected the application.' Wamble, 'Inter-Relations,' 412.
116 McBeth, *English Baptist Literature*, 14–19; SMYTH 1, 267. Also cited in Jordan, *Development of Religious Toleration* 3 (1603–1640), 269.

rapidly towards toleration, denying the role of the magistrate in regulating religion.[117] Like Hans de Ries, Smyth now accepted all believers as Christians. Earlier Smyth had fought the Church of England over ceremony and policy, and his fellow Separatists over trifles, but Smyth now asserted that 'all things of the outward church shall not cause [mee] to refuse the brotherhood of anie penitent and faithfull Christian whatsoever.' Like the Waterlanders, he rejected the use of the sword in self-defence. He still defended himself with the pen, but only with reluctance: 'My desire is to end controversies among Christians rather then to make and mainteyne them, especially in matters of outward church and ceremonies: and it is the grief of my hart that I have so long cumbred my self and spent my time therin.'[118]

A consistent advocate of religious toleration can hardly rely on a partisan God for support. Toleration implies a tolerant God, and vice versa. But Smyth did not believe he should make God after his own image; thus he could become tolerant towards others only because he had exchanged the God who elects and reprobates by decree for the God who enables human choice. Like Karlstadt and Hoffman and Menno Simons, Smyth now regarded God as universally benevolent.

Despite the rash excommunication of Smyth and his followers by Helwys and Murton, one does not need to imitate their censure as a historian. Historically there are many lines of continuity between Smyth and his former disciples. Thomas Helwys (ca 1570–ca 1615) was born into a Puritan family. He attended Gray's Inn in London as a law student. In Gainsborough he came under the influence of Smyth, and Helwys, who was a man of means, helped to finance the departure of Smyth's congregation for Amsterdam in 1607. Helwys sided with Smyth against the Separatists of the 'Old English Church' of Francis Johnson, and he received believers' baptism from Smyth (1608–9). When Smyth began to deny the validity of the baptisms he had performed and applied to the Waterlander Baptists for admission, Helwys assailed Smyth in the confessional statements that he and his followers presented to the Waterlanders.[119] The only obvious disagreement that originally divided Smyth and Helwys was Smyth's repudiation of the baptisms that he himself had administered. Helwys promptly charged Smyth with teaching succession, the bane of Separatists: 'And the whole cause in question being succession (for so it is indeed and in truth) consider wee beseech you how it is Antichrist's cheife hold, and that it is Jewish and ceremoniall, an ordinance of the Old Testament, but not of the New.'[120]

117 McBeth, English Baptist Literature, 20–27.
118 SMYTH 2, 755.
119 BURRAGE 2, 181–7. Cf Lumpkin, Baptist Confessions, 114–23.
120 BURRAGE 2, 185.

Fascinating here is Helwys's appeal to the ordinances of the New versus the Old Testament, which is basic to the Baptist position (whether Dutch or English), and which signals a sharp break with the Puritan and Reformed practice of harmonizing the Old Testament practice of circumcision with the New Testament practice of baptism. Helwys's definition of succession, moreover, is certainly not the traditional one; only an extreme Congregationalist would have agreed with Helwys. As for Smyth, he stoutly dismisses Helwys's argument:

> I deny all succession except in the truth, and I hold wee are not to violate the order of the primitive Church, except necessitie urge a dispensation; and therefore it is not lawfull for every one that seeth the truth to baptise, for then ther might be as manie churches as couples in the world and none have anie thinge to doe with other, which breaketh the bonde of love and brotherhood in the churches.[121]

The Waterlanders did not teach succession either, although De Ries had adopted the Calvinistic procedure of election of officers by acclamation. Helwys exaggerated the differences between himself and Smyth, perhaps following Smyth's earlier example in dealing with the 'Old Church' Separatists Ainsworth and Johnson.

Helwys clearly adopted Smyth's desire for accommodation with the Waterlanders, addressing them as 'beloved in the Lord' and *carissimi fratres fidei vinculo* (dearest brethren in the bonds of faith), and Helwys thanks the Waterlanders for 'the great love and kindness that you have shewed unto us.' He has also abandoned the Separatist position on predestination, and denies original sin, accepting Smyth's viewpoint.[122]

Helwys's doctrine of Christ is traditional and allowable in the ambiguous terms of the Waterlander Confession.[123] As for the ministry, Helwys distinguishes between the bishop (Karlstadt's and Hoffman's equivalent for minister) and the deacons as follows: 'The ministers of the church are the bishops, whose power has been delegated by the congregation and who preach the Word and administer

---

121 SMYTH 2, 758.
122 BURRAGE 2, 182:3–5: 'Quod deus necessitatem peccandum nemini imponit. Quod nullum sit peccatum per generationem a parentibus nostris. Quod deus vult omnes homines servari, et ad agnitionem veritatis venire, et non vult mortem morientis.' Compare this statement of Helwys in 1610 with Smyth's earlier statement, SMYTH 2, 682:3,5: 'Deum nullam peccandi necessitatem cuiquam imponere, sed hominem libere impulsu sathanae a deo deficere. Nullum esse peccatum originis, verum omne peccatum esse actuale et voluntarium viz: dictum factum aut concupitum contra legem dei: ideoque infantes esse sine peccato.'
123 Cf BURRAGE 2, 182:6, with art 4 of Dyck, 'The First Waterlandian Confession,' 9, or Lumpkin, *Baptist Confessions* 48:8–53:18.

baptism and the Lord's Supper, as well as the deacons, both men and widows, who on behalf of the church support the poor and infirm brothers in their needs.'[124] Here Helwys virtually reiterates article 16 of Smyth's confession, which reflects the Waterlander viewpoint, except where Helwys underlines the delegation of power 'by the congregation.'

Unlike Smyth, however, Helwys avoids phrasing his doctrine of justification as based in part on Christ's work and in part on the believer's sanctification.[125] But Helwys still comes close to Smyth in linking divine initiative with human response when he joins sanctification to the faith that apprehends Christ's obedience and justice. Thus Helwys avoids a forensic doctrine of justification.[126] Helwys's attitude towards the shunning of the excommunicated has virtually been copied from Smyth, and reflects the mild practices of the Waterlanders.[127]

During the next two years Helwys's warnings to the Waterlanders to deny Smyth admission went unheeded by Gerrits, who espoused the cause of Smyth. This may have caused Helwys to formulate the few differences still outstanding between himself and the Waterlanders more sharply in *A Declaration of Faith of English People* (1611).[128] Unlike Smyth, Helwys had not yet worked out his rejection of the doctrine of original sin to the point where he could flatly assert that 'infants are without sin.'[129] In *A Declaration* Helwys even seems to revert to some extent to the traditional position on original sin.[130] The fall of the human race is now held to be based on the imputation of Adam's sin to his descendants (art 2), but Helwys contradicts this assertion when he notes that the fall of humanity is the natural consequence of Adam's fall (art 4). The doctrine of imputation is in fact an alien element that is also vitiated by Helwys's claim, derived from the Dutch Baptists, that God has 'not predestinated man to bee wicked, and so to bee damned' (art 5).

Helwys's understanding of predestination, except perhaps for the doctrine of the fall of humanity in Adam, is anti-Calvinistic – in fact, typically Dutch Baptist. Any imputation of Adam's sin, or the natural effect of Adam's fall, is nullified with respect to salvation, since grace is granted to all, to choose for or against

124 BURRAGE 2, 183:13.
125 SMYTH 2, 683:10, to be compared with BURRAGE 2, 183:7–8.
126 For a contrary view, see Kliever, 'General Baptist Origins,' 314–15.
127 Cf SMYTH 2, 684:18: 'Excommunicatos quod ad civile commercium attinet non esse devitandos,' with Helwys, BURRAGE 2, 184:16: 'Quod excommunicati respectu civilis societatis non sint fugiendi.'
128 Lumpkin, *Baptist Confessions*, 116–23.
129 SMYTH 2, 682:5: 'Nullum esse peccatum originis, ideoque infantes esse sine peccato.'
130 Cf BURRAGE 2, 182:3–4: 'Omne peccatum esse actuale et voluntarium viz: dictum factum aut concupitum contra legem dei,' with Lumpkin, *Baptist Confessions*, 117, 118:4–5.

God.[131] All who accept God are then predestined to eternal life. This conditional form of predestination continues the late-medieval tradition and undercuts Calvinism.

After Smyth has died, Helwys in fact reasserts his earlier opposition to original sin, agreeing with Smyth and the Dutch Baptists that infants are innocent:

> And what doe you then hold of infants? That they are innocents as Christ teacheth: Matt 18:3f, 19:14, etc. 1 Cor 14:20. That they have no knowledge: Deut 1:39, Jonah 4:11. That God speaketh not to them, requiring anything at their hands. Deut 11:2, Matt 13:9, Rom 7:9, 1 Cor 10:15, and therefore they have not sinned, seeing sin is a breach of God's law. 1 John 3:4, Rom 4:15.[132]

It is possible that Helwys went in fact through such a development: namely, that he began to deny original sin, then reasserted the imputation of Adam's sin, contradicting it with other assertions, after which he again fully denied original sin. In that case Helwys went through a stage of uncertainty, amounting to confusion, in 1611. However, *A Declaration of Faith* represented the opinions 'of English People,' that is Helwys's whole group, which – though small – consisted of strong-headed individuals. It is therefore possible that what seemed to be a contradiction is in fact a compromise that Helwys found necessary to placate one or more of the others in his group. Lumpkin sums up the differences between Helwys and Smyth as follows:

> Mennonite influence is readily seen in [Helwys's and his congregation's] confession, for it shows a departure from the hitherto markedly consistent Calvinism of the Separatist movement. But it shows also decided signs of its author's Calvinistic background. It is anti-Calvinistic on the doctrine of the atonement and anti-Arminian in its views of sin and the will. Obviously it owed much to John Smyth, though it goes beyond his confession on a number of points: in urging the independence and autonomy of the local church ('though in respect of CHRIST, the Church bee one'), in denying a succession in church life, and in rejecting the Mennonite prohibi-

---

131 Kliever ('General Baptist Origins,' 315) describes the Dutch Baptist position as one that makes a 'man free to choose good or evil,' without noting that this natural freedom is itself the gift of God through the Holy Spirit to all of humanity. Then Kliever artificially contrasts this with Helwys by attributing to him the idea that humans, not being fully free, only 'have the ability to reject grace,' whereas Helwys plainly states (art 4) that man 'now being fallen, and having all disposition unto evil, and no disposition or will unto anie good, yet God giveing grace, man may receave grace, or may reject grace.' Thus Helwys teaches full freedom of choice.

132 Helwys, *Obiections Answered* (1615), 70.

tions against oaths, the bearing of arms, participation in government, and having dealings with excommunicants.[133]

Lumpkin exaggerates the differences between Helwys and the 'Mennonites' (and therefore also Smyth) in some respects. The Waterlanders accepted the magistracy, except for opposing it in principle when the government wields the sword or tries to coerce the consciences of its subjects, for example by seizing the property of religious or other types of dissidents. The succession issue, too, is extremely limited in scope. The Waterlanders forbade rash oaths, but one is allowed to invoke God's name to witness to the truth of a statement. Furthermore, Helwys's argument concerning civil relations with the excommunicated merely translates the statement he made in 1609, which, as we have seen, is derived from Smyth, and is fully consonant with Waterlander theory and practice. Finally, Helwys's doctrine of predestination, indebted as it is to the teachings of the Waterlanders, would have been too radical for Arminius.[134]

Helwys now found himself increasingly isolated in Amsterdam. Helwys's wife and children, who had remained in England, had been imprisoned. Over three quarters of Helwys's fellow Baptists had sided with Smyth, and the Waterlanders, too, disapproved of Helwys's excommunication of Smyth. Finally Helwys could communicate with the Waterlanders in Latin, but he found conversation in Dutch to be difficult.[135]

One understands Helwys's desire to return to England, except that these feelings were now turned into a new article of faith: one may never leave one's homeland in time of persecution.[136] Thus Helwys went back to England with a handful of followers. Like the Dutch *Doopers* or *Doopsgezinden*, they adopted the name of 'Baptists' for their faith. At Spitalfields, near London, they established the first Baptist congregation on English soil. Helwys had been influenced by Smyth and the Waterlanders on a point not yet mentioned, namely religious toleration. In 1612 Helwys published *A Short Declaration* in which his opposition to predestination undergirds his defence of religious freedom. Since God permits everyone to choose freely for or against him, the magistrates have no right to intervene in this free process, and even errors like Roman Catholicism must be tolerated.[137] Compulsory church attendance is unscriptural. Helwys's *Obiections Answered* begins as follows: 'Antichristian: "Why come you not to Church?"

133 Lumpkin, *Baptist Confessions*, 115.
134 See Bangs, *Arminius*, 350–5. Hudson, 'The Ecumenical Spirit,' 184, had preceded Kliever in claiming Arminian influence.
135 BURRAGE 2, 187.
136 Helwys, *A short Declaration* (1612, repr 1935), 204–12.
137 Ibid, 37–83. See also Jordan, *Development of Religious Toleration* 3 (1603–1640), 274–84; McBeth, *Baptist Literature*, 26–38.

Christian: "What should I do there?"' One is certainly reminded of the spirit of the *Brotherly Agreement* of Schleitheim (1527), which linked 'popish and anti-popish church attendance' with the frequenting of drinking-houses (art 4).

The Dutch experience had so alienated Helwys from the English Separatists that he taunted them as follows:

> You confesse your selves you were of the world before you made your seperation from [the Church of] England, and our Saviour Christ saith, that they which are of the world beleeve not in him. And who will not grant that they that beleeve not in Christ are infidells or unbeleevers? Then you, being of the world, were infidells or unbeleevers, and the Holy Ghost teacheth that infidells or unbelievers must amend their lives and be baptized, and by baptisme put on Christ (Mark 16:16). This strait are you now driven unto, either to confess that before your seperation you were infidells or unbeleevers, and then you must beleeve and be baptized, or els that you were beleevers and faithfull, and then you have seperated from a faithfull and beleeving people, and not from the world, and you must returne to your vomit with that false prophet, your first and cheife Shepherd [Francis Johnson] that hath misled you upon these false grounds.
>
> This is your constitution wherein you have erred as may plainlie appeare, for when you were called, and as you say seperated, you should have joined to Christ and have entered into his kingdome, which seing you have not done, you are not seperated from the world, nor have no fellowship in the Gospel.[138]

Despite Helwys's alienation from them he continues to address the Separatists in terms of the inner logic of their own system. This explains my earlier reluctance to choose sides in the debate over Baptist origins. Smyth and Helwys cannot simply be explained either in terms of English Puritanism or with sole reference to the Waterlander Baptists. However, with regard to the Baptist *distinctives* one simply *must* consider the demonstrable impact of the Waterlanders.

In England Helwys sent *A Short Declaration* to King James I, a defiant and heroic gesture, for he was no longer in Amsterdam, where such ideas were commonplace. On the flyleaf Helwys wrote the following dedication to King James:

> Heare o King, and dispise not the counsell of the poore, and let their complaints come before thee.
> The King is a mortall man, and not God; therefore hath no power over the immortall soules of his subjects, to make lawes and ordinances for them, and to set spirituall Lords over them.

138 Helwys, *A short Declaration*, selections from pp 126, 124.

If the king have authority to make spirituall Lords and lawes, then he is an immortall God and not a mortal man.

O King, be not seduced by deceivers to sin so against God whome thou oughtest to obey, nor against thy poore subjects who ought and will obey thee in all thinges, with body, life and goods, or els let their lives be taken from the earth.

God Save the Kinge

Spittlefeild

neare London.

Tho: Helwys.[139]

James I was an autocrat who did not like to have his immortality, or his divinity, or his ordinances questioned. Consequently Helwys was cast into prison, where he died some time in 1615.

In Helwys's absence the leadership had fallen on John Murton (also Morton), a furrier. Murton (1583–1626) had married Jane Hodgkin, a woman with Baptist sympathies, in Amsterdam.[140] Like Helwys, Murton had received his baptism from John Smyth, but he joined in Helwys's secession and returned to England with him. Under Murton's leadership the Baptists grew to five congregations, but there was a setback early in 1624 when Murton excommunicated a few members whose crudely modalistic speculations concerning the deity of Christ involved comparing Christ to a lump of God's incomprehensible and infinite substance or a ray from the divine sun. They seemed to be simple persons, noted for their Christian charity, but 'in their minds and brain' 'they do not understand this secret or mistery.'[141] Several persons, including Elias Tookey, who himself affirmed an orthodox Christology, objected to the excommunications, and as a result they too were ejected. Tookey and his friends then started their own group, which applied for membership with the Waterlanders.[142]

Upon Murton's death in 1626 the five congregations were left leaderless, and they decided to apply for Waterlander membership as well. In November 1626 they sent two delegates to negotiate in Amsterdam. They had read the Waterlander Confession, and concluded that they agreed with everything, except for oaths. They insisted on a weekly celebration of the Lord's Supper, claimed that unordained people may administer the sacraments when there is no other leader-

---

139 The dedication is photographically reproduced in Helwys, *A short Declaration* (repr 1935), [xxv], and Underwood, *English Baptists*, 48–9.

140 Extract from the marriage registers of Amsterdam, SMYTH 2, [761]: '1608. August 23. John Murton of Queynsborch [Gainsborough], furrier, 25 years, and Jane Hodgkin of Worchep [Worksop], 23 years.'

141 BURRAGE 2, 231.

142 BURRAGE 2, 222–33.

ship, and accepted Christians who were magistrates, regarding the holding of such offices as a secular matter.[143]

Hans de Ries responded cautiously when a letter reached him from Amsterdam, and I summarize his questions. Are the two representatives truly representative of the five congregations? Would they accept the fellowship of John Smyth's followers, whom the Waterlanders had accepted into membership, even though Helwys had declared them to be excommunicated? Do they still believe that Smyth's followers do wrong by remaining in Amsterdam? Do the English Baptists distinguish between lay and regular preachers? May anyone always serve the sacraments? Since they have no 'teachers,' do they have to celebrate the Lord's Supper *every* Sunday? If a brother does not wish to participate weekly in the Supper, will he be tolerated? Is the English oath merely an invocation of God to attest to the truth of a statement? May Christian government engage in war? Would the English Baptists take up arms on behalf of their king?[144]

Later correspondence shows that the possible problems in De Ries's mind were almost all satisfactorily resolved. On the matter of the oath the English Baptists and the Waterlanders came to agreement; there remained only a slight difference in practice, for whereas the Waterlanders did not call the invoking of God as witness an oath, the English Baptists did.[145] Rash excommunication remained a divisive issue, however. When one of the English Baptists attended a service of the Church of England, he was excommunicated. The Waterlanders rebuked the English Baptists for resembling Christ's disciples [the Sons of Thunder, Mk 3:17?] more than Christ himself. Furthermore, the English Baptists did not object to bearing arms.

It is understandable that the Waterlanders could not compromise on these issues. The Waterlanders themselves began as a protest movement against the practices of excommunication among the 'Mennists.' De Ries himself had left the Calvinists because he objected even to the display of arms, and De Ries had joined the Waterlanders because he disapproved of the 'Mennists' discipline. To the English Baptists these two differences did not seem crucial (*differentiae inter nos non sunt maiores*).[146]

The English Baptists felt disappointed and aggrieved by what they felt was Waterlander intransigence. Nevertheless, the Dutch admonitions were not without effect. Some English Baptist churches began to frown on the bearing of arms. Thus, the Speldhurst Church in Kent wrote:

143 BURRAGE 2, 239–41.
144 BURRAGE 2, 241–3.
145 BURRAGE 2, 235: 'De iureiurando nos nullam videmus discrepantiam'; 257: 'dat daer gheen onderscheyt was in onse houdinghe.'
146 BURRAGE 2, 234.

In answer to the enquiries about fighting we say that in some cases it may be lawful, but as the affairs of the nation now stand and is likely to continue till the appearing of the Lord Jesus, we account it exceedingly dangerous, and for officers of churches to enlist themselves either as private soldiers or commissioned officers – that is altogether unlawful.[147]

As late as 1660 the 'freewiller' Baptists of London condemned oaths and military participation: 'Marvel not O King at my single hearted conclusion, in that I said, I shall neither swear nor fight for thee.'[148]

In 1630, Jane, the widow of John Murton, had no difficulty agreeing with the Waterlanders on the points still under discussion, nor did she think it was wrong to return to Amsterdam. She received Waterlander membership as Janneke Morton.[149]

The Baptists in England, later known as 'General Baptists,' became the first Baptists in North America when Roger Williams founded 'Providence Plantations' (Rhode Island) in 1636.[150]

Finally, the Particular Baptists arrived on the scene in 1641. Their first congregation evolved from the Church of Southwark, London, which was founded by Henry Jacob in 1616, after he returned from Holland. As the Dissenters tended to settle their differences by hiving out, a group that separated from the Southwark Church, including Richard Blunt, who understood Dutch, concluded that baptism should be administered by immersion of adult believers only (like the Waterlanders, the 'General' Baptists still practised baptism by affusion). Blunt knew the Dutch situation well enough to have information on the Rijnsburg Collegiants, an aggregate of Baptists, Remonstrants who had been ejected from the Dutch Reformed (State) Church during the Synod of Dort (1618–19), as well as Calvinist sympathizers. Collegiant membership was open to all Christians (they baptized 'for all of Christendom'). The Collegiants first chose immersion with the baptism of Jan Geesteranus. As an Antitrinitarian Geesteranus was influenced by the Polish Brethren, like Christof Ostorodt whose own practice of immersion was inspired by the Spanish Antitrinitarian physician Michael Servetus.[151]

Blunt was now delegated to travel to Holland, where he visited the Collegiants. Blunt returned to England in 1641, and then

---

147 Cited in Underwood, *General Baptists*, 54.
148 Ibid, 90–1.
149 This is the Dutch version of Jane Murton's name. Thus John Murton had been known as Jan Morton by the Dutch. Cf BURRAGE 2, 225, 241.
150 Chronology alone would have made it clear that these settlers were General rather than Particular Baptists. The now dated study of the baptism of Roger Williams in 1639 (Whitsitt, *A Question in Baptist History*) confirms this.
151 Williams, *The Radical Reformation*, 312f.

> Mr. Blunt baptized Mr. Blacklock that was a teacher amongst them, and
> Mr. Blunt being baptized, he and Mr. Blacklock baptized the rest of their
> friends that ware so minded.[152]

The careful wording of this sentence seems deliberate, as does its ambiguity. If
Blunt had not been baptized, then Blunt and Blacklock baptized one another.
Then again, Blunt may have been baptized by the Rijnsburg Collegiants, in which
case he baptized Blacklock, who had already been elected their leader, whereafter
Blunt and Blacklock jointly baptized the rest. Burrage feels that the text concern-
ing Blunt and Blacklock involves a 'hopeless dilemma,' but one should not extri-
cate oneself, as Burrage did, by choosing one of two wild guesses made by Francis
Bampfield, on the basis that the alternative supposition can be disproved.[153]
Wamble interprets the quotation concerning the baptisms as implying that 'it is
highly unlikely that he [Blunt] was immersed by the Collegiants.'[154] However,
Payne flatly asserts that the Collegiants had immersed Blunt,[155] while Estep refers
to Blunt's 'commision to secure immersion at the hands of the Collegiate Mennonites in Rhynsburg, Holland.'[156] I accept Payne's and Estep's view, for, according
to the so-called Kiffin manuscript, the persons who founded the Particular Baptist
movement were 'convinced that baptism was not for infants' as early as 1638, but
they apparently did not dare to act on this conviction until three years afterwards.
They must have had scruples, unlike Thomas Helwys. Then they sent Blunt to
Holland:

> Mr. Richard Blunt with him being convinced of baptism, that also it
> ought to be by dipping the body into the water, resembling burial and rise-
> ing again, according to Col 2:12, Rom 6:4, had sober conferance about in
> the Church, and then with some of the forenamed who also ware so con-
> vinced. And after prayer and conferance about their so enjoying it, none
> haveing then so practised in England to professed believers, and hearing
> that some in the Nether Lands had so practised, they agreed and sent over
> Mr. Rich[ard] Blunt (who understood Dutch) with letters of commenda-
> tion, who was kindly accepted there, and returned with letters from them:
> John Batten, a teacher there, and from that Church to such as sent him.[157]

Why did this group send Blunt to the Rijnsburg Collegiants? Why did they, convinced of the rightness of such a course, wait until Blunt had returned from

152 BURRAGE 2, 302–3.
153 BURRAGE 2, 334, n 1.
154 Wamble, 'Inter-Relations,' 416.
155 Payne, Free Churchmen, 84–5.
156 Estep, 'A Baptist Reappraisal,' 56.
157 BURRAGE 2, 302–3.

Holland to institute believers' baptism by immersion? Why did they send letters commending Blunt to the Collegiants, unless he intended to accept their baptism? Why did the Collegiants commend Blunt to his own church, unless they certified that he had been baptized by them?

Torbet suggests that Blunt, as a Calvinist, would never have accepted baptism 'of Arminian Collegiants.'[158] This is a perplexing observation, for Blunt's fellow Calvinists would not have recommended him to the 'Arminian Collegiants' if they regarded them as unacceptable. But even if one assumes, for the sake of argument, that Blunt was less tolerant than his fellow Calvinists, and that he would have spurned baptism from an Arminian, such an obstacle would not have been serious, for the Collegiants were free to choose their own baptizer, and the Collegiants, making no exclusive claims to membership, counted Calvinists in good standing with the Dutch Reformed Church among their members.

There was, of course, plenty of incentive for the Particular Baptists to base their immersions on a baptism that had taken place in Holland. The case of John Smyth had been attended with extreme notoriety; it involved a se-baptism (which the Particular Baptists obviously avoided), and later Smyth had doubted the validity of the other baptisms he performed, on the assumption that the baptizer should already have been baptized. By sending Blunt to be immersed by the Collegiants, the Particular Baptists avoided both Smyth's problems. Nevertheless, the Kiffen manuscript is not explicit about Blunt's baptism. Particular Baptists would not have wanted to flaunt a Dutch connection to avoid that hateful and legally dangerous charge of being tainted with 'Anabaptism.'[159]

Stassen has shown that the Particular Baptist Confession of 1644 stands in the Dutch Baptist tradition with its interpretation of baptism.[160] In other ways this Confession seems to be a typically Separatist document, except that predestination is undercut, for God does not predestine anyone to damnation.[161] The Particular Baptists received many accessions from the earlier General Baptist congregations.[162] Although it is usually assumed that the General Baptists hardly influenced the Particular Baptists, this is merely an assumption. Certainly the name 'Baptist' must have been transmitted via the General to the Particular Baptists. Baptism is also called an 'ordinance' among the Particular Baptists, a usage current among Dutch Baptists ever since Hoffman published *Die Ordonnantie*

---

158 Torbet, *Baptists*, 43.
159 Hudson's argument ('Baptists were not Anabaptists,' 171–2) that the English Baptists were not influenced by the Dutch Baptists because they refused to be called 'Anabaptists' is unconvincing. See Payne's trenchant critique in 'Who were the Baptists?' 341. Mosteller's refutation in 'Baptists and Anabaptists,' 4–7, is devastating. Hudson never seems to have responded to Payne and Mosteller; he merely clings to his old viewpoint in 'The Ecumenical Spirit,' [182]–4.
160 Stassen, 'Origin of the Particular Baptists,' 322–48.
161 Lumpkin, *Baptist Confessions*, 157, art III.
162 Wamble, 'Inter-Relations,' 419.

Godts in 1530.[163] The Particular Baptists may have derived this usage from the General Baptists, or, to borrow Stassen's expression, 'a fresh breeze from Holland' may have been responsible.

The Particular Baptists tended to be more positive towards the magistracy than the General Baptists, but they rejected the Calvinistic theocratic position of the Separatists, following the Waterlander, General Baptist, and Collegiant position in denying that the rulers may legislate concerning religion. Thus the Particular Baptists continued the General Baptist legacy of advocating toleration. They could not appeal to the intentions of a tolerant God (as the Waterlanders and the General Baptists did), but they did use the Calvinistic, and devastating, argument that no ruler can either assist in or be an obstacle to God's decrees, hence the futility of religious intervention by the state.[164]

Furthermore, the Particular Baptists appear to have inherited the General Baptists' and the Waterlanders' liberal attitude towards confessional subscription. Even the Calvinism of the Particular Baptists may have been overstated. By being lenient on subscription they could always strengthen their Calvinism for apologetic reasons.[165]

Baptist influence did not always move from the General to the Particular Baptists. The General Baptists appear to have become somewhat more Calvinistic in their views on predestination, though they always resisted double predestination, and immersion became the commonly accepted mode of baptism among all English Baptists.

Thus, the Baptist movement advanced from continental Europe to England and there evolved further. Historically the Baptists of the Anglo-Saxon world have eclipsed the continental European Baptists. The advance of toleration in Holland was significant, but when it gained ground in England, its consequences were felt worldwide. It is the English Baptists, especially those that were transplanted to the United States, who have moulded modern notions of freedom of religion and the separation of church and state. Today the Mennonites and Baptists of continental European origin have about half a million members worldwide; the Anglo-Saxon Baptists count their members by the tens of millions.

To retrace our steps somewhat, it is not known whether Menno Simons was aware of his theological debt to Karlstadt. Hoffman, and for that matter the Swiss

---

163 Reprinted BRN 5, 145–70; English trans in Williams, *Spiritual and Anabaptist Writers*, 182–203.
164 See 'The London Confession' in Lumpkin, *Baptist Confessions*, 141–71.
165 Such apologetic motifs even surface nowadays, for example when Hudson honestly concedes that he wants to excise the Dutch Baptists from English Baptist history, in order 'to recover a reasoned apologetic for the Baptist position' *vis-à-vis* the Calvinists, and because 'proving "succession" through the Anabaptists runs counter to a central Baptist conviction,' and presumably history marches in accord with Baptist convictions ('Baptists Were Not Anabaptists,' 171, 179).

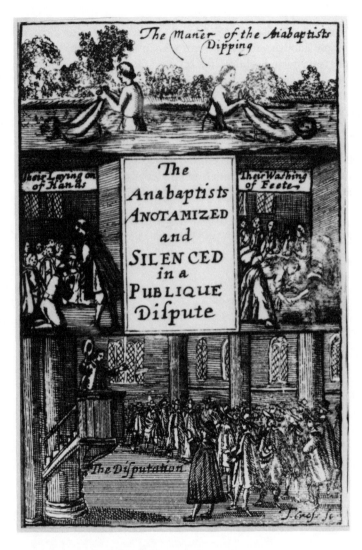

Frontispiece of Richard Carpenter's
The Anabaptist washt and washt and shrunk (1653).
Note the Dutch influence on what to a hostile opponent appeared to be the
most offensive Baptist distinctives. Baptism by immersion came by way of the
Rijnsburg Collegiants. The laying on of hands, after baptism, as a sign of one's
ordination to the priesthood of all believers, as well as the ordinance of foot
washing, was derived from the Dutch Baptists (Mennonites).
By courtesy of Bodleian Library, Oxford (Mason AA 125 frontispiece)

Baptists, would rather have disavowed Karlstadt's fathership, for to them he appeared to be simply another erudite waverer and an apostate. Yet, the Karlstadtian component is the main historical link between the northern and southern Baptists of Europe. Satisfying as the excision or the loss of Karlstadt from the history of the continental Baptists may have been from a later Mennonite confessional and emotional standpoint, Karlstadt's fathership of the Baptist movements in Europe is a historical fact that irrevocably alters one's perspective on the rise of the Baptists.

Moreover, historians should also recognize the links between the Dutch and the English Baptists.[166] Thanks to the Dutch and the English Baptists, and others, one can now safely affirm such linkage as a historical fact, without fear of being cast into Newgate or Clink Prison.

---

166 As this book is going to press, I have received proofs of Joseph D. Ban's defence of Hudson in 'Were the Earliest English Baptists Anabaptists?' to be published as a chapter to In the Great Tradition, ed Joseph D. Ban and Paul R. Dekar. Ban has twice argued his view with me: passionately, yet amicably. Those who would challenge my conclusions should consult Ban's chapter.

Karlstadt and Thomas Müntzer

Luther lumped Karlstadt and Thomas Müntzer together as violent Spiritualists in *Against the Heavenly Prophets* (WA 18, 62–214; LW 40, 73–224). Consequently Karlstadt has often been portrayed as a revolutionary in the secondary literature. The following primary documents have been translated from MS and WA to clarify Karlstadt's position vis-à-vis Müntzer.

1 / By late 1520 Müntzer had collected fourteen publications by Karlstadt (MS, 555, nos. 1, 6; 557, nos. 18–22, 24–31), of which nos. 27 and 30 are not properly identified. They are identical with FB 28 and 45, respectively.

2 / In 1522 Müntzer denigrated Luther, Karlstadt, Melanchthon, and Lang while conversing with Wolfgang Stein (MS, 565).

3 / Letter from Karlstadt to Müntzer (21 Dec. 1522), MS, 386–7.

> To Thomas Müntzer, highly esteemed brother and servant of Christ
> Peace to you from the Father of our Lord Jesus Christ.
>   I deem it necessary that you should choose that [peace], since I realize that you have fallen into a curse, not unlike the curse of Jeremiah.[1] I do not therefore approve of this, since, even in the case of Jeremiah, I perceive that a seed of grain had fallen into the earth.[2] It had not yet died. Like that man, it certainly seems to me that you taste the bitterness of mustard.[3] In spite of this, you have not yet been made the least of all

1 Jer. 20:14.
2 John 12:24.
3 There is an echo of this idea (was it derived from Karlstadt, or was Karlstadt just commenting on Müntzer's letter?) in *Protestation* (1524), MS, 231:16–17: 'Darumb ist [die schrifft] aber uns unwissenden menschen geschrieben, das der heylige glaube das senffkorns einen ydern also saur ankomme.'

men.[4] Indeed, if you would esteem yourself to be the least of all men, you would consider yourself unworthy of so much honour and glory as that with which that stepmother honoured Christ of Nazareth.[5] But of this, elsewhere.[6]

I observe in your letter the violent squalls of the sea in which you swim. Believe me, the Lord chastises the elect with judgment. Yet, if meanwhile it seems to you yourself that you have been smitten by the enemy, such judgment had to be rendered on account of sin. You know how easily it happens that we are not united with God's will. We withdraw ourselves from God as often as even our petty desires conquer us. We pass our time in a world of death. Thus the justice of Christ does not triumph in us, as long as we are subject to the life of the flesh. But of this elsewhere.

It pleases me greatly that there are some among the people of Zwickau who do not like some of the things that were accomplished. Nevertheless, I am not pleased when you rise and stand up with such little seriousness in the abyss of the divine will from which your birth is in the process of being accomplished. Where were you in the life of God? But of this elsewhere.

On this I congratulate you, that you have allied yourself only with us. I stay in the house of a certain citizen named Simon Fleischer and I propose that you look for me there. Indeed, I would see your face gladly. Not that that face entertains me at all, but thereupon I would confer with you to share what I should. Besides I would discuss what I do not wish to believe from sheets of paper. I would show you my new house which I have obtained in the country. I assume and hope that the labour would not displease you in any way.

I was not permitted to respond to all things. The Lord of my heart is powerful. His power and strong hand I have learned to know from experi-

---

4 Matt. 13:32.
5 The stepmother (noverca) is not Mary, for Karlstadt did not hold to a heavenly-flesh doctrine of the incarnation. Rather, we must think of Naomi, who adopted Obed as her own son (Ruth 4:14f). Obed is included in Christ's lineage in Matt. 1:5. Apparently, Müntzer's comments about the bitterness of Jeremiah had led to a reference to Naomi, since she calls herself Mara, i.e. Bitterness, in Ruth 1:20. Müntzer must have followed this up with a statement of hope, coupling it with a mystical reference to the Christ struggling to be born in us. Hence Karlstadt's reaction, upbraiding Müntzer for his lack of humility – another virtue held in high esteem by the mystics, but not by Müntzer.
6 The editor notes: 'sehr eilig geschrieben, siehe das viermalige De hoc alias' (MS, 386, n 1). This is possible, but, in view of Karlstadt's invitation to talk face to face, he probably indicated that he could not discuss everything freely, since his letter might be intercepted and reach Luther. At least this is Müntzer's interpretation in his next letter.

ence. In this place I have said more about dreams and visions than anyone among the professors.[7] About the remaining matters [let us talk] face to face. Farewell in Christ Jesus ...

Andreas Karlstadt

4 / Müntzer to Karlstadt (29 July 1523), MS, 393

To my most beloved brother Andreas Karlstadt, farmer in Wörlitz: Greetings, brother in the Lord!

I do not know what has kept you from writing anything, for you had promised to write me frequently. I do not know whether you are a lay-person or cleric, whether you are dead or alive, for you pass me over in silence, though time and again you have had suitable scriveners in Orlamünde. Remit, through whatever channels you could have communicated, the not so trifling amount of compound interest due on the old friendship.

I shall always answer your letters. It is useless to complain about letters being intercepted, as long as God administers our cause. I send you this man, Nikolaus, a brother in the Lord.[8] Assist him in the cause of our poor, for our nuns have disenfranchised the poor, to be rid of them. He himself will let you know the individual cases. To make sure, you will cross-examine him as you would examine the Lord.[9] He will not fail you. Trust this man. He is sincere in the Spirit of God. Farewell. Perhaps the Lord wants you for a procurator, to wash away the things you have perpetrated in the pompous court of the anti-Christ.[10]

To you, my dearest friend, I speak as to myself. Again, farewell.

Thomas Müntzer, curate of Allstedt

PS Greet your wife in the Lord Jesus. I abide in the old-fashioned fear of the Lord.

5 / Karlstadt to Müntzer (Orlamünde, 19 July 1524), MS, 415–16[11]

To the most esteemed brother in Christ, Thomas Müntzer, bishop of Allstedt

---

7 The ambiguity is deliberate. What Karlstadt had said about dreams and visions was censorious.

8 Nikolaus Storch was one of the 'Zwickau Prophets.' Müntzer expected Karlstadt to be antagonistic towards Storch; hence (as Wappler, *Thomas Müntzer*, 79, n 311, has already observed) Müntzer's repeated request to trust the man, who is a sincere brother.

9 1 John 4:1.

10 Matt. 27:24. The 'pompous court of the Antichrist' is probably an allusion to the University of Wittenberg, though Karlstadt had also served at the papal court.

11 For Barge's interpretation see BARGE 2, 114f.

Peace to you from the Father of Christ, Amen.

Since I love you, I cannot conceal my feelings, even if I shall not be echoing your sentiments. Neither should you kindle my anger, or suspect that anything is wrong, or [assume] that I have been alienated from you. It may be possible that he who not only harasses but in fact strikes you[12] is the one who loves you most, for the strokes of a conscientious man are better than the feigned kisses of an enemy.[13] In any case, I consequently answer your most friendly letter to me at greater length.

In accordance with Isaiah and Zechariah, I can hardly suggest a better signal with which the sheep of Christ are more happily gathered than with the whistling of the truth.[14] In any event, with blasphemies towards Christ the God I would not even have gathered the demons.[15] For the rest I do not appeal for rules from the trickier [passages of the] Scriptures. I both exhort and beseech you to cease elevating the host, for it is blasphemy towards the crucified Christ. Moreover, arousing the people with sacred hymns I consider either harmful or inconsistent with the divine principles.[16] At least you would have obscured to some extent the admonition I am about to write to the people and the fifteen villagers in Schneeberg.

I cannot at all sanction what you recommend, for it appears to me that such covenants conflict violently with the will of God, and with incredible spiritual harm they influence the hearts infected with the spirit of fear.[17] For trust in the blessings of the living God such covenants substitute trust in a man of abusive language,[18] that is, a staff made of reed.[19] You know how wicked that is! And to the extent that you thunder, this alienates from God and subverts these minds that are unskilled and lack ability to hear the voice of God. The Scriptures declare everywhere to those who are

12 Cf Gen. 32:24f.
13 See Prov. 27:6. Karlstadt deliberately alludes to a text that Müntzer himself had cited in *Protestation*.
14 Isa. 5:26; Zech. 10:8 (Vulgate).
15 Even the demons know the truth (1 Cor. 10:20–1; James 2:19).
16 Karlstadt alludes to Müntzer's *Kirchenamt*, which included not only Psalms (which Karlstadt tolerated) but hymns. We see in Müntzer's preface to the mass (MS, 163–5) a public response to Karlstadt, for there Müntzer attacks those who 'out of hateful jealousy' are accusing him of reintroducing 'papal gestures, masses matins and vespers' (MS, 163:1–10). Müntzer's rhetoric indicates that Karlstadt's critique had left him unsure, and when Konrad Grebel's Karlstadt circle sent a messenger to him, Müntzer admitted having doubts about the use of hymns (MS, 441:12–13). Even towards the end of his preface Müntzer had left the use of hymns optional (MS, 164:10–17).
17 2 Tim. 1:7 (Vulg.).
18 1 Sam. 17:8–9, 43–4.
19 Isa. 36:6. The idea of trusting in God, rather than in political leagues or human compacts, can be traced back in Karlstadt's thought to 1519. See Karlstadt, 'Militia Franciscana,' 73:11–24.

silent in a time of trial that [their thoughts] will be shouted abroad in the streets. In addition, that would mean having a heart with a thick fore-skin,[20] and placing one's trust and mind in men.

Besides, even if [your league] were about to wither away through the agency of us who have our eyes opened with respect to public opinion and anxiety, I know not whether and where there would be any sword sharper in ruining us. As regards you and your confederacy, I would desire that you refrain from local compacts of this sort and from writings that at this point will spawn a fear of enduring evils which we would have suffered, seeing that we have never been brigands or men of sedition.

How I am amazed at this brashness! How I do shrink back from it! And thus I shall publicly reveal it in the future, so all will know that I have nothing to do with all of you in such an undertaking and confederation.[21]

I counsel the same thing that Christ counsels and to which none of the prophets would object, namely, that you, in one accord with our dearest brethren, place your hope in the one God who has the power to confound your adversaries.

Again, if you planned to contemplate the judgments of God, you know I would owe my life to you and you [would owe your life] to me in return.[22] I shall gladly join you in proclaiming the truth of God and in [performing] works of approbation even unto death if I were to see a Philistine coming forth to obliterate the camp of God.[23]

You add greetings for my wife, which I have conveyed to her. She returns greetings to you and your wife with concern, and she wishes that you remain safe and sound.

I ask you to give this response your consideration, for I favour you and esteem you higher than myself.[24] Tell me why you would rather have my little boy named Abraham than Andreas, for I should like to know your reason.[25]

20 Jer. 4:4.
21 Karlstadt had already written the reply to Müntzer in the name of the people of Orla-münde, but here he announces his intention to publish it.
22 Philem. 19.
23 1 Sam. 17:4.
24 Phil. 2:3.
25 Andreas III had been born early in 1524, for on 23 Sept. the Council of Orlamünde noted that Anna Bodenstein was again 'sehr schwanger,' and that she had a child (KS 2, 56:24–5). In June 1525 Karlstadt refers to his one child in letters to Johann the elector (BARGE 2, 580) and to Luther (BR 3, 529). Since Karlstadt addresses Luther as 'Gevatter,' I agree with the edi-tor (BR 3, 530) that Luther was the godfather of Karlstadt's eldest son, Andreas Jr. This moves the date of Andreas Jr's birth to the winter of 1522–3 (he began his studies in Zurich in 1536).

A happy farewell in Christ Jesus. Greet and comfort our brethren in Christ.

Your Andreas Karlstadt

6 / Karlstadt and the People of Orlamünde to Müntzer (July 1524), MS, 571–3

Epistle of the People of Orlamünde to the People of Allstedt on How to Fight Like a Christian. Wittenberg: [Hans Lufft] 1524[26]

Peace from God through Christ our Lord
   Dear Brethren: we have carefully read the letter that you sent us, and we have perceived the reason why you wrote, which is to uproot and pluck up the Christians who are everywhere around you. Besides, you ask for our reaction and in return you want us to send you a written reply.

Andreas III died *before* 23 Sept. 1524, since the Council referred to only one child, i.e. Andreas Jr. Glatz refers to Anna's refusal to have her son baptized (BARGE 2, 219), but Barge was wrong in conjecturing that this took place in Jan. 1525, for Anna was expelled with her husband in 1524, despite her pregnancy. Barge failed to note that the request of the Council of Orlamünde to allow Anna to remain was tacitly rebuffed by the Council of Weimar (KS 2, 56–7). The whole family had fled to Strassburg by Nov. 1524 (BR 3, 379–80, n 4). Kaspar Glatz's letter is now seen as having been written in Aug. 1524 (WA 15, 325). According to Glatz, Karlstadt was absent and Anna refused to have Andreas III baptized. This fits the first week of August, when Karlstadt had been summoned to Wittenberg to settle matters related to his resignation, on 22 July, of the archdeaconate (WA 15, 326; SIDER, 304). Glatz's attempt to baptize Andreas III was no doubt prompted by the critical illness of the child.

Karlstadt referred to his *one child* in his letters in June 1525, although early in 1525 he had referred to his *children* (Bubenheimer, 'Karlstadt,' [46, 48]). Thus Anna must have given birth again, late in 1524, but this infant had then died in Rothenburg.

Early in 1526 Jakob was born in Bergwitz, with Käthe Luther, Justus Jonas, and Philipp Melanchthon as godparents at his baptism in Seegrehna (BARGE 2, 371–2). Adam was born in Kemberg in 1528 (Wackernagel, *Matrikel* 2, 17 n 19). When Käthe Luther questioned Karlstadt after having acted as sponsor, he expressed his understanding of Jakob's baptism obliquely, by noting that, indeed, Andreas III had been allowed to die without baptism (TR 2, no. 2667b).

Andreas Jr, Adam, and Jakob are the three sons of Karlstadt to whom Ulrich Zwingli alludes on 22 June 1530 (Z 10, 641). Barge is right about the other children, except that Küngold was a daughter (Bossert, 'Küngold Bodenstein,' 153). Wackernagel (*Matrikel* 2, 14, n 47) implies that Heinrich Bodenstein was a son of Karlstadt. This is unlikely, for when he enrolled at the University of Basel Heinrich paid the usual fees, whereas Adam, as son of the rector, paid nothing. Heinrich probably was a distant relative. Johannes Bodenstein (BARGE 2, 518) may have been another relative, but he could not have been a son of Karlstadt (see the list in BARGE 2, 517; and of the family tree in Bubenheimer, 'Karlstadt,' [53]).

26 Pointing out that the treatise was printed in Wittenberg, which is unthinkable without Luther's collaboration, Hoyer, 'Martin Reinhart,' 1604, notes: '[Das] lässt [Luthers] Vorwurf des "Allstedtischen Geistes" an die Karlstadt – Anhänger um so demagogischer erscheinen.'

Out of brotherly faithfulness we cannot conceal from you that (presuming we have understood your letters) we cannot have anything at all to do with worldly resistance. That is not what we have been commanded, since Christ bade Peter sheathe his sword and allowed him not to fight for Him, for the hour of His suffering was near.[27] Similarly, when the time is at hand that we are to endure some suffering for the sake of God's justice, let us not reach for knives and spears and drive away the eternal will of the Father with our own violence, for daily we pray: 'Thy will be done.'

But if you want to be armed against your enemy, clothe yourself with the strong breastplate and the invincible harness of faith, of which St Paul writes in Ephesians 6 [:13–17]. Thus you will dutifully vanquish and shame your enemies, so they will not harm even a single hair.

You have written that we should associate with you and make a covenant or entangle ourselves with you, and for support you cite 2 Kings [23:3], where Josiah covenanted with God and the people. We find in the same text that Josiah, having received the book of the Law, covenanted with God to walk in the ways of the Lord, to keep with his heart and all his strength His laws, commandments, and ceremonies, and to promote the words of the covenant. In other words, the king and the people made a covenant with God at the same time. For if Josiah had covenanted with both God and the people, his heart would have been divided, for he would have desired to please both God and men, about which Christ says: 'No one can serve two masters.'[28] Therefore, dear brethren, if we were to covenant with you, we would cease to be free Christians, having covenanted with men, and that would really raise an outcry against the gospel.

Then the tyrants would be overjoyed and say: 'They boast about the one and only God, but now they make a covenant with one another. Their God is not strong enough to fight for them. Besides, they want to establish their own sects, rebellion, and insurrection. Let us strangle and kill them before they overcome us.' Then we would have to die for such a reason rather than for the sake of the inalterable justice of God. What would God say to that? Would that not greatly dishonour and tear down the truth of God?

No, no, dear brethren, rather trust God alone, as King Abijah did in [2] Chronicles 13 when he had been surrounded by his enemies, or as the children of Israel did when they had been pursued by Pharaoh till they

27 Matt. 26:52.
28 Matt. 6:24.

came upon the Red Sea.[29] Yet, trusting God, they were miraculously delivered and saved. Therefore hear and receive only the true words of God, everyone according to his ability, and do not be concerned when the violence of tyrants arises to challenge you. For the apostles, all the saints of God, even Christ himself, could not avoid this.

Otherwise we shall gladly reply to your testimony, in so far as it is empty and removed from God, with the testimony of the Holy Spirit, and, having received the free gifts of God, we shall not spare you in any way. And if an accounting of our faith were to be demanded of us, [we would] come forward with joy to testify, even if every raging tyranny were to rise against us and persecute us unto death. Yet, all of this through the aid and power of God. Therefore dear brethren, learn only through the eternal will of God which our heavenly Father has revealed to us in the Holy Spirit through his only-begotten son Christ. Thus, in God, you will be peacefully delivered from all inner struggles [anfechtunge].

May God help us all, Amen.

The Congregation [gemeyn] of Christ in Orlamünde

7 / Müntzer's comments on the letter from Orlamünde
Müntzer to the people of Allstedt (7 Aug. 1524), MS, 433:29–434:13

Thus the whole world is filled with all the fear of the godless who despair, for they hear the rustling of the leaf on the tree and they imagine that an armoured man has appeared.[30] Therefore you should not be moved by their offence, which is none other than that of the godless, for when they wanted to arrest Christ, they were afraid of causing an uproar.[31] When one requites the oppressors, since they do not act justly and do not intend to do so forever, they are enemies of insurrection, which they themselves have provoked 'with all their thoughts, words, and deeds.'[32] In so far as one struggles against their folly, they claim one is rebellious. I have revealed my scheme to many friends of God and also to those of Orlamünde [to see] whether they wanted to support you, as they were boasting. Then they answered with a letter that gives an obvious cover for human fear, so it is a miracle, etc. I cannot accept that you also have become fearful, so that you, together with those of Orlamünde, wish to disavow the covenant of God, which you call the Old and New Testament, for the sake of the god-

---

29 Exod. 14:9f.
30 Lev. 26:36.
31 Matt. 26:5.
32 The line I have placed in quotation marks derives from the traditional confession, which Müntzer also used in his liturgy (MS, 166:5).

less. You certainly know that my writing has not been instigated against any rulers except against shameless tyranny.

8 / Luther's Reaction to Karlstadt

On 22 August 1524 Luther preached at 7:00 a.m. in Jena, and he implied that Karlstadt was in league with Müntzer. Karlstadt protested his innocence that afternoon in the Inn of the Black Bear. The following exchange took place (WA 15, 336:11–16):

KARLSTADT To this I add that you treat me with violence and injustice when you lump me together with the murderous spirit. I have nothing to do with the spirit of insurrection. This I protest publicly before these brethren, one and all.
LUTHER Dear Lord Doctor, that is not necessary. I have read the letter which you who are in Orlamünde have written to Thomas, and I certainly learned from it that you reject the insurrection.

Yet Luther repeated the charge in his *Heavenly Prophets*. First he distinguished between murderous prophets and those who have murderous intentions, placing Karlstadt in the latter category (WA 18, 72:15–18):

Therefore I did say Dr Karlstadt is not a murderous prophet. He does, however, have a rebellious, murderous, riotous spirit in him, which would reveal itself if there were an opportunity.

Then Luther scored Karlstadt's condonation of iconoclasm as incitement to insurrection, even though Karlstadt rejected this (WA 18, 88:6–9):

'But,' you say, 'Dr Karlstadt does not want to murder. That you can see from the letter which those of Orlamünde wrote to those of Allstedt.'
ANSWER 'I also believed this, but no longer. Now I no longer ask what Dr Karlstadt says or does.'

9 / Karlstadt explains how he wrote the letter of 19 July and the public reply on behalf of the congregation of Orlamünde (*Entschuldigung*, WA 18, 439:16–440: 27, 441:1–5)

Concerning Müntzer's unchristian attitudes, I can write before God with a clear conscience. As soon as I definitely understood Müntzer's plan, I opposed it, and it caused me as much sorrow as anyone living today, whatever his name. That I resisted Müntzer to the utmost of my ability can be vouched for by anyone who can still be reached and who saw the colour of my face and who heard with what haste I replied and complained about Müntzer's letter. They know how I condemned Müntzer's folly and predicted the evils that would follow. Many innocent people would be hurt, and some would perish, and intolerable damage would be done to the gospel, etc.

I complain to God that all this came true and everything came to pass as I predicted it. What I feared has also surrounded me. For I who am innocent was suspected and accused, and I have suffered much on account of Müntzer's rebellion, of which I have never approved, neither did I desire to take part in it. But this I must now commit to God who probably, for the sake of my sins, washes me in the bath of sorrow, so much so that I am nearly drawing my last breath.

However, I have helped to resist and prevent Müntzer's rebellion, and I can attest to this with the people of Orlamünde. Müntzer wrote the congregation [gemeine] in Orlamünde for support and a following, and they sent back a Christian and impeccable answer with godly sayings drawn from the Holy Scriptures. They resisted valiantly and admonished him zealously to fight with the Word of God and not with swords of iron. To this same letter I added one or two lines,[33] and I helped to quench and choke the fire just as much as the people of Orlamünde.

In this same letter one can also easily discover whether the bold incitement of Müntzer pleased or saddened me. It would be a good idea to obtain that answer, for the letter from Orlamünde was printed in Wittenberg a year ago, and it is not unknown in the German nation. Therefore its contents cannot be denied. From this same answer let all those judge who are understanding and honourable lovers both of justice and of innocence. Then let them accuse or excuse.

This is also true, that Müntzer, in addition to the letter he wrote to the above-mentioned congregation, wrote to me and tried to incite me to

---

33 First Karlstadt speaks of adding 'one or two lines,' but then he takes equal credit, and ultimately he identifies his own sentiments with the letter. Karlstadt was undoubtedly the author of this letter, which is thoroughly consistent with his teaching, but his contribution had to be concealed. Müntzer had written to Orlamünde; therefore a letter had to be issued in the name of the Orlamünde congregation. Moreover, as Karlstadt already had indicated in his letter of 19 July, he wanted to have the reply published, but he was no longer allowed to publish in Wittenberg. Karlstadt had been able to publish when Michel Buchfürer moved to Jena under the protection of Martin Reinhart, a friend of Karlstadt; see FB 110, 112, 114, 115, 119. On 14 Jan. 1524 Luther wrote to Chancellor Brück to repress Buchfürer. This effort was apparently successful. (See BARGE 2, 103, n 17, 115, n 59). Barge's surmise is confirmed by the few items which Buchfürer printed in Jena in 1524 (Hase, 'Johann Michael,' 131f). Thus, for quick distribution, the reply had to be printed in Wittenberg and Karlstadt's contribution could not be mentioned.

similar or even worse folly. But as soon as I read Müntzer's letter, my blood turned cold and I grew so fearful that I spontaneously tore it to pieces. Thereupon I considered that such a letter should at least be shown to someone, so at least some person would know the folly towards which Müntzer tried to incite me, and what foolishness Müntzer judged I would entertain, and for what a shallow simpleton Müntzer took me in assuming I would help him perpetrate such nonsense.

Therefore I soon mounted a horse and rushed towards Heilingen to Master Boniface. I complained about Müntzer's letter, his unchristian pressure, evil suspicion, trampling upon my personality, and defamation of my life. With all this Müntzer tried to crush me. Then we put together the pieces of the letter, and when we had read Müntzer's letter, Boniface became as impatient and incensed towards Müntzer as I. Then I explained that Müntzer had also written the congregation, and I hastily turned around towards Orlamünde and met some people whom I told that they should arm themselves with a sharp letter and answer blow for blow. This happened as I mentioned above.

For myself, however, I wrote an answer in Latin to Müntzer, and I wish that everyone knew what I had written in the letter I held in my hands, to conclude from that whether or not I was guilty. I hope I still have a copy of the same answer in Orlamünde ...[34]

I dislike writing this apology after Müntzer's death, and I would rather praise Müntzer too much than scold him slightly with the truth. But I am forced to write the truth, and I do not doubt that Müntzer, if he were still alive, would have defended me. I doubt not that, if he has been properly interrogated, he has defended me.

[Karlstadt continues with an account of the hostility of the peasants towards him, and how he had nearly been killed by them as well as robbed on several occasions.] Among the peasants I was like a hare among the hounds.

---

34 A whole sack of Müntzer's correspondence was preserved, including Karlstadt's letter. This was discovered in Müntzer's hiding-place in Frankenhausen.

The Imprisonment of Johannes Bebel and Thomas Wolf

The following documents are the reports the printers Johannes Bebel and Thomas Wolf had to make to the City Council when they were imprisoned from 7 to 10 December 1524 for printing Karlstadt's writings. Their depositions have survived in the archives of Basel, and they were published by Emil Dürr, but they have been overlooked in the secondary literature. These documents offer the basis for my claim that Felix Manz and his friends supported the publication of Karlstadt's most radical writings. The following material is a translation of *Aktensammlung zur Geschichte der Basler Reformation* 1, ed Emil Dürr, 174–6.

1 / The deposition of Johannes Bebel (alias Hans Welsch)[1]

Approximately one or two weeks before the fair in Frankfurt,[2] there came to my home Dr Gerhard Westerburg of Cologne,[3] and with him a young

---

1 Barge did not know these documents, but in spite of this, his observations in FB, 323–31, are almost entirely correct. I note the following differences: Barge assigns FB 126, 129, and 135 to the press of Andreas Cratander. The document translated here proves that Johann Bebel, alias Hans Welsch, printed independently. His types had been either rented or purchased from Cratander. Moreover, among the Strassburg reprints, FB 128 and 130 should be assigned to Johann Schwan rather than to Johann Prüss. Schwan had obtained Prüss's printing press by marrying his widow. For the period when the tracts were printed in Basel (late Oct. until early Nov.) see FB, 328f.

2 The pre-autumnal book fair in Frankfurt was established in June 1347, and it took place 'between the two days of our Lady,' i.e. 15 Aug. (ascension of Mary) and 8 Sept. (birth of Mary). In 1394 the duration was extended to 15 Sept. Not until the seventeenth century (when the Leipzig fair gave considerable competition) were the modern dates set (24 Aug. to 15 Sept.). See Dietz, *Frankfurter Handelsgeschichte* 1, 37–8. Since the tracts could not have been printed before the Frankfurt fair, Bebel and Wolf tried to convey the impression that they were victimized by Westerburg's 'evil scheme,' and that they were not responsible for the distribution of the tracts in the Swiss Confederacy.

3 Westerburg had married a sister of Karlstadt's wife. He was influential in spreading Baptist ideas to the Rhineland, and received adult baptism in Münster from Henrik Rol.

man from Zurich, named Felix Manz,[4] both of whom were unknown to me. They asked whether I would print one or two tracts at their expense. I then wished to see the tracts, so they showed me one with the title *Whether the Sacrament Forgives Sins*,[5] and they read some ten pages, but no more. I did not think it was bad, especially since it came from Karlstadt. So I told them to give it to me, for I wanted to show it to Oecolampadius.[6] Dr Gerhard wanted to accompany me, so we showed the same booklet to Oecolampadius, who read it hastily and said it was clear enough to him, but for the uninitiated it would be quite difficult. But if the doctor wished to have it for himself, I could print it at his expense, since I did not have anything else to print. Thus we agreed on three hundred [copies]. [Westerburg] would proofread himself if I were occupied with something else.

After the three hundred had been printed, he gave me the *Dialogue about the Sacrament*.[7] I then told him that I could not afford to print just three hundred [copies] – besides I did not know whether it was good or bad. He emphatically assured me that it contained nothing unchristian or evil. It was not directed against anyone, and it contained only the pure truth. Thus he ordered me to print a thousand copies. He would take three hundred, and the others he would take to Frankfurt if I could not sell them.

The same thing happened with the third booklet, entitled *Explanation of the Five Words*.[8] I also printed one thousand [copies] of it, as before. Then he promised me he would take six guilders' worth. When they were ready, he said I should [first] give him three guilders' worth. One of them [i.e. a companion of Westerburg and Manz] was a messenger on horseback

4 Manz was a native of Zurich. Prominent in Castelberger's Karlstadt circle, he was drowned for his Baptist convictions on 5 Jan. 1527.

5 *Missbrauch* (135).

6 Oecolampadius was consulted in his function as censor. Oecolampadius, Zwingli, and Bucer laid the basis for the early Reformed conception of the Lord's Supper, which included a critical acceptance of the main ideas of Karlstadt. In Strassburg the *Dialogus* (128), *Leyb* (130), and *Messen* (133) were reprinted by Johann Schwan, with *Messen* reprinted once more by Armand Farckall in Colmar, thirty miles southeast of Strassburg. The correspondence of the Strassburg reformers indicates that the tracts created a sensation. Bucer used them in the reconstruction of his views on the Lord's Supper. Since the reports of the printers show that Westerburg could not have taken more than 800 copies of the tracts (300 of *Missbrauch* and perhaps 500 of the *Dialogus*), Manz and Castelberger had a minimum of 5,300 copies of the tracts for distribution. They took most of the copies to Zurich where, according to Wolf and Bullinger, the Baptists sold them. Thus Karlstadt shaped the Baptist attitude towards the sacraments, and in Zurich Zwingli became the most radical proponent of the early Reformed understanding of the Lord's Supper.

7 *Dialogus* (126).

8 *Leyb* (129).

who needed them at once. When everything was finished, he would also take the remainder.[9]

In addition he gave me the fourth booklet *On the Baptism of Infants*.[10] He also wanted to take that for four guilders, and that is how he left me. He did not speak a word of leaving or going away, and I have never seen him since.

I handed the fourth booklet to the printer, to have it set in type. (I did not know then that the doctor had left town.) So [the printer] set two columns, and he told me that it was repulsive, and that I should look it over, for it was against Luther. I took it and brought it to Oecolampadius, who said I should tread carefully, for this was much too offensive. So I left it alone, not willing to print it. I looked for the doctor and I was told afterwards that, upon leaving my home, he had left town at once with Karlstadt.[11] The following day the above-mentioned Felix Manz came to me wanting to have the rest of the books, saying that both the doctor and Karlstadt had left. He was to receive the books and would also proofread the booklet about baptism. I then returned to him the same booklet and some more printed copies, and I told him that the doctor was an evil schemer, and that he had better leave, for I would print nothing more for him. Then he entreated me by the will of God, and offered me money to have it printed. But I would not do it at all. Consequently, I have, since then, seen neither the doctor nor Felix Manz of Zurich. But I heard that Felix Manz took to Zurich all the books that he had taken from me and Thomas Wolf, and he sold them there.

9 According to Wolf (see below) there was a bookseller to whom he sold many of Karlstadt's tracts. This may well be the same person, for he obviously intended to sell some of the tracts first to raise the money to pay for the remainder. Manz and Westerburg appeared to have enough money only for a run of three hundred copies of each booklet, but the printers insisted on larger quantities. Now who was the bookseller who visited Bebel's printing house without dismounting? This may well have been Andreas Castelberger, who was a bookseller, who had been the first to write to Karlstadt from Zurich, and who would have remained seated on his horse because he was crippled. He was known in Zurich as 'Andrew on the Crutches' (*Andres uff der Stülzen*).

10 The dialogue on baptism (see KS 2, 57:29–30) was submitted to Oecolampadius on or before 21 Nov. Oecolampadius had not yet read it, but he refers to it in a letter to Zwingli: 'De baptismo parvulorum libellum nondum legi' (z 8, 252). Since Bebel refers to this tract exactly as Oecolampadius does, its title was *Von dem tauff der kinder*. Barge conjectures that the treatise was confiscated by the magistrates (BARGE 2, 176), but Bebel says that he returned the booklet, i.e. the manuscript, to Manz. Since Karlstadt and Westerburg had already left, Manz tried to have it printed by Thomas Wolf (see below), but he was unsuccessful again. Manz then took it and recast it, turning it from a dialogue to a manifesto to the Council of Zurich (repr TQ SCHWEIZ 1, 23f).

11 Erasmus wrote on 10 Dec. that Karlstadt had been in Basel, but 'secretly' (FB, 326).

But, my dear sir, if you wish to understand the facts more fully, then you might send for Lorenz Weber ... at whose house they lodged together with Karlstadt.[12] He will probably know more about their actions than I, for I know no more about them.

Johannes Bebel, alias Welsch

2 / The deposition of Thomas Wolf

In the last few days there came to my house a red-bearded man, named Dr Gerhard Westerburg, from Cologne. I was not home at the time, so my wife told him I was drinking wine at The Saffron. He took a printer with him, who showed him The Saffron, and he called me out of the tavern. The above-mentioned Dr Gerhard – who was still unknown to me at the time – began and said, 'Sir, I have already waited more than a week for Adam Petri.[13] I have been told that he has travelled to Leipzig. This is taking me too long, and therefore I want to ask you to print me several German books. I shall pay you gratefully.' I said to him, 'Sir, I do not really like to print German when it injures the rulers or some worthy government. Against princes and lords I will not print in any way! I shall let it be known in the highways and byways that I do not approve of doing anything against them.'

The doctor answered, 'This has not been written against rulers or lords; neither is it against a whole government. It is only against the wicked papists who hold many prebends and destroy the gospels. I shall pledge my body and my possessions. If you get into trouble, I shall repay you twofold.' Then I said to him, 'Come to my home tomorrow and I shall let you know my decision.'

The following morning he entreated me with the words I have already mentioned and he prayed to have three hundred copies of each tract, for which he would pay me. I said, 'I cannot have them corrected, for my proofreader has been sent to Cologne for some Latin materials, so I have no one to correct them.' He answered that he would proofread them, just as it is written in the deposition of Hans Welsch. He dealt with me in the same way.

---

12 Lorenz Hochrütiner, a weaver by profession, had been exiled from Zurich in Nov. 1523 for having smashed the crucifix at Stadelhofen. On 24 July 1526 he was banished from Basel for his Baptist beliefs.

13 Petri had reprinted five of Karlstadt's previous publications (FB 9, 43, 48, 52 and *Apologia*). Another reason for approaching Petri was that Ulrich Hugwald printed for him. Hugwald was a radical who became a Baptist. (I owe this reference to M.I. Malich.)

I printed four booklets for him. Each of these was printed on sixteen sheets.[14] Of the first three I printed one thousand each, and eight hundred of the last one. I cannot remember even one of the titles, for I printed them directly from the copies I had before me. That is how it was done, and I offered them to the bookseller for sale.[15]

At last Felix [Manz] from Zurich came to me to print still another [tract], but I would not do it. I told him I had to print at the fair in Frankfurt. He was not satisfied with that. He ran after me for more than three days. Finally I said: 'My lords have given me orders about this booklet,' even though that was not true. With this I talked my way out of it. For the rest, I had the same experience as Hans Welsch.

Thomas Wolf

3 / The oath of peace (Urfehde)

The oaths of Thomas Wolf and Hans Welsch, printers in Basel

Saturday, the tenth day of December, they were set free, since they had been imprisoned for printing the booklets written by Karlstadt about the sacrament. Both of them swore the oath of peace. In addition they pledged that they would appear before my lords during a session of the council, and they will suffer without resistance or complaint whatever penalty my lords inflict upon them. This they have sworn by God and the saints.

A. Saltzmann

14 This is a deceptive diversion, for *none* of the tracts, which did not identify Wolf as the printer, had been impressed on sixteen sheets. The tracts are: *Christus* (124), *Messen* (131), *Gemach* (138), and *Gelaub* (139).

15 As we have seen, this is probably Andreas Castelberger.

The Woodcut
'Triumphus Veritatis'

The woodcut 'Triumphus Veritatis' ('Triumph of Truth'), shown on the cover, depicts a Palm Sunday procession. Two men spread their garments on the road (Matt 21:8). On the left the ark of the Scriptures is borne aloft by 'the patriarchs,' including Moses (with horns: cf Exod 34:29 Vulg), David (who is dancing before the ark), the bearded Aaron (who wears the high priest's turban), and Solomon (who wears the kingly crown). Prophets and apostles follow, for example, Peter (holding the keys), Paul (with the sword), and James the Small (with the saw). In the western iconographical tradition James the Small was identified with James the son of Alphaeus, who was also confused with James 'the brother of the Lord,' then regarded as the author of the Epistle of James. The presence of James in the woodcut is significant because, in opposition to Luther, Karlstadt had defended the Epistle of James as canonical.

In the centre of the procession the knight Ulrich von Hutten leads captive, tied to the tail of his horse (cf Rev 12:4), the traditionists who, claiming to be mediators, interposed themselves between Christ and the church. Among them are Pope Gregory I, whose double-barred cross is broken and whose tiara is falling down, and Augustine of Hippo, who also holds a broken crozier and whose mitre is blowing away; huddling behind them in cardinal's attire is Jerome. Like warlocks the theologians have donned animal disguises. They are, from left to right, Jakob Lemp (dog), Hieronymus Emser (goat), Johann Eck (boar), Thomas Murner (cat), and Johann Faber (holding a hammer and bellows). An ass (Augustinus von Alveld) follows them. Over their heads scurries a crowned black rat (Jakob van Hochstraten). The verse quoted above them states: 'Revealed is the Man of Sin, the Son of Perdition and Abomination, whom God smote with the rod of his mouth' (2 Thess 2:3, 8).

On the right the Saviour is seated on the open Bible, placed on a lectern in a lowly cart (a codex of the gospels), the wheels of which are decorated with laurel branches as in a secular triumphal procession, for example, as in an earlier woodcut entitled 'Triumphus Capnionis' ('The Triumph of Reuchlin'). (These woodcuts, which are similar in style, may have been the work of the same artist.) The cart of the Saviour is drawn by Mark (lion), Luke (ox), and John (eagle). Matthew is the youth who directs them and holds the banner with the inscription 'Now to the King of the Ages, immortal, invisible, the only God, be honour and glory for ever and ever, Amen' (1 Tim 1:17). Above Christ John 14 (not 10):6 is cited: 'I am the way, the truth, and the life.'

Martin Luther walks on stony ground (Mark 4:5–6, 16–17) on Christ's left hand (Matt. 25:31–46); he wears the cowl of an Augustinian monk and waves a quill. On Christ's right hand is Karlstadt; he, like the holy martyrs who follow, wears plain clothing and waves a palm frond (cf John 12:13). Only Christ and the evangelists are haloed. Christ, the Patriarchs, the Prophets, the Apostles, and the putti are barefooted (cf Exod 3:5; Matt 10:10; Luke 10:4); the captive priests wear sandals; Luther wears shoes. The putti on the right scatter flowers behind, not before, Luther. The artist expresses hostility towards the traditionists and Luther, mixed feelings towards Hutten, and respect for Karlstadt and the common people.

The 'Triumphus Veritatis' was probably published in Zurich by an artist from Nürnberg who identified himself pseudonymously as 'Hans Heinrich Freiermut' ('Freiermut' means 'one of free courage').[1] Because it has traditionally been assumed that the woodcut was produced by a Lutheran, the artist has not been identified.[2] I, however, assume that the artist had a Karlstadtian orientation, and thus it is likely that the artist was one of the so-called godless painters of Nürnberg and their associates. When one assumes that the pseudonym is appropriate (that is it reveals as well as conceals), Hans Greiffenberger is tentatively implicated, for his given name and most of the first syllable of his family name have been preserved in the pseudonym. The second given name, Heinrich, would then have served the purpose of concealment. Since the woodcut accompanied 2034 verses in praise of the Reformation, the simpler 'Hans Freiermut' might well have implicated the poet Hans Sachs. Greiffenberger and Sachs were friends; they even jointly published their religious disagreements.[3] Thus the pseudonym may have been chosen to protect Sachs as well as Greiffenberger.

It seems that Greiffenberger failed in concealing his authorship, for on 10 November 1524 he was reprimanded by the council of Nürnberg for his 'unor-

1 See Martin Luther und die Reformation in Deutschland, 221–2.
2 Ibid, 222; Scribner, For the Sake of Simple Folk, 63–5. Note my rejection of Scribner's date (1520).
3 Thus Sachs's Underweisung and Greiffenberger's Ob das Euangelium (the latter was also published separately as Ein Christenliche Antwordt) were published together in 1524. A bibliography of Greiffenberger's works was published in 'Hans Denck und die gottlosen Maler in Nürnberg,' Beiträge zur bayerischen Kirchengeschichte 8 (1901), 12–13.

thodox' artistic contributions.[4] This confirms the fact that Greiffenberger was not an obedient Lutheran.

The attribution of the woodcut to Greiffenberger is based on more than circumstantial evidence. In fact, the woodcut visualizes and synthesizes the themes found in Greiffenberger's literary legacy. In *Falschen Propheten* (1523) Greiffenberger attacks the pretended mediators who deceive the common people. Most Protestants would not have included Augustine among the false mediators, but Greiffenberger had attacked him for basing the authority of the gospels on the authority of the church.[5] This, coupled with Greiffenberger's defence of the Epistle of James, reveals his Karlstadtian perspective on the biblical canon. The verse concerning the 'Man of Sin,' which appears above the traditionists in the woodcut, is also cited by Greiffenberger when he contrasts the pomp and luxury of the 'Man of Sin' with the poverty of Christ, 'the humblest lamb.'[6] In confusing John 14 with 10 the artist was undoubtedly citing from memory: a logical error because chapters 14 and 10 have the same general theme. Elsewhere Greiffenberger similarly refers to John 10 when he is in fact citing John 14:17, 26 and 16:13,[7] although he also refers to this favourite text accurately.[8] Hutten removed the traditionists, and thus a few petals but no garments are spread in his way. Dragging away the traditionists at the tail of the horse fits apocalyptic speculations concerning Rev 12:4, but then Hutten's horse symbolizes the Red Dragon, that is Satan. Greiffenberger would have shared Hutten's aversion towards the clerics, but Hutten's use of physical violence would have appalled Greiffenberger as a Karlstadtian. On the frontispiece backing the woodcut the triumph of truth is achieved by the 'sword of the Spirit.'[9] Greiffenberger also cites 'Isaiah 2[:4]: "Turn your weapons into sickles and your spears into plowshares." [Rom 12:19, etc]: "Leave vengeance to God."'[10] Greiffenberger asserts that believers may not wield the sword or engage in war; moreover, only Christ will vanquish Antichrist.[11]

4 Packull, *Mysticism and the Early South German-Austrian Anabaptist Movement*, 39.
5 Greiffenberger, *Ein Christenliche Antwordt* (1524), A2: 'Allen elenden blinden gotlosen menschen, die da sagen das Evangelion sey nichts on der kirchen bewarung ... und buchen auf Augustinum. Antwort.'
6 Greiffenberger, *Falschen Propheten* (1523), A2v.
7 Greiffenberger, *Ein warnung vor dem Teüffel* (1524), Bv.
8 Greiffenberger, *Ein Christenliche Antwordt* (1524), A2, 3.
9 *Martin Luther und die Reformation in Deutschland*, 221.
10 Greiffenberger, *Ein Christenliche Antwordt*, [A4]: 'Esaie secundo. Macht zu sicheln ewer waffen, und zu pflugschar ewre spiess. Lasst got die rach.'
11 Greiffenberger, *Ein kurtzer begriff von guten wercken* (1524), [A2v]: 'Wo es aber antrifft oder belaydigt got oder sein wort, so mögen sie es nit leyden, mit worten zu verfechten, unnd nit mit dem schwerdt, oder krieg der waffen'; [A3–v]: 'Darumb so wacht und wart wenn Christus kumme und uns erlöse. Dann er allain muss den Antichrist und sein Reich stürtzen.'

Greiffenberger's aversion to Luther is obvious, but a few points remain to be considered. In the woodcut Luther waves the quill and wears the professorial cap. Greiffenberger frowns on outward assertions of scholarly accomplishment, and like Karlstadt he rejects the title 'Master': 'We are now becoming aware of the lies of those who call themselves "Master," although Christ, our only master, had forbidden this.'[12] Since Augustine was included among the captives, Luther's Augustinian cowl would have revolted Greiffenberger, but like Karlstadt he went further and attacked all clerical attire: 'I pay no attention to what they wear, black or blue, white or brown cowls: such shit means nothing before God.' 'It is purely the work of the devil when one pays attention to garments – those are not good works when one wears clothing that differs from the ordinary world or the common people.'[13]

In deference to the claims of the pseudonymous Hans Freiermut, 1524 is the generally accepted date for the publication of the 'Triumphus Veritatis.' Greiffenberger's problems with the council during that year would support this date. However, work on the woodcut must have begun in early 1523, for the prominence of Ulrich von Hutten in the centre of the woodcut supports a date of composition before news of the defeat of the knights (Franz Sickingen surrendered 6 May 1523) reached Nürnberg. The frontispiece, which was originally printed on the back of the left section of the 'Triumphus Veritatis,' was probably composed after Hutten's defeat. Here Christ (rather than Hutten) is depicted as casting the Roman hierarchy into hell; in the background lies a town with a white mountain (a literal interpretation of 'Wittenberg'). On the bottom of the frontispiece is a couplet that attributes truth's triumph to the conquests, accomplished with the spiritual sword, of the 'Wittenberg Nightingale,' that is Luther. The frontispiece, then, was probably cut after the appearance of Hans Sachs's extensive poem in praise of Luther, 'The Wittenberg Nightingale,' which was published 8 July 1523. At this stage Greiffenberger probably wanted to show appreciation for Luther in the woodcut; indeed, he may have done so, for there is a straight seam which divides the left and central portions of the woodcut from the section on the right. It seems that Greiffenberger may have removed the section originally on the right; alternatively, it is possible that he intended to use two sections, but this is not as likely, for then the right-hand section would have been better integrated.

12 Greiffenberger, *Ein Christenliche Antwordt* (1524), A3v–[4]: 'Wir werden yetz gewar, was das für larven sindt, die sich meyster lassen nennen, uber das, so es Christus unser meyster in verbotten hat, des haben sy nit geacht.'

13 Greiffenberger, *Ein kurtzer begriff von guten wercken* (1524), [A3v–4]: 'Ich acht nicht was sie an tragen, schwartz oder blaw kutten, weiss oder braun mantel, sollicher dreck gilt nicht für got'; 'Es ist eytel teüffels werck, wer darauff helt, darumb so seind sollichs nit gutte werck, das einer ein ander klayd tragt, dann die gemain welt oder menschen.'

Greiffenberger may have repeated the theme of the putti strewing flowers (be-hind Luther) in order to provide continuity between the sections. The contrast between the two sections is especially obvious in the foreground, where stones appear on the right although there is only sandy soil on the left. It is likely that when Greiffenberger was working on the left and central section, he did not yet anticipate depicting Luther as one who walks on stony ground. In fact, this detail in itself is very revealing, for in Christ's parable of the seed that fell on stony ground, the seed springs up immediately, and therefore seems promising, until it is scorched because of the shallow soil – an apt illustration in the 'Triumphus' of Greiffenberger's own attitude towards Luther. In Greiffenberger's writings this turning point in his view of Luther falls between the publication of *Falschen Propheten* (1523), where 'the evangelical Doctor Martin Luther' is referred to,[14] and the rather hostile *Die Weltt sagt sy sehe kain besserung von den, die sy Lutherisch nennet* ('The World says it sees no improvement in those whom it calls Lutheran') (1523).

In *Die Weltt* Greiffenberger gives evidence of having been persuaded by Karlstadt's attack on images (*Bylder* (88)). The 'godless' painters of Nürnberg, like Hans Sebald and Barthel Beham, as well as Georg Pencz, once they became convinced of the incompatibility of Christianity and the visual arts, turned to worldly themes and Renaissance art.[15] However, Greiffenberger considered Renaissance art offensive; although Luther told laymen to remain in their previous callings, Greiffenberger disagreed: 'One does not improve by engaging in a work or a trade that deceives or offends one's neighbour, especially if one refuses to give it up like certain idol carvers, painters, and woodcutters. "Ah," they say, "even if the saints are worthless, then I'll depict whores and pimps," as if money were everything. Such an attitude is false and unchristian; because of it the Word of God is slandered and mocked.'[16]

Greiffenberger ended his artistic career on a note of premonition and hope: 'Dear brethren in Christ, let us call on God (in Spirit and in truth) that he may grant us his power and redemption, to suffer joyfully according to God's will. Amen.'

14 Greiffenberger, *Falschen Propheten* (1523), B2: 'Das vatter unsers ausslegung von dem ewange-lischen Doctor Martin Luther.' Nevertheless, for the sake of brevity and clarity I have simplified. Even in *Falschen Propheten* there are already Karlstadtian tendencies in Greiffen-berger's rejection of secret confession, his claim of a specific promise attached to the commu-nion cup, his attack on the intercession of the saints, etc. The Lutheran and Karlstadtian ele-ments clash on occasion; one should for example contrast the praise of 'Doctor Martin Luther' on leaf B2 with the attack on the *doctores*, [A4]. Moreover, even in his final Karlstadtian phase Greiffenberger does show a foreign admixture of apocalypticism.

15 See Zschelletzschky, *Die 'Drei Gottlosen Maler' von Nürnberg*, 59.

16 Greiffenberger, *Die Welt sagt sy sehe kain besserung von den, die sy Lutherisch nennet* (1523), A3v–[4]: 'Der ist auch nit gebessert, der ein handel hat oder ein handwerck, damit sein

Two years later Greiffenberger's premonition was fulfilled. As a follower of Karlstadt Greiffenberger would have considered the Lutheran sacrament of the altar blasphemous. He therefore followed Karlstadt's alternative: a proper private celebration at home.[17] Having been caught celebrating the Lord's Supper at home with his wife, Greiffenberger was banished from Nürnberg by decree of its council.[18]

nechster betrogen oder vereergert wirt, unnd nit darvon lasst, wie etlich thun, als bildschnitzer, Maler und Formschneider, etc. Ey sagen sy gelten die hailigen nicht, so will ich huren und buben machen, ob die gelt gulten, dass ist falsch und unchristlich, sollich leutt machen dass man das wort gottes verlestert und verspot.'

17 For Karlstadt see BARGE 1, 489: '(112) Verum non illum condemno qui privatim celebrat, propter hoc quod Christus dicit. Accipite et non dicit accipe. (113) Si ex Christi cena legem et formam veritatis sumere liceret, sequeretur, quod laici non possent privatim celebrare, neque sacramentum accipere, quia cum Christo soli episcopi accubuerunt.'

18 Philoon, 'Hans Greiffenberger,' MQR 36 (1962), 64. This event took place in August 1526.

Abbreviations

ARBUSOW   Leonid Arbusow *Die Einführung der Reformation in Liv-, Est- und Kurland*, QFRG 3. Leipzig: M. Heinsius Nachfolger 1921

ARG   *Archiv für Reformationsgeschichte*. Leipzig; Berlin 1903f

BARGE   Hermann Barge. *Andreas Bodenstein von Karlstadt* 1–2. Leipzig: Friedrich Brandstetter 1905. 2d ed. Nieuwkoop: B. de Graaf 1968

BR   WA (*Briefe*)

BRN   *Bibliotheca reformatoria neerlandica*, ed S[amuel] Cramer and F[redrik] Pijper. The Hague 1903–14

BUBENHEIMER   Ulrich Bubenheimer. *Consonantia theologiae et iurisprudentiae*, 'Jus ecclesiasticum' 24. Tübingen: J.C.B. Mohr (Paul Siebeck) 1977

BURRAGE   Champlin Burrage. *The Early English Dissenters in the Light of Recent Research (1550–1641)* 1–2. 2d ed. New York: Russell & Russell 1967

CC   *Corpus catholicorum*. Münster 1919f

CR   *Corpus reformatorum*. Braunschweig; Leipzig 1834f

DB   WA (*Deutsche Bibel*)

DENZINGER   *Enchiridion symbolorum*, ed Henricus Denzinger and Adolfus Schönmetzer. Ed XXXV emendata. Barcelona: Herder 1973

DEPPERMANN   Klaus Deppermann. *Melchior Hofmann: Soziale Unruhen und apokalyptische Visionen im Zeitalter der Reformation*. Göttingen: Vandenhoeck und Ruprecht 1979

FB   E[rnst] Freys and H[ermann] Barge. *Verzeichnis der gedruckten Schriften des Andreas Bodenstein von Karlstadt*. 2d ed. Nieuwkoop: B. de Graaf 1965

KÄHLER   Ernst Kähler. *Karlstadt und Augustin: Der Kommentar von Karlstadt zu Augustins Schrift De Spiritu et Litera*, 'Hallische Monographien' 10. Halle: Max Niemeyer 1952

KS   *Karlstadts Schriften aus den Jahren 1523–1525* 1–2, ed Erich Hertzsch. Halle (Saale): Max Niemeyer 1956–67

KT   *Kleine Texte für theologische und philologische Vorlesungen und Übungen*, ed Hans Lietzmann. Bonn: A. Marcus & E. Weber 1902f

302 Abbreviations

LEENDERTZ	W[illem] I]zaäk] Leendertz. *Melchior Hofmann*, 'Verhandelingen rakende den natuurlijken en geopenbaarden Godsdienst uitgegeven door Teylers Godgeleerd Genootschap,' ns 11/1. Haarlem: De erven F. Bohn 1883
LINDEN	Friedrich Otto zur Linden. *Melchior Hofmann, ein Prophet der Wiedertäufer,* 'Verhandelingen rakende den natuurlijken en geopenbaarden Godsdienst, uitgegeven door Teylers Godgeleerd Genootschap,' ns 11/2. Haarlem: De erven F. Bohn 1885
LÖSCHER	Valentin Ernst Löscher. *Vollständige Reformations-Acta und Documenta* 1–3. Leipzig: Johann Grossens Erben 1720–9
LW	*Luther's Works* 1–53, ed Helmut T. Lehmann and Jaroslav J[an] Pelikan. Philadelphia: Muhlenberg Press / Saint Louis: Concordia Publishing House 1955f
MS	*Thomas Müntzer, Schriften und Briefe*, ed Günther Franz and Paul Kirn, QFRG 33. Gütersloh: Gerd Mohn [ca 1968]
MQR	*Mennonite Quarterly Review*. Goshen 1927f
PL	*Patrologia cursus completus, series latina* 1–222, ed J[ean] P[aul] Migne. Paris 1844–90
QFRG	*Quellen und Forschungen zur Reformationsgeschichte*. Leipzig 1911f
SIDER	Ronald J[ames] Sider. *Andreas Bodenstein von Karlstadt: The Development of his Thought 1517–1525,* 'Studies in Medieval and Reformation Thought' 11, ed Heiko A[ugustinus] Oberman. Leiden: E.J. Brill 1974
SMYTH	*The Works of John Smyth, Fellow of Christ's College, 1594–8* 1–2, ed W[illiam] T[homas] Whitley. Cambridge: University Press 1915
TQ	*Quellen zur Geschichte der Täufer*. Leipzig 1930f
TQ SCHWEIZ	*Quellen zur Geschichte der Täufer in der Schweiz*. Zurich 1952f
TR	WA *(Tischreden)*
WA	*D. Martin Luthers Werke*. Weimar: Hermann Böhlau 1833f
WB	*Die Wittenberger Bewegung 1521 u. 1522*, ed Nikolaus Müller. 2d ed. Leipzig: M. Heinsius Nachfolger 1911
ZKG	*Zeitschrift für Kirchengeschichte*. Gotha; Tübingen, etc. 1876f
ZSKG	*Zeitschrift für schweizerische Kirchengeschichte*. Stans 1907f
Z	*Huldrych Zwinglis Sämtliche Werke*. Berlin; Zürich 1905f

Bibliography

The bibliography is divided into three sections: I Karlstadt's Works; II Hoffman's Works; and III General Bibliography (this contains all primary writings of authors other than Karlstadt and Hoffman; collected primary materials, entered by title or name of editor; and secondary materials). In sections I and II the titles of Karlstadt's and Hoffman's works are listed alphabetically according to the short form used in the notes. In alphabetizing, numbers in titles have been disregarded; thus *151 Theses* is entered under *Theses*. In section I complete titles are omitted for items listed in FB, and the numbers assigned to the works in FB are added in parentheses after the short titles. For these items, where printers, dates, or places of publication are added, this is a deliberate correction of FB. To aid in identifying new titles for the Karlstadt and Hoffman bibliographies book size is assumed to be quarto, unless otherwise indicated. For works that are unique or very rare, the location of the item is given ('location' abbreviated to 'L'). Virtually all of Karlstadt's works are available in North America. They are listed in *The National Union Catalog Pre–1956 Imprints* 290 (Mansell 1973), 31–6. See also vol 739 (Mansell 1981), 451.

I Karlstadt's Works

Ablas (28)   Von vormugen des Ablas ... Wittenberg 1520
Abschiedspredigt   'Karlstadts Zürcher Abschiedspredigt über die Menschwerdung Christi,' ed and intro Calvin Augustine Pater, *Zwingliana* 14/1 (1974), 1–[16]
Anbettung (68)   Von anbettung vnd ererbietung der tzeychen. Wittenberg 1521
Apologia   CONTRA PAPISTICAS LEGES SACERDOTIBVS PROHIBENTES MATRIMONIVM APOLOGIA *pastoris Cembergensis, qui nuper, suae Ecclesiae consensu, uxorem duxit.* [Basel: Adam Petri 1521]. Repr Apologia pro M. Barptolomeo Praeposito qui vxorem in sacerdotio duxit. [Erfurt: Mathes Maler] 1521. Also repr Apologia pro M. Bartholomeo Preposito Kembergensi: qui Antichristi iugum abijcies: primus nostro secolo uxorem in sacerdotio duxit. Iunio MCCCCC xxiiij. Königsberg: [Hans Weinreich]. Cf *Eheweÿber.* Karlstadt's authorship has been controversial. For the older argument see CR 1, 421. For Barge see 'Karlstadt, nicht Melanchthon,' ZKG 24 (1903), 310–20. Barge's view is now accepted in *Supplementa Melanchthoniana* 6, 167.

Ausslegung (15) Ausslegung vnnd Lewterung etzlicher heyligenn geschrifften. Leipzig 1519

Axiomata (153) Axiomata, Dispvtationis Pro Receptione ad facultatem Theologicam gymnasij Basiliensis. Basel 1535

Bedingung (36) Bedingung: Andres Bodenstein von Carolstat. Wittenberg 1520

Bucher (46) Welche bucher Biblisch seint. Wittenberg 1520

Bylder (88) Von abtuhung der Bylder, Vnd das keyn Betdler vnther den Christen seyn soll. Repr KT 74

Christus (124) Ob man mit heyliger schrifft erweysen müge, das Christus mit leyb, blůt vnd sele im Sacrament sey. [Basel 1524]

1 Co 1 (75) Sendbryff Andres Boden. von Carolstatt. Erklerung Pauli. Ich bitt euch brüder das yhr alle sampt ein meinung reden welt. 1 Co. 1. Wittenberg 1521

Coelibatu (plus FB no.) Svper Coelibatv Monachatv et Vidvitate Axiomata. Wittenberg 1521. Several eds were used; see FB 59–62.

Concilio (45) Appellation: zu dem Concilio Christlicher vorstendiger vorsamelung. Wittenberg 1520. Repr with annotations in BUBENHEIMER, 292–300

10 Concl. Conclusiones decem christianissime, in CONTENTA Vlrichi ab Hutten (see BARGE 1, 236 n 131). Repr BUBENHEIMER, 290–1

13 Concl. in JNSIGNIVM THEOLOGORVM [Paris: Pierre Vidoué 1520] (see WA 1, 222A). Repr WA 6, 26–7. For authorship cf Kähler, 'Nicht Luther, sondern Karlstadt,' ZKG 82 (1971), 351–60.

405 Concl. (3) CCCLXX [CCCLXXX!] ET APOLOGEticae Conclusiones. Wittenberg 1518. Repr LÖSCHER 2, 76–105; CC 1, 38–75

Confutatio (27) Confvtatio Aduersus epistolam Joannis Eckij. Wittenberg: Melchior Lotter 1520

Contra Eccum (16) Conclusiones contra D. Joannem Eccum. Wittenberg 1519. Theses repr in LÖSCHER 3, 289–91

1 Cor 10 (142) Erklerung des. x. Capitels Cor. i. Das brot das wir brechen: Ist es nitt ein gemeinschaft des Leybs Christi. [Augsburg: Philippp Ulhart d. Ä. 1525]

Defensio (11) DEFENSIO aduersus Eximii. D. Joannis Eckii. Wittenberg 1518. Repr LÖSCHER 2, 108–70

De intentionibus (1) De intentionibus. Opusculum compilatum ad Sanctissimi emulorum Thome commoditatem. [Leipzig 1507]

De spiritu (12) Pro Diuinae graciae defensione. DE SPIRITV ET LITERA. Wittenberg 1519 (preface 1517). Repr KÄHLER

Dialogus (126) Dialogus Von dem missbrauch, des hochwirdigsten sacraments. [Basel: Johann Bebel 1524]. Repr KS 2, [5]–49. English trans with intro by Carter Lindberg, 'Karlstadt's Dialogue on the Lord's Supper,' MQR 53 (1979), 35–77

Dialogus [1529] DJalogus und gründtliche berichtung gehaltner disputation im land zů Holsten vnderm Künig von Dennmarck, vom hochwirdigen Sacrament, oder Nachtmal des Herren. Strassburg: Balthasar Beck [1529]. L: University of Pennsyl-

vania, attributed to 'Hoffmann.' Repr Dialogus und gründtliche berichtung gehaltner Disputation, im land zů Holsten. [Augsburg: Philipp Ulhart d. Ä. 1529].
Repr of Strassburg ed in G. Th. Strobel, *Beiträge zur Litteratur besonders des sechs-
zehnten Jahrhunderts* 2/1. Nürnberg; Altdorf: Georg Peter Monath 1786. Karlstadt's authorship, based on Hoffman's account, is not controversial. The best argument appears in Faust, 'Bemerkungen,' 96–8. Martin Bucer would have had a hand
in having the *Dialogus* printed. See Köhler, *Zwingli und Luther* 1, 791–2.

Disputatio (21)   Disputatio excellentium quae cepta est Lipsiae. Edition based on FB
21–3 and two manuscripts in Seitz, *Der authentische Text der Leipziger Disputation
(1519)*, 14–54, 219–47

Distinctiones (2)   Distinctiones Thomistarvm πολλακι και κηπωρος ανηρ
μαλα καιριον ειπεν. Wittenberg: Johann-Rhau Grunenberg 1508

Eheweÿber   DAS die priester eheweÿber nemen mögen vnd sollen. [Speyer: Hans
Eckhart 1522]. This is an expanded German trans of *Apologia*. In *Supplementa
Melanchthoniana* 6/1, 73–4, 148, three editions from Wittenberg, Augsburg, and
Strassburg are listed. The original ed is: Das die Priester Ee weyber nemen mögen
und sollen [Wittenberg: Nickel Schirlentz 1521], L: Cornell University, attributed to
Bartholomäus Bernhardi. Another version is Schutzrede vor Magister Bartholemeo
Probst zu Kemmerig [!] [Erfurt: Mathes Maler]. For Karlstadt's authorship see
Apologia.

Empfahern (54)   Von den Empfahern: zeychen: vnd zusag des heyligenn Sacraments
fleysch vnd bluts Christi. Wittenberg 1521

Emphahung (76)   Predig. Von emphahung des heiligen Sacraments. Wittenberg 1521.
An English trans of *Emphahung* (78) (excerpts) is found in *Karlstadt's Battle*, ed
Sider, 7–15.

Endschuldigung (146)   Endschuldigung des falschen namens der auffrür. Mit vor-
rhede Luthers. Wittenberg 1525. Repr based on FB 146–7 in WA 18, [431–8], 438–45
(KS 2, [105]–18)

Engelen (122)   Uon Engelen vnd Teüffelen ein Sermon [Strassburg: Johann Schwan
1524]

Erklerung (148)   Erklerung von dem hochwirdigen Sacrament und andere. Wittenberg
1525. Repr WA 18, 455–66

Fegfeür (95)   Ein Sermon vom stand der Christ glaubigen Seelen von Abrahams schoss
vnd Fegfeür, der abgeschydnen Seelen. 1523. [Augsburg: Philipp Ulhart d. Ä.]

Fritzhans (49)   Antwort geweicht wasser belangend: Wider Fritzhans. Wittenberg 1521

Fürbit Marie (108)   Ain frage ob auch yemant möge selig werden on die fürbit
Marie [Augsburg: Philipp Ulhart d. Ä.] 1524. Original ed 1523

Gebett   'D. Andreas Carolstads gebett zu sanct Peter,' aij–aiij of Gemeine Andächtige
gebett, so man alle Zynsstag zur bůsspredig in den vier Pfarkilchen zu Basel haltet,
für den grüwlich en Türcken. Auch für alles anligen der Christenlichen Kilchen.
In dem 1541. Jor angefangen. [woodcut with printer's signet] Joel. 1. Bekerend

euch zu eüwerem Herren got, dann er ist güttig vnd barmhertzig. 8°. L: Basel Universitätsbibliothek. The printer's signet (2 basilisks turned to the left, with the coat of arms of Basel, a bishop's staff turned right), is lacking in Heitz-Bernouilli, *Basler Büchermarken*. Cf BARGE 2, *Anl*. 57, 613–14.

2 *Gebotten* (121) Von den zweyen höchsten gebotten der lieb Gottes, vnd des nechsten. Mathei. 22. [Strassburg: Johann Schwan 1524]. Repr KS 1, [49]–71

Gelassen (104) Was gesagt ist: Sich gelassen. [Augsburg: Philipp Ulhart d. Ä. 1523]. Repr 1618, 1693, 1698, under pseudonym of Valentin Weigel, according to Wernle 'Ein Traktat'

Gelassenheyt (38) Missiue vonn der gelassenheyt. Wittenberg 1520

Gelaub (139) WIe sich der gelaub vnd vnglaub gegen dem liecht vnd finsternus halten. [Basel 1524]

Gelubden (50) Uon gelubden unterrichtung. Wittenberg 1521

Gemach (138) Ob man gemach faren, und des ergernüssen der schwachen verschonen soll. [Basel 1524]. Repr KS 1, [73]–9. Modern German trans in Fast, *Der linke Flügel*, 251–69; English trans (excerpts) in *Karlstadt's Battle*, ed Sider, 50–71

Geschwigen (110) Vrsachen das And: Carolstat ein zeyt still geschwigen. Jena 1523. Repr KS 1, [1]–19

Gewaldt (63) Berichtung dyesser red. Das reich gotis, leydet gewaldt, vnd die gewaldtige nhemen oder rauben das selbig Matthei. XI. Wittenberg 1521

Hauptartickeln (145) Anzeyg etlicher Hauptartickeln Christlicher leere. [Augsburg: Philipp Ulhart d. Ä. 1525]. Repr KS 2, [59]–104. English trans (excerpts) in *Karlstadt's Battle*, ed Sider, 127–38

Heylickeit (44) Uon Bepstlicher heylickeit. Wittenberg 1520

Himmel- und Höllenwagen Will Gott. Szo württ vortewtschte erklerung beder wagen. [Augsburg: Melchior Ramminger 1519]. One leaf, 30 × 40.7 cm. Repr *Bilder-Katalog zu Max Geisberg, Der Deutsche Einblatt-Holzschnitt in der ersten Hälfte des XVI. Jahrhunderts* (München n.d.), no. 611f. Also in *Luther* (1979/2), 60–1, and in Bubenheimer, 'Andreas Bodenstein von Karlstadt,' [9], [21], [23]

Iustificatione (13) Epitome De impij iustificatione. Wittenberg 1519

Job VII (155) Erlüterung disser reed Iob VII. welcher hinunder inss grab faart der kumpt nit widerumb heruff. Item Uon der künfftigen vnd nüwen welt. Basel 1539

Leyb (129) Auszlegung dieser wort Christi. Das ist meyn leyb Luce am. 22. [Basel: Johann Bebel] 1524

Litera (65) De Legis Litera Sive carne, & spiritu. Wittenberg 1521

Loci (156) Loci Commvnes Sacrae Scriptvrae. Basel 1540

Malachiam (93) Predig oder homilien uber den propheten Malachiam. Wittenberg 1522

Messe (71) Von beiden gestaldten der heylige Messze. Wittenberg 1521

Messen (131) WIder die alte vnd newe Papistische Messen. [Basel 1524]. Augsburg
repr: WIder die alte vnd newe Papistische Messen. Andres Carolstat; M. D. XXv;
[Arabesque]. Sole signature: Aij. L: Stuttgart, Württembergische Landesbibliothek;
Strasbourg, Bibliothèque Nationale et Universitaire
'Militia Franciscana seu militia Christi,' ed Gerhard Hammer, ARG 69 (1978), 72:
24–75:17
Missbrauch (135) Von dem wider christlichen missbrauch des hern brodt vnd kelch.
[Basel: Johann Bebel 1524]. English trans. of *Missbrauch* (136) in *Karlstadt's Battle*,
ed Sider, 72–91

Ochssenfart (90) Byt vnd vermanung an Doctor Ochssenfart. Wittenberg 1522
Opus a Deo (24) Epistola adversus Eckii argvtatoris, qvi dixit Opvs bonvm esse a Deo
totvm, sed non totaliter. Wittenberg 1519

Praefatio AD PHILIPPENSES ANNOTATIVNCVLA, Per *Leonem Iudae, ex ore Huldrichi*
Zuinglij, excepta. TIGVRI APVD CHRISTOFFERO *Froschouer. Anno* M. D. XXXI. A2–4v.
L: Zürich, Zentralbibliothek. Karlstadt's dedication to Count Ulrich von Dornum
dates from 10 December 1530. Repr BARGE 2, 588–91
Priesterthum (112) Von dem Priesterthum vnd opffer Christi. Jena 1523

Sabbat (115) Von dem Sabbat vnd gebotten feyertagen. Jena 1524. Repr KS 1, [21]–47.
Excerpts in modern German trans in Fast, *Der Linke Flügel*, 249–69
Scripturis (34) De Canonicis Scriptvris Libellus. Wittenberg 1518–20. Repr Credner,
Zur Geschichte des Canons, [316]–412
Sermon-Lichtmess 'D. Andr. Carolstadts Sermon am Lichtmess. Tag.' (i.e. 2 February
1518), *Unschuldige Nachrichten von alten und neuen theologischen Sachen*. Leip-
zig 1703. 119–25

Testament (143) Von dem Newen vnd Alten Testament. [Augsburg: Philipp Ulhart d.
Ä. 1524]
Teuffelischen falhs (114) Ap Got ein vrsach sey des Teuffelischen falhs. Jena 1524
Themata (154) Themata Istaec, Deo Propitio, disputabimus, Basileae. [1538]
151 Theses (26 April 1517) in JNSIGNIVM THEOLOGORVM [Paris: Pierre Vidoué 1520]
(see Barge 1, 463–4). Repr KÄHLER, 11*–36*

Verba Dei (26) Verba Dei Contra D. Ioannem Eckium, qui manifestarie dixit, aliud
dicendum theologistis, aliud gregi Christiano. Wittenberg 1520
Vertrieben (141) Ursachen der halben Andres Carolstatt auss den landen Zů Sachsen
vertryben. [Strassburg: Johann Schwan 1524]. Repr KS 2, [50]–8
Von dem Tauff Dialogue, ed in monograph form by Felix Manz: 'Protestation und
Schutzschrift,' TQ SCHWEIZ 1, 23–8. Manz added one line towards the middle of p 27
('sidmal sich meister Ulrich vermeint') as well as most of the section from 'ze reden
ist mir' to the end of the page, but its High German content points to a similar
appeal by Karlstadt, who argued that he had been driven out of Saxony without a

hearing: KS 2, 61:2; *Testament* (143), A2. Corrections are based on the manuscript in Zurich, Staatsarchiv, E II 340, fo. 8r–9v. Modern German trans in Fast, *Der linke Flügel*, 28–35. English trans in *Anabaptist Beginnings (1523–1533). A Source Book*, ed Estep. Nieuwkoop: B. de Graaf 1976. 55–8

Was bann (119) Vorstandt des worts Pauli. Ich begeret ein vorbannter seyn von Christo, vor meyne brüder. Rhoma: 9. was bann vnd achte. Jena 1524

Wasser (30) Von geweychtem Wasser vnd salcz. Wittenberg 1520

Willen gottes (102) Uon manigfeltigkeit des eynfeltigen eynigen willen gottes. was sundt sey. [Köln: Arndt von Aich] 1523

Wirtschafft (81) Sendtbrieff von Carolstadt meldende seiner Wirtschafft. Wittenberg: [Johannes Rhau-Grunenberg 1522]. L: University of Pennsylvania; Yale

II Hoffman's Works

All of Hoffman's writings were consulted, but Hoffman's Strassburg period has not been fully treated. A number in parentheses following a title refers to the numbers assigned to Hoffman's works in the most complete bibliography (found in DEPPERMANN, 345–9); these titles are not cited in full. Other titles are cited to the extent that clear identification is possible. Locations have been given only for those treatises not listed by Deppermann. Modern reprints are mentioned only when they have been used; other reprints are listed by Kawerau, *Melchior Hoffman*, 130–4.

Two items, *Magestadt* and *Tuchenisse*, are in the private possession of Mr Helmuth Domizlaff in München, who kindly provided me with photocopies. He purchased five of Hoffman's tracts, which are listed in *Auktionskatalog Karl & Faber*, no 19 (June 1940), 13–15. Three tracts – *Erklerung* (variant of *Erklerung* (48) ?), *Froudenryke Tuchenis* (only excerpts survive: *Zeucknus* (17)), and *Vrien Wil* (18) – were destroyed when Mr Domizlaff's bookshop was bombed during the Second World War.

Apoc. 14 (17) Das freudenriche zeucknus vam worren friderichen ewigen evangelion, Apoc. 14. 1532. Excerpts in LINDEN, [429]–32

Ausslegung (11) Ausslegung der heimlichen Offenbarung Joannis. Melchior Hoffman M. D. xxx. [Title frame]. 8°

Bekentnuss Bekentnuss des MELCHIOR HOFMANNS vom kindertauf. Publ. Hulshof, *Geschiedenis van de Doopsgezinden te Straatsburg*, 180–1. Manuscript: Archives municipales de Strasbourg, M.A.H.E., XI, fol. 393v

Cantica canticorum (7) Dat Boeck Cantica Canticorum: edder dat hoge leedt Salomonis: vthgelecht dorch Melchior Hoffman. Kiel: [Melchior Hoffman's Press] 1529. L: Prague, Státni knihovna ČSR: 25 G 433 / Adligat 6. fol. (LXVIII) = 4, A4–Q4

Daniel 12 (3) Das xij Capitel des propheten Danielis auss gelegt. Mdxxvj. [Title frame]. [Stockholm: The Royal Press]. L: Toruń (Poland), Biblioteka Główna Uniwersyetu Mikołaja Kopernika. Photostat: Uppsala

Dat Nikolaus Amsdorff (4)   Dat Nicolaus Amsdorff der Meydeborger Pastor, nicht
weth, wat he setten, schriuen edder swetzen schal. [Kiel: Melchior Hoffman's Press]
1528. Facsimile of single copy (Zürich Zentralbibliothek) in *Schriften des Vereins
für schleswig-holsteinische Kirchengeschichte*, Supplement 5. Preetz: Hansen
1928
Dialogus [1529]   See Karlstadt.

Erklerung (15)   WArhafftige erklerung, das der Satan Todt, Hell, Sünd, vnd dy ewige
verdam nuss im vrsprung nit auss gott sunder alleyn auss eygenem will erwachsen
sei. M. H. Osee xiij 8° [Ettlingen (Baden): Valentin Kobian] 1531. L: Utrecht,
Universiteits-Bibliotheek (title-page missing); Dublin, Trinity College
Euangelion (16)   DAs ware trostliche vnnd freudenreiche Euangelion welchs zů dieser
letsten zeit aller welt sol offenbart vnd für getragen werden, durch die waren Apostolischen geister, vnd knecht dess Herrn Jesu Christi. M. H. 1531

Forchte gottes (23)   EIn rechte warhafftige hohe vnd götliche gruntliche vnderrich-
tung von der reiner forchte Gottes. 8° [Hagenau: Valentin Kobian] 1533. Polderman,
who added the epilogue, probably smuggled the original manuscript out of prison.

Gelöfigen (2)   An de gelöfigen vorsambling inn Liflant ein korte formaninghe van
Melcher Hoffman. M. D. XXvj [Title frame]. Sign. A2–A5. [Stockholm: The Royal
Press]. L: Zürich, Zentralbibliothek
Gesicht (Ursula Jost) (12)   Ed Melchior Hoffman. Prophetische gesicht vnd Offen-
barung, der götliche würckung zů diser letsten zeit. [Title frame] 8° 1530
Enlarged copy of title-page in Kawerau, *Melchior Hoffman*, Abb. 4, 100–1. Excerpt
in modern German in Fast, *Der linke Flügel*, 298–308

Leüchter (13)   Der leüchter des allten Testaments vss gelegt. 8° 1529? 1530?.
Enlarged copy of title-page in Kawerau, *Melchior Hoffman*, Abb. 3, 68–9. Contents
in LEENDERTZ, 373–81

Magestadt (19)   Van der waren hochprachtlichen eynigen magestadt gottes, vnnd vann
der worhaftigen menschwerdung des ewigen worttzs vnd Suns des allerhochsten. 8°
1532?. Imperfectly transcribed excerpts in LEENDERTZ, [382]–5; LINDEN, [432]–7. The
text contains two of Ursula Jost's visions in a discussion of the incarnation. The
visions are based on an expanded ed of *Gesicht (Ursula Jost)*. Thus the twenty-
second vision in *Gesicht* is called the twenty-sixth vision here.
Matt. 1 (6)   Dat erste Capitel des Evangelisten St. Mattheus. Kiel: [Melchior Hoffman's Press] 1528. Only the preface survives. See Johann Melchior Krafft, *Ein
Zweyfaches Zwey-Hundert-Jähriges Jubel-Gedächtnis*. Hamburg: Johann Wolff-
gang Fickweiler 1723. 106, 440–5
Michael Wachter (27)   Eyn sendbrieff an den achtbaren Michel wachter. 1534, ed
Ernst-Wilhelm Kohls, 'Ein Sendbrief Melchior Hofmanns aus dem Jahre 1534,'
Theologische Zeitschrift [Basel] 17 (1961), [356]–65. There is *very* slight Dutch
influence (use of 'hondert,' *sc* for *sch*, etc). The tract is Hoffman's, but Cornelis

Polderman may have written it down in prison and must have arranged for its publication. It was published under pseudonym of Caspar Beck.

Nasengeist (5) Das Niclas Amsdorff der Magdeburger Pastor ein lugenhafftiger falscher nasen geist sey. Kiel: [Melchior Hoffman's Press] 1528. Facsimile in *Schriften des Vereins für schleswig-holsteinische Kirchengeschichte*, Supplement 4, ed Gerhard Ficker. Preetz: Hansen 1926

Ordonnantie (14) Die Ordonnantie Godts De welcke hy, door zijnen Soone Christum Jesum, inghestelt ende bevesticht heeft. Amsterdam: Claes Gerretsz 1611. Dutch trans of lost original dating from 1530. Repr BRN 5, [145]–70. English trans by Williams, *Spiritual and Anabaptist Writers*, 'Library of Christian Classics' 25, 182–203

Prophecey (10) PRophecey oder weissagung uss warer heiliger götlicher schrifft. Von allen wundern vnd zeichen, biss zů der zůkunfft Christi Jesu. 1530

Romeren (21) Die eedele hoghe ende troostlike sendebrief, den die heylige Apostel Paulus to den Romeren gescreuenn heeft. 8° 1533. Published anonymously

S. Jacob (25) Die Epistel dess Apostels S. Jacobs erklärt. 8° [Strassburg: Jacob Cammerlander] 1534. Published by Johannes Eisenburgk (Cornelis Polderman?). Title-page reprinted in *Stultifera Navis* 8 (1946), 87. Excerpt in *TQ Elsass* 2, 241–5

S. Judas (26) Die Epistel des Apostell Sanct Judas erklert vnnd gantzs fleissig von wort zů worten, aussgelegt. 8° [Hagenau: Valentin Kobian] 1534. Published by Cornelis Polderman, who wrote the preface. Title-page reprinted in *Stultifera Navis* 8 (1946), 86. Excerpt: *TQ Elsass* 2, 245–8

Sendbrieff (22) Eyn sendbrieff an alle gotts förchtigen liebhaber der ewigen warheyt, inn welchem angezeyget seind die artickel des Melchior Hofmans. 8° 1533. Published under pseudonym of Caspar Becker (Cornelis Polderman?), who wrote the preface

Summarium Summarium dess was Melchior Hoffman im Thurm uff 24 Tücher geschriben hat (1537), ed T. W. Röhrich, *[Niedners] Zeitschrift für die historische Theologie* 30 (1860), 104–6

Tuchenisse (20) Een vvaraftyghe tuchenisse vnde gruntlyke verclarynge wo die worden tho den Ro.ix.Ca.van den Esau vnde Jacob soldene verstaen worden. 8° 1532. Privately owned by Helmuth Domizlaff

Vrien Wil (18) Verclaringe van den geuangenen ende vrien wil des menschen. 8° 1532? Title-page lost. Repr BRN 5, [183]–98

Weissagung (9) WEissagung vsz heiliger götlicher geschrifft. Von den trübsalen diser letsten zeit. [Strassburg: Balthasar Beck 1529?]. L: Freiburg i. Br. Also: Weyssagung auss Heiliger Gotlicher geschrifft. [Strassburg: Wolfgang Köpfel] 1530. L: Amsterdam, Universiteits-Bibliotheek, Afdeling Mennonitica

Zeucknus (24) Worhafftige zeucknus gegen Die nachtwechter vnd sternen, Das Der
   Dott mensch jhesus christus amm Kreuzs vnd jmm grab, nit ein angenomen fleisch
   vnd blut auss Maria seÿ, sundern allein Das pawre vnd ewige wortt, vnd Der
   unenedliche sun Des allerhochsten. 1533. Original manuscript: Strasbourg, Archives
   municipales, no. 76/45, 2. Imperfect transcripts in LEENDERTZ, [386]–92; LINDEN,
   [438]–44
Zu Derpten (1) Jhesus. Der Christlichen gemeyn zu Derpten ynn Liefflandt wunschet
   Melcher Hoffman Gnad vnd fride. Published in Luther, Bugenhagen, Hoffman, Eyne
   Christliche vormanung. Wittemberg. M. D. XXV [Title frame] [Michael Lotter]. 2d
   ed Ein Christenliche vermanung. [Augsburg: Heinrich Steiner]. Repr WA 18, 426–30

III General Bibliography

[Ainsworth, Henry, and Francis Johnson]. AN APOLOGIE OR DEFENCE OF SVCH TRVE CHRIS-
   TIANS as are commonly (but vniustly) called *Brovvnists*. [Amsterdam?] 1604. 2d ed
   Amsterdam: Da Capo Press 1970
*Aktensammlung zur Geschichte der Basler Reformation in den Jahren 1519 bis
   Anfang 1534* 1, ed Emil Dürr. Basel: Staatsarchiv 1921
Aktenstücke zur Wittenberger Bewegung Anfang 1522, ed Hermann Barge. Leipzig:
   J.C. Hinrichs 1912
Akten und Rezesse der livländischen Ständetage 3 (1494–1535), ed Leonid Arbusow.
   Riga: J. Deubner 1910
Album academiae Vitebergensis 1, ed C[=Karl] E[duard] Förstemann. Leipzig: Carolus
   Tauchnitius 1841
Althaus, Paul. *The Theology of Martin Luther*, trans Robert C. Schultz. Philadelphia:
   Fortress Press 1966
Amelung, Fr[iedrich Ludwig Balthasar]. *Melchior Hoffman in Livland und die Ein-
   führung der Reformation in den Landkirchspielen Dorpat und Rüggen im Jahre
   1525*, 'Sitzungsberichte der Gelehrten Estnischen Gesellschaft 1901.' Jurjew (Tartu):
   C. Mattiesen 1902
Amsdorf, Nikolaus. Das Melchior Hoffman ein falscher Prophet vnd sein leer vom
   Jüngsten tag vnrecht, falsch vnd widder Gott ist. Niclas Amsdorff. 1528. [Title
   frame] [Magdeburg: Hans Bart]. Cited as *Falscher Prophet* L: Braunschweig, Stadt-
   bibliothek
– DAs Melchior Hoffman nicht ein wort auff mein Büchlein geantwort hat. Niclas
   Amsdorff M. D. XXViij [Magdeburg: Hans Bart]. Cited as *Nicht ein wort* L: Gotha,
   Forschungsbibliothek
– Ein vormanung an die von Magdeburg das sie sich fur falschen Propheten zu hüten
   wissen. Nicolaus Amsdorff. M. D. XXVij. Magdeburg: Hans Bart. Cited as *Vor-
   manung* L: Göttingen, Niedersächsische Staats und Universitätsbibliothek
Armour, Rollin Stely. *Anabaptist Baptism: A Representative Study*. Scottdale: Herald
   Press [ca 1966]
Arndt, Johann Gottfried. *Liefländische Chronik. Andrer Theil, Liefland unter seinen
   Herren Meistern, welche die alte Geschichte des Ordens und der benachbarten
   Völker erleuchtert*. Halle: Johann Justinus Gebauer 1753

Aus dem Kampf der Schwärmer gegen Luther. Drei Flugschriften, ed Ludwig Enders. Halle am Saale: Max Niemeyer 1893

De Avondmaalsbrief van Cornelis Hoen (1525), facsimile, ed and intr A[lbert] Eekhof. The Hague: Martinus Nijhoff 1917

Balke, Willem. *Calvin and the Anabaptist Radicals*, trans William Heynen. Grand Rapids: William B. Eerdmans 1981

Bangs, Carl. *Arminius: A Study in the Dutch Reformation*. Nashville: Abingdon Press 1971

Barge, Hermann. 'Die älteste evangelische Armenordnung,' *Historische Vierteljahrschrift* 11 (1908), 193–225

– 'Karlstadt, nicht Melanchthon, der Verfasser der unter den Namen des Bartholomäus Bernhardi von Feldkirch gehenden Schrift Apologia pro Bartholomeo Proposito,' ZKG 24 (1903), 310–18

– 'Luther und Karlstadt in Wittenberg: Eine kritische Untersuchung,' *Historische Zeitschrift* 99 (1907), 256–324

– 'Der Streit über die Grundlagen der religiösen Erneuerung in der Kontroverse zwischen Luther und Karlstadt 1524/25,' *Studium Lipsiense: Ehrengabe Karl Lamprecht*. Berlin: Weidmannsche Buchhandlung 1909. 192–213

– 'Über eine vergessene Schrift Karlstadts,' *Theologische Studien und Kritiken* 74 (1901), 522–33

– 'Die Übersiedlung Karlstadts von Wittenberg nach Orlamünde,' *Zeitschrift des Vereins für thüringische Geschichte und Altertumskunde* 21 (1913), 338–50

Bauch, Gustav. 'Andreas Carlstadt als Scholastiker,' ZKG 18 (1897–8), 37–57

Bauer, Karl. *Die Wittenberger Universitätstheologie und die Anfänge der Deutschen Reformation*. Tübingen: J.C.B. Mohr 1928

Beachy, Alvin J[ames]. *The Concept of Grace in the Radical Reformation*. Nieuwkoop: B. de Graaf 1977

Bender, Harold S[tauffer]. *Conrad Grebel c. 1498–1526, Founder of the Swiss Brethren*. Scottdale: Herald Press 1950

– 'Die Zwickauer Propheten, Thomas Müntzer und die Täufer,' *Theologische Zeitschrift* (Basel) 8 (1952), 262–78. English trans in MQR 27 (1953), 3–16

Benzing, Josef. *Die Buchdrucker des 16. und 17. Jahrhunderts im deutschen Sprachgebiet*, 'Beiträge zum Buch- und Bibliothekwesen' 12. Wiesbaden: Otto Harrassowitz 1963

Berendts, Alexander. 'Johann von Blankenfeld, Erzbischof von Riga, Bischof von Dorpat und Reval,' *Baltische Monatsschrift* 54, 23–60. Riga: Verlag der Baltischen Monatsschrift 1902

Bergendoff, Conrad. *Olavus Petri and the Ecclesiastical Transformation in Sweden (1521–1552)*. New York: Macmillan 1928

Biel, Gabriel. *Collectorium circa quattuor libros Sententiarum Prologus et Liber primus*. Collaborantibus Martino Elze et Renata Steiger, ediderunt Wilfridus Werbeck et Udo Hofmann. Tübingen: J.C.B. Mohr (Paul Siebeck) 1973

Bilder-Katalog zu Max Geisberg Der Deutsche Einblatt-Holzschnitt in der ersten Hälfte des XVI. Jahrhunderts. 1600 verkleinerte Wiedergaben, ed Hugo Schmidt. München: Hugo Schmidt n.d.

Bornhäuser, Christoph. *Leben und Lehre Menno Simons: Ein Kampf um das Fundament des Glaubens (etwa 1496–1561)*. Neukirchen-Vluyn: Neukirchener Verlag 1973

Bossert, G[ustav]. 'Küngold Bodenstein,' ARG 17 (1920), [153]

Böthfür, H[einrich] J[ulius]. 'Einige Bemerkungen zu Sylvester Tegetmeier's Tagebuch,' *Mittheilungen aus der livländischen Geschichte* 13/1, 61–84. Riga: Nicolaus Kymmel 1881

Brachmann, Wilhelm. *Die Reformation in Livland*, 'Mittheilungen aus dem Gebiete der Geschichte Liv-, Est- und Kurlands' 5/1. Riga: Nicolaus Kymmel 1849

Brecht, Martin. 'Herkunft und Eigenart der Taufanschauung der Züricher Täufer,' ARG 64 (1973), 147–65

Bredenbach, Tilmann. BELLI LIVONICI QVOD MAGNUS MOSCHOVIAE DVX, ANNO 1558. contra Liuones gessit, noua et memorabilis historia [Printer's Signet] 8°, Sign Aij–H5. COLONIAE, Apud Maternum Cholinum, Anno 1564. L: Kiel, Universitätsbibliothek. 2d ed in HISTORIAE RUTHENICAE SCRIPTORES EXTERI SAECULI XVI, 1, ed Adalbertus [= Wojciech] de Starczewski. Berlin: F. Reichardt 1841. L: Harvard University

Brieger, T[heodor]. 'Thesen Karlstadt's,' ZKG 11 (1890), 479–82

Brinkel, Karl. *Die Lehre Luthers von der fides infantium bei der Kindertaufe*, 'Theologische Arbeiten' 7. Berlin: Evangelische Verlagsanstalt [1958]

Brons, A[ntje]. *Ursprung, Entwickelung und Schicksale der Altevangelischen Taufgesinnten oder Mennoniten in kurzen Zügen übersichtlich dargestellt*, 3d ed. Emden: Th. Hahn Wwe 1912

Bruns, F[riedrich], and H[ugo] Weczerka. *Hansische Handelsstrassen* 1–3, 'Quellen und Darstellungen zur Hansischen Geschichte' 13/1–3. Köln: Böhlau Verlag 1962

Bruun, Christian. 'Skrifter i Anledning af Melchior Hofmans Laere,' *Den danske Literatur til 1550* 1. Copenhagen: 1870. 393–7

Bubenheimer, Ulrich. 'Andreas Rudolff Bodenstein von Karlstadt. Sein Leben, seine Herkunft und seine innere Entwicklung,' *Andreas Bodenstein von Karlstadt 1480–1541, Festschrift der Stadt Karlstadt zum Jubiläumsjahr 1980*. Karlstadt: Michel-Druck 1980. [5–58]

– 'Scandalum et ius divinum. Theologische und rechtstheologische Probleme der ersten reformatorischen Innovationen in Wittenberg 1521/22,' *Zeitschrift der Savigny-Stiftung für Rechtsgeschichte* 90, 'Kanonistische Abteilung' 59. [1973], [263]–342

Bugenhagen, Johannes. Acta der Disputation zu Flensburg [Title frame] 8°. Wittenberg: Joseph Klug 1529. L: Hamburg, Staats- und Universitätsbibliothek

– Eynne rede vam sacramente. Dorch Joannem Bugenhagen Pomeren tho Flensborch nha Melchior Hoffmans dysputatien geredet. 8°. Hamburg: [Jürgen Richolff d. J.] 1529. L: Copenhagen, Kongelige Bibliotek; Hamburg, Staats- und Universitätsbibliothek

Clasen, Claus-Peter. 'Anabaptist Sects in the Sixteenth Century: A Research Report,' MQR 46 (1972), 256–79

Clemen, Otto C[onstantin]. *Beiträge zur Reformationsgeschichte aus Buchern und Handschriften der Zwickauer Ratschulbibliothek* 1–3. Berlin: C.H. Schwetschke 1900–3

Continuity and Discontinuity in Church History, Essays presented to George Huntston Williams, ed F. Forester Church and Timothy George, 'Studies in the History of Christian Thought' 19. Leiden: E. J. Brill 1979

Cornelius, C[arl] A[dolf]. *Berichte der Augenzeugen über das Münsterische Wiedertäuferreich*. Münster: Theissing 1853

– *Geschichte des Münsterischen Aufruhrs in drei Büchern* 1–2. Leipzig: T.O. Weigel 1855–60

– 'Die Niederländischen Wiedertäufer während der Belagerung Münsters 1534–1535,' *Abhandlungen der historischen Classe der Königlich Bayerischen Akademie der Wissenschaften* 11. München: Verlag der K. Akademie 1870 [appeared in 1869]

Corpus scriptorum ecclesiasticorum latinorum. Milan, Vienna, Prague, Leipzig 1866f

Credner, Karl August. *Zur Geschichte des Canons*. Halle: Waisenhaus 1847

Crous, Ernst. 'Von Melchior Hofmann zu Menno Simons,' *Mennonitische Geschichtsblätter* 19, ns 14 (1962), 2–14

Davis, Kenneth Roland. *Anabaptism and Asceticism*, 'Studies in Anabaptist and Mennonite History' 16. Scottdale: Herald Press 1974

Denck, Hans. *Schriften*, ed Georg Baring, QFRG 24 (TQ 6), 1–2. Gütersloh: C. Bertelsmann 1955

Deppermann, Klaus. 'Hoffmans letzte Schriften aus dem Jahre 1534,' ARG 63 (1972), 72–93

– 'Melchior Hoffman. Widersprüche zwischen lutherischer Obrigkeitstreue und apokalyptischen Traum,' *Radikale Reformatoren*, 155–[166]

– 'Melchior Hoffmans Weg von Luther zu den Täufern,' *Umstrittenes Täufertum*, ed Hans Jürgen Goertz, 223–43

– 'Die Strassburger Reformatoren und die Krise des oberdeutschen Täufertums im Jahre 1527,' *Mennonitische Geschichtsblätter* 30, ns 25 (1973), 24–41·

Dexter, Morton. *The England and Holland of the Pilgrims*. Boston: Houghton, Mifflin 1905

Dietz, Alexander. *Frankfurter Handelsgeschichte* 1. Frankfurt: Hermann Minjon 1910

Documenta anabaptistica neerlandica 1, ed A[lbert] F[redrik] Mellink. Leiden: E. J. Brill 1975

The Dom Cathedral Architectural Ensemble in Riga, ed Yuri Vasilyev. Leningrad: Aurora Art Publishers 1980

Doornkaat Koolman, J[acobus] ten. *Dirk Philips. Vriend en medewerker van Menno Simons*. Haarlem: H.D. Tjeenk Willink & Zoon 1964

Douglas, Crerar. 'The Coherence of Andreas Bodenstein von Karlstadt's Early Evangelical Doctrine of the Lord's Supper: 1521–1525.' PHD thesis, Hartford Seminary Foundation 1973

Dunkley, E[rnest] H[ale]. *The Reformation in Denmark*. London: S.P.C.K. 1948

Dürer, Albrecht. *The Complete Woodcuts*, ed Willi Kurth, trans Silvia M. Welsh. New York: Dover 1963

Dyck, Cornelius J. 'The First Waterlandian Confession of Faith,' MQR 36 (1962), 5–13

– 'The Middelburg Confession of Hans de Ries, 1578,' MQR 36 (1962), 147–54

Edwards, Mark U. *Luther and the 'False Brethren.'* Stanford: University Press 1975

Egli, Emil, ed. *Aktensammlung zur Geschichte der Zürcher Reformation in den Jahren 1519–1533*. Zürich: J. Schabelitz 1879

– *Schweizerische Reformationsgeschichte* 1. Zürich: Zürcher & Furrer 1910

Erasmus, Desiderius. *Opera omnia*. Leiden: Peter van der Aa 1703. 2d ed London: Gregg Press [1961?]

Estep, William R[oscoe]. *The Anabaptist Story*, rev ed. Grand Rapids: Eerdmans [1975]

– 'A Baptist Reappraisal of Sixteenth Century Anabaptists,' *[Baptist] Review and Expositor* 55 (1958), [40]–58

Die Evangelischen Katechismusversuche vor Luthers Enchiridion 1, ed and intro Ferdinand Cohrs, 'Monumenta Germaniae Paedagogica' 20. Berlin: A. Hofmann 1900

Estes, James Martin. *Christian Magistrate and State Church: The Reforming Career of Johannes Brenz*. Toronto: University of Toronto Press 1982

Farner, Oskar. *Huldrych Zwingli* 1–4. Zürich: Zwingli-Verlag 1943–60

Fast, Heinold. 'Konrad Grebel. Das Testament am Kreuz,' *Radikale Reformatoren*, 103–[14]

– ed and trans. *Der Linke Flügel der Reformation, Glaubenszeugnisse der Täufer, Spiritualisten, Schwärmer und Antitrinitarier*, 'Klassiker des Protestantismus herausgegeben von Christel Matthias Schröder' 4. Bremen: Carl Schünemann 1962

Faust, Georg. 'Einige Bemerkungen zu Melchior Hofmanns "Dialogus,"' *Schriften des Vereins für schleswig-holsteinische Kirchengeschichte* 2d ser 3/1, 96–8. Kiel: Robert Cordes 1904–5

Fischer, E[rnst]. *Zur Geschichte der evangelischen Beichte* 1–2, 'Studien zur Geschichte der Theologie und der Kirche' 8/2, 9/4. Leipzig: Dieterichsche Verlags-Buchhandlung 1902–3

Friedensburg, Walter. 'Beiträge zum Briefwechsel der katholischen Gelehrten Deutschlands im Reformationszeitalter. Aus italienischen Archiven und Bibliotheken,' ZKG 16 (1896), 470–99, esp 492–3

– ed, *Urkundenbuch der Universität Wittenberg* 1 (1502–1611), 'Geschichtsquellen der Provinz Sachsen und des Freistaates Anhalt' ns 3. Magdeburg: Historische Kommission der Provinz Sachsen 1926

– 'Der Verzicht Karlstadts auf das Wittenberger Archidiakonat und die Pfarre in Orlamünde (1524 Juni),' ARG 11 (1914), 69–72

Fuchs, Gerhard. 'Karlstadts radikal-reformatorisches Wirken und seine Stellung zwischen Müntzer und Luther,' *Wissenschaftliche Zeitschrift der Martin-Luther-Universität Halle-Wittenberg* 3 (1953–4), 523–51

Garside, Charles, Jr. 'Ludwig Haetzer's Pamphlet Against Images: A Critical Study,' MQR 34 (1960), 20–36

– *Zwingli and the Arts*. New Haven: Yale University Press 1966

Gerdes, Daniel, ed. *Scrinium Antiquarium sive Miscellanea Groningana Nova ad historiam reformationis ecclesiasticam praecipue spectantia* 1–4. Groningen: Hajo Spandaw & G.W. Rump 1749–65. L: Boston, Public Library

Gerdes, Hayo *Luthers Streit mit den Schwärmern um das rechte Verständnis des Gesetzes Mose*. Göttingen: Göttinger Verlagsanstalt 1955

Goeters, J.F. Gerhard. *Ludwig Hätzer (ca. 1500 bis 1529) Spiritualist und antitrinitarier, Eine Randfigur der frühen Täuferbewegung*, QFRG 25. Gütersloh: C. Bertelsmann 1957

– 'Die Vorgeschichte des Täufertums in Zürich,' *Studien zur Geschichte und Theologie der Reformation, Festschrift für Ernst Bizer*, ed Luise Abramowski and J.F. Gerhard Goeters. [Neukirchen-Vluyn] Neukirchener Verlag 1969. [239]–81

– 'Zwinglis Werdegang als Erasmianer,' *Reformation und Humanismus Robert Stupperich zum 65. Geburtstag*, ed Martin Greschat and J.F. G[erhard] Goeters. Witten: Luther-Verlag 1969. 255–71

[Grebel, Konrad]. *Conrad Grebel's Programmatic Letters*, ed J[ohn] C[hristian] Wenger. Review by Alvin J[ames] Beachy, MQR 45 (1971), 153–6

Gritsch, Eric W[alter]. *Reformer Without a Church: The Life and Thought of Thomas Muentzer*. Philadelphia: Fortress Press 1967

Grossmann, Maria. *Humanism in Wittenberg, 1485–1517*. Nieuwkoop: B. de Graaf 1975

Haas, Martin. 'Michael Sattler. Auf dem Weg in die täuferische Absonderung,' *Radikale Reformatoren*, 115–[24]

– 'Der Weg der Täufer in die Absonderung,' *Umstrittenes Täufertum*, [50]–78

Hartfelder, Karl. *Philipp Melanchthon als Praeceptor Germaniae*. Berlin: A. Hoffman 1889; 2d ed Nieuwkoop: B. de Graaf 1964

Hartmann, Alfred. *Die Amerbachkorrespondenz* Basel: Verlag der Universitätsbibliothek 1942–74

Hase, E[duard Friedrich]. 'Karlstadt in Orlamünda,' *Mitteilungen der Geschichts- und Altertumsforschende Gesellschaft des Osterlandes* 4 (1858), 42–125

Hase, Martin von. *Johann Michael genannt Michel Buchfürer alias Michel Kremer*. 'Studien zur Deutschen Kunstgeschichte' 259. Strassburg: J.H. Ed. Heitz 1928

– 'Johann Michael genannt Michel Buchfürer alias Michel Kremer, Buchführer und Buchdrucker in Erfurt und Jena, Nachtrag,' *Gutenberg Jahrbuch 1957*, 131–6

Hätzer, Ludwig. Baruch der Prophet. Die Histori Susannah. Die histori Bel zu Babel Alles newlich auss der Bybli verteutscht. O Gott erlöss die gfangnen Anno M. D. XXVIII. Small 4°. [Zürich: Christoph Froschauer] L: München, Staatsbibliothek

– Ein vrteil gottes vnsers eegemahels wie man sich mit allen götzen vnd bildnussen halten sol vss der heiligen gschrifft gezogen durch Ludwig Hätzer. Getruckt zů Zürich Durch Christophorum Froschouer O Gott erlös die gfangnen: [1523]. L: Basel, Bibliothek der Universität

Hausmann, R[ichard]. 'Die Monstranz des Hans Ryssenberg in der K. Ermitage zu St. Petersburg,' *Mittheilungen aus der livländischen Geschichte* 17/2 (1899), [185]–95

– 'Zu Sylvester Tegetmeier's Tagebuch,' *Sitzungsberichte der Gesellschaft für Geschichte und Altertumskunde der Ostseeprovinzen Russlands aus dem Jahre 1898*. Riga: W.F. Häcker 1899

[Helwys, Thomas]. OBIECTIONS Answered by way of Dialogue. [London?] 1615. 2d ed Amsterdam: Da Capo Press 1973

- A SHORT DECLARATION of the mistery of iniquity. [Amsterdam?] 1612. 2d ed London: The Kingsgate Press 1935

Herminjard, A[imé] L[ouis]. *Correspondance des Réformateurs dans les pays de langue Française* 3. Genève: H. Georg 1870. 2d ed Nieuwkoop: B. de Graaf, 1965–6

Herriot, Duncan B. 'Anabaptism in England during the 16th and 17th Centuries,' *Transactions of the Congregational Historical Society* 12 (1933–6), 256–71

Hertzsch, Erich. *Karlstadt und seine Bedeutung für das Luthertum*. Gotha: Leopold Klotz 1932

- 'Luther und Karlstadt,' *Luther in Thüringen: Gabe der Thüringer Kirche an das Thüringer Volk*, ed Reinhold Jauernig. Berlin: Evangelische Verlagsanstalt 1952. 87–107

Heyer, Fritz. *Der Kirchenbegriff der Schwärmer*, 'Schriften des Vereins für Reformationsgeschichte' 56/2, no. 166. Leipzig: M. Heinsius Nachfolger 1939

Hillerbrand, Hans J[oachim]. 'Andreas Bodenstein of Carlstadt,' *Church History* 35 (1966), 379–98

- 'Luther's "Deserting Disciples": An Anniversary Reflection on the Anabaptists of the Sixteenth Century,' *McCormick Quarterly* 21 (1967), 105–13

- 'The Origins of Sixteenth-Century Anabaptism: Another Look,' ARG 53 (1962), 152–80

- 'Thomas Müntzer,' *Reformers in Profile*, ed B[rian] A[lbert] Gerrish. Philadelphia: Fortress Press 1967. 213–29

- 'Thomas Müntzer's Last Tract Against Martin Luther: A Translation and Commentary,' MQR 38 (1964), 20–36

Holl, Karl. 'Luther und die Schwärmer,' *Gesammelte Aufsätze zur Kirchengeschichte* 1. Tübingen: J.C.B. Mohr 1932. 420–67

- 'Melchior Hofmann,' *Mennonite Encyclopedia* 2. Scottdale, PA: 1956. 778–85

Horst, Irvin B[uckwalter]. 'Menno Simons. Der neue Mensch in der Gemeinschaft,' *Radikale Reformatoren*, 179–[189]

- *The Radical Brethren: Anabaptism and the English Reformation to 1558*. Nieuwkoop: B. de Graaf 1972

Howorth, Henry H[oyle]. 'The Origin and Authority of the Biblical Canon according to the Continental Reformers: 1 Luther and Karlstadt,' *The Journal of Theological Studies* 8 (1907), [321]–65

Hoyer, Siegfried. 'Martin Reinhart und der erste Druck hussitischer Artikel in Deutschland,' *Zeitschrift für Geschichtswissenschaft* 18 (1970), [1595]–1615

- 'Nicolaus Rutze und die Verbreitung hussitischer Gedanken im Hanseraum,' *Neue hansische Studien, Forschungen zur mittelalterlichen Geschichte* 17 (1970), [157]–170

Hubmaier, Balthasar. *Schriften*, ed Gunnar Westin and Torsten Bergsten, QFRG 19 (TQ 9). Gütersloh: Gerd Mohn 1962

Hudson, Winthrop S[till]. 'Baptists Were Not Anabaptists,' *The Chronicle* 16 (1953), 171–9

- 'The Ecumenical Spirit of Early Baptists,' *[Baptist] Review and Expositor* 55 (1958), [182]–95

Hulshof, Abraham. *Geschiedenis van de Doopsgezinden te Straatsburg van 1525 tot 1557*. Amsterdam: J. Clausen 1905
Husner, F[ritz]. 'Zwei unbekannte Wiedertäuferdrucke?' *Stultifera Navis* 8/3–4 (1946), 84–8

Ickelsamer, Valentin. Clag etlicher brüder: an alle christen von der grossen vngerechtikeyt vnd Tirannei, so Endressen Bodenstein von Carolstat yetzo vom Luther zů Wittenbergk geschicht. Valentinus Ickelschamer zů Rotenburg vff der thawber. [1525]. Repr *Aus dem Kampf der Schwärmer*, ed Ludwig Enders, 41–55
– Ein Ernstlich vnd wunderlich gesprech zwayer kinder mit einander. [Bamberg? Wertheim? Georg Erlinger] 1525. Repr 'Die Evangelischen Katechismusversuche,' ed Ferdinand Cohrs, [128]–42
– *Die rechte weis aufs kürtzist lesen zu lernen* (1527) and *Ain Teütsche Grammatica* (1537), ed Karl Pohl. Stuttgart: Ernst Klett Verlag 1971
Ingebrand, Sven. *Olavus Petris reformatoriska åskådning*, 'Acta Universitatis Upsaliensis, Studia Doctrinae Christianae Upsaliensia' 1. Lund: C.K.W. Gleerup 1964

Jäger, C.F. *Andreas Bodenstein von Carlstadt: Ein Beitrag zur Geschichte der Reformationszeit aus Originalquellen gegeben* Stuttgart: Rudolf Besser 1856
Jordan, W[ilbur] K[itchener]. *The Development of Religious Toleration in England* 1–5. London: George Allen and Unwin 1932

Kähler, Ernst. 'Karlstadt's Protest gegen die theologische Wissenschaft,' *450 Jahre Martin-Luther-Universität Halle-Wittenberg*. Halle-Wittenberg: Martin-Luther-Universität 1952. 299–312
– 'Nicht Luther, sondern Karlstadt' (zu WA 6, 26f.), ZKG 82 (1971), 351–60
Karlstadt's Battle with Luther: Documents in a Liberal-Radical Debate, ed and trans Ronald J[ames] Sider. Philadelphia: Fortress Press 1978. Reviews by Calvin Augustine Pater, *The Sixteenth Century Journal* 10/1 (1979), 107; Carter Lindberg, MQR 53 (1979), 86–7
Kawerau, Gustav. *Der Briefwechsel des Justus Jonas*. Halle: O. Hendel 1884. 2d ed Hildesheim: Georg Olms 1964
Kawerau, Peter. *Melchior Hoffman als religiöser Denker*. Haarlem: De erven F. Bohn 1954. Review by Henry Poettcker, MQR 45 (1971), 98–9
– 'Zwei unbekannte Wiedertäufer-Drucke,' ZKG 69 (1958), [121]–6
Keeney, William Echard. *The Development of Dutch Anabaptist Thought from 1539–1564*. Nieuwkoop: B. de Graaf 1968
Kleiner, John Walter. 'Andreas Bodenstein von Karlstadt's Eschatology as Illustrated by two Major Writings of 1523 and 1539.' THM thesis, Harvard Divinity School 1966
Kliever, Lonnie D[ean]. 'General Baptist Origins: The Question of Anabaptist Influence,' MQR 36 (1962), 291–321
Köhler, Walther. 'Aus Zwinglis Bibliothek, Randglossen,' ZKG 40 (1922), [41]–73; 42 (1923), 49–76; 45 (1927), 243–76
– 'Huldrych Zwinglis Bibliothek,' *Neujahrsblatt auf das Jahr 1921*, [1]–*49
– *Zwingli und Luther* 1, QFRG 6, 1924

Kohls, Ernst-Wilhelm. 'Ein Sendbrief Melchior Hofmanns aus dem Jahre 1534,' *Theologische Zeitschrift [Basel]* 17 (1961), [356]–65

Kolb, Robert. *Nikolaus von Amsdorf: 1483–1565, Popular Polemics in the Preservation of Luther's Legacy*. Nieuwkoop: B. de Graaf 1978

Kolde, Th[eodor von]. 'Wittenberger Disputationsthesen aus den Jahren 1516–1522,' ZKG 11 (1890), 448–71

Konung Gustaf den förstes registratur, första serien 4 (1527), ed J.A. Nordström. Stockholm: P.A. Norstedt & Söner 1868

Krafft, C. 'Mittheilungen aus der Matrikel der alten Cölner Universität zur Zeit des Humanismus,' *Zeitschrift für Preussische Geschichte und Landeskunde* 5 (1868), 467f

Krahn, Cornelius. *Dutch Anabaptism, Origin, Spread, Life and Thought (1450–1600)*. The Hague: Martinus Nijhoff 1968

– *Menno Simons (1496–1561) ein Beitrag zur Geschichte und Theologie der Taufgesinnten*. Karlsruhe i. B.: H. Schneider 1936

Krajewski, Ekkehard. *Leben und Sterben des Zürcher Täuferführers Felix Mantz*. Kassel: J.G. Oncken Verlag [1958]

– 'The Theology of Felix Mantz,' MQR 36 (1962), 76–87

Kriechbaum, Friedel. *Grundzüge der Theologie Karlstadts: Eine systematische Studie zur Erhellung der Theologie Andreas Karlstadts (eigentlich Andreas Bodenstein 1480–1541), aus seinen eignen Schriften entwickelt*, 'Theologische Forschung' 43. Hamburg-Bergstedt: Herbert Reich Evangelischer Verlag 1967

Krohn, Barthold Nicolaus. *Geschichte der Fanatischen und Enthusiastischen Wiedertäufer vornehmlich in Niederdeutschland. Melchior Hofmann und die Secte der Hofmannianer*. Leipzig: Bernhard Christoph Breitkopf 1758

Kühler, W[ilhelmus] J[ohannes]. *Geschiedenis der Nederlandsche Doopsgezinden in de zestiende eeuw*. Haarlem: H.D. Tjeenk Willink & Zoon 1932; 2d ed 1962

– *Geschiedenis van de Doopsgezinden in Nederland* Haarlem: H.D. Tjeenk Willink & Zoon 1950

Kuhles, Joachim. 'Die Unterdrückung der Volksbewegung und die Errichtung eines obrigkeitlichen Kirchenregiments zur Zeit der Reformation in den ostbaltischen Hansestädten,' *Neue hansische Studien, Forschungen zur mittelalterlichen Geschichte*, 17 (1970), 171–91

Laantee, Karl. 'The Beginnings of the Reformation in Estonia,' *Church History* 22 (1953), 269–78

Labes, E. 'Eine ungedruckte Rechtfertigungsschrift Andreas Bodenstein von Carlstadt's, in Betreff der Abendmahlslehre gerichtet and den Kanzler Brück in Weimar,' *Zeitschrift für wissenschaftliche Theologie* 17 (1864), [99]–112

Lang, Helmut W. 'Wiener Karlstadt-Drucke aus der presse Johann Singrieners (1521–1522),' *Gutenberg Jahrbuch 1970*, 212–17

Liber decanorum facultatis theologicae academiae Vitebergensis, ed Karl E[duard] Förstemann. Leipzig: Carolus Tauchnitius 1838

Lindberg, Carter. 'Conflicting Models of Ministry: Luther, Karlstadt and Muentzer,' *Concordia Theological Quarterly [Springfield]* 41 (1977), 35–50

– '"There should be no Beggars among Christians": Karlstadt, Luther, and the Origins of Protestant Poor Relief,' *Church History* 46 (1977), 313–34

Littell, Franklin H[amlin]. *The Origins of Sectarian Protestantism*. New York: Macmillan 1964

Locher, Gottfried W[ilhelm]. *Die Zwinglische Reformation im Rahmen der europäischen Kirchengeschichte*. Göttingen: Vandenhoeck & Ruprecht 1979

Lumpkin, William L[atane]. *Baptist Confessions of Faith*. Philadelphia: The Judson Press 1959

McBeth, H[arry] Leon. *English Baptist Literature on Religious Liberty to 1689*. New York: Arno Press 1980

McGlothlin, W[illiam] J[oseph]. *Baptist Confessions of Faith*. Philadelphia: American Baptist Publication Society 1911

McSorley, Harry J[oseph]. *Luther: Right or Wrong? An Ecumenical-Theological Study of Luther's Major Work, The Bondage of the Will*. New York: Newman Press / Minneapolis: Augsburg Publishing House 1969

Manz, Felix. 'Protestation oder Schutzschrift.' See Karlstadt, *Von dem Tauff*.

Martin Luther und die Reformation in Deutschland, Ausstellung zum 500. Geburtstag Martin Luthers, ed Germanisches Nationalmuseum. Frankfurt am Main: Insel Verlag 1983

Masin, E.M. 'Die Streitschriften des Andreas Bodenstein von Karlstadt,' Dissertation Wien 1977 (not available)

Die Matrikel der Universität Rostock 2 (1499–1611), ed Adolph Hofmeister. Rostock: G. Nusser 1891. Cited as *Matrikel Rostock*

Maurer, Wilhelm. *Der junge Melanchthon zwischen Humanismus und Reformation* 2. Göttingen: Vandenhoeck & Ruprecht [1969]

Meihuizen, H.W. *Menno Simons, ijveraar voor het herstel van de nieuw. testamentische gemeente*. Haarlem: Tjeenk Willink & Zoon 1961

– 'Who Were the "False Brethren" Mentioned in the Schleitheim Articles?', MQR 41 (1967), 200–22

Mellink, Albert Fredrik. *De Wederdopers in de Noordelijke Nederlanden 1531–1544*. Groningen: J.B. Wolters 1953

Møller, Jens G. 'The Beginnings of Puritan Covenant Theology,' *The Journal of Ecclesiastical History* 14 (1963), 46–67

Moore, Walter Lane, 'Between Mani and Pelagius: Predestination and Justification in the Early writings of John Eck.' THD thesis, Harvard Divinity School 1967

Mosteller, James D[onovan]. 'Baptists and Anabaptists,' *The Chronicle* 20 (1957), [3]–27, [100]–14

Mülhaupt, Erwin. 'Karlstadts "Fuhrwagen,"' *Luther, Zeitschrift der Luther-Gesellschaft* (1979), 60–76

Müller [Mollerus], Johannes. *Cimbria literata, sive scriptorum ducatus utriusque Slesvicensis et Holtsatici*. Havniae 1744

Müller, Johann Joachim. *Entdecktes Staatscabinet, darinnen so wohl das jus publicum, feudale, und ecclesiasticum illustriret wird*. 2d ed. Jena: Christian Pohl 1714

Müller, Karl. *Luther und Karlstadt: Stücke aus ihrem gegenseitigen Verhältnis.* Tübingen: J.C.B. Mohr 1907
Müsing, Hans Werner. 'Karlstadt und die Entstehung der Strassburger Täufergemeinde,' *The Origins and Characteristics of Anabaptism*, [169]–95

Neuser, Wilhelm H[einrich]. *Die reformatorische Wende bei Zwingli.* Neukirchen-Vluyn: Neukirchener Verlag 1977
Noll, Mark A. 'Luther Defends Melchior Hofmann,' *Sixteenth Century Journal* 4 (1973), 47–60
– 'Melchior Hofmann and the Lutherans: 1525–1529.' MA thesis, Trinity Evangelical Divinity School, Deerfield 1972

Oberman, Heiko Augustinus. *Forerunners of the Reformation. The Shape of Late Medieval Thought.* New York: Holt, Rinehart & Winston 1966
– *The Harvest of Medieval Theology: Gabriel Biel and Late Medieval Nominalism.* Cambridge: Harvard University Press 1963
– 'Wittenbergs Zweifrontenkrieg gegen Prierias und Eck,' ZKG 80 (1969), 331–58.
Olearius, Johann Gottfried. *Scrinium antiquarium* Halle: 1671
Oosterbaan, J.A. 'Een doperse christologie,' *Nederlands theologisch tijdschrift* 35 (1981), 32–47
The Origins and Characteristics of Anabaptism / Les débuts et les caractéristiques de l'anabaptisme, ed Marc Lienhard, 'Archives internationales d'histoire des idées' 87. The Hague: Martinus Nijhoff 1977
Oyer, John S[tanley]. 'The Influence of Jacob Strauss on the Anabaptists. A Problem in Historical Methodology,' *The Origins and Characteristics of Anabaptism*, 62–82

Packull, Werner O. *Mysticism and the Early South German-Austrian Anabaptist Movement 1525–1531*, 'Studies in Anabaptist and Mennonite History' 19. Scottdale: Herald Press 1977
– 'Some Reflections on the State of Anabaptist History: The Demise of a Normative Vision,' *Studies in Religion / Sciences religieuses* 8 (1979), 313–23
Pallas, K. ed. 'Urkunden, das Allerheiligenstift zu Wittenberg betreffend, 1522–1526' 2, ARG 12 (1915), [1]–131
– ed. 'Die Wittenberger Beutelordnung vom Jahre 1521 und ihr Verhältnis zu der Einrichtung des Gemeinen Kastens im Januar 1522. Aus dem Nachlasse des Professor D. Dr. Nik. Müller-Berlin,' *Zeitschrift des Vereins für Kirchengeschichte in der Provinz Sachsen* 12 (1915), 1–45; 13 (1916), 100–37
Pater, Adrian J[ohn]. 'A Study of Selected Doctrines in Melchior Hoffman.' ThD thesis, New Orleans Baptist Theological Seminary 1978
Pater, Calvin Augustine. 'Karlstadts Zürcher Abschiedspredigt über die Menschwerdung Christi,' *Zwingliana* 14/1 (1974), 1–[16]
– 'Melchior Hoffman's Explication of the Songs [!] of Songs,' ARG 68 (1977), 173–91
– Review of BUBENHEIMER and SIDER in *The Catholic Historical Review* 67 (1981), 124–5 .

Patrologiae cursus completus, Series graeca, ed J[ean] P[aul] Migne. Paris: Garnier Frères 1886f

Payne, Ernest A[lexander]. *Free Churchmen, Unrepentant and Repentant and Other Papers*. London: The Carey Kingsgate Press 1965
- 'Who Were the Baptists?', *The Baptist Quarterly* ns 16 (1955–6), 339–42

Pesch, Otto Hermann. *Theologie der Rechtfertigung bei Martin Luther und Thomas von Aquin, Versuch eines systematisch-theologischen Dialogs*, 'Theologische Reihe' 4. Mainz: Matthias Grünewald Verlag 1967

Petrus Lombardus. *Sententiae in IV Libris Distinctae*, ed tertia, I/II Liber I et II. Grottaferrata [Romae]: Editiones Collegii S. Bonaventura ad Claras Aquas 1971

Philoon, Thurman E. 'Hans Greiffenberger and the Reformation in Nuernberg,' MQR 36 (1962), 61–75

Pipkin, H[arry] Wayne. 'The Nature and Development of the Zwinglian Reformation to August 1524.' PHD Thesis, Hartford Seminary Foundation 1968

Pohrt, Otto. *Reformationsgeschichte Livlands. Ein Überblick*, 'Schriften des Vereins für Reformationsgeschichte' 145. Leipzig: M. Heinsius Nachfolger 1928

Pollet, J[acques] V. *Huldrych Zwingli et la Réforme en Suisse d'après les recherches récentes*. Paris: Les Presses universitaires de France 1963

Potter, G[eorge] R[ichard], *Zwingli*. Cambridge: University Press 1976

Preus, James Samuel. *Carlstadt's 'Ordinaciones' and Luther's 'Liberty': A Study of the Wittenberg Movement 1521–1522*, 'Harvard Theological Studies' 26. Cambridge: Harvard University Press 1974. Review by Carter Lindberg, MQR 52 (1978), 273–5
- *From Shadow to Promise, Old Testament Interpretation from Augustine to the Young Luther*. Cambridge: Harvard University (Belknap) Press 1969

Quednau, Hans. 'Johannes Lohmüller, Stadtsyndicus von Riga, ein Träger deutscher Reformation in nordosteuropa. Mit ein Auswahl aus seinen Schriften,' ARG 26 (1939), 51–67, 253–69

Quiring-Unruh, Liesel. 'Neues Licht auf das Geburtsjahr von Menno Simons,' *Mennonitische Geschichtsblätter* 24, ns 19 [1967], 54–71

Rad, Gerhard von. *Genesis: a Commentary*, trans John H. Marks. Philadelphia: Westminster Press [1973]

Radikale Reformatoren. 21 biographische Skizzen von Thomas Müntzer bis Paracelsus, ed Hans-Jürgen Goertz, 'Beck'sche Schwarze Reihe' 183. München: Verlag C.H. Beck 1978

The Reformation Crisis, ed Joel Hurstfield. New York: Harper & Row [1966]

Reinhart, Martin. *Anzaygung wie die gefallene Christenhait widerbracht Müg werden in jren ersten standt in wölchen sie von Christo vnnd seynen Aposteln erstlich gepflantzt Vnnd auff gebawet ist*. [Title frame]. [Augsburg: Heinrich Steiner] 1524
- *Wes sich Doctor Andreas Bodenstein von Karlstadt mit Doctor Martino Luther beredt zu Jena [Acta Ienensia]* 1524. 2d ed WA 15, [323–47]

Rich, Arthur. *Die Anfänge der Theologie Huldrych Zwinglis*. Zürich: Zwingli-Verlag 1949

Ritter, François. 'Elsässische Buchdrucker im Dienste der Strassburger Sektenbe-
wegungen zur Zeit der Reformation,' *Gutenberg Jahrbuch 1962*, 225–33
- *Histoire de l'imprimerie Alsacienne aux XVe et XVIe siècles*. Strasbourg: F.-X. Le
Roux 1955
Rogge, Joachim. *Der Beitrag des Predigers Jakob Strauss zur frühen Reformations-
geschichte*, 'Theologische Arbeiten' 6. Berlin: Evangelische Verlagsanstalt [1957]
Rörig, Fritz. *The Medieval Town*. Berkeley: University of California Press 1971
Ruhtenberg, Ralph. 'Die Beziehungen Luthers und der anderen Wittenberger Refor-
matoren zu Livland,' *Baltische Kirchengeschichte*, ed R[einhard] Wittram. Göt-
tingen: Vandenhoeck & Ruprecht 1958
Rupp, Gordon. 'Andrew Karlstadt and Reformation Puritanism,' *Journal of Theological
Studies* ns 10 (1959), 308–26
- 'Luther and the Reformation,' *The Reformation Crisis*, ed Joel Hurstfield. New
York: Harper & Row 1966. 21–31
- *Patterns of Reformation*. Philadelphia: Fortress Press 1969
- 'Word and Spirit in the First Years of the Reformation,' ARG 49 (1958), 13–26

Sachsse, Carl. *D. Balthasar Hubmaier als Theologe*, 'Neue Studien zur Geschichte der
Theologie und der Kirche' 20. Berlin: Trowitzsch & Sohn 1914. 2d ed Aalen: Scien-
tia Verlag 1973
Sandblad, Hendrik. *De eskatologiska föreställningarna i Sverige under reformation
och motreformation*, 'Lychnos-Bibliothek' 5. Uppsala: Almqvist & Wiksell 1942
Sasse, Hermann. *This Is My Body. Luther's Contention for the Real Presence in the
Sacrament of the Altar*. Minneapolis: Augsburg Publishing House 1959
Schmid, Walter, 'Der Author der sogenannten Protestation und Schutzschrift von
1524/1525,' *Zwingliana* 9 (1949–53), 139–50
Schmidt, Martin Anton. 'Karlstadt als Theologe und prediger zu Basel,' *Theologische
Zeitschrift [Basel]* 35 (1979), 155–68
Schnöring, W[ilhelm]. 'Johannes von Blankenfeld,' *Schriften des Vereins für Refor-
mationsgeschichte* 87 (1905), 1–115
Schottenloher, Karl. *Philipp Ulhart Ein Augsburger Winkeldrucker und Helfershelfer
der 'Schwärmer' und 'Widertäufer' (1523–1529)*, 'Historische Forschungen und
Quellen' 4. München: Freising 1921. 2d ed Nieuwkoop: B. de Graaf 1967
Schuldorp, Marquard, Breef an de Glövigen der Stadt Kyle wedder eeren Prediger Melchior Hoffman 1528. Title reconstructed by rendering into Schuldorp's Low German
the Latin translation of the original title given in Johannes Müller, *Cimbria literata*, 604.
The sole surviving tract begins with signature B: Marquardus Schuldorp gheeschet
vnd geordenth tho Schlesswick. On the basis of content, however, the tract seems
complete. [Hamburg: Jürgen Richolff d.J.] 1528. L: Copenhagen Kongelige Bibliotek, Sign. Hj 490b. 4
Schwarz-Lausten, Martin. 'Melchior Hoffman og de lutherske praedikanter i Slesvig-
Holsten 1527–1529,' *Kirkehistoriske Samlinger* 7. ser, 5/2, [237]–85
Scribner, Robert W. *For the Sake of Simple Folk: Popular Propaganda for the German
Reformation*. Cambridge Studies in Oral and Literate Culture 2. Cambridge: Cambridge University Press 1981

Seitz, Otto. *Der authentische Text der Leipziger Disputation (1519): Aus bisher unbenützten Quellen*. Berlin: C.A. Schwetschke 1903

Sider, Ronald J[ames]. 'Andreas Bodenstein von Karlstadt. Zwischen Liberalität und Radikalität,' *Radikale Reformatoren*, 21–[9]

– 'Karlstadt and Luther's Doctorate,' *Journal of Theological Studies* 22 (1971), 168–9

– 'Karlstadt's Orlamünde Theology: A Theology of Regeneration,' MQR 45 (1971), 191–218, 352–76

Siemelink, T[jaard] H[endrik]. *Melchior Hofmann; een voorbeeld van leekenprediking*, 'Geschriftjes ten behoeve van Doopsgezinden in de verstrooiing' 40 [1914]

Siggins, Ian D. Kingston, ed. *Luther*. Edinburgh: Oliver and Boyd 1972

Simons, Menno. *The Complete Writings of Menno Simons c. 1496–1561*, trans Leonard Verduin, ed John Christian Wenger. Scottdale: Herald Press 1956

– *Dat Fundament des Christelycken Leers (1539)*, ed H.W. Meihuizen. The Hague: Martinus Nijhoff 1967

Slaughter, Stephen S. 'The Dutch Church in Norwich,' *Transactions of the Congregational Historical Society* 12 (1933–6), 31–48, 81–96

Smyth, John. *The Works of John Smyth* 1–2, ed W[illiam] T[homas] Whitley. Cambridge: University Press 1915

Sources chrétiennes. Paris: Éditions du Cerf 1980f

Sprunger, Keith L. 'English Puritans and Anabaptists in Early Seventeenth-Century Amsterdam,' MQR 46 (1972), 113–28

Stassen, Glen H. 'Anabaptist Influence in the Origin of the Particular Baptists,' MQR 36 (1962), 322–48

Staupitz, Johann von. *Sämmtliche Werke*, ed J[oachim] K[arl] F[riedrich] Knaake. 1 'Deutsche Schriften.' Potsdam: A. Krausnick 1867. Pp 88–119 cited as *Liebe*; pp 136–84 cited as *Fürsehung*

Stayer, James M[entzer]. *Anabaptists and the Sword*. Lawrence: Coronado Press 1973, 2d ed 1976. Review by Walter Klaassen, MQR 45 (1971), 160

– 'Die Anfänge des schweizerischen Täufertums,' *Umstrittenes Taufertum*, 19–49

– 'Melchior Hofmann and the Sword,' MQR 45 (1971), 265–77

– 'Oldeklooster and Menno,' *The Sixteenth Century Journal* 9/1 (1978), 51–67

– 'Reflections and Retractions on "Anabaptists and the Sword,"' MQR 51 (1977), 196–212

– 'Reublin and Brötli,' *The Origins and Characteristics of Anabaptism*, [83]–102

– and Werner O. Packull, and Klaus Deppermann. 'From Monogenesis to Polygenesis: The Historical Discussion of Anabaptist Origins,' MQR 49 (1975), 83–121

Steinmetz, David C[urtis]. 'The Baptism of John and the Baptism of Jesus in Huldrych Zwingli, Balthasar Hubmaier and Late Medieval Theology,' *Continuity and Discontinuity in Church History*, [169]–81

– *Misericordia Dei: the Theology of Johannes von Staupitz in Its Late-Medieval Setting*, 'Studies in Medieval and Reformation Thought' 4. Leiden: E.J. Brill 1968

– *Reformers in the Wings*. Philadelphia: Fortress Press [1971]

Stiefel, Michael. *Ein Rechen Büchlin Uom EndChrist. Apocalypsis in Apocalypsin*. [Title frame]. 8°. Wittenberg: Georg Rhau 1532

- Ein sehr Wunderbarliche wortrechnung Sampt einer mercklichen erklerung etlicher Zalen Danielis vnd der Offenbarung Sanct Johannis. Anno 1553. [Title frame]

Stirm, Margarete. *Die Bilderfrage in der Reformation*, QFRG 45. Gütersloh: Gütersloher Verlagshaus Gerd Mohn 1977

Strauss, Jakob. Uon dem ynnerlichen vnnd ausserlichem [!] Tauff eyn Christlych begründt leer geprediget durch D. Ja. Strauss zů Eyssnnach Ecclesiasten Christus In der welt habt ir angst Aber seyt getrost ich hab die welt vberwunden. [Title frame]. Erfurt: [Johannes Loersfelt] 1523. L: Oxford, Bodleian; Heidelberg, Universitätsbibliothek. Cited as *Von dem Tauff*

- Wider den symoneisch. en tauff vnderkauften ertichten krysem vnd oel auch warin die recht cristlich tauff (allain von Christo auffgsetzt) begriffen sey, ein genötige sermon geprediget zu Eysssnach. Christus, In der welt habt jr angst. aber seyt getröst, ich hab die welt überwunden. D. Jacobus Straus Ecclesiastes. M. D. XXiij. [Title frame]. [Augsburg: Melchior Ramminger] 1523. L: Universitätsbibliothek Tübingen. Cited as *Wider den Tauff*

Stupperich, Robert. 'Anfang und Fortgang des Täufertums nach Ubbo Emmius,' *Nederlands archief voor kerkgeschiedenis* ns 50 (1969), [28]–55

Supplementa Melanchthoniana. Frankfurt 1968f

Swart, Peder. *Konung Gustaf den förstes krönika*, ed Nils Edén. Stockholm: Ljus 1912

'Sylvester Tegetmeier's Tagebuch,' ed Friedrich Bienemann. *Mittheilungen aus dem Gebiete der Geschichte Liv-, Est- und Kurlands* 12/3. Riga: Nicolaus Kymmel 1880. 502–5

Thomae Aquinitatis Opera omnia. Romae: Ex Typographia Polyglotta 1882–1906

Thompson, Alden Lorne. 'Tertius usus legis in the Theology of Andreas Bodenstein von Karlstadt.' PHD thesis, University of Southern California 1969

Tolmie, Murray. *The Triumph of the Saints: The Separate Churches of London: 1616–1649*. Cambridge: University Press 1977

Torbet, Robert G[eorge]. *A History of the Baptists*, rev. 6th ed. London: The Carey Kingsgate Press 1966

Troeltsch, Ernst. *The Social Teachings of the Christian Churches* 1–2. trans Olive Wyon. New York: Harper Torchbooks 1960

Tschackert, Paul. *Dr. Eberhard Weidensee (†1547), Leben und Schriften*, 'Neue Studien zur Geschichte der Theologie und der Kirche' 12. Berlin: Verlag Trowitzsch & Sohn 1911. 2d ed Aalen: Scientia Verlag 1973

Umstrittenes Täufertum, ed Hans-Jürgen Goertz. Göttingen: Vandenhoeck & Ruprecht 1975

Underwood, A[lfred] C[lair]. *A History of the English Baptists*. London: The Carey Kingsgate Press 1947

Vasella, Oskar. 'Zur Biographie des Prädikanten Erasmus Schmid,' ZSKG 50 (1956), 353–66

Vogt, Otto, ed. *Dr. Johannes Bugenhagens Briefwechsel*. Stettin [1888–99]; Gotha 1910. 2d ed Hildesheim: Georg Olms 1966

Volbehr, Friedrich. *Kieler Prediger-Geschichte seit der Reformation*, 'Mittheilungen der Gesellschaft für Kieler Stadtgeschichte' 6. Kiel: Schmidt & Klaunig 1884

Vööbus, Arthur. *Studies in the History of the Estonian People* 2, 'Papers of the Estonian Theological Society in Exile' 19. Stockholm: [Cultura Press] 1970

Vos, K[arel]. *Menno Simons 1496–1561, Zijn leven en werken en zijne reformatorische denkbeelden*. Leiden: E.J. Brill 1914

Wackernagel, Hans Georg, ed. *Die Matrikel der Universität Basel* 2. Basel: Verlag der Universitätsbibliothek 1956

Wähler, Martin. *Die Einführung der Reformation in Orlamünde: Zugleich ein Beitrag zum Verständnis von Karlstadts Verhältnis zu Luther*. Erfurt: Karl Villaret 1918

Walton, Robert C[lifford]. 'The Institutionalization of the Reformation at Zurich,' *Zwingliana* 13 [1972], 497–515

– 'Was There a Turning Point in the Zwinglian Reformation?' MQR 32 [1958], 45–56

– *Zwingli's Theocracy*. Toronto: University of Toronto Press 1967. Review by Franklin H[amlin] Littell, MQR 43 [1969], 339–40

Wamble, [Gaston] Hugh. 'Inter-Relations of Seventeenth Century English Baptists,' *[Baptist] Review and Expositor* 54, [1957], [407]–25

Wappler, Paul. *Die Täuferbewegung in Thüringen von 1526–1584*, 'Beiträge zur neueren Geschichte Thüringens' 2. Jena: Verlag von Gustav Fischer 1913

Watts, Michael R. *The Dissenters from the Reformation to the French Revolution*. Oxford: Clarendon Press 1978

Weidensee, Eberhard. *Eyn vnderricht vth der hillighen schryfft, Dem Dorchlüchtygen Hochgebarnen Forsten vnd Hernn, Herrn Christiarnn*. [Title frame]. [Hamburg: Jürgen Richolff d.J.] 1529. L: Copenhagen, Kongelige Bibliotek, Signature: Pal. 61 4^0

Wernle, [D.P.]. 'Ein Traktat Karlstadts unter dem Namen Valentin Weigels,' ZKG 24 [1903], 319–20

Westman, Knut B. *Reformationens genombrottsar i Sverige*. Stockholm: A.-B. Svenska kyrkans diakonistyrelses Bokförlag 1918

White, B[arrington] R[aymond]. *The English Separatist Tradition from the Marian Martyrs to the Pilgrim Fathers*. Oxford: University Press 1971

Whitley, W[illiam] T[homas]. *A History of British Baptists*. London: Charles Griffin 1923

Whitsitt, William H[eth]. *A Question in Baptist History*. Louisville: Charles T. Dearing 1896. 2d ed New York: Arno Press 1980

Williams, George Huntston. *The Radical Reformation*. Philadelphia: Westminster 1962

– 'Sanctification in the Testimony of Several So-called "Schwärmer,"' *The Church, Mysticism, Sanctification and the Natural in Luther's Thought*, ed Ivar Asheim. Philadelphia: Fortress Press 1967. 194–211

– 'Sectarian Ecumenicity: Reflections on a Little Noticed Aspect of the Radical Reformation,' *[Baptist] Review and Expositor* 64 [1967], 141–60

- and A.M. Mergal, eds. *Spiritual and Anabaptist Writers*, 'Library of Christian Classics' 25. Philadelphia: Westminster 1957

Wirth [=Hospinian], Rudolf. *Historiae sacramentariae* 2. Tiguri: Apud Iohannem VVolphium 1602

Wiswedel, Wilhelm. 'Melchior Hofmann,' *Bilder und Führergestalten aus dem Täufertum* 3. Kassel: J.G. Oncken Verlag 1952. 60–9

Wittram, Reinhard, ed. *Baltische Kirchengeschichte*. Göttingen: Vandenhoeck & Ruprecht 1956

Yoder, John. *Täufertum und Reformation in der Schweiz*, 'Schriftenreihe des Mennonitischen Geschichtsvereins' 6. Karlsruhe: H. Schneider 1962

Yoder, John H[oward]. 'Der Kristallisationspunkt des Täufertums,' *Mennonitische Geschichtsblätter* 29, ns 24 (1972), 35–47

- 'The Turning Point in the Zwinglian Reformation,' MQR 32 (1958), 128–40

- and Klaus Deppermann. 'Ein Briefwechsel über die Bedeutung des Schleitheimer Bekenntnisses,' *Mennonitische Geschichtsblätter* 30, ns 25 (1973), 42–52

Zerger, Fred J. 'Dutch Anabaptism in Elizabethan England,' *Mennonite Life* 26 (1971), 19–24

Zijpp, N[anne] van der. *Geschiedenis der Doopsgezinden in Nederland*. Arnhem: Van Loghum Slaterus 1952

Zschelletzschky, Herbert. *Die 'Drei Gottlosen Maler' von Nürnberg*. Leipzig: Veb E.A. Seemann Verlag 1975

Title-page of *Ursachen* (110),
published December 1523 by Michel Buchfürer in Jena.
In *Ursachen* Karlstadt first delineates a congregationally oriented church,
led by one who labours on weekdays 'in the sweat of his brow' and who
conducts his ministry among equals.
Reprinted from M[artin] von Hase, *Johann Michael* (1928)

Index of Names

Dutch patronymic names and surnames have been treated as family names; even Menno Simons is listed as Simons, Menno. In all three indexes page numbers are given in parentheses when the wording used in the text differs from that used in the index entry.

Index of Subjects

Index of Scriptural References

Because of their emphasis on biblical proof the secondary Reformers attempted to support their doctrinal arguments with biblical catenae that they borrowed from those whom they emulated. Every peculiar catena is potentially useful in settling questions of dependence.